Ple

ˈo

Oaksey on Racing

by the same author

The Story of Mill Reef
The History of Steeplechasing
(with Roger Mortimer, Peter Willett and Michael Seth-Smith)

John Oaksey
OAKSEY ON RACING

Thirty Years of Writing and Riding

Selections from *Horse and Hound*

Edited by Sean Magee

The Kingswood Press

All the pieces in this book
originally appeared in
Horse and Hound

This selection
first published in Great Britain 1991
by the Kingswood Press
an imprint of Methuen London
Michelin House, 81 Fulham Road, London SW3 6RB

Copyright © 1991 John Oaksey
The author has asserted his moral rights

A CIP catalogue for this book
is available from the British Library
ISBN 0 413 65230 0

Typeset by Falcon Typographic Art Ltd,
Edinburgh & London
Printed in Great Britain
by St Edmundsbury Press,
Bury St Edmunds, Suffolk

Contents

List of Illustrations

Acknowledgements and thanks are due to the following for permission to reproduce the photographs: Sport and General for 1, 7, 12, 23, 26, 31, 35, 38 and 69; Associated Press for 3, 14, 18 and 58; the Hulton-Deutsch Collection for 4, 10, 13, 19, 20, 30, 32, 44, 47, 49, 52 and 68; London Express Pictures for 5; Bob Thomas for 8; *Horse and Hound* for 9, 64 and 65; Paul Popper for 11; E. G. Byrne for 15; Charles C. Fennell for 16; Kicksports Foto for 17; Press Association for 21 and 33; London Photo Agency (Sport) for 22; F. Davidson for 24; W. Everitt for 25 and 45; World of Sports Photos for 27; Tony Edenden for 28 and 57; Alan Johnson for 29 and 55; R. Anscomb for 36; Desmond O'Neill for 37; Trevor Jones for 39; Alec Russell for 40; George Selwyn for 41, 42, 48, 51, 53, 56, 67 and 70; Bespix for 43, 50, 61 and 62; Stuart Newsham for 46; Sporting Pictures (UK) Ltd for 54; James Harrigan for 59; Jim Meads for 60; and Gerry Cranham for 63.

Special thanks are due to Jill Caudle at the *Horse and Hound* Picture Library for her help in collecting the photographs.

Foreword

by Michael Clayton
Editor of *Horse and Hound*

It is high time that the great achievements of John Oaksey in sustained sporting journalism were captured between hard covers.

This record of some of the best of his weekly racing diary, published in *Horse and Hound* for years, is a delight.

John Oaksey's regular reflections on the racing scene were enlivened by wit, wisdom, bubbling enthusiasm and the extra dimension during the winter months of a horseman's view from the saddle.

'You'll have to be ready with a sudden replacement for John's column in case he has a heavy fall on a Saturday,' my predecessor warned when I took over as Editor of *Horse and Hound* in 1973.

In those days John Lawrence, before his succession to his father's peerage, rode regularly as one of the most distinguished of National Hunt amateur jockeys. His lengthy, hand-written epistle to *Horse and Hound* readers had the special appeal of one who was experiencing the thrills and disappointments of the Turf and had the talent to convey those literal ups and downs with verve and a compelling style.

After his retirement from the saddle John continued to entertain and inform with undiminished vigour. He managed to combine a keep-fit regime with personal delivery of his manuscript, arriving in a track suit at our Thames-side offices early on a Monday morning with the precious racing diary.

'Bloke down 'ere in running shoes, says 'e's Lord Oaksey and 'e's got something for you,' a front doorman reported with some scepticism on the internal phone system.

As a distinguished rider, John was able to describe Fred Winter's fabulous win in the 1962 Grand Steeplechase de Paris on Mandarin, minus a bridle, with an insight which makes it a classic of sporting prose. His comments on standards of jockeyship were perceptive and fair – a notable contrast to some of the emanations from non-riding 'experts' in the grandstand.

With his legal training, John is capable of tackling racing politics robustly and with penetrating analysis.

'That Oaksey has libelled me again in your magazine. I shall have to sue, Governor,' complained the late Lord Wigg in one of his regular telephone calls to me. I assured him that John's knowledge of the law made this highly unlikely, and I backed him against any such accusation. No writs arrived from the former Levy Board boss who had curiously became the bookies' champion.

John has never over-estimated the importance of the sport he has so adored. He described it only recently, with endearing humility, as '. . . this lovely, enthralling, but, let's face it, basically insignificant pastime . . .' – a refreshing contrast to the impassioned utterances of those whose horizons are totally confined by the view through race-glasses or today's fixture list. It is not surprising that his engaging personality has gained him so many more friends from his regular appearances in the Channel Four TV racing team.

John's admirers, who have so relished the writing he has distilled from the sport, cannot over-estimate his contribution to the quality of life which his devotion to the Turf has produced for so many others.

Michael Clayton
Editor
Horse and Hound   June 1991

Editorial Note

The pieces included in this book were all first published in
Horse and Hound between 1959 and 1988, with the exception
of the article on Fulke Walwyn (pages 306–9), written for the
magazine in 1990 after John Oaksey had ceased to be Audax.
They are reprinted here in their original form, with a few very
minor amendments where necessary: typographic errors and
'errors in transmission' have been corrected, and a small
number of excisions have been made to remove irrelevant
futurology and to avoid inevitable repetitions – it might, for
instance, be wearisome for the reader of this volume to have
the details of Arkle's breeding offered more than once. The
headings of the pieces are, for the most part, as they originally
appeared in the magazine, and after each piece is given the
date of the issue in which it was published. The notes and
linking passages have been supplied by John Oaksey for this
book.

The task of putting together this selection has been, to borrow
a phrase from *Horse and Hound*'s main preoccupation, worth a
guinea a minute.

S.M.

Introduction

When I first wrote the Audax column in *Horse and Hound* thirty-two years ago, Arkle was an unbroken two-year-old, Lester Piggott had yet to become champion jockey, betting shops were still illegal and the Levy Board was no more than a twinkle in some Home Secretary's eye. Patrol cameras, starting stalls, overnight declarations and licensed lady trainers were all still in the future and the age of commercial sponsorship had only just been launched with the first Whitbread and Hennessy Gold Cups.

You could, I am sure, fill numerous books with an account of the transformation through which British racing has passed since then. But this, you will be relieved to hear, is not one of them.

There have only been three Audaxes since Arthur Portman (the first of them) started *Horse and Hound* in 1884 – and none of us has been noticeably reluctant to state a view on racing rules, controversies and 'politics'. But although such topics do find an occasional place in the pages that follow, they are mostly, as far as this particular book is concerned, beside the point.

For the best of my fun (to borrow a phrase from *Horse and Hound*), one way and another, has come either from riding horses or watching other people do it better. For more than half that period I had the amazing good luck to be paid, effectively, for doing the thing I loved the most in life – and was privileged, what's more, to do it alongside men like Fred Winter, Tim Brookshaw, Stan Mellor and their contemporaries.

No other sport I can think of gives a mere amateur scribbler the chance to share, however remotely and ineptly, the lives of his heroes. Certainly no other job could have enabled me to enjoy and attempt to describe, at such close quarters, the exploits of those even more deserving heroes, the horses on whose willing courage all of us depend.

No doubt all three Audaxes had special memories we treasured most. Arthur Portman, who loved shooting and was a first-rate shot, did not pay nearly as much attention as I have to the 'Winter Game'. The deeds of Golden Miller certainly inspired him but not, I suspect, quite to the same degree as those of Arkle did his successor!

David Livingstone-Learmonth, who took over when Arthur Portman was killed by a bomb in 1940, knew, and wrote, much more about breeding than I ever have. But, quite apart from plain ignorance in that regard, my excuse is that, during my time as Audax, breeding was covered with such scholarly eloquence by Peter Willett.

Here, anyway, are some of the scenes, personalities and subjects which stand out in my memory of thirty-two happy years. Except for a few shamefaced corrections and some very occasional editing – mainly to avoid too much tedious repetition! – this is how I saw and described them at the time.

I only hope you enjoy it half as much as I did.

J.O.
April 1991

The Grand National

John Lawrence (stripes) and Taxidermist about to come to
grief at Becher's first time round in the 1961 Grand National.
Just in front of him, Kingstel and George Slack take a
crashing fall.

Long before I first saw Aintree or had any idea what it was like, the Grand National was part of my dreams.

Bill Harris, the kindly Wiltshireman who helped my father teach me to ride, had been 'there the day Golden Miller won' and, understandably, never forgot it. So Mince Pie, my first beloved fat Welsh pony, must have jumped – or anyway, been asked to jump – a thousand imaginary Chairs, Becher's Brooks and Canal Turns. They were only faggots or knocked-down hurdles, and when she did not feel like it, Mince Pie quite often stopped. But Harris and I still went on dreaming.

Then, just before my eighth birthday (21 March has sometimes even been Grand National day) I drew Royal Mail in the family sweep – and listened enthralled as Evan Williams rode him home in triumph.

By that time Bob Lyle's Brown Jack, one of the first real books I ever read, had sown the seeds of my passion for racing. I knew that Royal Mail, like Brown Jack, was trained by Ivor Anthony at Wroughton. But how could I guess that Evan Williams's wife (Kim Muir's sister) would one day breed a colt by Ujiji and, for some unknown reason, call him Taxidermist.

OVER–UNDER THE PONY'S NOSE

'Mince Pie quite often stopped.' The 6-year-old John Lawrence and his first pony have a difference of opinion at the pony hunter trial, Purton House, Wiltshire, in 1935.

Taxi, alas, never ran at Aintree until well past his prime. But he was the best horse I ever rode and won both the Whitbread and Hennessy Gold Cups before giving me my first Grand National ride.

It ended, ignominiously, at Becher's – where Taxi was trapped, through no fault of his own, by the treacherous 'lip' which has now, thank Heaven, been ironed out.

The only unusual thing about my eleven unsuccessful National rides is that I always got back in time to describe them, after a fashion, in next day's Sunday Telegraph. *The resulting woefully incomplete accounts, blurred by adrenalin and fear, won no Pulitzer prizes. But until Marcus Armytage wiped our eyes triumphantly on Mr Frisk, I think John Hislop, third on Kami in 1947, was the only other to attempt the riding/writing double.*

But this chapter, you will be glad to hear, is much more concerned with the great race itself than with my attempts to win it. Quite often throughout this period, the Grand National has seemed in real danger of extinction. Here, perhaps, are some of the reasons why it has survived.

WIN OR LOSE, TIRED OR NOT, AINTREE IS UNFORGETTABLE

'I know you,' the little man said. 'You're the one who got tired before 'is 'orse.'

It was late at night under Piccadilly Circus and I had never seen the man before; but although he was speaking nearly fifteen years after Ayala caught Carrickbeg 50 yards from the post in the 1963 Grand National, I knew exactly what he meant. For all I know, in fact, he may be right!

Whether I got tired before him or not, Carrickbeg was not my first Grand National ride. I had been there twice before on the great day, riding an even better horse – the best I ever rode. But sadly, through circumstances entirely beyond his own control, Taxidermist never had a proper chance to prove himself round Aintree.

The first time we went there in 1961 his wind had just gone wrong and he ran with a tube in his throat. A year later it poured with rain for 48 hours before the race and Fred Winter won on Kilmore in the sort of swamp-like ground poor 'Taxi' always hated.

Fred's tactics were to drop right out and, as we started on the second circuit, I remember him asking, ever so politely, for 'a bit of room' along the rail. Since my role was already strictly that of a spectator, I cannot claim much credit for complying. But through he went to victory, following, as all his jockeys have since, the shortest route from start to finish.

Taxidermist's and my first National in 1961 was the year the Russians came, and I was dispatched on a scouting mission to Moscow by the newly-founded *Sunday Telegraph*. The BBC's

Peter Bromley came too and it would be hard to know who was more surprised – we by the pathetically small animals they were 'preparing' for Aintree in an indoor riding school, or they by the films of past Grand Nationals which we took to show them.

In the East European equivalent, Czechoslovakia's Grand Pardubice, it is, apparently, commonplace for the winner to have remounted at least once, and even Chris Collins was able to 'circle' after being carried out on the way to his epic victory.

Each nation has helpers poised at all the trickiest jumps ready to load up their fallen heroes and, try as we might, Peter and I could never convince the Russians that the pace at which Grand Nationals are run makes remounting a waste of time, except possibly late in the race or in some other special circumstances.

Sure enough, I was given personal proof of our failure to get this message across because, having fallen off 'Taxi' at Becher's (well, he *almost* fell), I was sitting cursing my fate when thump, down beside me came Russia's answer to Fred Winter, Vladimir Prakhov and his mount, the diminutive Grifel.

They must already have been a long way behind when disaster struck, but before I could start to commiserate, out of the crowd leapt the Russian *chef d'équipe*. This gentleman, a Mr Dolmatov, had been extremely helpful and hospitable to us in Moscow and I only hope (without much confidence) that the total failure of the Russian venture did not subsequently earn him a one-way ticket to Siberia.

Now he certainly seemed to have something like that in mind, because, heedless of my eloquent cries of 'nyet', he seized the unfortunate Prakhov and hoisted him willy nilly back aboard.

The field was long gone, well over Valentine's by this time – and to my delight, after going only a few yards in pursuit, Prakhov turned back and addressed Dolmatov.

I fondly imagined that he was taking my advice and telling his superior to jump in the Mersey – but not a bit of it!

What he said, in fact, was, 'Please, comrade, would you kindly pick up my whip?' – and when this had been done he set off again, gallantly soldiering on until the water!

John Lawrence walks away after parting company with
Taxidermist in the 1961 Grand National, as Vladimir Prakhov
remounts Grifel in the background.

No one had told the Russians, until too late, that, having not
run in 'qualifying' races in England, they would automatically
carry top weight. Their mission, in fact, was doomed to failure
before it began, but they were brave and cheerful sportsmen –
particularly Vladimir Prakhov, who is still warmly remembered
in at least one female heart in Southport!

After Carrickbeg, of whom more later, I was lucky enough
to be given a chance ride in 1964 on Crobeg. When I asked
his former trainer Bob Turnell how he jumped, the not very
heartening answer was 'flat and low' but, in fact, although five
letters of his name were the only things he had in common with
Carrickbeg, Crobeg jumped safely round to finish ninth behind
Team Spirit.

In 1965, with both Bill Rees and David Mould out of action, I
was invited (to my great pride) by Peter Cazalet to ride Kapeno.
But Kapeno himself did not think much of that idea so, having

ejected me at the Cheltenham water jump, he put a foot firmly in my stomach, bursting my spleen and ensuring that I watched Dave Dick ride him on television! They were still only cruising, too, at Becher's second time round when a loose horse crossed poor Kapeno and gave him no room to take off.

That was Jay Trump's year – an amazing one in several ways. Neither Tommy Smith, who rode the winner, nor Chris Collins, who was third on Mr Jones, had ever seen Aintree before that week – and Chris was in only his second season's riding.

Even more miraculous, the BBC, choosing two horses to follow in a documentary through their preparations for the National, picked Jay Trump and Freddie. Three months later the same pair drew clear together with the race between them over the last five fences.

Oh, that the BBC's modern documentary makers ('Forty Minutes' for instance*) could show comparable inspiration – or get even half as near the truth!

Neither Solimyth (on whom I had so many happy moments elsewhere) nor Master Mascus enjoyed Aintree much in 1966 and '68. In fact, by depositing me in Valentine's Brook, Master Mascus put considerable strain on Bob Glendinning and Bill Tadd, the faithful 'back-up' team provided by the *Sunday Telegraph* for most of the eleven Nationals I 'covered' from a saddle (or near it) on their behalf.

Although it hardly hurt at all (and I did get back in time for my 4.20 p.m. deadline), Master Mascus's fall was the nearest I ever got to emulating Captain Becher. I did actually take cover in Valentine's Brook while half the field passed overhead – and remember feeling sorry for my old friend John Ciechanowski, whose fall from Quitte Ou Double had left him in a far less desirable position – out fully exposed where the hooves were landing!

I'm afraid I probably did Red Alligator's triumph even less

---

* This is a reference to a deplorably slanted and biased 'Forty Minutes' programme about the Stable Lads' Welfare Trust. Filming the stable lads' Boxing Dinner in London – the SLWT's main annual fund-raising event – the programme-makers contrasted the revels of some admittedly well-lubricated owners, trainers and jockeys with the plight of out-of-work, injured and underpaid lads. They completely ignored the fact that the revellers had paid good money for their fun – money which would be used by the Trust to help stable lads.

justice than usual that Sunday. He was the first of Brian Fletcher's three winners – and on the morning of the race I remember my horror at finding Brian sweating hard in the steam room of the Southport Turkish Baths.

Since he weighed about 9st soaking wet, he could hardly be wasting for Red Alligator – and, in fact, it turned out that he was trying to 'do' a light weight in the last, a Flat race! It was also Brian's first ever visit to a Turkish Bath and no one had told him that you don't spend more than a couple of minutes in the steam room!

Happily, a glass of champagne and some wise advice, both supplied by Terry Biddlecombe, soon corrected the order of his priorities!

In between those comparative disasters, I had one of my best rides ever at Aintree on Norther – until the 23rd fence that is, because this, of course, was Foinavon's year.

Down to Becher's for the second time an abnormal, possibly even unique number of horses were still on their feet and going well. The three loose ones who led over the brook had been jumping so well and keeping so straight that I, for one, had stopped worrying about them.

The fence after Becher's is, after all, the smallest on the course and, second time round, bashed first time by a field of 44, it was barely 3ft high. But that, for some unknown reason, was three too many for Popham Down – who ran down the fence from left to right, cutting down the leaders like a row of thistles.

Just behind them Norther jumped a fallen rival and as he landed smack in the fence itself I jumped it really well without him. Stan Mellor landed beside me and (I'm not sure why) we both decided to get the hell out of there, instead of rolling up like hedgehogs as advised in all the manuals.

On Monday morning the *Daily Telegraph* carried a picture of the carnage, with two scampering fugitives in the foreground. Its caption – 'S. Mellor and Mr J. Lawrence running in search of their horses' – was one of the kindest, if not the most accurate, in the paper's history!

Apart from the kindness of Major Derek Wigan and Ken Cundell in letting me ride Regimental in 1971, his courageous clear round (eighth to Specify) had one permanent and invaluable result. For in those days some (nearly half, I think) of the

National fences were faced with prickly gorse, as opposed to the much softer, less vicious fir.

And when visiting Regimental at Compton a full week after the race, Major Wigan was horrified to find him still in considerable pain with his stifle and inside his hind legs torn and raw.

The gorse was clearly to blame and, luckily, Major Wigan had the energy, determination and influence to get something done about it. From 1972 on there has been no gorse at Aintree.

Just as well, because 1973 was to see by far the fastest, indeed, at least arguably, the greatest Grand National of all time.* Since most of the losers were off the bit and flat out from the start it was not a particularly 'comfortable' race – but I am prouder to have finished seventh (on Proud Tarquin) behind Red Rum and Crisp than of many victories.

The finish itself remains one of the saddest, most painful sights I ever saw on a racecourse – and Crisp's heroic 'failure' to give Red Rum 23lb after covering the 4½ miles nearly 19 seconds faster than Golden Miller, put him, for ever, alongside his conqueror that day, high among the immortals of Aintree.

By a tragic coincidence of dates, Proud Tarquin was not qualified to run next year – when, with blinkers, he was twice the horse. In seven days that spring he led Red Rum over the last fence in the Scottish Grand National, only to be swamped on the flat – and led The Dikler past the post in the Whitbread Gold Cup only to be disqualified!

So, although he would never have beaten Red Rum at Aintree in 1974, you cannot blame me for dreaming that he might have been thereabouts . . .

Now, back to that awful question asked under Piccadilly. *Did* I get tired before Carrickbeg?

* Incredible though it may seem, Red Rum's historic record was shattered in 1990 by Mr Frisk and at least seven of his opponents. Both the Cheltenham and Aintree Festivals took place on fast ground. No fewer than ten new records were set at the National Hunt Meeting and both the John Hughes Memorial (formerly the Topham) and the Seagram Foxhunters at Liverpool were run in record time.

But Mr Frisk and Marcus Armytage's 8 minutes 47.8 seconds still represents a truly amazing performance – more than 14 seconds faster than Red Rum and Crisp and over half a minute in front of the previous record-holder, Golden Miller.

I still don't know – but what I do know is that if only I could ride the race again, the first two places *would* be changed.

My first mistake, coming back from the Canal Turn second time, was to be anywhere near Out And About, who had been in front all the way. No one, not even Josh Gifford, could really hold him and I should have foreseen that he might fall.

Then, when he did, carving a great hole in the fourth from home – through which Carrickbeg dived (his only serious error) – I made my second mistake. Instead of taking a pull, sitting still and giving him time to recover, I stupidly asked him *at once* to make up those precious lost lengths.

He did so with such ease that we were in front before the last – and alone up that nightmare long run-in.

It was only passing the water, with less than 100 yards to go, that he lost the rhythm of his stride. Then I was tired all right – we both were – and then, perhaps a Fred Winter would have pulled him back together and held on.

It does not matter now – and, even all those years ago, the one truly heartbreaking moment came in January 1964 when, trotting up at Sandown, Carrickbeg broke down landing over the second last.

Only eight years old, he had improved by at least a stone and would, if only his legs stayed sound, have had three or four more chances.

But 'if only' is always part of the story of Aintree. I am just grateful to have been there – deeply grateful to the brave horses who carted me round and thankful that, with any luck, a lot more people are going to have the same matchless thrill of riding out at Aintree on Grand National day.

Win or lose, tired or not, they will not easily forget it!

31 March 1982

MOMENTS OF GLORY WHICH TURNED TO NIGHTMARE

There are 494 yards between the last fence and the winning post in the Grand National at Aintree – and, for about 480 of them, I was, last Saturday afternoon, the happiest man in the world. But the last battle is the only one to count – and for that, for those final, ghastly 14 yards, Carrickbeg and I had nothing left. So there, in a split second, the dream of glory became a nightmare and Pat Buckley swept past on Mr P.B. Raymond's Ayala to win the great steeplechase.

The pair of them won it fair and square because, together, with certain defeat staring them between the eyes, they had the courage and endurance to go on fighting what was an apparently hopeless battle.

A horse with slightly less bottomless stamina than Ayala, or a man slightly less strong, fit and determined than Buckley, would never have been able to seize the chance when it came.

At the time – at that bitter moment when Ayala's head appeared at my knee – I wished them both at the bottom of the deep, blue sea. Now, with admiration and only a little envy, I salute them for winning, deservedly, a truly wonderful race – a race, I think, as thrilling and spectacular as any Grand National since the war.

But besides the winner there was another hero. At the age of seven, in only his second season as a 'chaser, Carrickbeg had outjumped and outgalloped 46 older, more experienced horses for nearly 4¹/2 miles.

Steady as the rock of Gibraltar from the first fence to the

last, he was never for one single moment in danger of falling and, until his last reserves gave out ten strides before the end, he had answered my every call with cheerful, unhesitating obedience.

Unless he gives it me, I never expect to have a better ride at Aintree or anywhere else and, for those 9½ unforgettable minutes I offer him my heartfelt thanks.

They had begun as, with the long, nerve-racking preliminaries over at last, Mr Alec Marsh got the huge field off to a perfect start.

A bitter, biting wind had greeted us as we left the weighing-room and, by the time we turned in front of the stands to canter down, my spirits for one were at their lowest ebb.

Carrickbeg restored them slightly – striding out like a lion on the way to the post – but the last moments before a National will never be anything but a dreadful, goldfish-bowl ordeal and only when the first few fences are safely crossed can you begin to forget how much is at stake and settle down to enjoy the greatest thrill the sport of steeplechasing has to offer.

After our dismal experience together at Cheltenham,* those first few fences were, for Carrickbeg and me, especially important. But if he felt the same misgivings as his rider, Carrickbeg concealed them well. He measured the first to an inch and, even more encouraging, hit the top of the open ditch quite hard – and somehow made it feel no stiffer than a soft French hurdle.

As expected, Out And About (10st 7lb) had led from the start, but Josh Gifford held him well and the pace they set was nothing extraordinary. As the red and white flag fluttered its awe-inspiring warning over Becher's Brook, Jonjo (10st 6lb), French Lawyer (10st 6lb), Forty Secrets (10st 7lb), Chavara (10st 2lb) and Dandy Tim (10st 6lb) were in the leading group – and Carrickbeg (10st 3lb) sailed over like a bird not far

---

* After running well in the Leopardstown Chase (Britain was frozen throughout January and February), Carrickbeg started favourite for the Kim Muir at Cheltenham. But he was never going well and I fell off him at the last open ditch. It later transpired that one of his front plates had twisted into a murderous 'S'. Somehow he galloped back loose without carving holes in himself, but as a confidence-builder the experience left a good deal to be desired.

behind to land far out beyond the ditch and gallop on without a check.

Good Gracious (10st 7lb) fell at Becher's, Magic Tricks (10st) had gone at the first, Look Happy (10st) at the second, Merganser (10st 4lb) and Wingless (10st 3lb) at the third and Solonace (10st) somewhere thereabouts. But for most, as we swung round the Canal Turn, the fences were setting no great problems.

I personally had not seen one faller until Connie II (10st) ploughed through the tenth beside me, but the sickening crash she made was a violent reminder that this is still Aintree, where to take one liberty too many can mean a sudden end to all your hopes.

Ayala (10st), never far from the leaders, had, in fact, taken one at the Canal – carving a huge chunk from the fence, but failing completely to disturb either his own or Pat Buckley's equilibrium. I watched, with admiration, their recovery – and little knew how dear it was to cost me by and by.

On the long run back towards the stands, loose horses began to be a problem. Merganser, riderless, was a serious thorn in Josh Gifford's flesh, constantly unsettling Out And About and making him pull harder than ever, and, as we galloped towards the Chair – never an enjoyable moment – Wingless, dodging gaily about in front of Carrickbeg, made the towering cliff of the great fence an even less welcoming prospect than usual.

But all was well and now, with the water safely crossed, I found myself, for the first time ever, in a position from which the National had to be considered *as a race* – not merely as a struggle for survival. And the next 100 yards – swinging out into the country – were, in a way, more exciting than any in the whole $4^1/2$ miles.

There, deciding that the moment had come to get a bit closer, I picked Carrickbeg up for the first time – and the effortless power with which he surged up towards the leaders suddenly brought home the unbelievable truth that we were in the race with a real chance.

At Becher's the second time, in nine Grand Nationals out of ten, the shape of the finish can already be seen. And so it was now, for although Out And About was still in front together with Loyal Tan, French Lawyer and Dandy Tim, Ayala was close behind them, Springbok (10st 12lb) was improving steadily and, as Carrickbeg landed over the Brook, the leaders were not ten lengths ahead of us.

At the fence after Becher's, Loyal Tan and Dandy Tim dropped out exhausted and by the Canal there were (although I certainly did not realise it at the time) only six left in the race with a real chance. They were Out And About, now disputing the lead with French Lawyer, Hawa's Song (10st), Springbok, Ayala and Carrickbeg.

This list may be wronging some who were, in fact, still close enough to win at the Canal, but the fact is that from Valentine's on I saw only five horses.

And now it was a race in deadly earnest – no longer time to look about or manoeuvre for a clear run, but kick and push and get ground where you can.

The four fences from Valentine's to Anchor Bridge were as exciting as any I ever jumped – and at one of them, the fourth from home, the dice rolled fractionally against Carrickbeg for the first and only time in the whole race.

Understandably, having led almost all the way, Out And About was tiring now and, as French Lawyer went on, he crashed low through the fence and fell.

Perhaps three lengths behind, confronted with a gaping hole and a cloud of flying twigs, Carrickbeg hesitated for a split second, failed to take off when I asked, scrambled through the gap – and had then to swerve past his fallen rival.

These things happen so fast – and are so quickly driven from one's mind by what comes after – that it is all too easy to exaggerate their importance.

The newsreel film does not, unfortunately, show the incident in full, but it does, I think, prove that whereas Carrickbeg was bang with the leaders five from home, one fence later, after Out And About's fall, he had definitely lost at least a couple of lengths. Whatever the truth I do not offer it as an excuse. Such things happen in all Grand Nationals and the winner is the one who best overcomes them.

Probably, in any case, I should have given Carrickbeg a better chance to recover before asking him to go and win. But, passing Anchor Bridge, with the second last in sight, I saw Gerry Scott go for his whip on Springbok, saw the favourite stagger sideways, beaten – and, with Carrickbeg strong under me, it seemed that the time had come.

Until you have tried to ride a finish up it no one, I think, can fully appreciate just how long and wearisome the run-in at Aintree can be after 4 miles and 30 fences.

In the back of my mind now, as I sent Carrickbeg past Ayala and Springbok to join Hawa's Song at the second last, there was the foolish fear that something with a better turn of speed – Owen's Sedge, for instance – would come from behind and beat us all.

In fact, of course, what I *should* have feared was the dreadful strain put upon any horse who, after jumping for 4 miles, finds himself in front with neither fence nor company to help him up that final desperate, staring straight.

Next time, perhaps, I shall know better, but now, as Carrickbeg swept gallantly over the last with Ayala at his quarters, it still seemed possible. His stride had still not faltered and, straightening round the elbow half-way home with the roar of the crowd rising to a crescendo in our ears, the only feeling I remember was one of wild, incredulous hope that the dream first dreamt on a nursery rocking horse long ago was really coming true.

Until this moment, sustained by my horse's strength and by the heat of battle, I had felt no real physical strain, but now, all at once, the cold, clammy hand of exhaustion closed its grip on my thighs and arms.

Even to swing the whip had become an effort and the only thing that kept me going was the unbroken rhythm of Carrickbeg's heroic head, nodding in time with his stride. And, suddenly, even that was gone.

With a hundred yards to go and still no sound of pursuit, the prize seemed within our grasp. Eighty, seventy, sixty perhaps – and then it happened. In the space of a single stride I felt the last ounce of Carrickbeg's energy drain away and my own with it. One moment we were a living, working combination, the next, a struggling, beaten pair. There was still hope – but not for long.

As we passed Ayala before the second last, Carrickbeg had, to Pat Buckley himself, looked the winner bar a fall. 'Go on John,' he found the breath and good nature to say, but saying it, did not for one second relax his efforts. He had been riding hard for longer than I but, with the strength and determination of youth, managed to keep Ayala in the race.

Half-way up the run-in, still two lengths behind, it must have looked as hopeless to him as it did, I believe, from the stands. But he never gave up and, as Carrickbeg began to falter, pulled Ayala out for a final desperate effort.

The gallant chesnut cannot, I think, have quickened much if at all, but the depths of *his* stamina were as yet unplumbed, and so abrupt and complete was Carrickbeg's collapse that in half-a-dozen strides the gap was closed and the race over.

'I wished them both at the bottom of the deep, blue sea.' Pat Buckley and Ayala pass John Lawrence and Carrickbeg.

To my dying day I shall never forget the sight of Ayala's head beside my knee. Two heartbeats later he was half a length in front and, although I dropped my hands before the post, I can honestly promise any aggrieved supporter that it made not one yard of difference.

A wonderful race had been gallantly won and, though perhaps it is not for me to say it, almost equally gallantly lost.

Five lengths away, third, came Hawa's Song who, I believe, had made a bad mistake at the second last. Whether or how much this affected his chance I cannot say, but his running had, in any case, brilliantly justified Willie Stephenson's judgment in buying the horse from his cousin Arthur only a few days before the race.

Springbok, whose supposedly limitless stamina had, oddly enough, let him down three-quarters of a mile from home, tired on the flat and was beaten inches for fourth place by Team Spirit (10st 3lb). Mr R.B. Woodard's game little horse had, according to Willie Robinson, always been jumping too big, spending too much time and effort in the air.

From a hopeless position at the Canal, however, he ran on doggedly all the way home and there were no more delighted spectators on the course than his sporting American owners.

An even braver – and far sadder – story is that of old Kilmore, who landed on a fallen horse at Becher's the second time and, almost certainly, broke down in the effort of recovery. Even so, according to Fred Winter, he never once put a foot wrong and although never within striking distance of the leaders, struggled gallantly round to be sixth.

The old horse finished very lame and having, as his rider said, 'run the best and bravest race of his life', will never be asked to run again.

Behind Kilmore in seventh place came Owen's Sedge who, watched by his owner, Mr Gregory Peck, had jumped safely all the way. Going to the Canal Turn, Pat Taaffe thought he had a chance of being placed, but Owen's Sedge was baulked there by loose horses and could never thereafter get into the race.

French Lawyer, who, for a comparatively inexperienced 'chaser, had run a truly marvellous race – he was, remember, in front four fences from home – finished eighth, just ahead of Dark Venetian (10st 2lb) and Nicolaus Silver (11st).

The 1961 winner, despite going softer than he likes, had jumped as well as ever but never gave Bobby Beasley the slightest hope of success. Twelve more finished – 22 in all – and only 16 of the 47 runners fell or were brought down.

Among them was Jonjo who, until he over-jumped at Becher's second time round, had given his owner, the Duke of Albuquerque, a wonderful ride. Watching the newsreel, I noticed the Duke sitting up his horse's neck like a hero over the first eight fences, and Spain can be proud of its representative in the greatest steeplechase of all.

Frenchman's Cove (12st) made a hash of the first Canal Turn and, despite Dave Dick's vigorous efforts, would take no interest thereafter. Of the other well-backed horses, the worst disappointments were Dagmar Gittell (10st 5lb) and Loving Record (10st 12lb), both of whom were pulled up when hopelessly tailed off.

Mr Jones (10st 10lb), the sort of dour stayer who might have taken a hand in the finish, was unlucky enough to fall at the water and Forty Secrets (10st 7lb) lost any chance he had with a desperate blunder at the second last first time round.

No jockey was seriously injured, but Avenue Neuilly, alas, broke a foreleg and had to be destroyed after falling when already riderless at Becher's second time.

And that, I think, is the story of the 1963 Grand National, a race as fine and spectacular as any ever seen at Aintree.

As has been the case for the past two years, the modified fences presented no insurmountable problems to any reasonably competent jumper, and despite the huge field there was, so far as I could tell, practically no crowding or interference even in the first hectic mile.

The story of Ayala, like that of so many past Grand National winners, is studded with good and bad luck.

Now a nine-year-old chesnut gelding, he was bred by Mr J.P. Phillips at Dalham Hall and is by Supertello out of Admiral's Bliss by Admiral's Walk.

Ironically enough, Mr Phillips, when he has jumpers, now sends them to Don Butchers – so if things had gone differently Ayala could conceivably have become a stable companion of Carrickbeg's.

In fact, however, he was an extremely unpromising yearling with moderate forelegs who, as Mr Phillips's stud-groom C. Palmer recalls, was 'a real headache from the time he was foaled'.

Sent up, with his dam, to Newmarket sales (he was scouring so badly until the day before that Palmer despaired of getting him ready), Ayala was sold for 400 guineas to Mr G. Mostyn Owen – and, in the many transactions in which he has figured since, has never reached so high a price again!

Nor was poor Mr Mostyn Owen's money well spent, for when sent to Henri Jelliss at Newmarket, Ayala proved, in the words of the trainer, 'too slow to win a donkey race and too big even to get on a racecourse'. At the end of his second season he was, therefore, sold again, this time for only 40 guineas, to Mr N. Smith, who lives in Epping Forest.

It was then that Mr John Chapman, a tremendously keen and sporting enthusiast, heard of a potential hunter for sale and his wife, seeing Ayala one day on her way back from Newmarket, bought him 'for a song'.

Ayala was in fact a pretty bad hunter – as Mr Chapman's daughter soon discovered – so his owner decided to send him to Keith Piggott to be tried as a hurdler.

This venture, too, met with little success and, since he had another horse in training with Piggott of apparently greater promise, Mr Chapman told the trainer to send him to Epsom sales.

It was a tragic decision, for Mr Chapman, like most jumping owners, has dreamed all his life of getting a Grand National horse – and had he only held on a little longer, Ayala's true milieu would have become clear.

In fact, with Mr Chapman's full permission, Piggott bought the horse for 250 guineas and sold a half-share in him to Mr P.B. Raymond, the celebrated ladies' hairdresser.

In 1960–61, Ayala won three steeplechases and, although he had to be pin-fired last season, Piggott told Mr Raymond long ago that what they had was a potential winner of the Grand National.

That hope did not look very realistic when Ayala turned over at the open ditch on his reappearance at Cheltenham, but, next time out, he won well at Worcester and as Stan Mellor dismounted Mr Raymond told him 'you have just ridden the winner of the 1963 Grand National'.

Mellor, however, was already engaged for Frenchman's Cove and after asking at least one other jockey (Gene Kelly) Piggott approached Pat Buckley.

Only 19 years old, Buckley was born in Kildare and got his early riding experience there out hunting and as a member of the Pony Club. He joined Neville Crump's stable three years ago and quickly showed himself a tough, able horseman.

Last year, taking Gerry Scott's place on Springbok in the Grand National, he had the appalling luck to fall at the very first fence; but the fates did not wait long to give him ample repayment.

No one could have ridden a better or stronger race than Buckley did on Saturday – and who knows what further triumphs may be waiting in the long, bright future that stretches ahead of him.

I hope I shall be forgiven for holding over description of other events last week to our next issue. Perhaps I am prejudiced, but it seems to me that the 1963 Grand National was big enough to fill these pages on its own!

6 April 1963

The following January, Carrickbeg ran at Sandown Park.

I had set out, full of hope, on Carrickbeg (12st 2lb) for the Stanley Handicap 'Chase (3m) – only his second appearance since the National.

In his first, at Towcester in October, Carrickbeg had struck into himself just above the fetlock joint of his near-fore – but was never lame, never even flinched to pressure on the spot and had, according to the vets, bruised the tendon sheath without harming the tendon itself.

'It's only a blow' – how often I seem to have heard those words, and how often they turn out to be hollow, artificial grounds for hope. . . .

But none of that was in my mind on the Friday as, making the fences look and feel like so many upturned dandy brushes, Carrickbeg sailed round with the same easy, measured stride which carried him so close to triumph at Aintree last year.

I've said 'the same', but it wasn't really – for now, down the Railway straight, with only Jonjo (10st 13lb) and Mac's Leap (10st) in front, I felt like a man driving a supercharged Ferrari behind two Austin Sevens.

The plan had been to strike the front only between the last two, but Carrickbeg himself soon altered that, soaring eagle-like past Mac's Leap (to whom, remember, he was giving 30lb) at the third of the Railway fences and storming round to the Pond on a tight rein with the other floundering behind him.

And then, with the thought passing through my mind, 'We're going to win too far,' it happened. Fifty yards from the last – too late to do anything about it – the near-fore tendon gave way and Carrickbeg, though never attempting to spare himself, checked, changed legs and lost his action.

Even so, he stood back and flew the last and, with every stride increasing his agony, he held off Centre Circle (10st 13lb) by two lengths to win.

But no victory was ever gained at greater cost and no winning jockey ever returned to scale with a heavier heart.

It is still too early, as I write, to say just how bad the injury may be – but it is bad enough, and the one consolation now is that Carrickbeg, still only eight years old, has plenty of time ahead.

Perhaps, one day, he will come again to Aintree – and if he does, let them all beware.

18 January 1964

Poor Carrickbeg. Gay Kindersley, who had taken over his training from Don Butchers, gave him nearly two years' rest, but when we tried again in December 1965 it was soon painfully clear that the old fire was gone. Carrickbeg ran four times, and although I remember a moment at Sandown which raised my hopes, it was an illusion.

In retirement Carrickbeg became a superb hunter and particularly enjoyed himself with the Mid-Surrey Farmers' Drag, of which Gay was then Master. I had one glorious day on him, and have a picture by Peter Biegel which shows how relaxed he became.

ONE BIG
HARD LUCK STORY

The clock was put back 39 years last week and, as Mr C.P.T. Watkins's Foinavon plodded dourly home to win the 1967 Grand National, the ghost of Tipperary Tim walked once again at Aintree.

For out across the rainswept course – at the fence after Becher's, not a hundred yards from where, in 1928, the fallen Easter Hero decimated his opponents – a scene even stranger and more chaotic than that famous tragedy had taken place.

In far less time than it takes to write these words the wayward whim of one loose horse had smashed to smithereens what promised, till that moment, to be one of the finest, most spectacular contests in the National's history. And in all that history the race has surely never undergone a transformation half so sudden, violent and complete.

The disaster came, what's more, without the slightest warning, like a thunderbolt from a clear blue sky. Of the 44 runners, only 9 had failed to survive the first circuit – and no fewer than 30 landed safely over Becher's second time round.

As the leaders bore down on the 23rd fence – a small one on the left-handed elbow between Becher's and the Canal Turn – my guess is that at least 15 were close enough, and going well enough, to keep their jockeys' hopes alive.

Of these, the ones that I could see – for Norther (10st) was eighth or ninth, going as well as most – were Rutherfords (10st 11lb), Kirtle-Lad (10st 3lb), Princeful (10st 2lb) and Castle Falls (10st 3lb), the quartet who had shared the lead throughout. Close behind them, Rondetto (11st 7lb) was still pulling double, Terry Biddlecombe had got Greek Scholar (10st 9lb) tucked in near the inside rail, Kapeno (11st 1lb) and The Fossa (10st 2lb) were just in front of Norther and a moment earlier Different Class (11st 2lb) had appeared beside me as we went to Becher's.

Landing over it, David Mould had time to give him a pat of congratulation and if, at that moment, someone had asked me to name the winner my answer would have been Different Class.

But no one asked and in any case the time for easy speculation was long gone. For by Becher's second time – for those who have something left to go to war with – it is no longer merely a matter of survival. From there on it is a *race* and the most immediate question if, like me, you have jumped Becher's towards the outside, is how best to save ground around the two left-handed bends that follow. And it was now, as I edged Norther inward, that the sky fell on us all.

Long before, at the very first fence, Bassnet (10st 11lb), jumping too boldly, had crumpled up on landing and knocked over both Meon Valley (10st 7lb) and Popham Down (10st).

And so it was that, through no fault of his own, the blinkered Popham Down will go down in history as the horse who decided the 1967 Grand National.

I say 'through no fault of his own' – and mean it – for, to a riderless horse wearing blinkers, the sound and fury of a big field at Aintree must be terrifying and if, after jumping 22 fences perfectly normally, Popham Down decided that enough was enough, well, I for one don't blame him.

But the results of his decision were both dreadful and far-reaching. There may have been another loose horse involved, but my only clear memory is of Popham Down's blinkered head veering wildly across the field from left to right.

Rutherfords, Castle Falls and Princeful were probably his first victims, but in the next half-minute or so there were rather more urgent matters on hand than horse identification.

I don't, for instance, know the name of the unfortunate animal who, when Norther arrived at the 23rd fence, was lying directly in our path. Norther jumped *him* all right – but landed in the fence itself.

And that, alas, was the end of a supremely memorable ride – for, while I took the high road, he took the low and, when we came to rest, the fence, or what was left of it, lay between us.

Looking back, from the ground, the scene was reminiscent of those blood-curdling nineteenth-century sporting prints – with an added dash of nightmarish unreality.

Above the shattered fence, horses' heads were waving like demented serpents and, expecting one of them to join me at any moment, I waited no longer. 'Mr Lawrence dashing in search of his horse,' said one kindly newspaper caption – but 'Mr Lawrence running for his life' would have been much nearer the mark!

Stan Mellor (The Fossa), Pat Buckley (Limeking), Roy Edwards (Princeful) and Paddy Broderick (Kirtle-Lad) all fetched up, like me, without their horses on the landing side – but that is about all I can tell you from personal experience. The rest must be reconstruction from various sources and I do not vouch for its total accuracy.

One thing, however, is certain – that until the arrival of Foinavon (10st) no horse got over the fatal fence without either stopping or losing his rider.

Rondetto did, I think, jump it without falling, but Johnny Haine was knocked off as they landed and, although he got back aboard, Rondetto understandably declined his invitation to continue.

He had been going particularly strongly just before the disaster – almost running away in fact – and is one of the many whose supporters will always wonder 'what might have been'.

Apart from Rondetto – and Kirtle-Lad, who, like him, refused at the Canal Turn – 7 horses either fell at the 23rd or failed, for some reason, to get over it. They were Different Class, The Fossa, Norther, Dorimont, Princeful, Harry Black and Limeking – and as regards the last-named there is a grave injustice to be righted.

For, perhaps because photographs showed him lying in the bottom of the fence, several Sunday newspapers accused poor Limeking of causing – or helping to cause – all the trouble. In fact, of course, he did nothing of the sort, but was himself knocked over and winded in the *mêlée*. If horses could sue for libel, Limeking would never have to work again!

The bedlam at the 23rd fence in the 1967 Grand National.

His prostrate body (and, for a while, poor Norther's) did, however, serve to make the fence more or less unjumpable – and with some jockeys turning round to have another go, others trying to remount or find their horses, and still others coming up from farther behind, the situation on the take-off side was one of indescribable confusion. And it was into this cauldron of furious activity that John Buckingham now found himself galloping on Foinavon.

Twenty-six years old and riding, last week, in his first Grand National, Buckingham had only been engaged to ride Foinavon three days beforehand.

Setting out, understandably, with no great hopes beyond getting as far as possible, he found the horse a safe and accurate jumper – but not fast enough to stay near the leaders.

At Becher's, in fact, they were only three or four from last but (and this is significant) John Buckingham could see the favourite, Honey End (10st 4lb) not far ahead.

'We were a hundred yards from the leaders,' he says, 'but I

knew if I could stay somewhere near Josh [Josh Gifford, who rode Honey End] we wouldn't be far behind the winner in the end.'

But now, landing safely over Becher's, Buckingham saw the chaos up ahead – and here an episode from his past career is distinctly relevant. For on 5 March 1966, John Buckingham was riding a horse called Lira for his chief employer, Mr Edward Courage, in a steeplechase at Market Rasen.

There were ten runners and, at a certain stage of the race, faced with two alternative fences to jump, nine of them jumped the wrong one. Buckingham alone chose right and, after finishing second, got the race on an objection.

Here there was a fine example of quick thinking – and last Saturday the 23rd fence in the Grand National was a place where quick thinking paid rich dividends.

It is true, of course, in a way, that Foinavon won the National because he was too slow. Better horses had no time to take avoiding action simply because they were better and therefore closer to the trouble.

But that does not detract either from John Buckingham's cool horsemanship or from Foinavon's courage. The man saw that the only possible route to safety was on the wide outside – and the horse was bold enough to push his way between two riderless opponents.

Jumping almost from a standstill, he hopped safely over and, in that somewhat unspectacular moment, the 1967 Grand National was decided.

None knew it at the time, of course, not even Buckingham, who did not realise he was in front until and after Valentine's, and certainly not the Aintree crowd to whom, alas, the whole fiasco had been almost completely invisible.

But, in fact, as Foinavon cleared the Canal Turn, the pursuit had not even started. Kirtle-Lad was the first away, but he, as we've seen, refused to continue.

Packed Home (10st), Aussie (10st) and Greek Scholar were, I think, the first to get going, having, all three, jumped the 23rd fence at the second attempt.

Behind them quite a race developed – but it was all in vain. For Foinavon, to his own and his rider's eternal credit, never faltered or fumbled for an instant.

He may not have gone very fast (though his time was better than Anglo's last year), but he made no serious mistakes and he kept on galloping.

Just for a moment between the last two fences, as Honey End passed Greek Scholar to take second place, it looked on the cards that the tables might even now be turned. But Honey End – whom Gifford had taken back 50 yards to get a run at the 23rd fence – had done all he could and on the run-in Foinavon's lead remained intact.

It is, in the circumstances, easy to understand Josh Gifford's conviction that, with a clear run, Honey End would have won outright. But I wonder whether the facts really support it.

Admittedly, over the last mile the favourite did make up an extraordinary amount of ground. But the horses he was passing had all, to different degrees, been involved in the fiasco at the 23rd, and Foinavon, on whom, of course, he gained the best part of 200 yards is, to put it politely, no flying machine.

And don't forget that when Popham Down struck his blow, Honey End, as Gifford himself admits, was 20 lengths behind horses like Different Class, Rondetto, Kapeno and The Fossa.

Under Saturday's perfect conditions I don't see why *all* the leaders shouldn't have 'come back' – so, to win, Honey End had to make up 20 lengths from the Canal Turn on good horses who, at that point, were apparently still full of running. I don't say he wouldn't have done it – but I do say it wouldn't have been easy.

All that, however, is mere speculation. The facts are that Foinavon beat Honey End by 15 lengths, with Red Alligator (10st) 3 more lengths away, third.

Brian Fletcher – who had remounted Red Alligator with extraordinary speed – is just as convinced as Josh Gifford that he would have won 'if only'. But so are so many others that the whole race is really one big hard luck story.

In a couple of years' time I expect I shall feel pretty certain that Norther 'should' have won – but the name in the record books will still be Foinavon and that, really, is that.

Greek Scholar, trained, like Red Alligator, by Denys Smith, was fourth, Packed Home fifth and Solbina (11st 2lb) sixth.

I never personally saw Solbina in the race but he was apparently close enough at Becher's second time round, and made up a good deal of ground when he finally got away from the shambles.

The same certainly applies to What A Myth (12st), who refused the 23rd twice before he got over. But he, like his stable companion Honey End, was a long way behind the leaders at Becher's Brook.

It was, no doubt, a fine performance by What A Myth to finish ninth in the end, but I'm still not convinced that either of Ryan Price's pair would, other things being equal, have caught Different Class and Co.

Eighteen horses finished in all, but one, Vulcano (10st) had, alas, been destroyed after falling at the third fence. Almost unbelievably no jockey was even slightly injured.

And here it occurs to me that we should be heartily thankful for one thing – namely that what happened happened where it did and not one fence earlier. For Popham Down could just as easily have chosen Becher's and, had he done so, the probable results do not really bear thinking about.

Even as it is, these sensational events have, inevitably, given rise to talk of 'reforming' the National yet again, and in particular of tightening up the qualification for entry.

It seems to me, however, that no such change is needed. A field of forty-odd is perfectly reasonable at Aintree – *until* loose horses start to get in the way. And loose *good* horses are just as dangerous as loose *bad* ones.

Bassnet, for instance, might equally easily have caused Saturday's disaster. In fact, in a way, he did cause it.

So the answer, surely, is to get the loose horses out of the way as soon as possible – and that means doing away with (or leaving wide gaps in) the inside rail, particularly on the run down to Becher's.

I don't myself see anything much against this – so long as the fences have big, well-angled wings, but of course if you remove rails to let loose horses out you may also occasionally let one in who has fallen somewhere else.

Almost certainly a compromise solution can be found, and anyway there have, after all, been only two really serious fiascos of this kind in nearly forty years. So the main problem to be solved about the Grand National is still how to keep it going.

There is absolutely nothing wrong with the race itself – and the occasional total turn-up, however painful at the time, is perhaps a salutary reminder that this is still the National – a contest in which literally *anything* can happen.

It is also still by far the most exciting race I know to ride in and last week, on superlative going, the first circuit had, for most of us, been pure delight. There was always, it seemed, room to spare – and to jump these fences at speed on a bold horse remains, for me, a thrill I have yet to find anywhere else.

Mr Alec Marsh had to start us by flag on Saturday (the starting gates had given trouble all week), but he made a superb job of it. As usual the field was split into two schools of thought – the inside or 'Fred Winter' school, which, not unnaturally, is more fashionable at present – and the 'outside as far as Becher's' school, to which, I was reassured to see, Terry Biddlecombe belongs.

Bassnet, Popham Down and Meon Valley (a luckless first National ride for poor Andy Turnell) all fell as described at the first fence and April Rose (10st 8lb), usually so sure-footed, went at the third with Vulcano.

At the second Dun Widdy (10st 10lb) had pulled the reins out of Mr J. Edwards's hands, and, having got them back, but both on the same side, Mr Edwards managed miraculously to get as far as the 16th fence before he had to pull up.

Penvulgo (10st) and Princeful led over Becher's first time (where Border Fury fell) and these two, with Castle Falls and Rutherfords, made all the running first time round.

At the fence after Becher's, Norther made a slight mistake and Terry Biddlecombe, beside us on Greek Scholar, said sympathetically, 'That's a bastard, isn't it?' Just how big a bastard neither he nor I could know!

So on we went, and passing the stands, tracking Nick Gaselee on Kapeno (who jumped Becher's twice with ease) and Stan Mellor on The Fossa, I felt almost, if not quite, as much hope as Carrickbeg had given me at the same stage four years earlier.

The pace had not been slow (it could not have been considering Foinavon's time), and Anglo (11st 1lb), for one, found it beyond him. He had never been going well and was pulled up after making a hash of the Chair.

Freddie (11st 13lb) too was somewhat out-paced, but had, according to Pat McCarron, just begun to improve at Becher's.

It took him three attempts to get through the shambles at the 23rd and, finishing seventeenth in the end, he has probably run in his last Grand National.

Of the other well-fancied horses, Kilburn (11st) was going easily in the middle division when, for some unknown reason, he galloped straight on at the open ditch before Becher's second time round.

But so many of the rest were still standing and full of steam that the stage, I'm certain, was set for a battle royal.

This, as I've said before, was the best Grand National field for years and would have produced a magnificent race. Fate decreed differently – but there will be other days.

Bred in Ireland by Mr T.H. Ryan, Foinavon is a good-looking nine-year-old by Vulgan, whose position as leading N.H. sire is now consolidated.

The dam, Ecilace, by Interlace, also had a good 'chaser called Umm, who was well-fancied to win a Grand National some years ago.

Owned originally by Anne Duchess of Westminster and trained by Tom Dreaper, Foinavon accompanied Arkle on his first visit to England, but thereafter their paths diverged somewhat violently – and Foinavon's led to Doncaster Sales, where John Kempton bought him for 2,000 guineas on Mr Watkins's behalf.

The nine-year-old's record since has not been distinguished, but he had his hour last week and as long as the Grand National is run his name will remind us that no man who rides at Aintree need ever be completely without hope.

15 April 1967

TWO SEPARATE
SPORTING MIRACLES

At 3 p.m. last Saturday afternoon Lord Leverhulme, issuing the now traditional Senior Steward's pre-Grand National admonition, warned 38 somewhat preoccupied jockeys not to go too fast too soon.

And he added, lapsing understandably into cliché, that the eyes of the world would shortly be upon us.

About 27 minutes and 1.9 seconds later (the tapes went up at 3.18), 36 members of his Lordship's audience were wishing that the other two had taken more heed of his advice. And as for the eyes of the world, well, they were either bright with excitement or dim with tears at the wonder and pathos of two separate sporting miracles.

For they had seen Mr Noel Le Mare's Red Rum fulfil a dream first dreamt nearly 80 years ago, and they had also been privileged to watch Sir Chester Manifold's Crisp achieve a feat unequalled in all the National's long heroic history.

Superlatives like these are all too easy to misuse, but I have chosen my words with care and have the facts to back them.

There is absolutely no reason to doubt the official time of Red Rum's victory and Crisp, just three-quarters of a length behind him at the post, is fully entitled to share it.

At 30 m.p.h., the average speed of slower Grand Nationals than this, a horse covers 293 yards in 20 seconds. So, making every conceivable allowance for variable factors, Crisp would have passed the winning post *at least* 200 yards in front of Golden Miller, whose 38-year-old record he and Red Rum smashed by very nearly 19 seconds.

The alterations in 1961 to 24 of the National's 30 fences (it is often forgotten that neither the water jump nor, more important, the open ditches, were touched) have never, hitherto, appeared to have any effect on times. And, although the going was certainly lightning fast last week, there is nothing either new or strange about that.

At least twice in my own experience the race has been run under comparable conditions.

No, twist them as you please, the facts speak for themselves. And what they say is that these two horses treated the greatest steeplechase course in the world as it has never been treated before. They also say – and many millions will confirm – that of all the factors which combined to make this miracle, by far and away the most important was Crisp's fast, flawless, fearless jumping.

To my infinite regret I only saw it from afar – through the tangled, violent spectrum that is the average National jockey's point of view.

My last clear memory of Crisp is of the daring angle at which Richard Pitman asked him to jump the Canal Turn first time round. Already alone in front, the big horse, as television shows, cocked his ears in surprise at this unaccustomed command.

But the hesitation was only fractional – and next time, remembering, he cut the corner sharp of his own accord.

Many horses, of course, have jumped round boldly and well at Aintree without making a single mistake. But what Crisp achieved – over fences like nothing he had ever seen before – was a unique blend of speed and economy.

And again, as the clock confirms, the word 'unique' means precisely what it says.

The third fence in a National is the one many jockeys fear most – an upright cliff of an open ditch coming when the normal horse is still unaccustomed to the shape and size of Aintree.

But Crisp is far from a normal horse. All obstacles come alike to him – just one more problem to be solved as quickly and neatly as possible.

So, flicking over the great ditch now, he landed clear in front and, from that moment on, neither he nor Richard Pitman saw another horse until the end.

The Aintree fences are so constructed – loose furze on a foundation of unyielding thorn – that there is a precise minimum height, about six inches lower than their own, at which they can and should ideally be jumped. It is an irreducible minimum, though, a minimum under which lurk great black stakes as thick as your arm.

And, while six inches too low may be dangerous, six inches too high involves unnecessary effort.

The measure of Crisp's achievement last week is that, having struck this precious golden mean at once, he never wavered from it by a hairsbreadth. And for that achievement, needless to say, Richard Pitman, the finger on the trigger of this matchless weapon, deserves a lion's share of credit.

It was easy, afterwards, as it always is, to wonder whether, by giving Crisp a more pronounced 'breather' at some stage, Richard might have conserved the ounce or so of energy which, in the end, was all he needed.

No National was ever run without such questions and, since the same race is never run twice, they are never satisfactorily answered. But Pitman's answer – which I for one accept unreservedly – is that, sensing the precious yards Crisp was gaining at every fence, he determined to make his rivals win them back the hard way.

The fact that only one was able to do so – in the dying seconds of the race and with the third horse 25 lengths farther back – is surely all the vindication any man could need.

Thirty-eight horses set out in the 1973 Grand National and I make no apology for having so far mentioned only two of them. For there were, in effect, two races run last Saturday and in one of them only Red Rum and Crisp took a meaningful part.

But while one can make a triumph it takes two to make an epic, and it is time now to examine Brian Fletcher's feelings as, landing over Valentine's with only five fences left to jump, he saw Crisp still apparently going strong all of 30 lengths ahead.

His plan had been to ride a patient waiting race, but all too clearly now the time for patience was long gone. So he and Red Rum (10st 5lb) set sail in pursuit and the fact that 99 people out of 100 now wish they had failed in no way diminishes the gallantry and strength with which they attacked their apparently hopeless task.

It still looked hopeless at the second last – for Crisp stood back and flew, not at all the leap of a horse near the limit of exhaustion. But he *was* near it and only a moment later Richard Pitman felt the last dregs drain away.

What followed was the saddest, bravest sight I have ever seen on an English racecourse. Because, as Crisp started up the cruel, crooked quarter-mile of Aintree's run-in, his legs, so strong and certain until now, turned to rubber under him. With no rail to follow for the first 100 yards, he hung left-handed as if to go round again, and, when he wavered back on course, the rhythm of his gallop was lost beyond recall.

Seen from the stands – or on the television screen – these signs of exhaustion were a heartbreaking sight. But to Brian Fletcher they spelt hope and, calling on Red Rum for a final crucial effort, he set about closing the gap.

There was only just time even now and only a horse of quite exceptional courage could possibly have made it.

But Red Rum, whose racing career began in a humble two-year-old selling-race on this same course six years ago, has kept intact all the zest and enthusiasm of youth. Every ounce of the 23lb poor Crisp was trying to concede must by now have weighed a ton and, 50 yards from the line, as Red Rum's head appeared in the corner of Richard Pitman's eye, there was nothing left to do.

Nothing, that is, except lose gracefully, and an enduring memory of this supremely memorable race will always be the stoic sportsmanship with which Richard Pitman and Fred Winter bore their disappointment. In less than three weeks they had seen the two most important prizes in steeplechasing snatched from their grasp at the eleventh hour.*

To curse and cry would have been entirely forgivable – to smile, as they did, was magnificent.

But, leaving them for the moment in the bitter glory of a defeat worth a thousand victories, come back nine minutes to

* On 15 March Fred Winter watched Pendil stop on the Cheltenham hill and allow himself to be caught and beaten by The Dikler (pages 132–6). Crisp's heart-rending defeat came sixteen days later on 31 March and, just a week after that, Killiney, whom Fred thought the brightest prospect he had ever trained, was killed in a fall at Ascot.

the Melling Road and the close-packed jostling cavalry charge that is the start of a Grand National.

Red Rum (near side) gets up to beat Crisp.

Only Richeleau (10st) failed to survive the first fence and as Crisp (12st) began to build up his lead at the third, Ashville (10st 4lb) crumpled not far behind him.

My own feelings at that moment – apart from relief at Proud Tarquin's neat, unflurried jumping – was that such a pace could not possibly last.

But I was wrong. It never slackened for a moment, and as Crisp led us down to Becher's (he flicked it behind him like an upturned dandy brush) very few if any of his pursuers were on the bit.

Grey Sombrero (10st 9lb), Black Secret (11st 2lb), Endless Folly (10st), and, to his eternal credit, Mill Door (10st) were the first to follow him over the Brook and both Culla Hill (10st) and Beggar's Way (10st) were already well behind when they fell there.

Mr Vimy blundered too badly to continue and the great drop so unnerved Swan Shot (10st) that he refused to jump the next.

Highland Seal (10st) had made such a series of mistakes that David Nicholson pulled him up after the Canal Turn and a gallant adventure ended tragically here when the Duke of Albuquerque's stirrup-leather broke on Nereo.

Proud Tarquin made one of his few mistakes at the second ditch but I was much nearer to falling off than he to falling and on we went past Anchor Bridge with Crisp now about a fence in front.

Only one horse, Grey Sombrero, had even attempted to stay with the leader and for him the Chair brought tragedy. Landing on his own in second place, the handsome grey knuckled over for no obvious reason and, in what looked a harmless fall, had the cruel misfortune to break his shoulder.

Black Secret, Sunny Lad (10st 3lb), Rouge Autumn (10st) and Great Noise (10st 2lb) jumped the Chair in line abreast and now, for the first time, Red Rum appeared among the leading group.

The Chair is not only the biggest fence at Aintree but also the narrowest and, as Proud Tarquin sailed serenely over it, I saw and heard the beginning of the race's first real pile-up.

Proud Percy (10st) had somehow got his hind legs inside the guard rail and, bravely though he tried, could not hope to get the necessary height. As he crashed headlong, Canharis (10st 1lb) found no ground to land on and neither Charley Winking (10st) nor Red Rum's stable companion Glenkiln (10st) survived the *mêlée*.

On the turn in front of the stands a too enthusiastic photographer, leaning out over the rails, got a blow from my boot which must have hurt him even more than it did me – but I cannot pretend to feeling much sympathy at the time.

For now, of the 25 still standing, only 8 or 9 were in front of Proud Tarquin and, still reckoning the pace too hot to last, I had begun to hope for miracles.

Up in front – though still a fence behind the flying leader – Philip Blacker, Ken White, Bob Champion and Sean Barker had even better grounds for optimism on Spanish Steps, Rouge Autumn, Hurricane Rock and Black Secret.

And all the while Brian Fletcher was coolly biding his time on Red Rum, hoarding the energy which he alone, as things turned out, would have the chance to use.

Fortune Bay refused at the 19th – not before he had given his owner, George Sloan, some vivid memories to take back to America – and Rough Silk dropped out at the same fence.

Beau Parc pulled up before Becher's second time, and at the 27th, the final ditch, Astbury, Princess Camilla, General Symons, Mill Door and Sunny Lad were all involved in a traffic jam, the cause of which I cannot tell you. For these were already stragglers and as Red Rum drew clear of the rest at Valentine's the race, for most of us, was over.

Not quite for all, however. L'Escargot (12st), perhaps remembering his undeserved disaster in 1972, had jumped so cautiously early on that Tommy Carberry could take no sort of place. But now the former Gold Cup winner's class came into play and, storming past me at Anchor Bridge, he caught his old rival Spanish Steps on the flat to finish an honourable third.

Class, in fact, was superbly vindicated, for the top five horses in the handicap filled five of the first ten places.

Rouge Autumn (fifth), Hurricane Rock (sixth), Prophesy (eighth) and Endless Folly (ninth) were the only members of the huge 10st brigade to finish in single figures and, although I may be prejudiced, it seemed to me that Proud Tarquin (seventh) had enough steam left to suggest that for him, on softer ground and with no Crisp to chase, there may be another day. He had, in any case, given me an unforgettable ten minutes, and went home, I am glad to say, without a scratch to show for his adventures.

So that was the 1973 Grand National, the last, it seems, to be superintended by Mrs Topham, but surely far too fine a sporting spectacle to be the last of all. Seventeen horses finished, only poor Grey Sombrero was seriously hurt and even Crisp came back unscathed to eat his dinner as though it had been just any day.

In one's admiration for his heroism it would be easy to do the winner less than justice. So let it never be forgotten how Red Rum answered every call made on him when nine horses out of ten would have abandoned hope.

For his 85-year-old owner, Mr Le Mare, this was the fulfilment of a lifelong dream, and for his trainer, Ginger McCain, the culmination of a long-laid, brilliantly executed plan. They and

Brian Fletcher will not mind sharing the glory with Crisp, Richard Pitman and Fred Winter. For on 31 March 1973 there was glory to spare at Aintree.

6 April 1973

RED RUM –
THE GREATEST
'CHASER IN GRAND
NATIONAL HISTORY!

If Lottery, Cloister, Manifesto and Golden Miller had crossed the Melling Road together last Saturday afternoon, they would still have been no more than a respectful guard of honour. For you can only have one King, and as Red Rum sparkled home alone to win a third Grand National there was no longer any way that his claim to the Aintree throne can be disputed.

In five successive years he has jumped the great course five

Red Rum and Tommy Stack gallop their way into Grand
National legend.

times without making a single serious mistake. No other horse has ever won three Nationals, no other horse has been first or second five years running, and no other horse ever covered those 4$^{1}/^{2}$ miles as fast as Red Rum did to beat Crisp in 1973.

So let us, please, have no quibbling about easier fences, weaker opposition, lower weights or better going. Ever since he first went there ten years ago – to dead-heat in a two-year-old selling race over five furlongs – Red Rum has simply taken Aintree as he found it.

If 'luck' has sometimes seemed to favour him, it is because he has a genius for the place – and real genius jogs Fate's elbow.

There were several moments last week, for instance, when one of Red Rum's fallen rivals could so easily have brought him down and, from the Canal Turn second time, he and Tommy Stack never had less than two loose horses to contend with.

But that's the National. That is Aintree, and the weapons needed to survive there are cunning, foresight and agility. No other horse has ever blended them more perfectly and the success of Red Rum's unique method has now been far too regular and consistent to be ascribed to luck.

In one respect, admittedly, the Fates were kind last week, because a good deal of rain had fallen at Aintree before the meeting opened and although the ground was drying up on Friday morning there followed a nightmare afternoon of gales, rain and sleet.

They looked like producing the sort of going Red Rum hates and, if repeated next day, they would have made the National an ordeal difficult to bear and quite impossible to enjoy.

So, next morning when the sun came out again, and a drying wind repaired the damage, it was indeed a sort of miracle. As the 42 runners circled the paddock, Red Rum's quarters glittered like a beacon of hope and there was no trace of favouritism in the judges' decision to give his devoted attendant Billy Beardwood the prize for 'best turned out horse'.

The biggest crowd seen at Aintree for many years had already had its appetite whetted by two supremely exciting races starring the Champion Two Mile 'chaser Skymas and the Champion Hurdler Night Nurse.

Either would have made any normal day and, as the 42 runners lined up, in light so crystal clear that the Canal Turn was perfectly visible from the stands, the pessimistic thought occurred that, after such curtain-raisers, even the National might turn out an anti-climax.

So, sadly, it did for some, because the first fence produced its longest casualty list since the disastrous eleven-horse pile-up in 1951.

The starter was in no way to blame this time, but seven either fell or were brought down.

The Senior Steward, Lord Derby, had, as usual, reminded the jockeys that a $4^1/2$-mile steeplechase is not a five-furlong sprint, but I'm afraid that even good advice like that is apt to go in one ear and out the other in the nerve-jangling minutes before a Grand National start.

Anyway, whatever the reason, Willy What was, as far as I could see, the first to go and he undoubtedly brought down War Bonnet. High Ken was knocked over, too, through no fault of his own, while for various reasons Spittin Image, Duffle Coat, Huperade and Pengrail also got no farther.

It is hard to exaggerate the piercing disappointment of a fall so early in a National. Before this of all races it is impossible not to build up hopes of a sort and, however remote and unjustifiable they may have been, it is a real heartbreak to find them shattered when the race has scarcely begun.

So to these seven jockeys, whose sad fate I shared not all that long ago, I offer heartfelt, if useless, sympathy.

Sebastian and Boom Docker were disputing the lead as Red Rum and the other survivors picked their way through the first-fence carnage, but the third, that horribly large and staring open ditch, claimed an even more distinguished victim.

I did not see exactly what happened to the Gold Cup winner Davy Lad, but since he had never fallen in his life before it seems fair to give him the benefit of any doubt that is going.

What can be said for certain is that Royal Thrust hit the fence so hard that Colin Tinkler could not possibly be blamed for going into orbit. Inycarra also fell or was brought down and although I understand that some interested party accuses Miss Charlotte Brew and Barony Fort of causing Burrator's downfall, I can only say that if that was the case Burrator must have been undesirably and, at that stage, hazardously far behind. Because Miss Brew had sensibly set off as near the outside rail as she could get and, by the fence before Becher's (only two after the third), Barony Fort was already more or less tailed off. I very much doubt whether he did anyone any serious harm – and if he did it was the sort of accident which is often inevitable among no-hope backmarkers in a National.

Talking of backmarkers, the greatly and understandably fancied Gay Vulgan was, by this time, among them. Whether through his own fault or not he had undergone an experience at the first fence which made him wish he was somewhere else.

Many of the sons of the great Vulgan have loved Aintree and flourished there but on this one, sadly, it had the opposite effect. Gay Vulgan quickly chose discretion instead of valour and, although Bill Smith somehow managed to get him round once, he had very wisely pulled up before Becher's on the second circuit.

The even better bred Fort Vulgan was brought down by Harban at the fourth and as Sebastian V landed over Becher's in the lead, his forelegs failed to withstand the extra strain. He did not, technically speaking, fall but Ridley Lamb would have needed a safety harness to stay with him.

To Sebastian's eternal credit he carried on riderless to the bitter end, jumping straight, causing no trouble and actually finishing either first or second. But now he was gone and behind him the famous fence claimed a much more tragic victim when Winter Rain crumpled landing over it and broke his neck.

Castleruddery fell at Becher's too, so as Boom Docker led Prince Rock and Brown Admiral round the Canal Turn, the original 42 had been reduced to 26.

So much for the theory, so often advanced from the safety of the stands, that the Aintree fences have been made 'too easy' nowadays.

But at least Red Rum had avoided all the carnage – sidestepping at Becher's, for instance, like a Welsh three-quarter – and the only other faller as Boom Docker led them down to Anchor Bridge was Prince Rock.

Having presumably frightened himself by a slight mistake at the 11th, an open ditch, he swerved and stopped so violently at the next that poor Graham Thorner was fired out as if from an ejector seat.

In fact, Prince Rock did eventually follow him over – but at such an angle that the horses behind him were lucky to escape.

Prince Rock's owner, Mr Michael Buckley, has had some wonderful moments this season, but last week, I'm sorry to say, the Fates demanded a cruel double repayment for their favours. The second instalment was even sadder, because second time round the Hennessy Gold Cup winner Zeta's Son was still very much in the race and making ground when he fell at Valentine's and had to be destroyed. He and Winter Rain, the other fatal casualty, were two high-class 'chasers of the kind we can least afford to lose.

Jumping magnificently, Boom Docker came to the Chair a good 15 lengths in front – and his lead was doubled when Sage Merlin hit the top of the biggest fence on the course and failed to get his undercarriage down in time.

As he struggled to his feet, Red Rum landed over the Chair behind him, and, as usual, chose correctly to jink left instead of right. For that was the way Sage Merlin went and the great horse could easily have taken him amidships.

But all was well, the water caused no pain (though Lord of the Hills pulled up there) and as Barony Fort cleared it two furlongs behind the leader Miss Brew got a sympathetic cheer.

But the jockey who needed sympathy next was John Williams, to whom Boom Docker had, till then, given such a memorably exhilarating ride.

No one will ever know what passed through Boom Docker's head as he galloped alone towards the first fence second time round. Perhaps he remembered where the stables are, or perhaps his carefree exertions had begun to tell. Whatever the reason, he ran down the 17th, refused to take off at all and is just one more of those problems in equine psychology which Aintree so often produces.

So, for the second time, the lead was violently altered and as Andy Pandy pulled his way clear going down to Becher's, Fred Rimell's long-held opinion that this was the best of his four runners looked easy to understand.

At this stage last year I remember thinking that Golden Rapper might be going almost too well for his own good, and perhaps the same was true of Andy Pandy. For although he only just brushed the top of Becher's, that, at 30 m.p.h., was just too much.

Failing to reach the level ground beyond the brook, he toppled over, and, landing safe behind him, Red Rum danced elegantly past what was probably, although we did not know it then, the only serious remaining danger.

But for Tommy Stack a much more serious worry at that moment was the loose horse on his left, sandwiched between him and Jeff King on What A Buck as they jumped the 23rd.

No one can say where a loose horse will go at the Canal and the last place you want him is half a length in front on your inside. So Tommy took the only possible precaution, and when he asked Red Rum to accelerate the answer was both immediate and immensely reassuring.

Taking off just in front of his riderless companion, the old horse guided him round towards Valentine's like a kindly schoolmaster, and between them, he and Tommy Stack had yet again avoided possible disaster.

There were still loose horses round him though, and now, as What A Buck dropped back (soon to be overtaken by his younger half-brother The Pilgarlic), Churchtown Boy moved easily into second place.

Only two days earlier he had won the Topham Trophy so easily that his trainer Taffy Salaman immediately decided to go for a unique double. The last horse to come anywhere near it was Irish Lizard, who finished third to Early Mist in 1953, two days after winning the Topham, but now, poised on Red Rum's heels, Churchtown Boy looked ominously full of running.

But safe jumping and the art of self-preservation are not the only qualities which have gone to make up Red Rum's Aintree record. His relentless brand of stamina is just as rare and just as vital – and now, with less than a mile to go, he began to call up the reserves which only he possesses.

Poor Churchtown Boy was, in any case, almost certainly fighting a losing battle, but, in fact, he also contributed to his downfall by meeting the last three fences just wrong. By the time the third of those mistakes used up his remaining strength, Red Rum had already measured the last precisely, and flicked over it fresh as paint. The loose horses had run out by that time, so just 494 yards remained between him and immortality.

With the crowds pressing forward by the winning post, the run-in looked to Tommy Stack like a rapidly shrinking funnel. 'I was frightened they might put him off,' he said afterwards, 'or that I might just go and fall off.'

But Red Rum has never been afraid of crowds. If anything they inspire him and as he galloped towards this one, his stride never faltered.

Of the next few moments I can, I am afraid, give no clear or coherent account, because like 50,000 others at Aintree and millions more in front of television sets, I was screaming my head off with tears in my eyes.

But no earthquake occurred, no chasms opened up and the gremlins who waylaid poor Devon Loch were busy elsewhere last week. So the most famous, best-loved English steeplechaser there has ever been galloped cheerfully past the post, politely accepting the onrush of an hysterical mob as he pulled up and walked calmly back with his police escort to the hallowed spot where no horse ever appeared before on three different Grand National days.

You can call it sentimental if you like, but I honestly do not believe that an English horse race can ever have produced a happier scene. When Brown Jack won his sixth Queen Alexandra Stakes they say that elderly ladies pulled up their skirts in the race to welcome him. The skirts may be shorter nowadays, but the feeling at Aintree was the same – a mixture of wonder, excitement, delight and love.

The only casualty I heard of in the rush was Ginger McCain's wife Beryl, who took a crashing fall down the stairs from the top of the stands. But despite a cut eye, she was still there beside Red Rum before he reached the winner's enclosure. So was a laughing, crying Billy Beardwood and so, very soon, was Ginger McCain himself.

On Friday, before kindly allowing me to ride beside Red Rum in his final wind-up gallop, Ginger had expressed the fear that he might be 'a week short of his peak. I just can't bear to be as hard on him as I used to,' he said, 'we've got too fond of him, that's the trouble.'

But that fondness and the loving care which Red Rum has enjoyed ever since he arrived in Southport lie very near the root of his success. On Friday morning, watching him storm along his favourite strip of sand, and paddling afterwards in the sea, you would have thought him nearer three years old than twelve, a happy, supremely healthy athlete doing the job he loves. For that miracle, and for other miracles it has made possible, Ginger McCain deserves the lion's share of credit – and the honour of training such a paragon could not possibly have gone to a nicer man.

Apart from the gallant Churchtown Boy, who made his own piece of history by finishing second, Eyecatcher stayed on bravely to be third just as she had twelve months ago. The Pilgarlic was fourth, adding fresh glory to the name of his dam, What A Daisy, who not only produced L'Escargot but whose other son, What A Buck, was sixth on Saturday, separated from his brother by Forest King.

Five others finished – Happy Ranger, Carroll Street (who had been badly baulked early on), Collingwood, Hidden Value and Saucy Belle. Both the last two had been remounted and so was Barony Fort, after his and Charlotte Brew's adventure had ended in the ditch which guards the fourth from home.

Unhurt and undismayed, Miss Brew tried several times to negotiate the offending obstacle but Barony Fort decided he had done enough. He had from the start been predictably and totally outclassed, but Miss Brew still jumped all but four of the Grand National fences, which is a great deal more than her less friendly detractors had predicted. She enjoyed every moment, she says, and came back determined to try again as soon as possible.

No doubt other girls will follow her example, hopefully on more suitable horses than Barony Fort, and, though I am personally still unconvinced of their wisdom, nothing happened last week to prove that one of them won't one day stand in the winner's enclosure.

For the man who did stand there on Saturday, no praise could be too high. Tommy Stack may modestly pass on all the credit to Red Rum and, of course, in a way he is right. But even great horses deserve and need great jockeys and this one was given a flawless ride by an ex-champion who is even better now than when he held the title.

Spare a thought, though, for the other man in Red Rum's story. Brian Fletcher was as delighted as anyone at Aintree last week and let it never be forgotten that his skilful hands were on the reins in three of Red Rum's five Nationals.

8 April 1977

BOB CHAMPION AND ALDANITI KEEP THEIR DATE WITH HISTORY

'Never mind – we'll just have to wait and come back together.'
When Bob Champion spoke those words at Sandown Park on
30 November 1979, it would have been easy to dismiss them as
mere defiant wishful thinking – understandable and deeply to
be admired, but sadly out of contact with reality.

Bob himself, though let out for that one day from hospital,
still looked desperately ill, and Aldaniti, whose return to racing
he was at Sandown to watch, had just been pulled up lame for
the third time in his life.

No one in his senses could have predicted with any confidence that either would race again – let alone together and
triumphant.

But Bob Champion was not the only one who refused to recognise defeat. Aldaniti's owners, Nick and Valda Embiricos,
ranged themselves firmly behind him – and although Josh
Gifford says now that he 'thought they were crackers to go on',
neither he nor his wife Althea (whose father had persuaded him
to buy Aldaniti in the first place) even wavered for one instant
in their loyalty to the Findon stable jockey.

So, as you can see, there was a special magic in the air last
Saturday – the sort you feel when a human heart and mind and
spirit come out on top against the odds.

Just to find a healthy, fit Bob Champion going to the post on
a sound, enthusiastic Aldaniti involved at least two miracles.
And when they came back it was, I honestly believe, a perfect
end to the happiest, most romantic tale ever told in all the
National's long, eventful history.

48 *Oaksey on Racing*

Nor, incredibly, were the winning pair last Saturday's only heroes. For while it seems pretty safe to assume that no jockey recovered from cancer had ever ridden a Grand National winner before, you can say with even greater certainty that no 54-year-old has ever been seriously involved in the finish – let alone an honourable second after losing the best part of three stone in two months!

That was John Thorne's unique achievement on Spartan Missile and perhaps the happiest moment of this glorious sunlit day came as the winner and second pulled up – and John reached across to fling a congratulatory arm round Bob Champion's shoulders. 'I'm very proud of my horse, but prouder still of Bob,' he said afterward – and went on to pay his own special tribute to the way Josh Gifford has stood by his ailing jockey.

Being trainer as well as owner, breeder and rider of the second, John will also have appreciated the masterly skill with which Josh had prepared Aldaniti.

It must be hard enough to win a Grand National with any bad-legged horse – but harder still to produce him at Aintree fit to run for his life after *only one race* since his breakdown sixteen months ago!

My only doubt about this genuine masterpiece of training is whether Josh will be able to follow it through, as he promised before the race last week, by giving up smoking!

As the 39 runners paraded past buzzing, crowded stands in bright sunshine, it certainly was not easy to believe that either the Grand National or its home are now on their last legs. But Mr Davies is, allegedly, asking £8 million for the place – and even contemplating another attempt to run the meeting on his own.*

Perhaps it is just as well that you cannot put a price on happiness or a tariff on tears of delight. Either would have

* Property developer Bill Davies had bought Aintree racecourse from Mrs Mirabel Topham in 1973. At the end of 1973 he made an arrangement whereby the bookmakers Ladbrokes ran the course on a seven-year lease, and in 1982 the Jockey Club launched an appeal for Mr Davies's then asking price of £7 million. When the appeal brought in an amount well short of that sum, the deadline was extended, and eventually on 20 May 1983 the course was acquired for £3,400,000 and passed into the control of the Jockey Club under the umbrella of Racecourse Holdings Trust.

made Aintree a goldmine last week, but such scenes may never be repeated and certainly cannot be guaranteed.

All you can hope is that the Grand National's claim to be a British sporting institution worth preserving will turn out to have been strengthened by the universal appeal of this latest amazing chapter in its history.

The future may not be secure but, as Bob Champion and Aldaniti have proved so gloriously, that is no reason for giving up hope.

Looking back now it chills the blood to remember how close the whole story came to disaster before it had properly begun. For after lining up (like Spartan Missile) towards the outside, Aldaniti hit the first fence really hard and might so easily have been betrayed by the slight unexpected drop. But all was well and Bob Champion now regards this early error as a blessing. 'It taught him a real lesson,' he says, 'and that was the only mistake he made.'

Bob Champion and Aldaniti clear Becher's Brook on the second circuit.

Certainly, from the moment they appeared in the leading group after eleven fences, Aldaniti's jumping was a joy to watch. At fence after fence he and his rider were in perfect unison – Bob seeing the stride far out, asking a rhythmic question and getting a bold, surefooted answer.

At the 12th, for instance, when he actually hit the front, Aldaniti took a clear length off Zongalero in the air.

His progress from the back had no doubt been eased by other such leaps and throughout the second circuit the story was the same. The economy of effort this implies is the stuff of victory round Aintree.

Pacify had been one of the early leaders along with Tenecoon (who fell at the 11th) and Choral Festival. The latter must have given 18-year-old Mark Low some memorable thrills – staying near the front for most of the first circuit and finally getting knocked over with only two fences left to jump.

Barney Maclyvie and Another Captain fell at the first and, although the big open ditch caused no trouble, several bold adventures ended at the fourth – notably Aidan O'Connell's on Chumson (he remounted, but fell again) and John Carden's on Bryan Boru.

Frank Berry, taking Liam O'Donnell's place on Delmoss, also fell here and so did Niall Madden on Kilkilwell.

No Gypsy fell at Valentine's after several blunders, but in the meanwhile Carrow Boy had led the whole field safely over Becher's. He got a scurvy reward, poor fellow, because a loose horse crossed him violently going to the fence after Valentine's and Carrow Boy was not at all to blame for losing both his concentration and his balance.

Jim Wilson's chance of a Gold Cup/National double had disappeared (with Another Prospect) at the Canal Turn and the Swiss amateur Marcus Graffe was unable to survive Drumroan's blunder at Valentine's.

It is not clearly visible on the video I have seen, but Bill Smith reported later that Coolishall had been badly baulked at the Canal. The horse's unfortunate owner, Brod Munro-Wilson, once again missed his eagerly longed-for ride by dislocating a shoulder and cracking two ribs on the Thursday.

Apart from the Canal, Coolishall jumped round as safely as ever to finish eighth. Probably the ground was not quite as soft as he really likes and, sadly, I'm afraid by far his best chance of glory went with that broken stirrup in 1980.

At the 10th, Zongalero took over the lead, but all this while without fuss or waste of effort, Aldaniti had been smoothly improving his position.

As I've said, he landed clear over the 12th and as they galloped back towards us across the Melling Road, the group with him included Sebastian V, Zongalero, Rubstic, Royal Stuart and Royal Mail.

The last-named, beautifully ridden by Philip Blacker, had followed the inside 'Fred Winter' route and as Aldaniti, Zongalero (who 'fiddled' it cleverly) and Sebastian V led them over the Chair, Royal Mail's trainer, Stan Mellor, must have been a happy man.

All his three runners – Royal Mail, Royal Stuart and Pacify – were within striking distance and as they set out on the second circuit Royal Stuart carried an exhilarated Hywel Davies up to dispute the lead.

Poor Hywel had come back thrilled to the core by his first ride over the big fences on Daviot in the Topham and during it had made a characteristic recovery, from a serious blunder at Becher's.

So now I could not believe my eyes when, for what looked, by his standards, a wholly inadequate reason, he suddenly toppled off Royal Stuart.

There *was* a reason, of course – yet another broken stirrup-leather – so both the jockey and all who backed Royal Stuart are fully entitled to feel hard done by!

A moment later disaster struck again for Royal Stuart's trainer – because Pacify hit the top of Becher's and, landing in third place behind Aldaniti and Rubstic, just failed to get his undercarriage down. Stan Mellor's three-strong team had been cut, almost at a stroke, to one.

But that one, Royal Mail, was going beautifully and as he followed Aldaniti and Rubstic round the Canal Turn it is time to take a look back at events behind them. Because now the race was rapidly taking on something like its final shape.

Zongalero had already lost his place when he fell at Becher's and, as we found out later, it was at one of the previous fences that John Thorne's troubles had begun.

Apparently Spartan Missile stood off too far, pitched on landing and 'lost' his feet in a soft patch of ground. 'It knocked the stuffing out of him for a while,' says John, 'and then I went and got cut off at the Canal!'

No one, of course, can measure the precise effect of such disasters, but when Aldaniti led Royal Mail across the Melling Road for the second time, Spartan Missile must have been nearly 20 lengths adrift. Four of those were the lengths he was beaten by – which, of course, gave the jockeys in the stand a chance to say, 'Oh, he came too late. A professional would have won.'

Well maybe, but before you make any such assumptions remember (a) that the professional in question would have had to get on as well as John does with Spartan Missile and (b) that even professionals sometimes meet interference in Grand Nationals.

John Thorne reproaches himself for not getting over to the inside earlier on the first circuit – and plans to start off there next time. But in every other respect I believe that he gave Spartan Missile an admirable ride.

There was certainly no sign whatever of fatigue about his finishing effort – and the one mistake described above (which may well have cost more than four lengths) could happen to anyone.

Departures I have not already mentioned include those of Lord Gulliver (fell at the 13th), Three Of Diamonds (fell at the second Canal Turn) and Martinstown (brought down when well behind at the 27th). Dromore, Son And Heir, My Friendly Cousin, The Vintner, Casamayor and Deiopea all either refused or were pulled up.

Deiopea carried Mrs Sheedy faithfully – but not quite as far or as prominently as Sandwilan did Mrs Hembrow in 1979.

The Vintner drew a magnificent recovery from Chris Grant at the Chair, but even that did not teach him to pay the fences adequate respect.

So, with four left to jump, the stage was set. Rubstic, for whom perhaps the ground was still just too soft, had begun to lose his place, but both Three To One and Senator MacLacury had moved up close enough behind Aldaniti and Royal Mail to take advantage of any lapse the leaders made. And now, at last, Spartan Missile was with them – still many lengths behind the leading pair, but gaining steadily.

For the moment, however, Royal Mail and Philip Blacker were much the more obvious threat and, sensing their presence, Bob Champion moved over close to the wing at the second last.

It was a perfectly fair and sensible precaution. No one, at this particular stage of his career, was going to get past on R. Champion's inside! But just conceivably it was also decisive – because now, switched right-handed behind the leader, Royal Mail failed, for some reason, to adjust his stride.

Until then his great namesake, the winner in 1937, must have been looking down with pride, but here, getting fatally just too close, the New Zealander hit the second last a dreadful thump.

The blunder never looked like disturbing Philip Blacker's seat, but although they were quickly back on an even keel to jump the last still in second place the precious impetus and energy were gone.

Royal Mail had more than justified his right to a place high up in the original weights and his rider had confirmed his own tenacious long-legged claim to a very high one among modern Aintree jockeys.

But now the four heroes of this wonderful race had the stage to themselves at last and, just for a moment, as Spartan Missile stormed past Royal Mail, he was gaining so strongly that anything looked possible.

'Every time I felt I might win I kept telling myself not to be stupid,' Bob Champion said afterwards. 'But then when we got to the elbow [half-way up the run-in] I started to pray.'

Well, of all the many prayers which have been offered on that historic stretch of turf, none has been more deserving of an answer and now, sure enough, Aldaniti found the strength to keep his stride unbroken.

I doubt if he quickened and Spartan Missile certainly did not falter. It was just that over the last 100 yards the space between them suddenly stopped shrinking.

So Bob Champion and Aldaniti kept their date with history. As the jockey had promised they 'came back together' and I never expect to see a happier, more emotional scene on a British racecourse.

Admirably ridden by Mr Geordie Dunn, Three To One finished fourth, a rapidly vanishing neck behind Royal Mail, and Senator MacLacury was fifth another 12 lengths away.

For some reason I do not seem to have mentioned Royal Exile, but he and Ben de Haan had been quietly soldiering on near the inside all the way.

Royal Exile's 83-year-old American owner, Mr Rigg, was born in Liverpool and had not been back for 77 years. But now, an honourable sixth, his little ex-French 12-year-old did him proud.

The other six to finish were, in this order – Rubstic, Coolishall, Rathlek, So, Sebastian V and Cheers.

Aldaniti, the first winner since Sundew (in 1957) to lead throughout the final circuit, was bred by Mr Thomas Barron in Co. Durham. The name is a combination of his four grand-children – Alistair, David, Nicola and Timothy.

Aldaniti's dam has no other obvious claim to fame and although his sire, Derek H, has now produced the very useful Sunset Cristo (one of the few to beat Silver Buck over fences) there was nothing much in the Doncaster catalogue to tempt Josh Gifford. It was only on the insistence of his father-in-law, George Roger-Smith, that he paid 3,200 guineas for the unbro-ken three-year-old and it was in Althea Gifford's colours (with Bob Champion wearing them) that Aldaniti ran and won his first hurdle race at Ascot.

He was then sold to Nick Embiricos, whose wife was for-merly Valda Rogerson. Her mother and father owned Pas Seul and Salmon Spray and Valda herself is a skilful horsewoman.

As Josh Gifford says, it was her patience and care which brought Aldaniti through the long, boring but vital months of walking and trotting on the roads which laid the foundations of his recovery.

In fact, two days before the Grand National Mrs Embiricos had the horrid experience of losing her very promising young 'chaser, Stonepark, who broke his neck in the Topham Trophy won by Mr Marlsbridge. For a moment she and her husband were undecided whether to risk Aldaniti but, by the grace of God, they felt unable to disappoint Bob Champion so late in the day!

Neither he nor Aldaniti are a penny the worse for their triumph – or the celebrations which followed. In fact the horse may even run again this season.

So may Spartan Missile – perhaps the 'Horse and Hound'

at Stratford – but he came home pretty tired and is having a well-earned rest. John Thorne, believe it or not, plans to stay light and ride on the Flat this season. What a man . . .

His heroic display had been foreshadowed, in the Haig Foxhunters on the Thursday, when Dick Saunders (a mere chicken of 47) produced a flawless clear round on Frank Gilman's Grittar. I hope Dick will forgive me for doing him less than justice, but feel pretty sure he will agree that Bob Champion and our old friend and rival John Thorne deserve pride of place this memorable week.

In fact, if as seems probable, Grittar is given a chance to emulate Spartan Missile next season, Dick may easily find himself up there with them on Grand National day.

10 April 1981

Spartan Missile did run again that season – finishing lame when second to Roadhead in the Mahonia Hunters' 'Chase at Ascot. That, alas, was the last time his gallant owner rode him, because John Thorne was killed the next year riding a different, younger horse in a point-to-point (see pages 303–5).

After being fired and missing a season, Spartan Missile came back and ran in two more Nationals when trained by John's son-in-law, Nicky Henderson. Put down at the age of thirteen, the horse won twenty-four races including two Aintree Foxhunters and one at Cheltenham. He also finished fourth in a Cheltenham Gold Cup, second in both the Whitbread and the Grand National and ran in the Grand Steeplechase de Paris.

Dick Saunders, of course, came back to Aintree twelve months later to win on Grittar and become, at 48, the oldest man ever to ride a Grand National winner.

IT'S TIME WE TOOK THE TRAP OUT OF BECHER'S

For well over twenty years I have been criticising the water jump on the grounds that the ditch on its landing side represents an unfair 'trap' by which horses, who do not know it is there and have never been taught to cope with it, can be caught and injured through no fault of their own.

Happily, nowadays, the actual ditch has been made so shallow that a horse unlucky enough to drop his hind legs in it is no longer likely to break his back, as Sundew and too many others did in the bad old days.

It was while we were discussing Dark Ivy's tragic death that Peter O'Sullevan, with whom the welfare of horses has been a life-long preoccupation, pointed out that the same objection applies, with even greater force, to the landing side of Becher's Brook.

I tried very hard to find a flaw in his reasoning, but failed completely – and am now convinced that he is right.

In 1961 a riderless horse ducked in front of Taxidermist and me very much as Attitude Adjuster did in front of Dark Ivy. Taxi 'fiddled' brilliantly and popped over, scarcely touching a twig. At any other fence in the British Isles, he would have been as safe as houses.

But not at Becher's. At all Aintree's other drops, the landing, though lower than the take-off, is on flat ground. At Becher's alone it slopes up from the bottom of the Brook so that the forefeet of a horse landing even half a yard short meet turf inclined quite sharply against him. It is not a feeling you easily forget and at 30 m.p.h. or thereabouts you need an awful lot of luck to survive it.

That day in 1961, Taxi's nose hit the ground soon after his feet and we were down for a fall which he, at least, had done absolutely nothing to deserve.

It has, I admit, taken me a long time to recognise the fact but I am now convinced that those few sloping yards on the landing side of Becher's are the only unfair part of the Grand National course – and a part which could be altered without damaging the race in any way.

(a) *left* Becher's Brook as it looked when this article was written – the 'landing side represents an unfair trap'.
(b) *right* Becher's Brook as John Oaksey proposed it should be, with the brook drained and the lip filled in to provide a drop fence without the 'treacherous slope'. This is almost exactly the change made for the 1990 race.

No one will ever exclude luck, good and bad, from steeplechasing. But the truth is that the slope at Becher's causes undeserved falls – by trapping good jumpers who see a nice, straightforward plain fence and stand back a yard too far or, for whatever reason, put in a short one and come down a bit too steep.

The sad fact has also to be faced that the same slope greatly increases the chance of serious injury to fallers. Dark Ivy hit the fence plenty hard enough to fall anywhere, but, with level ground to land on, he might still have survived.

It is absurd to throw up your hands in horror at the thought of any alteration to the Grand National fences. One way and another, they have been changing ever since Lottery demolished the stone wall in front of the stands in 1840.

In 1885, according to Hoadley Munro, no fewer than 10 of the 30 'fences' were, in fact, gorse-laced hurdles only 3½ft high. As late as 1960 the most important and beneficial change of all was made when the 'bloody great green walls' were so sloped on the take-off side that they became positively inviting.

'Filling in Becher's Brook' certainly sounds like sacrilege but, for the vast majority of horses, the alteration I propose will make the great fence no easier to jump.

The drop will still be there but, with the ditch filled in to the foot of the fence itself, the whole landing area will be flat.

No doubt the drop will find some horses out but at least none will be trapped and tripped by a treacherous slope they did not know was there.

30 April 1987

No change was made for the 1988 Grand National but in 1989 Becher's was once again the scene of unacceptable carnage. The Irish horse Seeandem failed to clear the Brook and broke its neck, while the amateur-ridden Brown Trix, who crashed headlong into the ditch, was dragged out, lifeless, not long before the field came round again.

An enquiry was set up under Peter Greenall and it was decided to fill in the Brook, or at least reduce it to a shallow trickle inches wide. The drop remains, but wherever you land the ground is flat. The treacherous lip is gone forever and the rail on the outside of Becher's has been straightened to keep onlookers back out of a horse's eye-line as he approaches the fence. This, it is hoped, will avoid the tendency to jump Becher's at a sharp left-handed angle.

Arkle

Arkle (Pat Taaffe) at Kempton Park on the day of his final
race, 27 December 1966.

How many animals can you remember who never once disappointed you or fell below your expectations? My answer would be two dogs, one cat (of whom I had not expected much in the first place) and the hero of this chapter. For of all the racehorses I have known, watched and admired, none has come closer than Arkle to my idea of absolute, impeccable perfection.

Did he *ever* disappoint us? Well, I suppose that first Hennessy in 1963 was, at the time, a disappointment of sorts – but not if you listened to Pat Taaffe.

Twelve months later there was emphatically no disappointment whatever about Arkle's second defeat. Read about it on pages 80–4 and see if you agree. As for the third – as for failing by three-quarters of a length to give Stalbridge Colonist 35lbs in the Hennessy Gold Cup of 1966, well, far from a disappointment, that was perhaps the clearest proof we have ever had of Arkle's unique supremacy.

In the next two Gold Cups after Arkle was forced to retire, Stalbridge Colonist finished second and third – beaten a total of two lengths. The Gold Cup after that was won by What A Myth, who had finished third in Stalbridge Colonist's Hennessy, a length and a half behind Arkle, from whom he was receiving 33lbs!

Then, of course, there was the final, bitterest disappointment of them all. I was riding at Wincanton on 27 December 1966, and can still remember the shock with which we heard the news in the weighing room. Arkle second to Dormant? It didn't make sense. Just conceivably he might have fallen. But *beaten* by Dormant, giving him only 21lbs? No. They must have got it wrong.

But they hadn't. It was all over. The sun had gone in and, only four years later, Arkle was dead. I do not believe that he ever seriously disappointed anyone in his life.

In the pieces that follow you will, I'm afraid, find a surplus of superlatives. But if I apologise, it is only because they are inadequate.

When Arkle appeared for the last time at the Horse of the Year Show, Anne Duchess of Westminster, his devoted owner, was asked what tune she would like the band to play. 'Please play "There'll never be another you",' she replied – and no band ever played a truer song.

*

Though trained in Ireland, Arkle made his steeplechasing debut, in November 1962, at Cheltenham.

Saturday's third outstanding performance had been the effort-less victory, first time ever over fences, of the Duchess of Westminster's Arkle, who, ridden like Fortria by Pat Taaffe, jumped round like a seasoned veteran to carry off the Honey-bourne 'Chase (2m).

It is true that both the Queen Mother's Dargent and Joms-viking fell quite early on, making Arkle's task a good deal easier, but the fine big five-year-old was always cruising on a tight rein, and after disposing of Billy Bumps without dif-ficulty down the hill, ran home to win in a style ominously reminiscent (from an English point of view) of Fortria himself in his younger days.

24 November 1962

Arkle was back at Cheltenham the following spring.

The Irish had to wait an unexpectedly long time for their first success on the Tuesday, but when it came, though not, I sup-pose, financially very helpful, Arkle's victory in the Broadway 'Chase was a heart-warming sight for any lover of a good horse, whatever his nationality.

No real doubt existed that Arkle was a good horse – and the opposition was not all that impressive. But the way Arkle dealt with it had to be seen to be believed.

Coming to the third last sandwiched between Brasher and Jomsviking, Arkle jumped it less well than either of his rivals and looked for a moment in grave danger of getting squeezed out.

At the next fence, too, he gained no ground and, in front of me a partisan with an Irish air groaned – whether from heart or pocket or both I could not tell – 'Begod he's beat.' But the next ten seconds made him eat his words.

Without a visible signal from Pat Taaffe, without the slightest apparent effort, Arkle was a dozen lengths clear. He simply shot from between the two English horses like a cherry stone from a schoolboy's fingers. It was done in less than 50 yards and neither of the others was stopping.

It is, of course, both tempting and downright useless to make comparisons between this performance and that of Mill House in the Gold Cup. In my opinion, Mill House is, at present, a better and faster jumper than Arkle – but further than that I would not go.

One can only pray that both keep sound and well until they meet – and hope that whenever and wherever that meeting takes place we will all be there to see it.

There has, in my short memory, been no comparable pair of six-year-old 'chasers in training at one and the same time and if they are ever to come to the second last together in a Cheltenham Gold Cup the man who would, at this moment, predict the outcome with confidence is either a fool or has second sight.

23 March 1963

Arkle and Mill House were, of course, to meet well before the 1964 Gold Cup, and the controversial race for the 1963 Hennessy is described in the 'Horses' chapter under Mill House (pages 180–5). At the time, it merely made the arguments even more heated – and the English even more confident . . .

THE FASCINATION
OF NEXT WEEK'S
GOLD CUP

The field for the 1964 Cheltenham Gold Cup will almost certainly be the smallest in the history of the race. It now seems more than likely, in fact, that Mill House and Arkle will go to the post by themselves next week. And yet – although two-horse races are by no means everyone's ideal – I seriously doubt whether a straightforward match, at least under N.H. Rules, has ever generated more widespread fascination and excitement.

There are those, of course, who consider it an insult to the great Mill House even to contemplate a struggle. Has he not (they ask with scorn) met Arkle once already in the Hennessy Gold Cup, given him weight and galloped him into the ground? And *that* (they add with a tolerant smile as if to settle the matter once and for all) was Mill House's first race of the season. He will be much fitter now and Arkle's best chance of beating him – if he ever had one – has gone.

Well, of course, they may be right, but if so a very unusual situation now exists in the steeplechasing world; for Arkle is every bit as far in front of his contemporaries in Ireland as Mill House is – and if, between these two, an appreciable gap exists, the balance of power between their respective countries must be uniquely tilted.

So I, for one, prefer the view that there will be precious little in it. All we can do is attempt to measure the strengths and weaknesses (if any) of two truly great 'chasers – and pray that no untimely accident robs us of a final, indisputable decision.

To take Mill House first, there is really very little left to say. Since he reached the prime of life (if indeed he has reached it!), his powers have never once been fully tested. With an abnormal degree of sheer physical strength, he combines the ideal temperament and outlook for a 'chaser – bold but not headstrong, fearless but not foolhardy.

For any normal horse, the fact that, at Cheltenham, he may well have to make his own running would be a grave disadvantage. But Mill House has already shown, in the Hennessy, that this worries him not at all.

For him, racing is still a joy and, as he pricks his ears and quickens going to a fence, no other encouragement is needed than the sheer exuberant delight of his own strength.

When he meets one right there is almost certainly no horse in the world capable of jumping as fast, as far and with as little effort.

Probably it was an attempt to do so that undid Arkle on their only previous meeting.

It is almost impossible (touch wood) to imagine Mill House falling. The fence strong enough to stop him, one feels, does not exist – and he is, in any case, unbelievably quick and clever for his size.

So where, you may ask, is the doubt? What is the chink in these apparently impregnable defences through which a rival may hope to strike a mortal blow? I can only think of one – and it is no more than a bare possibility.

The fact does remain, however, that almost all Mill House's victories have been won a long way from the finish. Always, at least in the last two seasons, he has battered the opposition insensible well before the second fence from home.

He has not yet shown – because he has never needed it – the power to accelerate when challenged at or just after the last. And it is here, surely, that Arkle's only hope must lie.

If Mill House has that power, then he is, I believe, truly invincible – the complete 'chaser, the goal towards which men have striven ever since two Irishmen decided, for fun, to race their hunters from one church steeple to another. It is the possibility of seeing that goal reached which will bring the hopeful to Cheltenham in their thousands.

But the doubt remains and, to tell the truth, Mill House's final wind-up at Sandown last week did little or nothing to allay it. In the Gainsborough 'Chase (3m) he had only one serious rival

– that incurable tearaway Out And About – and, as Mill House strode effortlessly past to lead round the final bend, the latter had, it seemed, done no more than give him the gallop Fulke Walwyn so urgently wanted him to have.

In the paddock beforehand, Mill House looked superb and, judging by the line of hard muscle along his flank, pretty near the peak of fitness. But he has always been a lazy worker at home and now, between the last two fences, it was suddenly clear just how badly he needed this race.

Going to the last the big horse changed his legs uneasily. He met it right to stand off, and Willie Robinson, who usually sits so still, must have sensed the need to make up his mind. So he asked – and Mill House, looking, for a change, like an ordinary mortal, took not the slightest notice. Instead, he got far too close, hit the fence hard and, though never in danger of falling, landed on the flat a very tired horse.

Now it would clearly be ridiculous to draw from this performance any serious conclusions. Without a race since Boxing Day (and even that little more than a half-speed exercise), Mill House was perfectly entitled to feel the strain in sticky ground and giving, as usual, lumps of weight.

He will be a very different horse next week – as fit as Fulke Walwyn can make him, which means as fit as he can be made.

Nevertheless, had Arkle been at Sandown, and had he landed on the flat within hail of his rival, I personally have very little doubt that we should now have a different favourite for the Cheltenham Gold Cup.

For again and again, throughout his career over fences, the Duchess of Westminster's brilliant horse has shown the one thing Mill House may, just conceivably, lack – the ability to produce, at the end of a fast-run race, a really blistering turn of speed.

On four of the five occasions I have watched him, Arkle has finished almost literally running away. Once this season, admittedly, he was fully extended by Loving Record, but those who saw that race agree that the farther they went the farther he would have won.

Arkle is not, perhaps, quite as brilliant and effortless a jumper as Mill House – though by all accounts he is getting better at it every time he runs. Even so, it would clearly be unwise in the extreme to ask him to gallop beside the English champion for more than a couple of fences.

And here the absence of other runners may set Pat Taaffe a real problem; for Arkle is, I understand, a very hard puller indeed.

In a fair-sized field he can be settled down but there'll be an awful lot of daylight at Cheltenham, and I don't imagine that Willie Robinson would be exactly heartbroken to see his rival tearing away in front from the start.

Mill House, too, takes a pretty considerable hold, but the faster they go the better it will suit him, and if someone's throat is going to be cut, the challenger looks the more vulnerable.

So, added to the thrill of seeing the two best 'chasers in the world, there will be next week the fascination of a duel of wits and tactics between two great Irish horsemen.

They are the firmest of friends and, ironically enough, it was Pat Taaffe who gave Mill House his early education and rode him first time out over hurdles.

When the big horse joined Fulke Walwyn's stable, Robinson, disappointed with his slovenly work at home, rang Taaffe for reassurance! 'Don't worry,' he was told, 'he's the best I ever sat on.' At that time Arkle had yet to show his full potential and now, no doubt, Pat Taaffe would not be so encouraging. He may still have been right, though – as to that, we can only wait and see.

You will, I'm afraid, get no selection here – for two excellent reasons. One is that Audax, fortunately, cannot tip – the other that he simply does not know his own mind! And in truth, except for those personally bound to either camp, does it really matter? Far more important than the actual result is the race itself.

If all goes well, if these two young giants come to the last together, the Cheltenham crowd will surely get something no money can buy – a spectacle never excelled and very seldom equalled in the long, drama-studded annals of National Hunt racing.

29 February 1964

ARKLE – THE GREATEST 'CHASER SINCE PRINCE REGENT

In more ways than one the 1964 Cheltenham Gold Cup defied belief. It was, for a start, almost unbelievable that the race should live up in full to such tremendous advance publicity – and to most of us in England it was quite unbelievable that, barring accidents, Mill House should be beaten by as much as five lengths. Yet both these wonders came to pass and, by achieving them, the Duchess of Westminster's Arkle proved himself beyond question the greatest steeplechaser seen in Europe since Prince Regent.

With so much at stake, so much could have gone wrong – a single slip, a fall, a tiny error of judgment. Any of these might have left a nagging doubt in the mind – but none of them transpired. There can never have been a race more perfect in every way – or a triumph more complete.

One day, of course, perhaps with the help of a pacemaker, Mill House may get his revenge. The man who denies that possibility is a fool. But last Saturday afternoon there was no doubt. England's champion was beaten fair and square and it is the measure of Mill House's greatness in defeat that, to overcome him, Arkle had to produce a display of flawless majesty, speed and power – and a record time to boot.

Everything conspired, it seemed, to set the scene ideally for an historic sporting occasion. The first three races on Saturday were run in blood-curdling cold and intermittent showers of snow. But the last of these had cleared as the rugs came off and, as the four horses in the Gold Cup field cantered past the stands, Cheltenham was bathed in hard, clear sunlight.

Trotting calmly back towards the start, Mill House was a sight I shall never forget. So relaxed that Willie Robinson needed but one hand on the reins, he suddenly broke, for a few strides passing the first fence, into an extravagant, extended gait that would have done the High School in Vienna proud.

Behind him Arkle, eager to be off, twisted his head impatiently against the bit.

If Pas Seul and King's Nephew knew they were outclassed, it did not show and, as all four turned to inspect the first fence, the atmosphere was electric with a brand of suspense and fascination I never felt before on any British racecourse.

Both champion and challenger, needless to say, looked supremely hard and fit. Save perhaps in height, Mill House is just a size bigger all round, but Arkle, though leaner behind the saddle, has almost equal depth and strength in front.

The tactics, like everything else, lived up to expectations. Mill House swept over the first two fences four lengths clear and although, to begin with, Arkle pulled hard for his head, Pat Taaffe, without apparent difficulty, settled him down to dispute second place with Pas Seul. Here – and I think throughout – King's Nephew brought up the rear.

First time round the order never changed, but now, looking back, you can see that in one respect the writing was already on the wall. For although, in the Hennessy Gold Cup, it had been Mill House's tremendous jumping that gained the day, this time it was he who fiddled the occasional fence – while if Arkle made a mistake I personally never saw it.

At the open ditch in front of us, the favourite took off far too close for comfort – but sailed on undisturbed and, as Willie Robinson let out a reef going down the hill, appreciably increased his lead.

Here, against any normal rivals, the race would have been over. Soon after the water Pas Seul and King's Nephew were already feeling the strain, but although Pat Taaffe had not yet noticeably moved a muscle, Arkle never let the gap get dangerously wide.

Instead he closed it without effort, and for the first time – even for Mill House's most convinced adherents – the awful spectre of defeat was plain to see.

Turning downhill towards the third from home, the favourite, as we know now – and as poor Willie Robinson must have suspected then – had his last chance to poach an advantage that might neutralise his rival's fearsome final speed.

On the verge of despair, one felt – like a baited bear struggling to loose the bulldog's hold – he threw an enormous leap, and Arkle, rising barely a length behind, matched it with cruel, almost careless, ease.

Until the second last, which Arkle jumped the better, neither horse had been asked for his ultimate effort. But ten strides after it, for perhaps the first time in his life, Mill House felt the whip, gave all he had – and found it nothing like enough.

For now it came in all its glory – that blistering, explosive burst of speed in which, all along, we had known that Arkle's only hope of victory must lie.

Now, well before the last, it was no longer hope but certainty. Mill House never gave up, never even faltered, but, in those few decisive yards, he, of all horses, was made to look like just another beaten 'chaser.

And as Arkle stormed victorious up the hill, though every throat was sore with cheering, in many – mine for one – there rose a choking lump of sadness, too.

Arkle and Pat Taaffe return to the unsaddling enclosure after beating Mill House in the 1964 Cheltenham Gold Cup.

The scene that followed – with half Ireland surging off the stands to welcome back their hero – would make most Epsom Derby days look like a Salvation Army meeting. Arkle, patted from head to tail on every side, took it all just as he had the race, with a champion's calm assurance. He did not say, 'I am the greatest,' but it was said for him many times – and it was true.

Now, with all the tumult and shouting only a memory, it is time to attempt some measurement of Arkle's achievement.

On time alone, there is no doubt that this was an outstanding Gold Cup, for Arkle won in four seconds less than Saffron Tartan three years ago over the same course on even faster going. This, I think, disposes at once of the theory that Willie Robinson should – or could – have set a more testing pace on Mill House. Neither Fulke Walwyn nor anyone else in a position to judge gives this as an excuse for the favourite's defeat.

To my mind, Mill House was beaten largely because he hardly ever succeeded in outjumping his rival. If anything it was the other way round, for Arkle, with the incentive of another horse to lead him almost throughout, never lost an appreciable amount of ground in the air and never made a single serious mistake.

I have seen it written several times that soft or heavy going would have been in Mill House's favour. This may be so, but the records scarcely confirm it, for many of Arkle's Irish victories have been gained in the mud and I long ago heard Pat Taaffe say that it could not be too soft for him.

Is there, then, any real reason to hope that, with the score at present one-all, Mill House will one day turn the tables?

If an excuse exists, it must surely be that the favourite was forced, on Saturday, to make all his own running. That is, even for a horse of Mill House's courage and boldness, a dreadful handicap.

For three miles he never saw or heard another horse – and this, I believe, may well be why his jumping, though always safe, was never quite the deadly weapon it has been in the past.

In last year's Gold Cup, for instance, Mill House did not hit the front until the 14th fence – a very different matter from leading all the way – or disputing the lead as he did for much of the Hennessy Gold Cup.

Even with a pacemaker – and a suitable one won't be easy to find – there can be no certainty that Arkle, whose stamina, after all, is not in doubt, would not still find a decisive burst of final speed.

For the answer to that question we can only await the next time, but the possibility does exist and always will until Mill House has been beaten in a race run flat out from end to end.

For the moment, however, Arkle can only be assessed on what we know – namely, that he conquered by five lengths a horse who is all that and more in front of any 'chaser now trained in England. For on Saturday, don't forget, while Pas Seul ran a gallant race to be third, 25 lengths behind Mill House, King's Nephew, winner of the Great Yorkshire 'Chase and no slowcoach by any standards, was 15 lengths farther away.

Tom Dreaper, to whom so large a share of credit for Arkle's triumph must go, is not yet prepared to compare the new champion with Prince Regent or the brilliant but ill-fated Royal Approach – the two best 'chasers he has hitherto trained. But Pat Taaffe, who rode Royal Approach, has no such doubts. 'Arkle,' he says emphatically, 'is the best I have ever ridden. I was never worried throughout the race and, at the third last, knew I would win easily.'

That, certainly, was how it looked from the stands, for even when Mill House was the best part of six lengths ahead crossing the water, Taaffe, to all appearances, might have been riding in an unimportant selling 'chase with a stone or two in hand!

It is easy to over-praise a winning jockey, but of this one all that need be said is that a great horse got the ride he deserved.

With Willie Robinson, who did all that any man could, and Fulke Walwyn, who produced Mill House fit to run for his life, everyone must feel the deepest sympathy. Both they and the horse's owner, Mr W. H. Gollings, bore their bitter disappointment bravely – and all three believe that there will be another day.

It was four years ago that Tom Dreaper, acting on behalf of Anne Duchess of Westminster, paid 1,150 guineas for a bay colt by Archive at the Dublin Sales. He had good reason to do so, for Archive, who died in 1961, was by Nearco out of Lord Astor's St Leger winner Book Law – and Dreaper himself had trained both Arkle's dam, Bright Cherry, and his grandam, Greenogue Princess.

Both were by well-established jumping sires and both were themselves good racehorses. Bright Cherry, by Knight of the Garter, was brilliantly fast, but only barely stayed two miles over fences – and then only on top of the ground. Greenogue Princess, a member of a long-established Irish jumping family, was by My Prince out of Cherry Branch II by Cerasus.

Arkle's pedigree is, therefore, a fascinating mixture of top-class blood from both the jumping and flat-race worlds. Book Law, dam of Archive, was a really good filly who, apart from winning the St Leger, was second in both the One Thousand Guineas and the Oaks and had, as a two-year-old, won the Queen Mary Stakes at Ascot.

Her best son was the Eclipse winner Rhodes Scholar and though Archive was moderate on the racecourse, he has had a good deal of success at stud, siring Arcandy, who won a Stewards Cup, Farrney Fox and 'chasers such as Mariner's Log (who was near the top class when he chose to exert himself), Regal Arch and Loving Record.

Arkle's maternal grandsire, Knight of the Garter, by the great stayer Son-in-Law, was himself a fast horse who won the Coventry at Ascot as a two-year-old. He has sired one winner of the Irish One Thousand Guineas and, of course, many more under N.H. rules.

Greenogue Princess bred four winners on the flat and, besides Arkle's dam, Bright Cherry, two 'chasers – one of whom, Greenflax, I remember riding at Cheltenham for Fulke Walwyn. He used to hit almost every fence extremely hard, sometimes causing his rider grave discomfort – but never fell himself.

My Prince, sire of Greenogue Princess, was, of course, with Cottage, one of the two greatest jumping stallions of modern times. He sired three Grand National winners, Gregalach, Royal Mail and Reynoldstown – and two of the best horses ever to run at Aintree without winning, Prince Regent and Easter Hero.

Further back in Greenogue Princess's pedigree you find the top-class hurdler General Peace and an ancestress of that brilliant classic filly Bella Paola.

So on both sides of his family tree Arkle has a rare mixture of all the qualities that go to make up a great steeplechaser – class, courage, stamina, a turn of speed and jumping ability. They have combined to produce a phenomenon, but now, being wise after the event, it would be hard to dream up a pedigree more likely to do just that . . .

14 March 1964

Three weeks later, Arkle won the Irish Grand National, and the following season won at Gowran Park before meeting Mill House again in the Hennessy.

ARKLE – THE COMPLETE, FINAL, FLAWLESS ANSWER TO THE PERFECT 'CHASER?

So now we know for sure. The long argument is over, the last remaining question answered. And, on the minds of those who watched the 1964 Hennessy Gold Cup, the manner in which that answer was given – clear, ruthless, utterly decisive – will be for ever indelibly engraved.

For this, one felt, as Arkle and Mill House galloped together past the crowded, buzzing stands at Newbury last week, this is what steeplechasing is about.

Since Messrs Blake and O'Callaghan set off to race from Buttevant Church to St Leger Steeple 212 years ago, thousands of men and women all over Great Britain and Ireland have worked and schemed and dreamed to produce the perfect 'chaser.

From time to time their dreams have been close to fulfilment. Perhaps, who knows, they were fulfilled. Cloister, Manifesto, Jerry M, Easter Hero, Golden Miller and Prince Regent – all these and other deathless names have kindled in men's hearts the self-same fire that burnt so bright at Newbury last Saturday afternoon.

Comparisons are pointless. All one can say without fear of contradiction is that no horse – certainly no seven-year-old – has ever looked more the complete, final, flawless answer than the Duchess of Westminster's Arkle.

To predict that Arkle might beat Mill House a second time last week and win the Hennessy, no crystal balls were needed. But the way in which his victory was gained, that, I believe, no one could conceivably have foreseen, not even those convinced disciples to whom the Cheltenham Gold Cup winner had already proved for ever his superiority over England's champion.

For that superiority was based, we thought, on the single, deadly stab in the back to which, at Cheltenham, Mill House, with all his boldness, strength and resolution, found no answer.

If, last week, Arkle and Pat Taaffe had merely repeated that manoeuvre, waiting behind to strike at a moment of their own choosing, the doubts might still remain. But they didn't wait, not even for a single fence – and their triumph, won the hard way, is all the more complete and cruel.

The first fence of the 1964 Hennessy Gold Cup: left to right, Arkle, Mill House, Pappageno's Cottage, John O'Groats.

Prepared as we were for a battle of wits – the rapier against the bludgeon – it seemed little short of a disaster for Ireland when, at the second fence on Saturday, Arkle (12st 7lb) jumped past Mill House (12st 4lb) and Vultrix (10st) to take the lead.

Those who had backed the favourite – and those who merely wished him well – felt something like the seconds of a classic defensive boxer who, pitted against a slugger, rushes out from the first bell trading punches, toe to toe.

To Willie Robinson, hoping, without much confidence, that

one of the lightweights would give Mill House some company, this unlooked-for opposition must have seemed the answer to a prayer. And to Pat Taaffe, powerless, as he admitted afterwards, to contain Arkle's volcanic energy, those first few fences were, no doubt, a nightmare.

A lesser horseman, the muscles of his arms and back stretched taut against the reins, might well have fought a losing battle, and wasted his own as well as his mount's reserves. But Pat is far too old in the game to make any such mistake. Rock steady, cool as could be, he let Arkle have his way and, storming up the straight, though still pulling desperately hard (spurred on by Mill House's presence at his quarters), the favourite began to settle down.

Fulke Walwyn has always believed – and who shall blame him – that if Mill House could get upsides with Arkle his relentless stride and explosive jumping would tip the scales. And now, five strides off the water, Willie Robinson put this theory to the test.

Picking up half a length behind his rival the big horse landed half a length ahead, and in the roar that greeted his enormous leap the heartfelt hopes of England could be heard.

But one jump seldom wins a horse-race and this was the first, last and only time that Arkle gave a yard away. Down the back side, chased now, as almost throughout, by Ferry Boat (10st) and The Rip (10st 2lb), the two leaders galloped shoulder to shoulder and, although Robinson had not seriously asked him yet for a further effort, it was Mill House who showed the first ominous signs of strain.

This, I believe, was the crisis of the race, the moment of tragedy as well as truth, for, at fence after fence, fighting like a cornered lion, Mr Gollings's gallant horse struggled to wear his rival down – and struggled, all too obviously, in vain.

Instead of the lovely, effortless arc we know so well, his jumping became more and more a series of flat, desperate gambler's throws. He was hurdling the fences now and when, at the last on the far side, six from home, Arkle made his only serious mistake, it came too late to make the slightest difference.

For Mill House had given his all – and it simply wasn't enough. No one but a mindless, heartless dolt could feel anything but sympathy with his downfall, and I hope that some of the cruel inanities I heard spoken about him after Saturday's race will, one day soon, be thrown back in their authors' teeth.

Three times in his last three races now, Mill House has attempted the impossible and failed with honour. He looked – and doubtless was – fit to run for his life last week and I personally have no doubt at all that, with Arkle out of the way, he would have won a second Hennessy Gold Cup.

It only remains to hope and pray that these three desperate unavailing struggles will not leave a permanent mark on a wonderful horse who, after all, has done at least as much as Arkle in the past two seasons to raise public interest in N.H. racing to its present record level.

But the loser is all too easily forgotten in racing, and this time Mill House, beaten fair and square at his own game, was not even to be granted the sour reward of chasing Arkle home.

He weakened, finally, down the hill and Ferry Boat swept past him to turn into the straight no more than two lengths off the leader – the only conceivable danger left bar a fall or wholesale blunder.

Arkle, meanwhile, had recovered from his solitary mistake as if the big birch fence was a clothes brush. He stood off, in fact, a whole stride too far and, as Pat Taaffe put it later, 'The only thing that got over was his head.' But the strength and balance of this fantastic animal are such that he barely seemed to hesitate – and was off again in a flash like a schoolboy released from class.

Just once, before the first fence in the straight, Pat Taaffe glanced round to measure up the opposition and, although to us in the stands Ferry Boat looked uncomfortably close, we could not know the reserves of power Taaffe felt between his knees.

Clearly they were enough – for he never moved – and, even when Arkle screwed a little awkwardly over the second last, the least excited man at Newbury seemed to be his rider.

And no wonder – for now, between the last two fences, the race, as a race, was over. Ferry Boat, having gallantly done his part, was under extreme pressure and, well before Arkle landed safe on the flat, a deafening roar went surging out to welcome him home.

Half-way up the run-in Taaffe tapped him gently down the neck and, unbelievably after such a race, Arkle lengthened his stride to draw even farther away.

In a hundred yards he more than doubled his lead over Ferry Boat and at the line was ten lengths clear, still galloping on with incredible zest for a horse who had carried 12st 7lb for 3¼ miles and led very nearly throughout.

Newbury last Saturday had its biggest ever crowd for a November meeting – 10 per cent more than the year before – and I cannot believe that there was one spectator who failed to be moved by this extraordinary performance.

To the cheers which greeted the winner in the unsaddling enclosure there was, naturally, an Irish flavour, but the English were cheering as well.

Standing there, his long ears pricked (they almost meet in front of his forehead), Arkle certainly did not look a tired horse and it is no particular surprise to hear that he will run this afternoon in the Massey-Ferguson Gold Cup.*

I may as well add, however, that, in my opinion, he is probably being asked a much more searching question at Cheltenham than ever he was at Newbury.

It is, after all, on the cards that Mill House, having suffered two bitter, arduous defeats at the end of last season, may not be quite the force he was twelve months ago. And well though Ferry Boat ran on Saturday, he cannot, on recent form, be put in the same class with horses such as Buona Notte, Scottish Memories and Wilmington.

All three, as I write, are intended runners against Arkle today and, with a 3lb penalty, he has to give them 26lb, 33lb and 32lb respectively.

If, seven days after a race like the Hennessy Gold Cup, he fails to do so there will be no dishonour in defeat, and if he wins, well, with the ragbag of superlatives already exhausted, there will be precious little left to say . . .

To return to Newbury, Mill House struggled on bravely in third place until the flat, but had to surrender it there to The Rip, who finished quite strongly 12 lengths behind Ferry Boat and 10 lengths ahead of Mill House.

* See pages 80–4.

I am glad to report that as the big horse was unsaddled a large and sympathetic crowd gathered around him. They at least had not forgotten the past.

Apart from Mill House's total eclipse, the one sad note on Saturday was that Arkle's trainer, Tom Dreaper, was prevented by a bout of 'flu from coming to Newbury. If, as I sincerely hope, he watched the race on television, there could surely be no more effective cure.

It was Dreaper, of course, who bought Arkle for the Duchess of Westminster five years ago, and his choice, as usual, was dictated partly by conformation and partly by breeding.

Last Saturday as the rugs came off, Arkle not only looked a perfect picture of health and fitness (his coat carries a summer gleam and is so fine that it scarcely needs clipping) but had also put on weight and muscle since last season.

Apart from his lovely, almost feminine head, the most notable thing about him is that great, deep chest in which so fabulous an engine lies concealed.

At Newbury Arkle no longer looked small beside Mill House – and this was not entirely an illusion. He is bigger and stronger than ever before, and doubtless better, too.

And until some flaw is revealed in Arkle's armoury, I for one shall continue to believe that, in him, we are lucky enough to have seen the perfect, complete 'chaser.

12 December 1964

FLEETING SHADOW OF
A CHANCE TURNED
INTO TRIUMPH

In the space of seven days and two races, the Duchess of Westminster's Arkle has raised the repute and standing of National Hunt racing to a peak unequalled in its long and varied history. His name has become, quite literally, a household word wherever men talk of horses and I don't believe there was a single man, woman or child who, watching the Massey-Ferguson Gold Cup (2m 5f) at Cheltenham last Saturday afternoon, did not feel a very real pang of grief that his greatness had to be robbed of the victory it so richly deserved.

For while the Hennessy Gold Cup had been a unique pearl of sheer flawless excellence, this was a many-sided diamond reflecting from its facets all the qualities that go to make the sport we love.

Arkle's own heroic failure showed us how defeat can be made to seem at least as glorious as victory. The wonderful, heartening performance of Mr H.J. Joel's Buona Notte showed how, in such company, youth and strength, however great, cannot quite make up for the hard-won wisdom of experience. And, last but by no means least, Mr Raymond Guest's lovely grey mare Flying Wild showed how courage and tenacity can grasp a fleeting shadow of a chance, hold on, and turn it into triumph.

Indeed, however great (because on them depends the future) one's fascination with her mighty victims, this must and should be the story of Flying Wild. For it was her grey nose that crossed the line in front and her name that will be written, deservedly, in the record books.

As I write it is undecided whether she will race again but what more fitting swan song could you wish for than to beat, in fair fight, the greatest steeplechaser in the world and one of the only two who might, one day, just conceivably, challenge for his title?*

It is four years now since Mr Guest, having missed his plane to America at Dublin airport, was invited to while away the time with a visit to Dan Moore's nearby stable.

Shown round by the trainer's wife, Mrs Joan Moore (who hunted Team Spirit as a four-year-old and who, as I recently saw proved in Co. Limerick, is still better than most men across a country), the sporting American saw a four-year-old mare in one of the boxes – and fell in love on sight. He rang up his agent, Tom Cooper (now of the Irish B.B.A.), and, although till then his racing interests had been mainly on the flat – Larkspur won the Derby in his colours – soon became the owner of one, as yet, more or less untried jumper.

Between that day and this, fate has more than once played less than fair with Flying Wild.

Starting a red-hot favourite, she fell at the first fence in the N.H. 'Chase at Cheltenham; she was upsides with Arkle and going great guns when she fell (suffering a painful injury) in the Leopardstown 'Chase last season; the first fence claimed her again in the Grand National; and, on a lesser plane, when carrying me to what seemed certain victory in a valuable hurdle race at Leopardstown, she took off too soon and put her forefoot through the top bars of the second last flight!

Scattered among these disasters there have, of course, been victories – eight over fences and hurdles before last Saturday, including the Stone's Ginger Wine 'Chase at Sandown in which Flying Wild gave Mill House's conqueror, Dormant, 18lb and a two-length beating.

So when, after Saturday's race, Dan Moore, who has trained the mare all her life, wondered aloud how any horse could give her 32lb, it wasn't just the wisdom of hindsight.

In the Leopardstown 'Chase, in fact, Arkle had been set to

---

* Flying Wild did not run again that season but she did win a two-mile 'Chase the following year and ran her last race at Galway, aged ten, in July 1966.

concede only 26lb, so, since Flying Wild would at least have run him close that day, the magnitude of his task at Cheltenham needs no underlining.

And how close, how very close he went! In the paddock beforehand, the focus of many thousand anxious eyes – each wondering how much his Newbury effort might have cost him – Arkle settled my doubts, at least, the moment he was stripped.

Dancing gaily round, head high, ears pricked, he looked – and surely was – as eager as ever for the fray. Conceivably he might have run up a fraction lighter behind the saddle than at Newbury but that's a quibble. The whole picture was one of a fit, fresh horse, bursting out of his skin with strength and health.

The others, however, were by no means dwarfed. Flying Wild is cast in a rather lighter, more fragile mould but, of her type, is very hard to fault. And Buona Notte, though the race will certainly have brought him on, has clearly flourished since last season and is a mass of well-proportioned bone and muscle.

Almost throughout the first two miles Arkle (12st 10lb), pulling hard, but wasting no unnecessary energy, alternated in the lead with The O'Malley (10st). He wasted no time in the air either but, perhaps because among his rivals there were several of the quickest jumpers in the game, seemed slightly less supremely spring-heeled than at Newbury.

Behind the two leaders until Happy Spring (10st 5lb) began to weaken at the top of the final hill, the rest were always racing in a tight-packed bunch, first one then another gaining a yard or two by a particularly brilliant leap.

Among these battle-hardened rivals – mostly far more experienced than he – Buona Notte (10st 2lb) kept his place without apparent effort. He made only two mistakes, but the first one came at a vital stage, just as Pat Taaffe sent Arkle ahead, turning downhill for home with only two to jump.

It was more a slip than a blunder, but it cost Buona Notte at least two lengths and these he had to make up with the heat well and truly turned on as they stormed towards the second last.

Here, for some strange reason unknown to me, The O'Malley slipped up on the flat and, as the race swept on towards its final act, he and Paddy Broderick were left, a tangled heap like flotsam in the wake of a wave.

Miraculously, none of the others was impeded, and neither horse nor jockey was badly hurt.

And now, I'm afraid, there were few thoughts spared for them – for as Wilmington (10st 6lb) and Scottish Memories (10st 5lb) began to crack beneath the strain, Arkle came under pressure round the final bend and Buona Notte ranged up beside him, with the grey head of Flying Wild (10st 6lb) showing between them, struggling tigress-like to keep her place.

And 'struggling' was the word, for throughout that desperate race to the last, the mare, sandwiched between two more powerful horses, had precious little room. Had her determination faltered for a single heart-beat, the race would have gone the other way – but it didn't and, 50 yards before the fence, it was Arkle who, though far from giving up, was most clearly near the end of his resources.

I must say that, at this moment, with my loyalties almost equally divided, it seemed to me that Buona Notte had the race sewn up. Johnny Haine has, in common with Lester Piggott, the misleading faculty of making horses do all, or nearly all, they can without much visible encouragement – but even so, allowing for that, I believe Buona Notte was going best of the three, and what happened next confirms that impression.

For now, going to the last, perhaps a neck in front of Flying Wild, Mr Joel's fine horse made his second, most serious mistake. He took off half a stride too close and hit the top six inches hard.

This, by itself, would not have mattered, but landing, ever so slightly unbalanced, Buona Notte's hind legs skidded on the damp and greasy turf.

For an awful moment, as Flying Wild and Arkle shot away, he was almost sideways on. Then he was straight again – and running – just a second or less too late.

Up the hill, hanging doggedly at Flying Wild's quarters, Arkle fought the awful, dragging dead-weight strapped across his back. It was this which beat him – this alone – and I know no higher compliment than to say that his utter refusal to admit defeat reminded me of Mandarin.

But there were other things to think of – for Buona Notte

was not finished and, yard by yard, with the time running out against him, he closed on Flying Wild.

Nothing is impossible on Cheltenham's cruel hill and, as they flashed together past the post, poor Johnny Haine thought he had won. Or, anyway, returning to unsaddle he rode into the first enclosure and, for what seemed an age (the loudspeaker announcement was inaudible), no one knew for sure.

In the end it was Bob Turnell, his own slender hopes dashed by some sharp-eared bystander, who ended the suspense, 'You've won, Dan,' he called across to his brother-trainer, and it was true – Flying Wild by the width of a nostril.

Arkle was third a bare length behind, giving the winner 32lb and the second 26lb. He appeared to have a desperately hard race but was, in my considered opinion, facing, at these weights, a task considerably more severe than that which he accomplished so brilliantly in the Hennessy Gold Cup.

No disrespect to Mill House is intended, but the shorter distance at Cheltenham was almost certainly against Arkle and he had, in the previous seven days, undergone an arduous 3¹/₄-mile race with 12st 7lb on his back, two long road journeys and several nights in a strange stable.

Singly, these might not be serious handicaps. Taken together, they are hardly the ideal preparation for carrying 12st 10lb against two such horses as Flying Wild and Buona Notte.

He failed – and all honour to those who brought about his failure – but Arkle is still the king and nothing we saw on Saturday suggests that he is likely to be dethroned in the foreseeable future.

19 December 1964

For reasons beyond my control – falling off – Audax produced no account of the 1965 Cheltenham Gold Cup. It was probably Arkle's easiest – with poor Mill House a respectful 20 lengths behind in second place.

A facile victory under 12st 7lb in the Whitbread Gold Cup wound up Arkle's 1964–5 season, and in November 1965 he was back at Sandown for his fourth meeting with Mill House.

TEARS AND FULL THROATS GREET TRIUMPHANT ARKLE

Saturday, 6 November 1965: Sandown Park, Esher, near London, England. The date and place are worth remembering.

The sky was a clear, cold blue and at 2.48 p.m. or thereabouts the sun hung low already over the racecourse stables. Around the empty unsaddling enclosure a sea of faces spread and grew, fed by a stream of men and women running, pell-mell from the stands.

They ran, uphill, with thumping hearts and eyes alight, as if the devil was behind them or the Holy Grail in front.

And, in a way, it was.

For, however great or small the part played in their lives by racing, there was not, I believe, one single soul in that whole motley, rushing throng who did not feel, for certain, that he was living through a piece of history. Not war, not death, not politics – but history just the same.

The cause of all this fever-heat was walking calmly up the self-same hill, his long ears pricked, courteous as always to those who pressed to touch him, his heart, I suspect, beating no faster than theirs.

His name, of course, was Arkle and – perhaps I should have mentioned it before – he had just won the three-mile Gallaher Gold Cup.

He had won it, the history books will show, by 20 lengths from Rondetto, with Mill House third, four lengths away. But what they cannot show is the manner of his triumph and its meaning.

They can't record how we who watched him felt, the tears

in many eyes, the choking lumps, in many throats, the volume
of our cheers – the overwhelming sense of greatness.

No doubt such scenes have happened before on English
racecourses – but never, in my experience, quite like this.
The only comparable moment in my memory is Mandarin's
Grand Steeplechase de Paris and even that was different. Then
it was courage and skill in adversity which inspired us. Now
it was greatness pure and simple.

Arkle clears
the last in
the Gallaher
Gold Cup.

That Arkle should win was no surprise at all – that he should
win as he did, in record time, giving 26lb and 16lb to horses like
Rondetto and Mill House, was more than even his most fervent
worshippers could possibly foresee.

It established him, to my mind and, I believe, to the minds of the vast majority of those who were at Sandown, as the greatest steeplechaser there ever was or ever will be.

Perhaps, who knows, time and some other horse will one day call those words in question. But I write them now without fear of contradiction. They represent the facts as we know them at this moment. There is no longer any room for doubt.

For this unforgettable day nature had set the perfect scene. The turning leaves, the sky, the cold, clean wind – all conspired, as we packed like sardines round the parade ring, to produce a sense of almost unbearable expectation.

It showed in the applause which greeted both Arkle and Mill House as they appeared, followed them down to the start and – something I've never heard before – continued almost unbroken, though in various keys, throughout the race.

The first cheers were, deservedly, not for Arkle but for Mill House. Achieving at once a perfect understanding with his new rider, David Nicholson, the big horse jumped from start to finish as well as I have ever seen him – which is to say as well as any horse can jump.

Led by Candy (10st) over the first two fences, Mill House (11st 5lb) brushed him imperiously aside down the Railway straight – and each succeeding giant leap drew a roar of appreciation from the crowded stands and rails.

Some lengths behind him Arkle (12st 7lb) had, unusually for him, settled calmly in Pat Taaffe's hands. But clearly there's a compass in his handsome head for, swinging round towards the Pond, he suddenly decided it was time to go.

I can't remember a more obvious display of understanding in a racehorse. No one had told Arkle the distance of the Gallaher Gold Cup, but he knew Sandown – and would tolerate no leader up the well-remembered hill.

Sweeping over the open ditch before the stands, he and Mill House were cheered again and realising that this was not, after all, the end, Arkle settled once more, saving his strength and letting his rival draw ahead.

This, of course, is hindsight. At the time, as Mill House stormed majestically down the Railway straight, recalling with every stride the days of his supremacy, there seemed, to us in the stands, a very real chance that he would win.

David Nicholson's orders were to press on from the water and, obeying them superbly, he gained a length at each of the three close fences. Was Pat Taaffe waiting, or had he, perhaps, seen the spectre of defeat? We could not tell – but the answer was not long delayed.

For now, round the final bend, without coming off the bit, without, apparently, the slightest encouragement, Arkle unsheathed his sword. It flashed once, brilliant in the sunshine, and, before the Pond, for the fourth and surely the last time, poor, brave Mill House saw destiny sweep by.

I doubt if he has ever run a better race. No other living horse could have done more and, in that moment, sympathy and sadness mingled with our admiration for his conqueror.

Now, with two fences left, there was only one horse at Sandown.

Going to the last, Arkle was still, almost literally, running away. Landing over it Pat Taaffe just shook the reins and, unbelievably, he quickened. I seriously doubt whether the 300 yards of the run-in has ever been covered much faster – and certainly no winner ever came home, on this or any other course, to a greater, more rapturous welcome.

Twenty lengths behind Arkle, Rondetto deprived Mill House of second place and deserves his full share of credit. It was the little chesnut's first race of the season and, until the water jump second time, he had been sailing along hard held close behind his two great opponents.

From then on, according to Jeff King, lack of an outing began to tell and it was, in the circumstances, no mean achievement to catch Mill House.

The latter had, of course, borne the brunt of Arkle's awesome challenge, and David Nicholson treated him humanely when all hope was gone. But nonetheless I am far from certain that Rondetto was not second best on merit at these weights, and their next meeting (without Arkle) is something to look forward to.

'Without Arkle' – how often, I wonder, are those words going to be thought or spoken over the next few years? For after all the tumult and the shouting died away last week, N.H. racing found itself face to face with a situation unknown since the days when judges used to call: 'Eclipse first the rest nowhere.'

With 12st 7lb on his back – the heaviest weight the rules now allow him to carry – Arkle smashed the three-mile chase record at Sandown on Saturday by *11 seconds*. The concession of 16lb to Mill House made not one ounce of difference and I am personally convinced that had Mill House carried 10st or even 9st 7lb, the result, though possibly not the distance, would have been the same.

So where, it has to be asked, do we go from here? The Hennessy Gold Cup (for which the weights have already been published), the King George VI 'Chase and the Cheltenham Gold Cup – all these are, barring accidents, as good as over and done with. They won't be dull – watching Arkle could never be that – but they will, unless something quite unforeseeable happens, be both uncompetitive and repetitive.

In the great conditions races clearly there is nothing to be done. We can only hope (and what a hope!) that a new star will arise capable of extending the champion. Until that happens – or until Arkle's powers begin to wane – I for one am quite content to thank Heaven for the chance of seeing such flawless perfection.

It only remains to congratulate Tom Dreaper for turning the great horse out a picture of health and fitness without a previous race in public, and Pat Taaffe once again for giving him an irreproachably perfect ride.

Pat, incidentally, calls this one of Arkle's easiest successes. That, in the end, was how it looked to me and, if true, strongly suggests that he is still improving. With any normal horse one would also say that he should be 'better for the race' – a truly awe-inspiring thought for any would-be future rivals.

13 November 1965

Arkle's next race was the Hennessy Gold Cup, in which he carried 12st 7lb, started at 6–1 on, and beat Freddie (10st 3lbs) by 15 lengths. He then went to Kempton Park for his first King George VI 'Chase.

ARKLE'S GREAT TRIUMPH SADDENED BY MISFORTUNE

Tragedy walked in the footsteps of triumph this week when one of the biggest crowds ever seen at Kempton Park watched Arkle win the King George VI 'Chase (3m). For as the greatest horse in the world cantered calmly home to a thunderous welcome, Dunkirk, who had challenged him so bravely, lay dead with a broken neck far out across the course.

Attempting the impossible, he had, almost literally, broken his heart on the anvil of Arkle's greatness and the men who, twenty-five years ago, fought and died on the beaches that bore his name would surely be proud to count him a member of their gallant company.

We know now that Dunkirk's death was caused not by his fall but by the supreme effort he had made. It would, in any case, have been in vain, but without him the King George would have been a hollow procession, and so to him, to his owner, Colonel Whitbread, and most of all to his rider, Bill Rees, those who were at Kempton – and millions more who watched on television – owe a debt no words of sympathy can pay.

Often in the past, for Mill House, for Brasher and perhaps for others, the price of challenging Arkle has been exhaustion and undeserved defeat. Now, for Dunkirk, it was death, for Bill Rees a broken thigh and months of painful inactivity.

I need hardly say that Arkle's owner, Anne Duchess of Westminster – and no doubt the great horse himself, could he express his feelings – must regret as bitterly as any this tragic *dénouement* to their latest triumph. But they were not to blame. No one was to blame. The cause of Dunkirk's death was his own fighting heart which, to the end, acknowledged no superior.

And, ironically, it was the wayward English climate that had set the scene for his last and greatest race. But for the torrential rain which fell at Cheltenham, Dunkirk would have run there a week ago and, with a few more degrees of frost, he would never have run at Kempton.

To run at all was a bold and sporting decision taken by Colonel Whitbread and Peter Cazalet more for the good of the game than with any real hope of victory.

But after one circuit on Monday that hope looked, for a moment or so, just barely on the cards.

Setting off as if the devil was at his heels, Dunkirk had at one time been almost a fence in front. Relaxed and confident, neither Arkle nor Pat Taaffe showed the slightest sign of uneasiness, but to some in the stands at Kempton it seemed conceivable that if Dunkirk could get a second wind they might at least have a battle on their hands.

But that expectation was short-lived. From the water jump on, without apparent effort, Arkle began to close the gap and, as they swung right-handed down the back side, Dunkirk must have heard behind him the hoof-beats of his fate.

Till then he had jumped superbly. Now, at the sixth from home, he made his first mistake and Pat Taaffe, coolly measuring the situation, decided to run no risk of interference should he fall.

Letting out an inch or so of rein, he sent Arkle up beside his rival to rise at the fatal open ditch perhaps half a length in front.

But poor Dunkirk never rose at all. A second earlier his lungs had filled with blood and, crashing headlong through the fence, he died as quickly and as bravely as a horse can die.

I hope – and surely it is probable – that he died without knowing he was beaten. And, like a captain on the bridge of a sinking ship, Bill Rees sat tight – too tight, for his leg was trapped and crushed under Dunkirk's body.

So ended an heroic enterprise, and courage was never more scurvily rewarded.

The rest was all Arkle. Alone, magnificent, his only danger

the cheering crowds which threatened to engulf him, he hesitated briefly at the second last, put himself right, and stormed away, so fresh that Pat Taaffe's hardest task all day was to pull him up.

Of his victory it only remains to be said that, judging by the effortless accuracy with which he measured the big, black, unfamiliar Kempton fences, Arkle would make Aintree look like shelling peas.

The magic of his presence had packed the stands at Kempton and I honestly don't believe we need fear that lack of opposition will ever weaken the magic hold Arkle has established on the imagination of the public.

That hold is no longer confined to the racing world. The other day in a national newspaper Arkle was included among the ten most 'glamorous' figures of 1965.

It must be doubtful whether any racehorse has ever been better or more widely known and loved. Heroes like Brown Jack and Golden Miller – about the only two remotely comparable examples I can think of – had no television screen to spread their fame and Arkle's value to racing in terms of publicity and advertisement is, quite literally, incalculable.

1 January 1966

Arkle started at 10 to 1 on for a third Cheltenham Gold Cup victory in 1966.

The story of the 1966 Gold Cup is the story not of a race – for there was no race – but of a fence.

Coming down the hill at the end of the first circuit Arkle had already taken the lead from Dormant and was sailing serenely along.

No one, alas, can say what passed through his mind as he galloped towards the 11th fence – the last, that is, next time around. Perhaps he was thinking about St Patrick – in whose honour a sprig of shamrock adorned his browband – or perhaps, more likely, he was looking at the crowd and enjoying, as he undoubtedly does, their undivided attention.

Anyway, meeting the fence dead right to stand back, he simply galloped straight on, parted the birch with his chest – and drew from the stands a great groan of horrified surprise.

But what followed this cataclysmic blunder was even more surprising – for the level flow of Arkle's stride was not interrupted by so much as a nod of his head. Pat Taaffe never moved (*that* was no surprise) but, as he said afterwards, he got no feeling of impact. The fence might just as well have been made of cotton wool and, as if to calm his admirers' shattered nerves, Arkle proceeded to clear the next (the open ditch) by an effortless couple of feet. My first impression of this incident was a simple confirmation of the fact that no modern steeplechase fence (save possibly at Aintree) is ever likely to upset Arkle's flawless strength and balance. Probably that is the case, but, oddly enough, of all the obstacles at Cheltenham the great horse chose precisely the right one to take on.

For walking round on the Wednesday evening, a N.H. official had noticed that the birch in this last fence had, through repeated battering, become far looser than any of its fellows. I understand that orders were given to repair it before the Thursday's racing but, for one reason or another, this, if done at all, was done to only a very small extent.

The gratitude of the whole (well, nearly the whole) steeplechasing world is due to the man responsible, for, had he obeyed his orders too zealously, no one can say for sure that history might not have been tragically altered.

The whole story only goes to show that Arkle was born under the right star, or, as an Irishman put it recently, that 'the good Lord must have a half-share in him'.

The rest needs little telling. Dormant chased the champion gallantly until the third last fence but then Pat Taaffe decided enough was enough. Arkle glided easily away, flicked over the offending obstacle clean as a whistle and won by 30 lengths.

Dormant, deservedly, kept Snaigow out of second place and so Anne Duchess of Westminster's magnificent horse joined Golden Miller and Cottage Rake in the select company of those who have won three Cheltenham Gold Cups.

At present, apart conceivably from Flyingbolt, there seems no earthly reason why he should not indefinitely extend that sequence.

26 March 1966

ARKLE – GLORIOUS
IN DEFEAT!

As Mr R.J. Blindell's Stalbridge Colonist galloped home last week to win the Hennessy Gold Cup a child in the stands began to sob. 'Don't you cry,' his mother told him, 'leave the crying to the Irish.'

But he was right to cry and she was wrong to scold him, for in the finish they had just watched there was a kind of sadness that had nothing whatever to do with national pride.

The inevitable had happened. Arkle had been beaten at last – by an English horse, and a supremely popular English jockey. But the cause of his defeat was far too clear – and its manner far too courageous – for any great rejoicing in the huge, predominantly English crowd.

We had seen a very good horse beat a great one, but the real victory was the handicapper's. It took 35lb – all the weight at his disposal – to bring the champion down and, in Arkle's 'failure', there was more glory than in many of his triumphs.

Appearing in public for the first time in eight months, Anne Duchess of Westminster's wonderful horse had looked to me, beforehand, every bit as good as ever. I could detect no sign that he might need the race and, striding eagerly round the paddock, his long ears proudly cocked, he had the air, as always, of a kindly monarch come to accept the homage of his subjects.

But, on the other side of the stands, in the hubbub of Tattersalls' and along the busy rails, there was an ominous rumble of opposition. The bookmakers had weighed up Arkle's disadvantages – his weight, the lack of a previous race, the probability that he might have to make the running – and the known ability of his rivals particularly of What a Myth (10st 2lb), to whom he must give 33lb.

Their conclusion was cautious, but definite – that Arkle faced his hardest task in England since December 1964, the day of his last defeat.

Opening at 2 to 1 on, he could soon be backed at 6 to 4 on and, although the faithful flocked to take that price, it never shortened further.

And almost at once the special tactical handicap under which Arkle so often has to labour reared its head again. Freddie (10st 7lb) led him over the first fence, but at the second he soared past into the lead.

Thereafter, until the last dramatic scene of all, nothing headed or even joined him. Though setting no great gallop and not, by his standards, pulling particularly hard, Arkle had nevertheless to be in front for more than three miles – with all the extra strain, mental as well as physical, which that involves.

He has, of course, often done likewise in the past and on Saturday, watching him measure each fence with the same old blend of accuracy and abandon, the spectre of defeat seemed far away.

Behind him the others were all closely bunched, but What A Myth's jumping was already leaving a good deal to be desired and down the back side second time round he was the first to come under pressure.

Before that, though, Arkle had enjoyed his usual triumphal procession past the stands, and graciously rewarded those who clapped and cheered him with a special staglike bound across the water.

He has so often done something spectacular like this within earshot of the crowd that I honestly don't believe it can any longer be coincidence. You could, I suppose, call it 'showing off' – I prefer a born entertainer's wish to please.

Anyway, turning into the back straight, two more explosive leaps hotted up the pace, but still his lead did not increase and still the pack snapped at his heels.

The first to weaken was, surprisingly, last year's second, Freddie. He had shadowed Arkle from the start, jumping much better than at Sandown, but now, almost certainly, the strain of that hard race – and of three gruelling journeys the length of England – told its tale.

And as he dropped back we waited expectantly for the relentless surge of acceleration with which, at this stage in the past two years, Arkle has asserted his authority.

But somehow, ominously, it never came. On the turn for home with four to jump, Pat Taaffe had not begun to ride, but nor had Stan Mellor, two lengths behind him on Stalbridge Colonist (10st). And now, for the first time, moving into second place three fences out, the little grey emerged as much the biggest danger.

Indeed the only danger, for Master Mascus (10st), 'on a tight rein at three miles', according to Jeff King, had failed to stay a yard beyond that distance.

Kellsboro Wood (10st), who had never been out of the first three (and who, for a six-year-old, ran another wonderful race), was under pressure – and What A Myth, handicapped both by his own mistakes and by the slow early gallop, was struggling to challenge.

So, as Arkle swept over the second last two lengths ahead of Stalbridge Colonist, the cheer that went out to welcome him was a confident, exultant one – the battle-cry of his adoring public.

Even to Stan Mellor it seemed, at that moment, as if the favourite must win. 'Arkle sprinted from the second last,' he says, 'and I thought, oh well, that's it.'

But suddenly Stalbridge Colonist was sprinting too and, hurtled into the last with the furious, fearless energy that is Mellor's trade mark, he took off at Arkle's quarters, passed him in the air – and landed running, with his head in front.

It was the impetus that counted more than the leap itself and, into his stride like quicksilver, the grey snatched a vital length in the first 20 yards of the run-in.

To poor Pat Taaffe, feeling that his beloved companion had no more to give, the race seemed over there and then. 'I thought we'd be beaten easily,' he says, but he, of all men, should have known that Arkle would never acknowledge defeat, however inevitable, without a fight.

And now, although defeat was inevitable (for Stalbridge Colonist never faltered), the champion threw all his heart and remaining strength into a desperate bid to ward it off. He pulled back nearly half a length and with 100 yards to go it still looked on the cards.

But Stan Mellor, three times champion jockey, and Stalbridge Colonist, the winner of eleven races last season, are not the pair to pass up such a chance.

So, together, they hung on – but half a length behind them, their wonderful, indomitable rival earned more than half the glory.

In those last hectic moments few had eyes to spare for What A Myth, but, with the future in mind, his performance should not be forgotten.

Fully six lengths behind Arkle at the second last, it was only from then on that his stamina came properly into play. But in the end, gaining on the two leaders with every stride, What A Myth finished third, beaten only one and a half lengths by the favourite.

The *dénouement* of the 1966 Hennessy: the grey Stalbridge Colonist comes to collar Arkle.

In a faster run race, on softer ground or over a slightly longer distance, he must have gone desperately close. And so, with Kellsboro Wood fourth, Master Mascus fifth and

Freddie last, the tenth anniversary Gold Cup went into the record books – as fine and memorable a race as any of its predecessors.

And a race, moreover – as *The Times'* leading article said on Monday – 'when a loss is as good as a win'. For, to set against the sadness of seeing Arkle so narrowly beaten, there were many consolations.

No man now riding, for instance, has done more for the reputation of N.H. racing – or for the welfare of his brother jockeys – than Stan Mellor.

After three successive championships, he was only robbed of a fourth by a horrible fall at Aintree in which his face was smashed beyond recognition. Neither that disaster nor several short spells of bad luck since have had the slightest effect on his courage or sense of humour. And, as I've written so often before in these pages, there is no more stirring sight in N.H. racing than Stan 'winding one up' over the last two fences of a steeplechase.

And if the man is a universally popular figure with the jumping crowd, so, in his way, is the horse. For Stalbridge Colonist's record last season was one of unbelievable reliability. In fourteen attempts, he won eleven races, was only unplaced once – and then set off for France where the swamp-fever ban marooned him until November!

A grey seven-year-old, on the small side but beautifully made, Stalbridge Colonist has been trained for the last two years by Ken Cundell, to whom enormous credit is due, not only for keeping him fresh throughout last season but also for producing him fit to beat Arkle so soon after the upheaval of a return journey from France.

Mr Harry Dufosee, who bred Stalbridge Colonist, has for many years now been producing a steady stream of jumping winners from his farm near Wincanton.

The foundation of his fortunes as a breeder was laid when, in the late 1920s, Lord Stalbridge asked him to keep a mare called May Bush. By By George! out of Queen of the Hawthorns by Lesterlin, May Bush had finished third in the Irish One Thousand Guineas and was bought at Ballsbridge by Owen Anthony for £1,500.

Lord Stalbridge paid Mr Dufosee £1 a week to board her and,

after a few years of unsuccessful breeding attempts, let him have the mare for a year's keep – £52!

May Bush then produced, in two years, Stalbridge Weston (the dam of that fine hurdler Spring Corn and other winners) and Stalbridge Common, dam of Eesofud and, therefore, gran-dam of the Hennessy winner.

Eesofud herself was not much good on the racecourse, but had broken a bone in her knee point-to-pointing and could never use that leg properly afterwards. Before the surgery, however, her work at home had suggested she might be better than Spring Corn. She has, incidentally, a three-year-old son by Domaha who has never been beaten in thirteen appearances in the show-ring!

And apart from the sterling qualities of the winning pair, the Hennessy result was, in another way, welcome as well as sad.

Arkle's reputation stands as high as ever but the jumping world has seen it proved that he *can* be beaten. So, while there is no sign whatever of a genuine challenger for his title, his mere presence in a handicap should never again dry up the opposition altogether.

The crowds will still flock to see him whenever he appears, but, in handicaps at least, they will have the prospect of real rivalry.

Lastly I must record my own firm belief that Arkle is every bit as good as ever. It is true that he did not appear to show quite his old acceleration in the straight at Newbury, but the race had been slowly run and he had behind him a fast seven-year-old capable of winning in good class at two miles.

It is also at least arguable that, in the circumstances, forced as he was to make all his own running, the lack of a previous race in public this season just turned the scale between defeat and victory.

But that is all speculation. The story of a magnificent race, of a fine winner and a great loser should perhaps end with Pat Taaffe's parting words – 'God help them next time he runs . . .'

3 December 1966

The next time he ran was in the SGB Handicap 'Chase at Ascot on 14 December 1966, and he easily resumed his winning ways. It was then back to Kempton for a second King George.

TRAGEDY STRIKES CRUEL BLOW AT KEMPTON

In the seven years I've been responsible for filling it, this page has not been written with a heavier heart: for Arkle may never run again – and if that nightmare should come true then 27 December 1966 was as black a day as any in the history of National Hunt racing.

On it, the record books will show that Anne Duchess of Westminster's Arkle (12st 7lb) was beaten a length by Mrs Doris Wells-Kendrew's Dormant (11st) in the King George VI 'Chase (3m) at Kempton Park. But behind this sensational, well-nigh unbelievable result there lay a sad and all too ordinary explanation; for Arkle – who had never before shown his adoring public the slightest sign of weakness or unsoundness – hobbled sadly out of the unsaddling enclosure last Tuesday afternoon like an old soldier on whom the years are suddenly weighing heavy.

Minutes later he could hardly walk at all and was carried back to the racecourse stables in a horsebox. There he was examined by the two official vets on duty and with remarkable and admirable speed an X-ray was obtained of Arkle's off-fore foot. And so, less than three hours after Dormant's victory, news of his world-famous victim was flashing down the wires to be heard, with shock and sadness, wherever men care about horses.

It was bad but might have been much worse. The main (pedal) bone is fractured inside Arkle's off-fore hoof, but the X-ray revealed no displacement.

If none occurs, as Mrs Tom Dreaper and Arkle's regular vet, Mr Maxie Cosgrove, agreed on Tuesday night, there is at least an even-money chance that the great horse may recover completely – enough to race again in twelve months' time. But he could not, in any circumstances, race before 1968 and will probably have to stay in his box at Kempton for at least three weeks.

A great deal – almost everything in fact – depends on how things develop during that time. But though I've no wish whatever to minimise the disaster, it can be argued (touching all available wood) that, if the only injury is a simple fracture of the pedal bone, the odds on recovery are rather better than even money.

Since the bone in question is completely surrounded by the hoof – which serves it as a natural and effective splint – displacement is much more the exception than the rule.

An experienced racehorse vet to whom I spoke last week could not remember a case in which permanent lameness was caused by such a fracture. He cited the instance of Mr Oliver Gilbey's Wingless, who broke a pedal bone at Kempton on 30 November – and who is already walking perfectly sound.

All this, however, is mere guesswork and may well be wishful thinking. The hard fact is that Arkle, rising ten years old, will be eleven before he can conceivably be fit to run again. It will indeed be a miracle if at that age, after so serious an injury, he recovers in full the unique brilliance which over the past three seasons has set so many racecourses on fire.

And I've no doubt at all, knowing the love his owner and trainer bear him, that the flame of that brilliance will never be allowed to burn low. The sad descent from greatness to mediocrity can never be for Arkle.

And so, hoping with all my heart for the best, here, as well as I can piece it together, is the story of what may have been the last appearance of the greatest steeplechase horse the world has ever seen.

It began with the frost leaving the ground on Tuesday to produce surprisingly good going – and with the news that Mill House, having pulled a muscle in his quarters, would not run.

So slipped away the big horse's last and, as things turned out, almost certainly his best, chance of taking some revenge upon his old familiar rival.

Of Arkle's remaining six opponents, only two, Woodland Venture (11st 7lb) and Dormant, could conceivably be called 'dangers' in theory – and that was how it proved in practice.

For, although Arkle set off in front as usual, those two had no great difficulty in staying with him and almost from the first there were grounds for suspicion that all might not be well.

To Pat Taaffe the signs were even more ominous. His old friend reached uncharacteristically for the second fence, never really took hold of the bit and, most significant of all, soon began to hang outward away from the rails – and away from his off-fore leg.

He had never done this before and Taaffe, who believes that the injury was probably caused by striking the guard-rail of a fence, is now convinced that Arkle was feeling it for much the greater part of the race. If he is right – and no one is in a position to argue – then this is a story of tremendous courage as well as tragedy.

Passing the stands after one circuit, Dormant passed Arkle to take the lead, and among the crowd an anxious buzz greeted the unaccustomed sight of the champion in second place. As Dormant went by, Arkle's ears lost, for a moment, their normal confident poise. He looked, to one sympathetic observer, 'like Samson must have looked when he found his strength gone with his hair'.

But Arkle's strength was by no means all gone yet. Soon after the water he was back in front and then, just as his supporters began to kick themselves for worrying, he made, at the 14th fence, the last and by far the worst of several minor blunders.

This, in fact, was not minor at all. It made even Pat Taaffe sit back, and many horses, less powerful, agile and superbly balanced, would have fallen.

No one can say how much it may have cost in terms of pain and energy, but even so Arkle would not give up his lead. Round the final bend as Pat Taaffe began to ride, he answered heroically – but beside him on Woodland Venture Terry Biddlecombe was sitting ominously still.

Terry believes – and I wholeheartedly agree with him – that, as they went to the second last, the younger horse had the race at his mercy.

In the light of what happened afterwards, he must surely be

right, but we'll never know for sure. For now, taking off beside Arkle two from home, Woodland Venture just clipped the top foot of the fence, lost his balance and fell. He had done nothing at all to discourage my belief that he is the best young potential staying 'chaser in England.*

The last water jump Arkle ever took: with him in the 1966 King George VI 'Chase at Kempton Park is his eventual conqueror, Dormant (Jeff King).

And now, some ten lengths clear of Dormant with only one fence to jump, Arkle's troubles were surely over. As if to make even more certain, he threw at the last one of his special grandstand leaps and, to those standing by the fence, it looked inconceivable that he could be beaten.

As Dormant landed apparently without a chance on the flat, Jeff King, to his eternal credit, had still not given up. And, as he sat down to ride, Arkle, still far ahead, must suddenly have

* Woodland Venture was all out to win the 1967 Gold Cup by three-quarters of a length (at level weights) from Stalbridge Colonist, who had, as we have seen, needed a concession of 35lb to beat Arkle in the previous year's Hennessy. So even if Woodland Venture 'had the King George at his mercy', it was only by virtue of his great rival's disability.

begun to feel the full, agonising, strength-sapping effects of his injury.

Now too he had no fence ahead on which to concentrate his mind and, until Dormant appeared beside him 50 yards from the line, no visible enemy to fight.

Small wonder then, in all the circumstances – with 12st 7lb on his back and a broken bone in his foot – that even this peerless, unconquerable fighter could fight no more. And as his strength drained away it seemed, as often happens in finishes such as this, to be flowing into his rival. For Dormant, give him his due, did quicken after the last.

Half-way up the run-in, his prospects still looked remote, but for poor Arkle the winning post might just as well have been a million miles away.

Fifty yards from it, for only the fourth time in his steeple-chasing career, he had to acknowledge defeat. That in itself was sad enough – but what is one defeat compared with our loss if we are never to see him race again?

31 December 1966

A PROUD WARRIOR
WHO FOUGHT TO THE
BITTER END

For a moment last week the election, the Derby, the World Cup and all the other preoccupations of an English June seemed unimportant. A single four-word news announcement put them abruptly in perspective – and sent a stab of almost personal bereavement through who knows how many million hearts.

'The end of Arkle,' the radio said, and, as the voice droned on, laconic, uninvolved, the rest of its sad message was drowned in a flood of memories.

With them, at first, came bitterness – anger at the cruel fate which has cut short the happy retirement Arkle so richly deserved. For he was only thirteen years old and might fairly have looked forward to another decade of sweet grass, warm beds and careless ease.

He was far too intelligent to be one of those horses who pines when his active life is over and, after all, if from time to time he wanted to hear the roar of the crowd again, what racecourse or showground in the world would not have been proud to receive him?

So it *is* cruel – to Arkle himself and perhaps even more to those who loved him best. Almost everyone who owns a domestic animal has to face, sooner or later, the dreadful decision Anne Duchess of Westminster faced last week.

Once it was clear that the pain in Arkle's feet could not be cured and would get worse, there could only be the one decision. But only one person could take it and this great horse, unlike so many others, was lucky enough to have an owner who both deserved and appreciated the gift from the gods that he was.

But to set against his sad, untimely ending, Arkle was lucky in other ways as well. Throughout his life, in a world it takes all sorts to make, his selection of human beings was as unerring as his jumping.

An owner who wanted to bet, a trainer who specialised in hurdlers or a jockey with clumsy hands – any one of them could have sent his life careering off down false, dark-ending trails. But the Duchess was prepared to wait, Tom Dreaper saw the big, ungraceful youngster's full potential, Johnny Lumley, Paddy Woods and all the others at Greenogue worked long and hard to develop it – and in the end, in Pat Taaffe's gentle, steely fingers it flowered to the thing of magic that was Arkle.

So he was lucky in his friends, and even luckier perhaps never to know the downward sag to mediocrity and failure which is, inevitably, the lot of so many.

That tragic Boxing Day at Kempton, Arkle's supremacy was as great as it had ever been. Not for him the agonizing battle with advancing years, the steady, too slow progress down the handicap, the defeats by younger horses, the excuses, the knowing nods and patronising words – 'I told you so – he's gone.' No one ever said that about Arkle.

To the very end there was no hint of deterioration and now there never will be. Our memories of him may fade with time, but they can never be tarnished by failure – and of all the great 'chasers since the war I can think of only one, Mandarin, who went out on anything like so high a note.

But if, in these ways, Arkle was lucky, how much luckier were we who lived to watch and enjoy his greatness. And how lucky – though not all racecourse managers might agree – that television came in time to convey that greatness to millions for whom, without it, Arkle would only have been a name.

Of all those millions each will have his memories. My own are so many and vivid that it is difficult to choose, but, oddly enough, a defeat, one of the only four he ever suffered over fences, stands clearest in my mind.

Only a week before, Arkle had turned the Hennessy Gold Cup

into a hollow procession beating poor Mill House by 100 yards and looking, quite literally, invincible.

Even with 12st 10lb on his back, even over two miles and five furlongs, a distance patently short of his best, he was still made a red-hot favourite for the Massey-Ferguson Gold Cup. And it was only between the last two fences at Cheltenham as Flying Wild and Buona Notte went past him, that we realised he wasn't invincible after all.

But the moment I remember came *after* the last fence that day. Buona Notte, who had blundered horribly, was fighting back in a vain attempt to catch Flying Wild and the two of them, the elegant, grey mare and the massive, powerful bay, would in any case have made a thrilling sight.

But look back behind them and you will see something far more memorable. Head low, dog-tired, giving 32lb to one rival and 26lb to the other, Arkle *gained ground* up the Cheltenham hill.

With everything against him, he never for one moment thought of giving up and even now, shutting my eyes, I can see the angle of his out-thrust neck with every nerve and sinew strained to the limit and beyond.

It wasn't, thank heaven, how we usually saw him. Far more often, of course, it was the others who struggled in vain and he who toyed with them.

But a lot has been written of Arkle's alleged 'conceit' – a ridiculous and inaccurate word in any case to describe the natural elegance and gaiety which were his outward trademarks. And even if he had an air of pride, conceit is still the wrong description. For conceit is a balloon that can all too easily be pricked.

In all his four defeats – that fatal, misleading slip at Newbury, against Flying Wild and Buona Notte, trying to give Stalbridge Colonist 35lb and, finally, on three legs in the King George VI 'Chase – Arkle's courage never once deserted him.

So used to victory, he might so easily have sulked when things got tough – but the tougher they got, the harder he tried. Effortless supremacy is one thing – dogged persistence in pursuit of the impossible quite another.

It is very hard to shift, as Arkle did, from the first to the second without losing either his own or anyone else's respect.

So call him proud if you like, for proud he was. But not, I beg of you, 'conceited' – for braggarts seldom fight, as he did, to the bitter end.

The facts and figures of Arkle's record are too well known to bear repeating in detail. Only six horses ever beat him over fences. Mill House and Happy Spring did so in the 1963 Hennessy Gold Cup, after one of the only two mistakes which ever affected Arkle's career.

The second, at the last open ditch in the 1966 King George VI 'Chase, was the one which smashed his pedal bone, brought about his defeat by Dormant and drove him into premature retirement.

Between those two disasters I can only remember seeing Arkle hit two fences hard. One was the second in the Railway straight at Sandown (he took off a full stride too soon) and the other was the last fence first time round in his third and final Cheltenham Gold Cup.

He had the shamrock in his bridle for St Patrick that day and, looking at the crowd instead of where he was going, he simply galloped straight on. But so great was his strength, so perfect his balance that the shamrock never even nodded and Pat Taaffe never moved.

In public I suppose he must have jumped well over 500 steeplechase fences and, even if you add a few mistakes unnoticed from the stands, his record – unblemished by a single racing fall – can never have been excelled by any 'chaser, let alone one who was so often asked to concede huge weights in top-class handicaps.

I have no wish to revive the sterile argument comparing him with Golden Miller, but to suggest that the Aintree fences would have been too much for Arkle has always seemed to me insulting nonsense.

From the moment when, as a headstrong yearling, he came off second best in an argument with a strand of barbed wire, only one obstacle ever *did* prove too much for him. That was a schooling hurdle and the crashing fall he took over it taught him a lesson he never forgot.

Perhaps that, in the end, was the underlying secret of his greatness. For while there may well have been horses with hearts, lungs, muscles and bones as efficient as Arkle's – horses who could gallop as far and as fast – there has never been one who combined with those physical qualities the intelligence, co-ordination and timing to jump 500 fences at racing pace and misjudge only five or six.

Had Arkle ever gone to Aintree, I for one have not the slightest doubt that, barring sheer bad luck, he would have carried any weight up to 12st and won any of the Grand Nationals run during his lifetime.

But there is no need for such speculation. The facts alone are quite enough. They are, simply, that no other horse in steeplechasing history ever dominated his contemporaries half

Arkle and Pat Taaffe at the Dublin Horse Show.

as completely as Arkle did. No other horse in the whole history of Thoroughbred racing was ever so much loved and admired by so many people, and to no other horse does the sport and all who follow it owe so huge and unpayable a debt.

It is a slightly sobering thought that, in under three minutes this week, a three-year-old colt will, by galloping 12 furlongs on the flat, have earned nearly as much (£60,000) as the total (£75,000) Arkle won by galloping almost 100 miles and jumping 500 fences and hurdles.

Such are the topsy-turvy values of modern racing – but it wasn't for money that Arkle ran his heart out. He did it because he had been bred for the job and taught to do it well by kindly men whose kindness and skill he was glad to repay.

He did it because he loved his own speed and strength and agility – and perhaps because he loved the cheers they brought him. He was, more certainly than any other Thoroughbred I can think of, a *happy* horse who enjoyed every minute of his life.

In that sense perhaps the human race did repay some small part of the debt it owed him and at least when his life ceased being a pleasure it was quickly and humanely ended.

But mostly the debt remains unpaid. We can only try to pay it by remembering Arkle as he was – brave in defeat, magnificent in victory, kind and gentle in repose.

Now he is gone and we must search for others to warm our blood on winter afternoons, to fill the stands and set the crowds on fire. No doubt we shall find them – but they will be pale shadows of the real thing. For those who saw Arkle will never forget the sight and, until they see another like him, will never believe that two such miracles can happen in a lifetime.

5 June 1970

Races

Jonjo O'Neill punches the air in triumph after Dawn Run's
Gold Cup victory.

Ten races is not many in thirty years and it would not be hard to pick as many more. But all of these were occasions when I genuinely did feel lucky to be there. Most of my greatest equine heroes figure, not all of them as winners. I admired Pendil, for instance, more than The Dikler, Sea Pigeon more than Monksfield and Bustino more than Grundy. But these contests are chosen more for themselves, as races, than for the horses who took part. Here, in fact, 'The play's the thing'.

I notice, by the way, that the ratio of six jumping races to four flat is the same which the Levy Board uses when distributing prize money. Except that, unfortunately, they have it the other way round . . .

TRIUMPH OVER IMPOSSIBLE ODDS

Grand Steeplechase de Paris, Auteuil, 17 June 1962

From Agincourt to D-Day, France, I suppose, has been the scene of more brave deeds by Englishmen than any other country in the world. Mostly, of course, they were inspired by the horrid waste of war, but sport, in its less serious tragic way, can also lift a man to heights of daring and achievement, and as Fred Winter and Mandarin came back last Sunday after winning the Grand Steeplechase de Paris, I like to think that the ghosts of long-dead English horsemen rode beside them, glad and proud to know that the flag for which they fought and died still flies, even in this sad, dull, mechanical age.

To win at all would have been a famous victory – to win as Winter and Mandarin did was an heroic triumph over odds so steep that no normal man or horse could have been blamed for giving up long before the end.

None of this, of course, could even be guessed at, as, in the atmosphere of a Turkish bath, the 14 runners swept gaily past the stands for the first of three intricate, twisting circuits.

So far as one could see in the friendly but chaotic tangle that serves Auteuil for a parade ring, the French horses were not a wildly impressive sight. Nor, to someone who had never seen him before, would Mandarin have been, but to the large band of English supporters, the sheen on his coat, the hard muscles writhing over his quarters, and the way he pulled 'Mush' Foster round the paddock, all told their own encouraging tale.

Sure enough, after flicking neat and fast over the preliminary hurdle jumped on the way to the start, Mandarin was soon upsides in front and passed the stands pulling, as usual, like a train. He has always been a 'heavy-headed' ride, with precious little feeling in his mouth, and always runs in a rubber-covered snaffle to save his lips and jaws.

Joe Lammin, Fulke Walwyn's head lad, serves Mandarin his daily bottle of stout.

At the beginning of last season a brand new bridle was bought and Mandarin had worn it only half-a-dozen times, including his victories both in the Hennessy and Cheltenham Gold Cups. But the trouble with rubber bits is that a fault or wear can develop unseen in the steel chain – and this, no doubt, is what had happened now.

After the first, sharp, left-hand bend the Grand Steeple course comes back towards the stands and there, going to the fourth, a soft but staring privet fence the best part of six feet high, the bit snapped clean in the middle, inside Mandarin's mouth. I remember thinking at the time, 'He got a little close to that one,' but for another full circuit none of us in the stands realised the dreadful truth.

In fact, of course, Fred Winter now had no contact whatsoever with the horse's mouth or head. The reins, kept together by the Irish martingale (or 'rings') were still round Mandarin's neck, and they, together with the thin neck-strap of the breast-girth, were Winter's only hand-hold.

To visualise the full impossibility of the situation you must remember first that when a racehorse, particularly a hard-pulling chaser, is galloping on the bit, much of the jockey's weight is normally balanced, through the reins, against that of the horse's head and forehand. Now, for both Fred Winter and Mandarin, this vital counterbalance was gone completely. The man, with no means of steering but his weight, had to rely entirely on grip and balance; the horse, used to a steady pressure on his mouth, had to jump 21 strange and formidable obstacles with his head completely free – a natural state admittedly, but one to which Mandarin is wholly unaccustomed.

Small wonder then that, at the huge 'Rivière de la Tribune' – the water in front of the stands – he fiddled awkwardly, landing only inches clear of the bank and disaster. Thereafter, save for another nasty moment at the same fence next time round, the little horse jumped unbelievably well, and Fred Winter, sitting still or driving on as the need arose, matched his every move with the sympathetic rhythm that is nine-tenths of horsemanship.

But the fences, needless to say, were only half the problem. Walking the course that morning with Winter, Dave Dick and Joe Lammin, Fulke Walwyn's head lad, we had all wondered afresh at the many turns, and countless opportunities for losing your way. The Grand Steeple is, roughly, two figures of eight in opposite directions and one whole circuit outside both. There are at least four bends through 180 degrees, and to negotiate them all as Winter and Mandarin did, without bit or bridle, was, quite literally, miraculous.

The answer lies, of course, in many things – in the matchless strength of Winter's legs, in Mandarin's own good sense, and in the absolute determination of them both never to give up while there was one shot, however forlorn, left on the board.

It is also, I think, only fair to give some credit – and our thanks – to the French jockeys, several of whom could, had they pleased, have taken advantage of the disaster and, without much risk to themselves, got rid of the biggest danger. Instead, at least one – Laumas on Taillefer – and probably several others actually did their best to help, proving gloriously that the comradeship of dangers shared can, in some sports at least, count far more than international rivalry.

Throughout the race, save for a moment on the last bend, Mandarin was up in the first four, and, as he jumped the Rivière for the last time, the full horror of his situation dawned upon us in the stands.

From that moment on, the nerve-wracking suspense, the wild impossible hope, plunging to black despair and back again, were like nothing I have ever known on a racecourse – or for that matter anywhere else.

Mandarin cleared with ease the tricky post and rails at which he hesitated fatally three years ago, and came to the junction of the courses close fourth – close enough to lift the hearts of those who knew his and Winter's invincible finishing power.

But now disaster almost struck. Before the last right-handed turn, a large bush must be passed on the left – but can with equal ease be passed on the right. Mandarin, on the inside, with no rail to guide him, could not know until the last moment which way to go. For a few heart-stopping strides he hesitated, Winter threw all his strength and weight into one last desperate swerve – and somehow they were safe.

But priceless lengths had been lost and now, round the final bend, with only two obstacles to jump, Mandarin was only fifth, some six or seven lengths behind the leader.

On the turn, of course, Winter could hardly ride at all, but then, facing the Bullfinch, in a straight line for home at last, it was a different matter. From the stands we saw the familiar crouching drive of the shoulders, and Mandarin, responding as he always has and always will, thrust out his gallant head and went for the Bullfinch like a tank facing tissue paper.

None will ever know what the little horse felt or thought between those last two fences. I have always believed he knows just what it means to win – and now none will ever convince me otherwise. In a hundred desperate yards he passed three horses as if they were walking and, as he landed in front on the long run-in, my eyes, I am not ashamed to say, were half-blind with tears.

But it was not over yet. Mandarin was deadly tired and Winter, the reins gathered useless in his left hand, could do nothing to hold him together. He could only push and drive – and how he drove. Even so, inch by inch, Lumino, the only French horse able to accelerate, crept nearer and nearer.

In the final desperate strides, not knowing the angle, not one of us could really tell who had won. Fred Winter thought he had got up, but *he* could not speak, so for several ghastly moments we had to sweat it out. But then, there it was – number one in the frame – and as Mandarin came back, mobbed as no film star has ever been, head down, dog-tired, sweating – but surely happy – a cheer went up such as I have never heard on any racecourse.

For Fred Winter it was not the end. Riding a dream of a race, he went on, 40 minutes later, to win the Grande Course de Haies on Beaver II. I have neither time nor space to describe that race and, triumph though it was for Beaver's trainer, Ryan Price, it only served as the perfect ending to an historic afternoon. For on Sunday, Fred Winter and Mandarin had earned themselves a place among the immortal names of sport. I have never seen a comparable feat, never expect to – and can only thank God that I was there.

23 June 1962

THE HISLOPS' BELIEF IN 'BRIGADIER' PAYS OFF

Two Thousand Guineas, Newmarket, 1 May 1971

In one of his more famous exploits, as described by Sir Arthur Conan Doyle, Brigadier Gerard killed a fox – with a single, well-aimed stroke of his sabre – in full view of the Duke of Wellington and the British army.

But although the gallant Hussar caused quite a stir on that occasion, it was nothing compared with the sensation at Newmarket last Saturday afternoon as, with a single, equally deadly stroke, his modern reincarnation, Mrs John Hislop's Brigadier Gerard, mowed down the two best-known three-year-olds in Europe.

Mill Reef and My Swallow duly fought out their long-awaited return match last week, but as they came together on the sunlit Rowley Mile, Joe Mercer picked up his whip two lengths behind them.

The light, back-handed slap he gave Brigadier Gerard looked, at the time, the gesture of a jockey in trouble – for neither Geoff Lewis on Mill Reef nor Frankie Durr on My Swallow had yet made any comparable move.

But then, with nearly three furlongs of the 1971 Two Thousand Guineas left to run, the picture changed as dramatically and completely as any Classic I remember.

For that one gentle reminder had been all Brigadier Gerard needed. Momentarily, it seemed, he became unbalanced but, if so, Joe Mercer was ready, and, back straight and level in a flash, the big bay lengthened his stride with the sudden explosive power that is flat racing's most memorable sight.

In a dozen strides he drew level with Mill Reef, and Geoff Lewis, who was just deciding, happily, that he had My Swallow beaten, knew with greater certainty that the game was up.

'The moment Joe appeared it was all over,' he said afterwards, and so it was, for now, coming out of the Dip, Brigadier Gerard left his two distinguished rivals as though they were caught in an Irish bog.

I don't know what proportion of the huge crowd at Newmarket had backed the winner, but, certainly, of the many assembled experts very few, in their hearts, expected him to win.

So it is all the more delightful to record that this was, perhaps, the most universally popular Classic victory seen in England since Sir Gordon Richards won the Derby.

Because, as he swept majestically home last week, Brigadier Gerard was striking an unforgettable blow for the attitude of mind which sees racing more as a sport and a source of pleasure than as a means of making money.

No one, least of all John Hislop, would deny that money plays a vital part in bloodstock breeding. Without it the whole complex, infinitely chancy business – about which he knows as much as any living man and a great deal more than most – would topple like a house of cards.

But the belief to which Mr and Mrs Hislop gave such selfless support when they refused a quarter of a million pounds for Brigadier Gerard last year is simply that money is not everything. Having spent his whole adult life (except for a war in which, though refused on medical grounds for the army, he parachuted into France with the Special Air Service and won a Military Cross) in various branches of the racing world, John Hislop long ago reached the top in at least three of them.

A high-class amateur over fences and hurdles (third in the Grand National on Kami), he was far and away the best to ride on the flat in England since the war.

As a breeding expert, his advice has long been sought all over the world and as a journalist and author he has described the racing scene with more warmth, colour and style than any other living writer.

I can honestly say that his *Steeplechasing* was a major factor in my own determination to become an amateur rider and for anyone else with ambitions in that direction it remains quite outstandingly the best book ever written on the subject.

But throughout this long and highly successful career, John Hislop has quietly, and with no great capital investment, been applying his own theories in search of a high-class racehorse. And when Brigadier Gerard, whose grandam Brazen Molly he bought for 400 guineas, crowned an unbeaten two-year-old season by winning the Middle Park Stakes, it seemed to him that his long search might have reached the rainbow's end. And for such a man, in the circumstances, such a horse, as John said in the winner's enclosure last week, was 'simply not for sale'.

Brigadier Gerard with Jean and John Hislop after his Two
Thousand Guineas victory.

But the gamble involved was none the less a tremendous one – and all the more so in a season blessed with two other colts quite obviously so far above the average. For until now, do not forget, it seemed perfectly possible that Brigadier Gerard might be good enough to win, say, six Two Thousand Guineas out of ten – and still finish third in 1971.

He could then hardly have been worth more than £50,000, so in hard cash the Hislops' gamble represented a bet of £200,000 at even money on a horse who started out at 11 to 2!

Such was the background to this unforgettable race – and

such are the reasons why, in the cheers that greeted Joe Mercer and the Brigadier on Saturday, there was the special, heartfelt warmth of an English crowd hailing not only an English horse, but also the sort of Quixotic sporting gesture for which, even in these days of blackguarded referees and whining cricketers, the English, or some of them, still have a special feeling.

Everything had conspired to set a perfect scene for this eagerly awaited clash. The sun shone, a huge crowd packed the Rowley Mile, and the field, though small, was a sight to treasure.

In sheer size, strength and evident well-being, My Swallow inevitably made his five opponents look almost insignificant. A mass of hard, shiny-coated muscle, he danced eagerly through the parade, so bursting with power that confirmed Mill Reef supporters like myself could hardly bear to watch him.

But size isn't everything, we told ourselves, and the little American colt has never looked better or more elegant. Beside him Minsky seemed almost common – a massive chestnut cast in a typical sprinting mould.

Indian Ruler is a nice colt of medium size, and Good Bond, though he probably ran below his form, had already looked outclassed in the paddock.

In describing the winner it is hard to avoid wisdom after the event – but even harder to find a fault in his conformation.

Almost as tall, I imagine, as My Swallow, Brigadier Gerard has slightly more quality, expressed in a truly beautiful head, a fine sloping shoulder and great length from hip to hock.

He is, in fact, a really lovely colt and although some thought he looked less fit than his rivals before Saturday's race, I stood one yard from his nostrils four minutes after it and a candle held against them would hardly have been extinguished.

No better testimonial could be imagined to the skill of Dick Hern. Together with John Hislop he had long ago taken the bold decision not to give the Brigadier a race before the Guineas, and last week, producing the colt fit to run for his life, he proved that in this, as in everything else, they had been absolutely right.

The early stages of the Two Thousand Guineas had gone pretty much as expected, with My Swallow racing wide in the middle of the course just ahead of Mill Reef on the stands side. Minsky, who had tracked My Swallow, was beaten after six furlongs and as My Swallow and Mill Reef joined battle soon after halfway, Joe Mercer moved into position inside and just behind them.

Neither Indian Ruler nor Good Bond ever got into the race with a chance and Jimmy Lindley, who rode the latter, was emphatic that this was far and away the best Two Thousand Guineas in his experience.

And why not, after all? For if Mill Reef had beaten My Swallow three-quarters of a length (as he did), with Minsky five lengths away (as he was), we would have accepted the result as confirmation of last year's form, when these two dominated all their contemporaries in Europe.

Well, not quite all – because Brigadier Gerard never met either of them. And now here he was, three lengths in front and sailing merrily away – an unexpected result perhaps, but one with a perfectly reasonable explanation, namely that Mrs Hislop's colt is, at a mile, much the best of his age in Europe.

I saw no excuse for either of his victims, nor was any offered. So let us be thankful for that rare and precious thing: an entirely satisfactory Classic race, won by the best horse, by an English horse and by a horse, what's more, who is not likely either to be sold abroad or rushed off prematurely to stud.

7 May 1971

A GREAT RACE IS WON
AS IT SHOULD BE WON

Prix de l'Arc de Triomphe, Longchamp, 3 October 1971

By winning the 1971 Prix de l'Arc de Triomphe, Mr Paul Mellon's Mill Reef laid several separate and valid claims to immortality. Neither his time, his earnings nor, almost certainly, his value have ever been surpassed by a racehorse trained in Europe.

And I believe that, last Sunday afternoon at Longchamp, cheered by a huge adoring crowd and watched by millions more on television, Mill Reef may have set another record – harder to prove but arguably even more worthwhile.

For racing has always been primarily a source of entertainment and the question I wish to ask on Mill Reef's behalf is whether, in the history of the sport, any other three-year-old colt has, by the end of his second season, given mankind as much sheer pleasure, excitement and emotion as this small, infinitely gallant bay.

It is not, I admit, a claim you can substantiate in black and white, but certainly, in twenty years of fairly regular attendance, I have never seen a flat racecourse more full of happy, delighted human beings than Longchamp was last week.

Arkle inspired the same warm glow of universal satisfaction – a feeling that somehow the frivolous, artificial game we love has, briefly, been transformed and lifted far above its normal self.

But Arkle is already both immortal and unique and, through

no fault of his, the public he entertained was probably smaller than Mill Reef's.

Ribot and Nijinsky were, at times, as much household words as Mr Mellon's colt, but the great Italian only ran three races outside his native land and the enormous pleasure Nijinsky undoubtedly gave was marred in the end by the dying fall of his career.

So, quite apart from any comparison in terms of merit with the great ones of the past (and only two post-war middle-distance horses, Ribot and Sea Bird II, can now stand such comparison), it seems to me that Mill Reef may fairly claim to share, with Arkle, the title of champion entertainer.

And his services to racing – already of incalculable value – are, with any luck at all, nothing like over yet.

The English used to put modesty high on the list of qualities they value in a hero, and although the likes of Cassius Clay and Dave Bedford sometimes seem to have changed all that, there is still, for many of us, something irresistibly attractive about the champion who holds his peace and lets his deeds speak for him.

That, certainly, is Mill Reef's way. In size, shape and temperament he has neither Nijinsky's flamboyance nor Arkle's swagger. This week, in fact, watching him wander diffidently round the sunlit Longchamp paddock, the contrast with some of his larger, stronger, more exuberant opponents was almost painfully apparent.

Mentally, it was clear, he had never been more completely relaxed but, although the journey from Kingsclere had been brilliantly stage-managed, the signs of its effect – followed by three nights in a strange box – were there for all to see.

Behind the girth and down his quarters, Mill Reef had run up undeniably light and the awful question asked itself – might not what looked like relaxation be, in reality, the apathy of a horse 'gone off the boil'?

Some such thoughts must have passed through many heads – and none more agonizingly than Ian Balding's. For months now he can have had few, if any, waking moments without a picture of Sunday's scene in his mind's eye and, of all that long and anxious period, the last half-hour – with no more to do but wait and hope – must have been in many ways the worst.

But for Ian and for all Mill Reef's nerve-wracked supporters, reassurance was at hand. No sooner had Geoff Lewis settled in the saddle than the little horse seemed to grow.

And then, as he turned to canter down, the adjective 'little' no longer applied. Neck stretched as usual, he bounded eagerly away and suddenly, as those insignificant-looking quarters bunched and sprang, you could almost feel their abnormal power.

Unlike Nijinsky, Mill Reef had an ideal draw – six off the rail with both Ramsin and his pacemaker Ossian inside him. A Parisian paper had carried the headline *'Ossian va tenter tuer Mill Reef'* – and, sure enough, after half a furlong the two stable companions were lying first and second, going, I suspect, as fast as they could lay legs to the ground.

But so far from 'killing' Mill Reef, the gallop Ossian set was, if anything, to the favourite's advantage. Because Geoff Lewis, determined never to be out of the first half-dozen if he could help it, had jumped off so smartly that Mill Reef took a stronger hold than ever before.

Had the early pace been slow, Geoff might have had a battle on his hands, but as things were he was able to settle calmly in fourth place while Ossian and Ramsin led them behind Le Petit Bois.

As in so many of Mill Reef's races this season, one had the feeling that things were going almost too much according to plan and, although he lost a length or so swinging downhill towards the turn, Geoff Lewis can't remember a single moment of real anxiety.

For us in the stands, however, that moment came as they straightened out for home. Duncan Keith on Ortis and Lester Piggott on Hallez had both moved past Mill Reef to join Ramsin in the lead and, for several endless, breathless seconds, the gold cross and white noseband to which our eyes were glued disappeared behind a line of horses four abreast.

In fact, foreseeing that Ossian was certain to tire, Geoff had eased out from the rail for a hundred yards or so. But to challenge on the outside would have involved coming round at least four horses and so, with Mill Reef strong under him, he decided to bide his time.

For the fleeting seconds those calculations took to make, the position, from the stands, looked by no means secure. We held our breath and wondered gloomily if history was about to be repeated.

But the waiting was very nearly over. In the twenty-three years since Charlie Smirke and Migoli won the Prix de l'Arc de Triomphe, Longchamp, for English-trained horses, has seen a long trail of disappointment, near misses and disasters. And now, when the tide turned at last, it was, for the thousands who had come from England and Ireland to cheer Mill Reef, a supremely memorable, dramatic moment.

With two furlongs left, he and Geoff Lewis were still almost entirely hidden, and, as the horses in front of them came under pressure, the danger grew with every stride that they might be carried back, helpless, in a pocket of exhausted rivals, while something else came past on the outside.

It is often and truly said that instant acceleration is the one essential hallmark of a great racehorse and what happened next was a vivid living proof of that. For now, as Ortis and Hallez faltered in front of Mill Reef, a narrow gap materialised between them.

It can't have been very wide and may not have stayed open very long, but for Mill Reef, at this, the climax of his career so far, it was more than enough.

One moment we were searching anxiously down a line of jumbled colours, nodding heads and waving whips – the next, they parted and, like some projectile thrown from an angry crowd, a small, dark, utterly unmistakable shape detached itself.

I have no very clear idea of the next twenty seconds or so, because even the Press Box, full of supposedly hard-hearted scribes, exploded in something very like hysteria. We know now that Geoff Lewis waved his whip for no more than 50 yards, that Pistol Packer came out of the bunch in vain pursuit – and that Mill Reef won, in the end, by three clear lengths.

But what mattered *then* was the unmistakable fact that, when he hit the front a furlong and a half from home, there was no way he could be beaten.

A great race was being won as it should be won by a great horse with a single deadly rapier-thrust of speed.

Drawn 18 – the worst possible position – Pistol Packer justified in full her claim to be Europe's outstanding three-year-old filly and, a length and a half behind in third place, her old rival Cambrizzia reproduced to a pound the form they have shown all season.

Mill Reef wins the 1971 Arc.

Caro (fourth) was the first of the older horses to finish – and he, too, confirmed the form book, beaten about the same distance by Mill Reef as he had been in the Eclipse.

Of the first six horses home, five were ridden by English jockeys and Lester Piggott, fifth on Hallez, was followed closely by Joe Mercer on Lady Beaverbrook's admirable Royalty.

Then came Bourbon, Arlequino and the Canadian horse One For All, but Miss Dan, Ramsin and Irish Ball were all well back among the also-rans.

Apart from Pistol Packer's draw, there was no trace of excuse or hard luck story, and when Mill Reef's time was announced – a clear record for both track and race by seven-tenths of a second – it merely served to confirm what everyone at Longchamp knew already, that this had been one of those rare, completely decisive, indisputably right results.

No praise can be too high for Geoff Lewis's handling of Mill Reef, not only here but in all his races this season. He may be, as Geoff says, the sort of horse all jockeys dream of riding, but no one can do better than perfection and, at Epsom, Sandown, Ascot and now at Longchamp, Mill Reef has covered 5³/4 miles in the highest grade of competition without once being in anything less than an ideal position.

But if the jockey's record is flawless, what about the trainer's? Mill Reef's first race this season was on 17 April. Between that day and 3 October, Ian Balding has produced him at, or very near, his best on five different occasions.

For six months he has walked the trainer's nightmare tightrope with too much work on one side and too little on the other, and, where so many have tried and failed in the past, he has succeeded brilliantly all along the line.

No one who has not himself had charge of a great public favourite like Mill Reef can possibly tell what it costs in terms of sleepless nights, anxiety and strain. But, through it all, Ian Balding has, outwardly at least, remained as calm and unshakable as he used to be when, as full-back for Cambridge, the Oxford pack exploded round his ears.

The unfailing courtesy and kindness with which he treats the racing press are to be recognised by a Derby award this year and you would search the racing world in vain to find three men more deserving of a horse as good as Mill Reef than Mr Paul Mellon, Ian Balding and Geoff Lewis.

It was confirmed at Longchamp that Mill Reef will stay in training next year and, whatever the outcome of his eagerly-awaited meeting with Brigadier Gerard, the long-range target will be a second attempt upon the Prix de l'Arc de Triomphe. So, for the moment, grateful for all the pleasure he has given and with fingers crossed for his continued health and fitness, let us leave Mill Reef to the rest he has so nobly earned.

8 October 1971

The story of Mill Reef's career as a four-year-old is too sad to bear much repetition. After proving himself every bit as good as ever with a spread-eagling victory in the Prix Ganay, he only scraped home from Homeric in the Coronation Cup. Subsequent tests established that Mill Reef was suffering from rhinopneumonitis – usually an abortion-producing scourge of brood mares but also one of the viruses which crippled so many stables during the seventies. That Coronation Cup was, alas, to be the little horse's final bow.

A whole series of ailments and accidents kept Mill Reef out of the Eclipse – run on soft ground he would have loved – and the Benson and Hedges, which was, of course, the scene of Brigadier Gerard's only defeat. But in August Mr Mellon's American vet Charles Allen (sent over for a special 'second opinion' examination) pronounced him fit, well and ready to start his preparation for another Arc de Triomphe. Mr Mellon had just announced that Mill Reef would stay in training as a five-year-old when, in a quiet half-speed gallop on the morning of 30 August 1972, Fate struck its last and cruellest blow.

The complex and difficult operation which saved Mill Reef's life can also be said to have saved the National Stud. Siring a succession of top-class horses (some of them named in his obituary on page 218), he soon became one of the world's most sought-after stallions. After his death, the National Stud had to be reorganised on completely different lines.

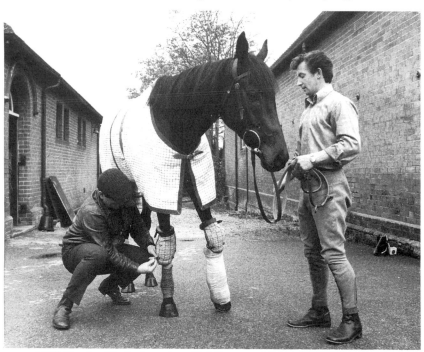

Mill Reef with trainer Ian Balding and lad John Hallum in October 1972, two months after the accident which ended his racing career.

THE FINEST HOUR OF
AN EXTRAORDINARY
HORSE

Piper Heidsieck Cheltenham Gold Cup, Cheltenham,
15 March 1973

It would have seemed well-nigh inconceivable on the Thursday morning of last week that Pendil could jump round Cheltenham without making a single serious mistake, settle satisfactorily all the doubts about his stamina – and *still* not win the the Piper Heidsieck Cheltenham Gold Cup.

Yet all those things did happen on the Thursday afternoon, and while there were many factors which helped to make them possible, by far the most important was the courage, strength and determination of the big, white-faced bay horse known as Mrs Peggy August's The Dikler.

It is tempting to see the 1973 Gold Cup as 'the race Pendil did not win' – tempting, but most unfair. It should be remembered rather as the race The Dikler and Ron Barry won together – as a masterpiece of training and jockeyship and as the finest hour of a very extraordinary horse.

Ever since The Dikler first appeared at Cheltenham three years ago, everything about him has been on a grand scale – not least his sins, failures and omissions.

Even in his last race before the Gold Cup he had, if you remember, behaved like a naughty, overgrown schoolboy, and got disqualified for his pains.

But somehow all those trials and tribulations, all that unfulfilled promise and misapplied strength, seemed to crystallise last week into one unforgettable, irresistible performance.

No horse has ever covered the modern Gold Cup course as fast as The Dikler did – and *I've* never seen a horse, not even Arkle, who more obviously threw his whole heart and mind into the business of covering the distance between the second last fence and the winning post at Cheltenham in the shortest possible time.

For most of that distance this seemed to be just another of The Dikler's many brave but unsuccessful endeavours. Because all eyes were fixed on the favourite and, as I say, it seemed inconceivable that he could fail.

A moment earlier, ranging easily up to The Dikler's gallant stable-companion, Charlie Potheen, Pendil had landed over the second last in front and darted clear.

Now, with the bitter wisdom of hindsight, Richard Pitman blames himself for not waiting a little longer. At the time, with Pendil strong and full of running under him, he was absolutely right to go when he did. No one not blessed with second sight could possibly foresee what happened next.

For although Pendil has occasionally tended to idle after hitting the front, he has always hitherto kept up the rhythm of his gallop. And there has never, hitherto, been a challenger close enough or good enough to take advantage.

Perhaps it was partly the crowd – certainly the biggest and most vociferous in his experience – perhaps it was partly the daunting sight of that final lonely hill, and perhaps after coming so far his reserves were running low.

But now, for whatever reason or combination of reasons, Pendil faltered, changed his legs and lost more than half the momentum which, till then, had been carrying him home.

In nine races out of ten it still would not have mattered, but this was different. And what made it so was the unique reserve of power which Ron Barry had managed to hoard in The Dikler's giant frame.

Riding the big horse for only the second time in his life (the first had been a brief 'school' the previous week), Ron had found, at once, the key to his complex personality.

Even cantering down they had looked at peace with one another and, in the race, helped, admittedly, by the pace at which Charlie Potheen set off in front, The Dikler settled more rapidly and more completely than ever before.

The result, as Fulke Walwyn had predicted, was a very different proposition from the tired horse who, twelve months earlier, led over the last fence only to 'die' half-way up the hill.

Round the final bend, as Pendil shot clear, Ron Barry had suffered one brief check as he tried unsuccessfully to pass between Charlie Potheen and the rails. But then, pulling out, still at least five lengths behind the flying Pendil, he called for a final supreme effort.

From there to the line the only break or alteration in The Dikler's long, relentless stride was the one enormous leap which catapulted him over the last fence. It was here, in fact, that he won the Gold Cup for, as he landed safe and hurtled on, Pendil was just beginning to lose his concentration.

They made an unforgettable contrast, these two – the little horse wavering, suddenly fragile, and the big one surging forward like a breaking wave. It was as if Goliath had got up, plucked the stone from his forehead and taken David suddenly by surprise.

But now, in the moment of defeat, Pendil showed his quality – and proved that whatever else beat him it was not lack of stamina.

Fifty yards from the line, The Dikler was at least a neck and probably half a length in front. Ten strides past it, Pendil had overtaken him once more.

It was as close as that and I honestly don't see how you could hope for a better, more exciting steeplechase.

It was not, of course, a two-horse contest and, at least arguably, The Dikler could not have won without the bold, front-running, assistance of Charlie Potheen. His and Terry Biddlecombe's reward was an honourable third place, six lengths behind Pendil and five ahead of L'Escargot.

I have written a good deal in the past years about Fulke Walwyn and his horses and was convinced long ago that there has never been a finer trainer of staying steeplechasers. But even in Fulke's long, triumph-strewn career there can have been few memories to match the moment last week when he stood in the Cheltenham winner's enclosure with The Dikler and Charlie Potheen.

And as he would be the first to acknowledge, neither of these supremely difficult, headstrong individuals could ever have reached that enclosure without the skilful, nerveless horsemanship of 'Darkie' Deacon, who does and rides them both in all their work at Lambourn.

The white face of The Dikler just heads Pendil in the 1973 Cheltenham Gold Cup.

The early stages of the Gold Cup had been notable mainly for The Dikler's evident relaxation and for Pendil's comparative lack of it.

At the top of the hill first time round, Richard Pitman had to change his hands and yank at the favourite's mouth to stop him running clean away – and even in the last mile he was still bounding along with too much exuberance for his own good.

In the opinion of one experienced trainer, this, because of the fast, dry ground, was the best chance Pendil will ever have of winning a Gold Cup and certainly such conditions are the exception, not the rule, at Cheltenham in March.

But I'm not sure that any such pessimistic view is justified by the facts.

Even running as free as he did, and after striking the front two fences from home, Pendil had enough energy left to quicken in the last 50 yards of a fast-run race. That was not the performance of a doubtful stayer and, if he can be persuaded to calm down a bit early on, I see no reason why even softer ground should rob him of a second chance. He is, after all, only eight years old.

Of the others, L'Escargot ran a most gallant race, bang there between the third and second last fences and only beaten for speed thereafter. Spanish Steps, though passed in the end by Garoupe, was also far from disgraced. He, L'Escargot and Crisp will add a real flavour of class and quality to the Grand National field next week.

23 March 1973

Pendil again started an odds-on favourite for the 1974 Gold Cup – and was cruising when the 100 to 1 outsider High Ken fell slap in front of him at the third last fence and brought him down. Captain Christy, who went on to win easily from The Dikler despite a last-fence blunder, did subsequently beat Pendil in a King George. But in my opinion Pendil was nevertheless not once but twice an unlucky loser of the Cheltenham Gold Cup. He was ante-post favourite again when he broke down in 1975 and, although he and John Francome won three races in 1976–7, Pendil, who broke down finally aged thirteen, never had a third try at the Gold Cup.

At least one prediction came true. Crisp was an heroic second in Red Rum's first Grand National (see pages 31–8), L'Escargot, the National winner two years later, was third and Spanish Steps was fourth. I am still proud of having finished seventh in that race on Proud Tarquin.

A RACE THAT CAUGHT
US BY THE THROAT

*King George VI and Queen Elizabeth Diamond Stakes, Ascot,
26 July 1975*

'The best flat race I've ever seen' . . . Superlatives are dangerous
things, often inviting contradiction, argument and maybe even
scorn. But of all the millions who watched the 1975 King George
VI and Queen Elizabeth Diamond Stakes on television or in the
flesh last week I never expect to meet a single man or woman
who could honestly deny that here, for a moment, two horses
and two men came as near to perfection as any of the great
ones around whom the history of the Turf is built.

It would, of course, be foolish to assert that Dr Carlo
Vittadini's Grundy is the best horse there has ever been –
or that either he or Lady Beaverbrook's Bustino is the bravest.
But no drama can be measured solely by the excellence of those
who act it out. The play's the thing and here, from overture to
curtain, the play caught all who saw it by the throat, leaving
us full of wonder, gratitude and pride.

In our gratitude there were, admittedly, some special selfish
elements. Both Grundy and Bustino were bred in England and,
while control of one has already been bought by the National
Stud, the other belongs to one of British racing's most faithful
and generous supporters. He too will stay in England as a stallion and, at a time when the sport, plagued by inflation, taxation
and many heedless Governments, is increasingly dominated by
American blood, the simultaneous emergence of two world-
class home-bred horses is Manna from heaven indeed.

The setting too was perfect – Ascot on a flawless summer day with the watered turf an emerald stage designed for heroes. The Queen, to whose stud Bustino will go, was there with her mother, the stands were happily packed and perhaps it was appropriate that this supremely successful piece of showmanship should be adorned by the presence, among many other famous names, of Mr Fred Astaire, himself no stranger to perfection.

I am sure he admired the graceful dancing stride with which Grundy cantered down and perhaps, as Dahlia threw a brief tantrum before the starting stalls, he remembered some other leading ladies demanding special treatment.

Dahlia, in fact, was installed first, more than a minute before the last of her rivals and then, as the flag went down, no doubt the great dancer appreciated the well-rehearsed routine put on by Bustino and his entourage.

Bustino's own first steps were not in the script, I suspect – for he broke like a sprinter and led for 50 yards. But order was soon restored as both his two pacemakers were hustled to their places – Highest leading Kinglet for the first six furlongs at a gallop which immediately had the eleven-horse field strung out in single file like so many three-mile 'chasers.

Only five horses, in fact, even got into the foreground, for while the German five-year-old Star Appeal was bold enough to thrust his way up into third place, Bustino was never farther back than fourth and Patrick Eddery, taking aim between Joe Mercer's shoulders, poised Grundy two lengths behind him.

Dahlia soon came next and the others, by the look of them, were finding it quite hard enough to stay even reasonably well in touch.

Whatever your view of pacemakers in general, there is no denying that the impression of careful teamwork added to the drama, and as Highest fell back exhausted after six furlongs, Kinglet struggled past to make his contribution.

But try as he might, the pace had been too much for any ordinary horse and although there was still half a mile to go Joe Mercer decided it was time to answer the £100,000 question once and for all.

What followed set countless pairs of hands and race glasses a-trembling and destroyed for ever the insulting theory that

Bustino is just a one-paced stayer. Because, as he stormed clear towards the final bend, Patrick Eddery, though fully alive to the danger, found Grundy unable to stay as close as he wished and had intended. 'I just could not go with him,' he told us afterwards and, as a result, as Bustino swung into the short Ascot straight, there were at least three and maybe as much as four lengths of ominous daylight showing between him and the Derby winner.

And so the stage was set. The pace-makers had disappeared, Star Appeal was beaten and on Dahlia, doing her utmost though she was and holding all the rest, Lester Piggott knew that her historic hat-trick simply was no longer on the cards.

But all the disappointments which that sentence contains were needed to make the agonising climax possible. Only four actors were left, but to two of them, as to all of us, the race still seemed wide open.

Once straightened out for home, Patrick Eddery drew his whip and now it was Grundy's turn to smash for ever the canard that he is just 'the best of a bad lot'.

Bustino's stride had never wavered, but in less than a furlong his lead was swallowed up. To poor Joe Mercer, Grundy's blond mane and white-slashed face must have been the least welcome sight in all the world, but needless to say it never broke the rhythmic thrust and drive on which his supremely stylish finish is based.

As he called for a counter-punch and got it, the two horses battled together head to head and at that moment, as Eddery said later, 'it could still have gone either way.'

He paid tribute to Bustino's dogged heroism, and no wonder, for don't forget that, by this time, the older horse had been alone in front for three furlongs. For just a moment, as he fought back again inside the distance, the thought crossed my mind that Grundy might find yet another battle one too many. And no doubt, if there had been the slightest flaw in his stamina or courage, that would have been the end.

But there was no flaw and now, as the chesnut head showed just in front, it was poor Bustino who finally reached the bottom of even his reserves. Tongue out, dog-tired, he staggered briefly towards his rival – and then, as Joe Mercer straightened him, ground on indomitably to the end.

'The best flat race you could ever hope to see': Grundy
(right) and Bustino fight out the finish of the 1975 King
George.

A stone, age or no age, is a lot of weight in this class and
at this speed and last week, as Grundy's number went up, the
winner by half a length, I'm sure there were many who wished,
as I did, that this could have been a finish with no loser.

But that was not to be, and don't suppose that in praising
Bustino's courage I mean to belittle Grundy's. To him and
his rider early in the straight the task ahead must have had a
daunting look indeed and the willing determination with which
Grundy tackled it and carried it through simply proves that he
has a heart and mind to match his ability. The combination is
both rare and deadly.

Of the beaten horses last week by far the most important
is, of course, Dahlia, who finished third, five lengths behind
Bustino and a length and a half in front of her old rival On My
Way. Card King came next, then Ashmore, Dibidale, Libra's
Rib and Star Appeal. The last-named's running with Grundy
shows how incredibly misleading was the line drawn through
Nobiliary, whom he (Star Appeal) beat so easily in the Eclipse
Stakes.

But to return to Dahlia, the crucial question clearly is how close she ran to the form of her two previous victories in the race, in the first of which two years ago she slammed Rheingold, the subsequent conqueror of her great rival Allez France.

Well, first of all, without any doubt Dahlia, believed by her trainer Maurice Zilber to be back at the excellence she usually achieves by this time of year, ran far better than in any of her three previous races this season.

In those races, Card King had beaten her once, Ashmore twice and, in the Grand Prix de Saint-Cloud, both he and On My Way finished in front of her. At Ascot by contrast she beat all three of these tough, consistent colts – and beat them decisively.

Dahlia's appearance is never wildly impressive, but to my eyes last week she looked, by her standards, fit and well. Lester Piggott did not make any excuses for her and the final clinching argument to show that she ran near her best is, of course, the time. Because, while both Grundy and Bustino were clocked together at 2 minutes 26.98 seconds – 2.36 seconds faster than the previous record – there is no doubt that Dahlia and several others too ran the mile and a half faster than it had ever been run before.

There is, in fact, as far as I can see, every reason to conclude that Dahlia was at least as good last week as she had been twelve months earlier – and very probably as she had been the year before that.

And who, in all the circumstances, needs more evidence that this unforgettable race was won by a great three-year-old from a four-year-old who has improved enormously with age?

Bustino, who is a whole size bigger than Grundy, looked an absolute picture of health last week – a long, rangy bay standing over an enormous stretch of ground and showing, in his handsome, masculine head, all the courage and honesty which mark his running. Lady Beaverbrook may have waited a long time for her first Classic winner, but the wait was infinitely well worthwhile.

Bustino was having only his second race this season and it speaks volumes for Dick Hern's skill and confidence that he was able to produce a big, mature horse fit to run for his life on so light a public preparation. As for Joe Mercer, he is, I believe, incapable of making an ugly, ungraceful or inefficient movement on a horse's back and now the inspiration of a great occasion merely added strength to the already flawless perfection of his style.

It was on this course that his brother Manny died and the service Joe did for British racing last week was a fitting memorial.

Like Joe Mercer's, Patrick Eddery's style is firmly built on the conventional Anglo-Irish model – smooth, rhythmic and with none of the exaggeration which has so often come in recent years from the unsuccessful attempts of lesser men to imitate Lester Piggott.

In a sense, Eddery had as much at stake as anyone last week, and in that awful moment of doubt as Bustino led into the straight, he could easily have been forgiven for losing his head. Instead he rode like the champion he is and, of all the many reasons we have to remember this finish with pride, not least is the skill and poise of the two men who shared its glory with their horses.

That brings us to the hero of the story, who is, I am glad to say, back safe and sound in his box at Seven Barrows, where his first action on returning was to make a beeline for the manger. Walking into the winner's enclosure at Ascot, Grundy looked, understandably, more exhausted than ever before, but I am assured by those who know him best that it will neither last nor leave a mark.

The measure of Peter Walwyn's achievement this season is that Grundy has looked bigger and stronger every time we've seen him. No doubt his wonderful temperament has helped, but if you give a great artist superlative material to work with, the result is likely to be a masterpiece. And that, in Grundy, is what Peter and his staff have produced.

I add the words 'and his staff' not only because they are true, but also because Peter himself is always first to share the credit. He paid a special tribute last week to Matt McCormack, the work rider who has so greatly helped Eddery to settle Grundy down; but you don't have to spend very long in Seven Barrows before you see that, like all great stables, it has a loyal, close-knit spirit of its own. Teamwork may no longer be a very fashionable word but the greatest trainer ever born would not saddle many winners without it.

Peter Walwyn quite rightly dismissed the future briefly and unprintably last week. 'Who cares now?' he asked, and I don't blame him.

What's more, as I hope Peter Willett will be pleased to hear, I no longer claim that Grundy has been inadequately tested. I still believe that, for the good of British breeding, top-class horses should, as a rule, be kept in training as four-year-olds, but if Grundy can pass on the qualities we saw last week then the good of British breeding may well be best served by getting him off to stud as soon as possible.

Anyway, the Levy Board and its advisers are heartily to be congratulated on doing far and away the best bit of business achieved by any (if they will forgive the expression) nationalised concern this year.

British racing can bask in a glow of warmth and glory, treasuring the memory of two brave, willing and brilliant horses who were born and bred in England and who, if all goes well, will die here. And if, before that happens, they can even occasionally reproduce the qualities which caught our hearts last week, then the 1975 King George VI and Queen Elizabeth Diamond Stakes may come to be remembered not only as the best flat race you could ever hope to see, but also as the beginning of a golden age.

1 August 1975

Sadly, Grundy, who failed completely when an odds-on favourite for his only other race, the Benson and Hedges Gold Cup, was also a comparative failure at stud. After several not particularly productive years at the National Stud, he was sold to Japan.

Thanks largely to his daughter, Height of Fashion, dam of Nashwan, Bustino was champion brood mare sire in 1988 and 1989. He has sired the winners of over £2 million including the Ascot Gold Cup winner Paean and, still extremely fertile, stands at the Queen's Wolferton Stud in Norfolk.

COLONIAL CUP HERO GRAND CANYON WON THE HARD WAY

Colonial Cup International Steeplechase, Camden, South Carolina, 27 November 1976

It is 200 years since General Cornwallis marched out of Camden, South Carolina, for the last time, and at that time the Americans were undoubtedly well pleased to see him go. But they gave his countrymen a wonderful welcome back last week for the seventh Colonial Cup, and I cannot help feeling that the general may have turned proudly in his grave.

In fact, he may well have reflected that if his Redcoats had shown the sort of determination which got Ron Barry and Grand Canyon home in front on Saturday, the War of Independence would probably have had a different end.

In the past three months, Grand Canyon had won two flat races in Italy, one high-class hurdle race in France and one in England. Indeed, since coming round the world from New Zealand to be trained in Sussex by Derek Kent, he had run sixteen times and only twice been beaten when he completed the course.

But this, needless to say, was a trial of strength entirely different from anything Mr Pat Samuel's big six-year-old had hitherto attempted.

In six previous Colonial Cups, no horse trained in Europe had even gained a place, Grand Canyon had never in public jumped fences before and, quite apart from eleven of the best jumpers in America, his opponents included the ex-Champion Hurdler Lanzarote and the best French four-year-old hurdler of the day, Beau Dad.

The Colonial Cup course is just over two miles and six furlongs in length, with seventeen identical brush fences about four-and-a-half feet high. Built brand new this year, they consist of a thick foam-rubber base covered with green carpet and a soft brush top, through which, as Grand Canyon proceeded to demonstrate, a horse can gallop with impunity.

Nevertheless, the base, which is three feet high, has to be jumped and, at the pace they went last week, these were by no means insignificant obstacles.

The ground at Camden is so sandy that it never gets soft, even after heavy rain. In fact, as on a beach, water tends, if anything, to make it firmer, and the rain which fell last Friday had precisely that effect.

It had always seemed probable that the race would be run at a tremendous gallop and, in fact, the time, 5 minutes 12 seconds, would have broken most hurdle race track records over a comparable distance in England.

This was not, as it turned out, exclusively due to Grand Canyon, because, though a natural and habitual front-runner, he was led for the first two miles by a mare called Life's Illusion. But that only shows the furious pace she set, because as Grand Canyon cantered down, doing his best to pull Ron Barry's arms out, it was clear he was in no mood to hang around.

While he was being led to the course, the field for an earlier race had galloped by and well before the start his nerves – or, anyway, his impatience to get on with it – were threatening to betray him.

'He never settled at all,' Ron Barry told us afterwards, and although Life's Illusion led him by several lengths at the first fence, Grand Canyon was as near to running away as makes no difference.

He was certainly going too fast to jump, and as he dived headlong through the fence his supporters had the first of many agonising moments. Whether standing back too far or getting too close, or simply galloping straight on, this extraordinary horse proceeded to give one of the most hair-raising exhibitions of jumping – if you can call it that – which I have ever seen.

But, incredibly, thanks to Grand Canyon's own great strength and the nerve and skill of his rider, there was never a moment when they looked in serious danger of coming unstuck.

The risks they took did not even cost them much ground and, throughout the first two miles, with Life's Illusion tearing away a dozen or more lengths in front, Grand Canyon was equally far ahead of the others.

Among these, Lanzarote was jumping superbly and, given a glorious ride by John Francome, never strayed far from the inside rail. The French four-year-old, Beau Dad, lay close to him for a long way, but before the last half-mile both Irish Fashion and The Bo-Weevil were clearly finding the pace too hot.

So, eventually, did Life's Illusion, whose rider claimed the full allowance and, on this occasion at least, was unable to restrain her. The mare, who belongs to Raymond Guest's daughter, Virginia Van Allen, is a former 'Steeplechaser of the Year' and, if she was ever brought to England, would, in my opinion, be unbeatable at two miles over either hurdles or fences.

Now, however, she could do no more and, as Grand Canyon went past her four fences from home, a group which included the grey Temple Gwathmey winner Fire Control, Crag's Corner and Lanzarote, had all moved up to within half-a-dozen lengths.

They were plenty close enough, but at the third last fence Lanzarote made the first of his only two mistakes. It was not a bad one but, landing flat-footed, he lost impetus just when he needed it most.

In John Francome's opinion it was this, and not the much more obvious blunder he made at the last, which cost him the race. For now the chips were down in deadly earnest and, round the long final turn, Fire Control gained relentlessly on Grand Canyon.

The leader had made one of his worst blunders three fences out, but it was now, just when his previous extravagant antics might have been expected to tell, that Grand Canyon proved himself not only strong but infinitely brave.

As he ran at the last, half a length in front of Fire Control, Lanzarote, only two lengths behind them and still far from beaten, stood off too far and landed in a heap. Gallantly though he struggled to recover, it was the final straw, and at the line Crag's Corner kept him out of third place by a fast disappearing nose.

So, up the long run-in, all England's hopes rested squarely on Ron Barry's shoulders and, for everything Fire Control threw at them, he and Grand Canyon somehow found an answer.

Grand Canyon beating Fire Control in the 1976 Colonial Cup.

At the line they still had half a length to spare, and since Mandarin's Grand Steeplechase in Paris I cannot remember a pair of whom I have felt more proud in a foreign field.

As they walked back to a rapturous welcome, it was announced that Fire Control's rider, Doug Small, had claimed a 'foul'. I do not know when he reckoned it took place. Nor, I suspect, do the stewards, because it took them less than a minute to disallow a claim which, had it succeeded, would almost certainly have caused a riot.

Fourth in the end, as I have described, Lanzarote pulled up lame and had probably knocked himself in that last-fence blunder. Though still sore next morning, he seems to have suffered no serious injury, and deserves his share of credit for running a wonderful race on going much harder than he really likes.

But no excuses are needed for him, or for any of the other horses. They were beaten fair and square by a horse whose extraordinary strength, balance and will to win had overcome what, for any normal steeplechaser, would surely have been a disastrous series of mistakes.

Had Grand Canyon stayed calmer and jumped as well as we know he can, he would presumably have had a great deal more to spare. But to win as he did was, in the circumstances, an even more remarkable achievement and a triumph not only for him and Ron Barry but also for New Zealand and, above all, for Derek Kent, who had produced him as hard and fit as any racehorse can be made.

It only remains to say thank you, on behalf of all of us visitors lucky enough to see this unforgettable race, for the equally unforgettable hospitality of our hosts.

The American jumping world may, by our standards, be a small one but, thanks largely to the generosity of Miss Marion Dupont Scott (who not only owns Camden but had also provided almost the whole $100,000 prize), it produced, last week, the nearest thing you could find to a genuine world championship. To those who organised it, everyone who loves the sport owes an unpayable debt of gratitude.

3 December 1976

On his retirement Grand Canyon served for a while as a charger with the Household Cavalry.

A RACE SO MOVING
THAT IT BROUGHT
TEARS TO THE EYES

Waterford Crystal Champion Hurdle, Cheltenham,
14th March 1979

It was not difficult to be rude about life at Cheltenham last week. In fact, with consistently foul weather, unsatisfactory going, unpredictable results and a new grandstand which pleased only a small minority, it was sometimes pretty hard to be polite.

But not for the first time, luckily, the horses came to the rescue. In race after race their willing courage overcame all drawbacks to remind us yet again that, despite its manifold shortcomings, this is still the greatest jumping meeting in the world. And, on Wednesday afternoon, in the Waterford Crystal Champion Hurdle, two of them lifted the sport clean across the magical borderline which separates a merely thrilling spectacle from an experience so mysteriously moving that it can and does bring tears to the eyes of normally reasonable and unemotional spectators.

Such, without any doubt, was the finish in which Dr Michael Mangan's Monksfield beat Pat Muldoon's Sea Pigeon for the second year running. These, of course, are no ordinary horses. Both have been with us for a long time and both, despite many hard races, are still ready, as we saw again last Wednesday, to put every ounce of energy on the line.

Sea Pigeon, the older by two years, was running in his fiftieth race, 26 jumping and 24 on the flat. He was seventh in Morston's Derby and his 24 victories include two Chester Cups.

Until the other day at Haydock, he had never been beaten in

a handicap hurdle and, in three attempts at the championship he has now been fourth once and second twice.

Although shorter, Monksfield's career has been even busier – a total of 64 races, 38 over hurdles (of which he has won 11, including 2 Championships) and 26 on the flat, where, despite lacking Sea Pigeon's speed, he has won five times.

The two horses have, in fact, quite a lot in common. Both have been wonderful servants to their owners – but in other ways they are, of course, completely different.

It is, for instance, improbable to say the least that Sea Pigeon could have compiled his record as an entire horse. He was, in fact, gelded as a three-year-old – but Monksfield remains a stallion and, at the age of seven, has never yet shown the slightest sign of resenting any part of his job.

In fact, there is every reason to believe that part of his excellence comes from a quite exceptional appetite for hard work.

All this season doubters like myself have been wondering whether his devoted trainer Dessie McDonogh was not asking too much of a small, seven-year-old entire – first by running him several times on the flat and then by asking him to concede huge weights in handicap hurdles; so when Monksfield finally ran, by his standards, a really disappointing race in the Erin Foods Hurdle, even the trainer himself may, for a moment, have felt his faith shaken.

But not for long. All last week reports of the arduous work which Monksfield had been doing went round Cheltenham and on Monday Dessie McDonogh told me: 'He very nearly got away with me this morning. If I'd changed my hands he'd have gone and I couldn't have pulled him up till we passed Arkle's statue.'

The fact is, of course, that Monksfield is a phenomenon. Like Red Rum he needs – and can absorb – more work than a normal horse, and like Red Rum he is lucky enough to have found a trainer who thoroughly understands him.

So, in a different way, has Sea Pigeon and, last week, sad though it was to see Monksfield's old rider Tommy Kinane removed from his accustomed place, these two extraordinary horses had, in Dessie Hughes and Jonjo O'Neill, two of the best and strongest jockeys in the business.

Tommy Kinane, in fact, gave Champion Hurdle day the

perfect curtain-raiser by coming from behind on the wide outside to win the Waterford Crystal Supreme Novices' Hurdle with Monksfield's stable-mate Stranfield.

That must have warmed Dessie McDonogh's heart – and it may also have helped Dessie Hughes to reach one or two vital tactical decisions, because, by the time the Champion Hurdle field set off, 67 horses had run over the old hurdle racecourse – in conditions not all that far short of waterlogging.

Most, though not all of them, had followed a more or less conventional route near the inside and, as a result, the ground there was inevitably more ploughed up than any other part. (I cannot, personally, see why a fresh course is not saved for the Champion Hurdle as, apart from the Foxhunters, it is for the Gold Cup – but that is by the way.)

In any case, having chosen to lie up with Monksfield and force the pace if necessary, Dessie Hughes also decided to steer round the wide outside – giving ground away in search of better, fresher going.

Four other jockeys followed his example and, considering that the five who did not filled the last five places at the finish, I don't think there can be much doubt who was right.

In one other respect Dessie's rivals played into his hands because, at least from the stands, it seemed that they all gave Monksfield three lengths' start – some of them even more.

But, anyway, off he went in front and, quite apart from the other thrills and pleasures he had in store for us, proceeded to give a display of bold, accurate hurdling as fine as anything ever seen at Cheltenham.

There are eight flights in a two-mile hurdle and Monksfield met every single one of them precisely in his stride. He did not waste energy by standing too far back, he certainly never got too close and if he touched a hurdle at all it was only the timed, intentional flick which professionals sometimes give the padded top bar.

Apart from a few strides round the stable turn, Dessie Hughes stuck boldly to his chosen route – followed by Kybo, Sea Pigeon, Within the Law and Beacon Light.

As they turned uphill at the far end of the course, it cost him so much ground that Birds Nest, in the inside group, was able briefly to show in front. But Monksfield brushed him aside with another flawless leap at the cross hurdle – and turned downhill for home with Kybo, Beacon Light and Sea Pigeon on his heels and all the rest beginning, in various degrees, to feel the strain and show it.

There followed the race's only tragedy. Rising for the second last alongside Monksfield, Kybo stood off a yard too far, hit the top on the way down and, slipping as he landed, failed to find the necessary extra leg.

No one can possibly blame Josh Gifford and Bob Champion for feeling 'robbed'. My own view is that Sea Pigeon, two lengths behind when Kybo fell, was going every bit as strongly. And that, as we shall see, was not quite strongly enough.

But for Pat Muldoon, Peter Easterby and all the rest of this wonderful horse's admirers, the next few seconds must have been an agonising mixture of hope and heartbreak. Because round the final bend, leaving Beacon Light and all the others trailing, Sea Pigeon sailed up to Monksfield with Jonjo O'Neill sitting poised and motionless. Against any other horse the result from then on would have been a foregone conclusion and, as they stormed dead level into the last, Sea Pigeon was not out-jumped as he had been twelve months before.

But Monksfield is not just any other horse. Three rhythmic slaps from Dessie Hughes's whip in time with his last three strides produced the usual flying leap, but Sea Pigeon was just as good and, a fraction quicker into his stride, he set off up the hill a neck in front. So there you had it – the bell for the final round with the champion looking defeat between the eyes.

'Though small, I gave my all, I gave my heart.'

Paul Mellon wrote those words about Gimcrack and I can think of none better to describe what Monksfield did on the Cheltenham hill last week. Head down – so low, Hugh McIlvanney wrote, that mud on his nose would have been no surprise – the little brown horse tore back at his bigger, darker rival like a terrier going for the throat.

Halfway up the hill they were level and Jonjo went for his whip. But he hardly had need to use it.

In ground much softer than he likes, on a course which has never really suited him, Sea Pigeon too was giving his all. He may never have run a finer race, but on this day and against this rival it was not enough. For everything Dessie Hughes asked of him, Monksfield had a reply. Inch by inch he thrust his head further in front and at the line there was three-quarters of a length to spare.

Sea Pigeon (near side) and Monksfield hammer and tongs in the 1979 Champion Hurdle.

When Monksfield and Night Nurse dead-heated at Liverpool two years ago, I never expected to see a better hurdle race, but this, except for the sadness that there had to be a loser, may just have been the one.

I have certainly not seen so much excitement and emotion on a racecourse since Grundy beat Bustino and, since such a race deserved to be crowned with grace and sportsmanship, I am delighted to be able to record that Pat Muldoon was one of the first to push through the crowd around Dessie McDonogh to shake the winning trainer's hand.

'You cannot be sad to be part of something like that,' he said and in Jonjo O'Neill's face too, as he dismounted, there was far more happiness than pain.

I don't know what he and Dessie Hughes told each other in the weighing room, but hope that, like Gerry Wilson and Billy Speck after Golden Miller beat Thomond II, they raised a glass and said, 'When we are old we can sit back in our chairs and tell them that we did ride at least one day of our lives.'

Beacon Light was 15 lengths behind in third place, but this, apart from Kybo, was strictly a two-horse race.

Its chief hero, apart from the horses themselves, was undoubtedly Dessie McDonogh. It can never be easy for a small trainer to handle a horse as much in the public eye as Monksfield, but Dessie has always had not only the courage of his convictions, but also the good humour to smile and forgive those who disagree, carp and criticise. Like his horse, in fact, he has a heart out of proportion with his body.

Breeders get little credit in the jumping world, but at least Mr and Mrs P.C. Ryan had the pleasure of greeting Monksfield in the winner's enclosure last week. They produced him by sending their beautifully-bred mare Regina to the American horse Gala Performance (by Native Dancer), so Monksfield's pedigree contains high quality blood on both sides.

His dam is half-sister to the successful New Zealand sire Pakistan II (by Palestine) and his maternal great-grandam Theresina not only won the Irish Oaks herself but bred an Irish Derby winner, Turkhan, and a wartime Ascot Gold Cup winner, Ujiji.

That, with Monksfield's future as a sire of jumpers in mind, rings an eloquent bell in my memory because Ujiji was the sire of Taxidermist, winner of the Hennessy and Whitbread Gold Cups and the best steeplechaser I was ever lucky enough to ride.

If Monksfield can manage to produce a son with a combination of his own and 'Taxi's' qualities, I just hope I live long enough to see (and back) him!

23 March 1979

THERE WERE NO LOSERS IN THIS WHITBREAD FINISH!

Whitbread Gold Cup, Sandown Park, 28 April 1984

Grundy and Bustino will, quite rightly, never be forgotten, but I honestly doubt whether anyone lucky enough to watch the 1984 Whitbread Gold Cup will ever again feel safe in calling their King George VI and Queen Elizabeth Diamond Stakes 'the race of the century'.

Comparisons are unnecessary, but I for one never have seen, and almost certainly never will see, a finer, more thrilling or, in all the circumstances, more heroic finish than the four-sided battle which Queen Elizabeth the Queen Mother's Special Cargo fought and won last week against Lettoch, Diamond Edge and Plundering.

To understand the tangle of hope and emotion which this epic struggle aroused you must remember first its extraordinary many-sided background.

The colours carried by the winner would alone, of course, have made it unforgettable – the Queen Mother's greatest triumph as an owner in the thirty-four years since the late Lord Mildmay persuaded her and her daughter, then Princess Elizabeth, to enter National Hunt racing as joint owners of Monaveen.

But the hope that Special Cargo might, against all veterinary odds, give his owner her first Whitbread was only one question among many as the 13 runners came into line last Saturday.

Could Michael Dickinson (Lettoch and Ashley House) clinch another trainer's championship by winning his first Whitbread in his fourth and last jumping season?

Or could Fred Winter (Plundering), already seven times champion trainer but now £11,000 behind in prize money, snatch the title back?

Could Fulke Walwyn (Diamond Edge and Special Cargo), the 74-year-old doyen of his profession, add a seventh Whitbread to the record six he had already won?

And lastly, could Diamond Edge, at thirteen, become both the oldest and the first ever three-time Whitbread winner, enabling his old friend and companion-in-arms Bill Smith, to bow out on a victorious triumphant note?

With all that at stake, and the sun blazing down on a huge expectant crowd, the dangers of anti-climax were very evident. But what gives the 1984 Whitbread such a uniquely powerful claim to be called 'the perfect steeplechase' is the fact that, as Plundering and Lettoch rose together at the last fence, every single one of these issues was still wide open and undecided.

Oddly, in fact, at that stage a Royal victory looked the least likely *dénouement*. Kevin Mooney had been riding for dear life from the Pond and it was only between the last two fences that Special Cargo, still only fourth and some lengths behind Diamond Edge in third place, began to close the gap.

But before I attempt to describe the next few hectic, scarcely believable moments, let us go back to the start of a race in which, for most of the way, the veteran Diamond Edge was a majestic, dominating figure. He has always taken a strong hold and his attitude to steeplechase fences has always been disdainful.

Last week, swinging gaily off in front, he attacked them with the bravado of a carefree six-year-old. It used, occasionally, to cost him dear but now he made no appreciable mistake – often standing far back and 'flattening' like a hurdler but, on balance, gaining far more ground in the air than he lost.

Behind him at the downhill third, luck took a hand for the first, last and only time. Robert Earnshaw had settled Lettoch towards the rear and now, as Donegal Prince became the race's only faller, he found the way ahead completely barred.

'We just had nowhere to go,' says Earnshaw, and by the time he and Lettoch got going again they must have lost between 10 and 20 lengths.

Looking back now, that makes them desperately unlucky

losers and this, the race's only valid hard-luck story, is also its only real flaw as a perfect sporting trial of strength.

At the time, Ashley House looked a pretty adequate Dickinson substitute. He, Plundering, Polar Express and, to begin with, Skegby, were Diamond Edge's closest pursuers and companions – with Special Cargo and Fortina's Express never far behind.

Going to the Railway fences for the last time, in fact, it was Ashley House at Diamond Edge's quarters who seemed to spur the old horse on. Diamond Edge jumped the three close fences like a stag inspired – so well that Bill Smith felt able to ease him round the final turn.

I have heard this called a mistake – the critics' theory being that Bill should have made the best of his advantage and kicked for home. But he, after all, knows Diamond Edge better than anyone and, in view of what followed, I am convinced that the 'breather' he gave the old horse going to the Pond was not only right, but, in the circumstances, a stroke of ice-cool tactical inspiration.

By the second water, miraculously, Robert Earnshaw and Lettoch had beavered their way back into the race. Around the bend, as Fortina's Express and Ashley House began to weaken, Lettoch and Plundering passed both them and Diamond Edge and, as the two seven-year-olds led the thirteen-year-old past the Pond, the stage looked set for a straightforward Winter – Dickinson confrontation.

At the second last it still seemed very much that way and even now, looking back on film, what followed would be quite impossible to predict. You can see, it is true, that Bill Smith had not yet asked Diamond Edge the ultimate question – but Special Cargo did not even jump the second last particularly well and, landing over it, an outside chance of a place seemed all Kevin Mooney could reasonably hope for.

Several times last Saturday we showed on pre-race TV a film of the final thrust with which Bill Smith and Diamond Edge drove between Father Delaney and Ottery News to win in 1981. And now, as Plundering and Lettoch started up the run-in together, the two old friends behind them played the same last card – a glorious attempt to do it one more time.

For me, this will always be the most moving mental picture

from an unforgettable afternoon – Diamond Edge, at full stretch, hurling himself between his younger rivals and, for a few heart-rending strides, quite clearly getting his head in front.

'I just hope he still thinks he won,' Cath Walwyn said afterwards – and anyone who dismisses such words as 'over-sentimental' should understand that, just after three o'clock last Saturday afternoon, Sandown Park was not too full of cold, hard-headed realism.

At the last in the 1984 Whitbread, Plundering leads Diamond Edge, with Kevin Mooney on Special Cargo (left) starting to rally.

Personally, as Diamond Edge stormed past Plundering and challenged Lettoch, I was screaming so hysterically at my TV monitor that, without an action replay, I might never have noticed Special Cargo's eleventh-hour appearance. Nor, almost certainly, did Diamond Edge – so, although the gallant Lettoch also fought back again to deprive the old horse of second place in the end, I suspect that Mrs Walwyn's hope was justified.

No one can tell if horses know (or care) whether they have crossed the line in front. But they certainly recognise, remember and enjoy the warmth and pleasure with which winners are welcomed back. And at Sandown last Saturday none of the placed horses can possibly have felt a loser as they walked down into the crowded, noisy, happy cauldron of the winner's circle.

Special Cargo, it now appears, had made up at least four lengths from the last fence and maybe more. And that, mind you, to pass three horses who were by no means going backwards.

The best previous time for Sandown's three miles and five furlongs is down in the record books as 7 minutes 11.5 seconds, achieved by The Dikler in the 1974 Whitbread. I think I can be forgiven for reminding you that it rightfully belongs to Proud Tarquin, who, whatever view you take of the course his rider steered, did cross the line with his head in front.

But now, in any case, a new record stands of 7 minutes 10.6 seconds – just one of many reasons why Special Cargo's name will live for ever in jumping history.

By a particularly happy chance, the Hoechst monthly N.H. breeder's award – for March, not April – was presented at Sandown last Saturday to Mrs R.J. King, whose mother, Mrs Abbott, bred Special Cargo near Dorchester eleven years ago, by Dairialatan (a big, headstrong horse who once ran away with me in a flat race at Worcester and still won!) out of Little Tot (a Flush Royal mare who is still alive, aged twenty-two).

Special Cargo was sold to Ireland as a six-month-old foal and the Abbott family, not surprisingly, lost track of him until, to their delight, he reappeared in the Royal colours as a staying hurdler of enormous promise.

But already Special Cargo's legs were giving trouble. Blistered in his hurdling days, he broke down before he won a 'chase and missed a whole year after being fired between December 1979 and December 1980.

In the season which followed, Special Cargo won three times, was never out of the frame and ended up beating the Hennessy winner Approaching at Sandown on Gunners' day.

But next season disaster struck again and, running second to Royal Judgment over three miles six furlongs in heavy ground at Chepstow, the nine-year-old broke down really badly.

'If he had not shown so much ability it would not have seemed worth persevering,' the Queen's stud manager Michael Oswald says. But one last attempt was decided on and the Lambourn vet Michael 'Spike' Kirby implanted carbon fibre 'frameworks' into Special Cargo's battered tendons.

Like many of the Queen's and Queen Mother's horses, young, old and convalescent, Special Cargo spent most of the next eighteen months on Major Eldred Wilson's farm near Sandringham.

When, eventually, he went back to Saxon House, his legs, I understand, looked like 'a horse coper's nightmare'. But Spike Kirby's magic had worked and now, in the hands of an even greater magician, Special Cargo started on the long road back.

He had already become the joint-hero of one of the season's happiest stories when, ridden by John Oxley's son Gerald, he won the *Horse and Hound* Grand Military Gold Cup. Soon after that race the Whitbread was discussed, but I remember the Queen Mother saying, with characteristic consideration for her trainer, 'I am not sure, because I know how badly Fulke wants to win it with Diamond Edge.'

Already a winner of one Hennessy and two Whitbreads, the older horse had spent his convalescence quietly on the West Country farm of *his* owner, Mr Sam Loughridge. Himself a skilful and experienced vet, Mr Loughridge relies, I understand, on rest as opposed to operations.

But his patience sent Diamond Edge back to Lambourn sound – and all that was needed then was the double miracle of training and stable management by which, at the age of 74, Fulke Walwyn produced two gallant invalids fit and fresh to run the races of their lives.

I have said and written many times – and have even less fear of contradiction now – that Fulke Walwyn stands confirmed, yet again, as the greatest trainer of steeplechasers there has ever been.

4 May 1984

SHE WAS BEATEN –
BUT NOBODY TOLD HER

Tote Cheltenham Gold Cup, Cheltenham, 13 March 1986

Jonjo O'Neill and Mrs Charmian Hill's Dawn Run looked defeat
between the eyes in last week's Tote Gold Cup – and stubbornly
refused to recognise it. Instead, combining their own special
brands of daring and determination, they turned it into victory
– a triumph as moving, memorable and uproariously welcomed
as any in the history of Cheltenham's greatest race.

Dawn Run's duel for the lead with Run And Skip had made
the 1986 Gold Cup a nail-biting spectacle from the start, but as
the race approached its climax there were two especially crucial moments – one two fences from home, the other halfway
up the final hill.

Going to the second last, with Wayward Lad and Forgive
'N' Forget both ominously strong beside him, Jonjo could see
that something well beyond the norm was needed even to keep
Dawn Run in touch.

Throwing his heart far over the other side, he asked for a
long, long leap. You won't find the form of his request in many
textbooks and there was more than a hint of desperation about
Dawn Run's reply. But somehow it still worked. The big mare
landed running, with neither ground nor momentum lost.

Even so, as they rose at the last, third place still seemed the
best that she could hope for. Mrs Hill 'thought she was beaten
then' and Tony Mullins, watching from the members' lawn,
'saw her land safe and turned away'.

In one respect at least their despair was premature because

Mark Dwyer's plans for Forgive 'N' Forget, so carefully laid and stylishly carried through, were suddenly left in ruins when last year's winner hit the last fence hard.

But Wayward Lad's final leap was characteristically precise and, landing a full length in front of Dawn Run, he quickened brilliantly to treble that advantage. That, however, was his last card and, playing it, he wavered to the left. 'I suddenly saw he was tiring,' Jonjo told us afterwards – '*and so did she.*'

In the first three-quarters of the race, the great Irishman had repeatedly proved what a superlatively sympathetic horseman he is – helping Dawn Run to overcome her inexperience and sitting rocklike through her one serious mistake.

But Jonjo O'Neill is also a great *jockey* and now, faced with perhaps the most urgent and difficult tactical problem of his noble career, he solved it as though they had all the time in the world.

As Wayward Lad went left, Jonjo eased Dawn Run gently to her right – and took three precious strides to get her perfectly balanced. No time was ever less wasted because now, seeing daylight and a tired horse ahead, Mrs Hill's great mare showed the indomitable will to win which made her the Champion Hurdler of three countries.

Poor Wayward Lad was out on his feet and neither Forgive 'N' Forget nor Run And Skip had an ounce of energy left. So Dawn Run galloped home to claim her kingdom by a length and, as Jonjo raised his right arm in triumph, one of the biggest crowds ever to watch a Cheltenham Gold Cup roared its collective head off in admiration for a heroine and affection for the best-loved and most universally respected jockey of his day.

Not all the scenes which followed were a source of pride – and several frantic admirers are extremely lucky that Dawn Run was too tired to use her hind legs in the unsaddling enclosure. But it was a real joy to watch the warmth with which the other jockeys hailed her and Jonjo as they came back.

Tony Mullins was soon adding his congratulations and, typically, Jonjo lost no time in expressing his gratitude publicly for Tony's freely given help and counsel.

This, in fact, was British jumping at its sporting, admirable best – a day when even losers smiled. And the great race had, as I've said, been a drama from the start.

As Dawn Run sailed cheerfully over the first two fences, Steve

Smith Eccles, beside her on Run And Skip, served clear notice that this was to be no unopposed lap of honour. In fact, first blood went to the mare because Run And Skip hit the third fence hard – and hit it again the next time round.

By that time sheer bad luck had eliminated another possible claimant for the lead when Alan Brown's leather broke on Cybrandian, leaving him with no chance of controlling so hard a puller. But Run And Skip's presence seemed to encourage and inspire Dawn Run and throughout the first circuit her jumping left little or nothing to be desired.

The first sign of fallibility was a splash as she dropped her hind legs in the water – and you can hardly blame an old anti-water-jump campaigner for reflecting how much more serious this might have been!

Nowadays, though still, in my opinion, a pointless obstacle (at least when sited out in the country), the water is kept too shallow to inflict the sort of undeserved, back-breaking wrench which killed Sundew and other good horses.

The slight check still probably disturbed Dawn Run – and allowed Run And Skip to go on plaguing her. 'I wanted to give her a breather,' Jonjo says, 'but Steve [Smith Eccles] would never let me . . .'

An unusual view of the last fence in the 1986 Gold Cup: Dawn Run takes off in pursuit of Wayward Lad (no. 12).

Dawn Run took the last open ditch, scene of poor Tony Mullins's downfall, in her stride, but at the next, for the first and only time, the channel of communication between her and Jonjo missed a beat.

The stride he asked for was not, I think, quite as long as the desperate 'penultimate' one I've already described, but this time Dawn Run did not accept the signal. The 'short one' she substituted was quick as light and Jonjo never budged. But Dawn Run's tail flew up as she crashed through – a flag of encouragement to her pursuers.

Of these – with Run And Skip still just in front – Wayward Lad and Forgive 'N' Forget were now poised on the leaders' heels.

Earls Brig had fallen at the 15th, Von Trappe was out of it when he went four fences later, Combs Ditch, carried out at the same fence, had never threatened to take a serious part and, as they turned downhill for home, Righthand Man and Observe were both finding the pace too hot.

So the stage was set – and the last act was entirely worthy of its prelude.

This, perhaps, is the place to congratulate the losing jockeys. Steve Smith Eccles on Run And Skip, Graham Bradley on Wayward Lad and Mark Dwyer on Forgive 'N' Forget all rode races *precisely* designed to give their mounts the best conceivable chance.

Dwyer (until the last) and Bradley (for 100 yards after it) must have tasted victory only to have it snatched away.

I am sorry to qualify this well-deserved praise, but if the jockeys concerned watch this historic finish again I wonder how many strokes of the whip they can count *which made the slightest difference*. Precious few, in my opinion – but that unfortunate modern tendency was the only regrettable thing about the 1986 Gold Cup.

The first horse ever to complete the Champion Hurdle–Gold Cup double, Dawn Run is more than ever a match, in terms of courage, for her indomitable owner.

It was just twelve months before she paid 5,800 IR guineas for the big three-year-old Deep Run filly that Mrs Hill had been carried off Thurles Racecourse much nearer dead than alive.

Two years later, with the withdrawal of her permit already hanging over her, she rode Dawn Run to her first victory. It is a wonderful sporting fairy tale and, with any luck at all, there are plenty of chapters left.

Paddy Mullins is, by nature, so quiet and self-effacing that his vital part in the story tends to be overlooked. For him and his whole united family the controversy over who should ride Dawn Run must have added a lot of unnecessary strain, but at least in the end it had a happy ending and the great mare, needless to say, was brought out at Cheltenham fit to run for any kingdom.

20 March 1986

Audax's obituary of Dawn Run appears on pages 233–6.

HARWOOD'S HERO
LIFTED ALL OUR
HEARTS

*Trusthouse Forte Prix de l'Arc de Triomphe, Longchamp,
5 October 1986*

With one long, graceful sweep, like a sharp scythe through long grass, Dancing Brave mowed down a high-class international field to win the Trusthouse Forte Prix de l'Arc de Triomphe at Longchamp.

The French Derby winner Bering finished second, the English

Dancing Brave powering home from Bering (dark sleeves)
and Triptych in the 1986 Prix de l'Arc de Triomphe.

and Irish Derby winner Shahrastani was fourth and the German Derby winner Acatenango seventh. So there can no longer be the shadow of a doubt that Prince Khaled Abdulla's Lyphard colt is a truly great middle-distance racehorse.

Equally, there is no longer any question that Dancing Brave should never have been beaten. He did not give Shahrastani quite as big a start in the Longchamp straight as he did that sad day at Epsom but the even more vital difference now was his own attitude and style of racing.

Settling calmly in the first half mile, he was still nearer last than first turning into the straight – but instead of the eager, unbalanced schoolboy who sprawled round Tattenham Corner in the Derby, Pat Eddery found beneath him a poised and deadly machine, with all its power still intact.

For Dancing Brave's legion of supporters in the stands, mind you, the first furlong of the straight was agony. 'Ah, well,' we began to think, 'he *has* been in training since April' – and then, when Pat picked up his whip: 'Oh no, it's going to be the Derby all over again.'

But no one lucky enough to see what followed will ever forget it. Two taps from the whip were all Dancing Brave needed and, when you remember the records of his opponents, the charge which brushed them aside like autumn leaves must rank among the great moments of racing history.

Darara, rather surprisingly, led for the first three furlongs – with the Aga Khan's intended pacemaker Dihistan never able to reach the front. Then, after Baby Turk had taken over round the downhill swing for home, the Irish colt Nemain had a brief moment in the limelight. But he was soon swamped by a line of green as, two furlongs from home, the Aga Khan's trio, Shardari, Shahrastani and Darara came on virtually in line abreast. Acatenango and Triptych were at their heels with Bering closing fast on the outside.

Drawn beside Bering, Pat Eddery had wisely chosen him as the one to follow and it was now, seeing Gary Moore go for home, that he sounded the charge on Dancing Brave. The result, as I had said, was sensational. No sooner had one Derby winner, Shahrastani, got his head in front than another, Bering, stormed past him – but now, to us in the stands, it was clear that all our fears were groundless.

The season had *not* been too long for Dancing Brave and, at full stretch, he was an awesome sight. Bering, who smashed the French Derby record at Chantilly, looked for a moment almost stationary, and so great was Dancing Brave's impetus that, hitting the front only half a furlong from home, he won, going away, by a length and a half.

So this eagerly awaited day lived right up to, if not beyond, our wildest dreams – an unforgettable race won brilliantly by the best horse in Europe, almost certainly the best we have seen since Mill Reef.

Unfortunately, from a cross financial point of view, the French were infected by their visitors' enthusiasm to such an extent that Dancing Brave started favourite!

But this was a day when money seemed strictly incidental, a golden Indian summer afternoon when Pat Eddery and Dancing Brave lifted our hearts and made any trouble easy to forget.

Behind them Bering was clearly in no way disgraced. No doubt he would have preferred slightly softer ground but no one offered that as an excuse. Indeed, so far as I heard, no one offered an excuse of any sort.

Only half a length behind Bering and a short head in front of Shahrastani, Triptych ran perhaps the finest race of her extraordinary career. I heard her trainer Biancone quoted the other day as saying that Triptych 'does not always do everything she can'. Well, maybe not, but if so, who can possibly blame her? She has, after all, no reason, on past form, to expect any lengthy holidays!

On this occasion anyway, dividing two Derby winners with a dozen good horses strung out behind her, I hope no one will accuse this wonderful mare of doing less than her best.

Beaten fair and square though he was, Shahrastani must have delighted Walter Swinburn by beating Shardari (a neck!) to confirm his choice. Clearly the Derby winner did give his true running this time, reversing Ascot form with Shardari but still well beaten by a better, faster horse. All honour to the Aga Khan and Michael Stoute for taking the risk and trouble to bring him back for this much more honourable farewell.

Shardari ran only a fraction below his best, if that, and one and a half lengths behind came Darara, not quite living up to the previous record of Prix Vermeille winners, but still not at all disgraced. Nor, two lengths behind her, was the German four-year-old Acatenango. He had been up near the leaders for 10 furlongs and Steve Cauthen was full of praise. 'My only complaint,' he said, 'is that Dancing Brave and six of the others went so much faster.'

Dihistan, for an unwelcome change, did not get any bouquets for his efforts. Tenth, just behind Mersey and Saint Estephe, he apparently even at one stage got somewhat entangled with his stable-companions. But no one suggests it made much difference.

So, in fact, as far as Europe is concerned, a golden seal was set on the long and brilliantly conducted campaign which began when Dancing Brave first appeared (on ground much softer than he likes) at Newmarket in April.

For a horse who was then being trained specifically for the Two Thousand Guineas and only almost as an afterthought for the Derby, six months is a long time and no praise can be too high for the skill and care with which Guy Harwood and his faithful team at Pulborough have not only kept Dancing Brave fresh and well but also converted him from an inexperienced and somewhat explosive beginner into the highly tuned racing machine we saw last week.

No doubt their task was made easier by the colt's willing and equable temperament – but that only makes it even better news that he is to stand in England. No one, alas, can predict which of his many qualities Dancing Brave will prove best at passing on – but this is now such a complete racehorse that it will be a cruel freak of heredity if he does not succeed at stud.

For the moment, we can only be thankful to have seen him – and keep our fingers crossed that, if he does go to California, the tight turf circuit at Santa Anita will not incommode him. Blessed as he is with the speed of a top-class sprinter, I cannot see why it should.

9 October 1986

Dancing Brave never looked like winning the Breeders' Cup. But I think that the blame for this, his only 'failure', was much more likely to lie with the long, hard season to which a Two Thousand Guineas, King George and Arc de Triomphe winner must inevitably be subjected than with the conformation of the Santa Anita track.

Horses

Silver Buck (Sooty White) winning the Limes Handicap
'Chase at Market Rasen in 1983.

Sea Bird II to Blazing Scent – Pas Seul to Baulking Green. It takes all sorts, and winning great races is only one of many ways in which horses can make you remember them. Here are some of the heroes who, for all sorts of different reasons, earned a place in Audax's private Hall of Fame.

It includes two of my greatest and most admired 'rivals' – The Dikler and Baulking Green – and several even greater favourites.

I wrote a whole book about Mill Reef, and had the honour of sitting, briefly, on Pas Seul (one slow canter when he was three), Mill House (a day's hunting with the VWH when he was a long way past his prime) and Flyingbolt – who, though also well past his best, ran away with me for about three miles at Roddy Armytage's!

Night Nurse and Sea Bird often thrilled me in different ways and although Dawn Run's Gold Cup is dealt with in 'Races', her somehow unnecessary, even rather pointless, death in France was an even bigger shock than Triptych's in Kentucky.

As for Desert Orchid, many of his triumphs came outside the period covered by this book – and, as I write this, they may not even be finished yet – but his Whitbread (my favourite race whoever wins it) is a very precious memory.

THE STORY OF PAS SEUL

For perhaps ten seconds last Thursday afternoon, thousands of people at Cheltenham and many more in homes all over the country held their breath as a big bay horse galloped towards a steeplechase fence. Of all those who watched and crossed their fingers and prayed, only one man could do anything about it. For Bill Rees, the rider of Pas Seul, those seconds must have seemed a lifetime. They ended, as we know, in triumph, but behind this victory in the Gold Cup lies a story which, so it seems to me, contains all the romance and fascination that make men spend their lives in the breeding and racing of Thoroughbred horses.

When, twenty-one years ago, Hitler's war swept over Europe, Fred Darling, the most famous trainer in England, found his world dissolving around him. He had in his yard two yearlings who, as Sun Chariot and Big Game, were later virtually to sweep the board in the wartime classics of 1942, but he had also the mares, foals and yearlings of his own stud, and for these, with all the big bloodstock sales in abeyance, the future was grim and uncertain.

Mr Darling kept a few Guernsey cows to graze his paddocks, and through these he met Mr Harry Frank, a highly successful farmer who also kept Thoroughbred mares and was himself a fine horseman and judge of horses.

One day while looking at the Beckhampton yearlings, a bay filly by Royal Dancer caught Mr Frank's eye and he bought her there and then for £40 to make a hunter. She was her dam's second foal and, since the first, sold as a yearling for 850 guineas, had already won two races, Mr Darling was probably right when he said that her price at the Doncaster Sales would have been nearer to two thousand than one.

But there were no Doncaster Sales, so Pas de Quatre (as the filly was called) came to Mr Frank's farm near Crudwell in Wiltshire instead of joining some high-class flat-race stable. She was, as it turned out, the only one of her dam's seven foals never to win, but that fact does not seem important now that she has bred two winners of the Gold Cup!

From the time she was first broken, Pas de Quatre proved herself utterly fearless but distinctly wilful. She has never, all her life, allowed anyone to put a foot in the stirrup to get up on her, preferring them to jump aboard as she walked on and making her feelings clear to anyone who tried otherwise.

Bob Turnell, a lifetime friend of Harry Frank's, had helped to break the mare and, while stationed nearby in the Army, was the first to take her out hunting. After the first attempt, he told Mr Frank that Pas de Quatre never once offered to refuse but – a foretaste, perhaps, of things to come – was apt, sometimes, to hit a fence low down!

In training for a while with A. Kilpatrick, Pas de Quatre ran well several times over fences at Cheltenham, ridden mostly by Turnell, but never managed to win. After one season Mr Frank decided to breed from her and sent her to Gay Light, a stallion quartered in Gloucestershire who had, inadvertently, failed to get a premium from the Hunters' Improvement Society.

As a result of this union, Pas de Quatre foaled, unassisted, while turned out for a morning graze and her first son, who damaged one eye at birth and bears the mark – a clouded pupil – to this day, became famous as Gay Donald, winner of the 1955 Gold Cup.

Bought by Jim Ford for Mr P.J. Burt, a Wiltshire farmer, his is another story, but his owner figures also in the oddest chapter of all in the history of Pas Seul.

For some years later, after two more foals, both fillies (one of whom, Irish Dancer, ran unsuccessfully in Mr John Rogerson's colours), Pas de Quatre was given to Mr Burt when Harry Frank decided to cut down on his breeding activities.

The mare had been covered by Erin's Pride that season, but had shown herself in use several times during the summer and, as the result of two tests, was certified to be barren. A condition of the gift had been that she should have a good home and, with Mr Frank's permission, a girl groom of Mr Burt's rode her during the spring of 1953 in *three hunter trials* and *two ladies' point-to-points*. In all these ventures, as we now know, she was accompanied by her unborn son, later to be known throughout the land as Pas Seul!

At this point in her career, however, Fate took a hand once again, for Mr Burt died suddenly and his wife was unable to keep the horses on.

Harry Frank's one wish was still to give Pas de Quatre a good home, and with this in mind he passed the mare on to her old friend and admirer, Bob Turnell. He, in turn, sent her to the Littleton Stud near Winchester where, incredible though it may seem, she cheerfully allowed Royal Tara to cover her.

And there, to the complete bewilderment of all who knew her history, Pas de Quatre proceeded, calmly, some weeks later, to produce her second Gold Cup hero.

To him she transmitted a little of her own wayward character and all the fearless courage and toughness that marked her extraordinary life. She gave also the brilliant speed and stamina that we saw displayed at Cheltenham as Pas Seul stormed up the hill to beat Lochroe.

Pas de Quatre herself is still going strong and her four-year-old son by Domaha, Travel Alone, is in training with Bob Turnell. She has also a filly foal this year by Drury. She is twenty-one now, but that is nothing in her family, for after he had won the Gold Cup, Pas Seul received a telegram of congratulation from his grandam, Baroness VI, by Weissdorn out of American Beauty by Teddy, who, at the ripe old age of thirty-one, is still alive in Cheshire!

I hope I will be forgiven this long digression, but the story itself seemed at least as well worth telling as its happy outcome.

This began, on the last and brightest day of the N.H. meeting, as Kerstin and The Major led the Gold Cup field out into the country.

It was a marvellous race to watch – fast, clean and virtually free from interference. Kerstin was always in the first three and, at the water second time round, Hayhurst sent her to the front.

With the exception of Lotoray, who was soon tailed off, Mac Joy was the first to be beaten and Knightsbrook blundered away any chance he may have had at the fence after the water.

Pas Seul (left) and Lochroe at the last in the 1960 Gold Cup.

Rees had waited patiently on Pas Seul, and save for one slip at the water had been given no cause for anxiety. Now, going up the hill, he improved steadily to a position just behind Kerstin, while Lochroe made ground with equal ease at his quarters.

Three from home, Kerstin was under pressure and, a moment later, Lochroe and Pas Seul had drawn clear with the race between them.

Pas Seul lost, perhaps, a length at the second last and his incredible twelve-year-old rival, who had been quite beautifully ridden by young David Mould, looked anything but a beaten horse as he darted gaily into the last. For the final crucial strides before the fence, Rees sat like a statue and then, sensing that all was well, gave Pas Seul the office.

To us in the stands the race seemed over as they landed safe on the flat, but Lochroe and Mould thought otherwise.

Into his stride like a flash, the little horse again poached half a length and it was only his strength – never his courage – that dwindled on that desperate hill. As Pas Seul wore him down, an exhausted Kerstin fell at the last and, an ironic twist of fortune, so impeded Roddy Owen that he lost third place to Zonda.

After his tragic blunder last year, no one could grudge Pas Seul's triumph. His owner, Mr John Rogerson, is one of the most faithful supporters of the game and there has never been a better or more hard-working senior steward. For Pas Seul's trainer, Bob Turnell, and for his rider, Bill Rees, it was a just reward for many heartbreaks and years of hard work.

And, among many happy faces in the unsaddling enclosure, none was more filled with joy than that of Jack Beasley, Pas Seul's faithful lad. Well over fifty now, Beasley, who won the Lincolnshire Handicap on White Bud in 1923, has been with Turnell ever since the war and rides Pas Seul in much of his work.

Quite apart from Pas Seul's well-known erratic jumping, it was a fine feat of training to get him to the post fit enough to win so great a trial of strength. He has not looked a robust horse all this winter and to make things worse had sustained a severe overreach in his last race.

Since that race, it must be added, he has been given regular treatment by Mr N. Brooks, whose 'impulse change' worked miracles on Aureole and other highly strung horses.

No one can say how great an effect this may have had on Pas Seul, but Mr Brooks gave his services voluntarily and free of charge and deserves his share of credit.

If one felt at Cheltenham that Pas Seul deserved to win, so, surely, did Lochroe, who ran the finest race of his wonderful career and beat all the other better-fancied horses out of sight. It was cruel luck for Mr Edward Cazalet to miss this memorable ride, but I feel sure he rejoiced that his old favourite so covered himself with glory and that his place was taken by David Mould.

19 March 1960

MILL HOUSE AT THE LAST FENCE IN THE HENNESSY

As Mill House came alone to the last fence in the Hennessy Gold Cup on Saturday afternoon, National Hunt racing achieved one of those rare, precious moments in which a mere game lifts men out of themselves above and beyond the ordinary humdrum level of their normal lives. For the thousands who watched and cheered him at Newbury, this huge bay horse was doing something even the greatest human artists do only once or twice in a lifetime.

He was, to us, what Shakespeare may have been to Elizabethans on the first night of *Hamlet*, what Garbo sometimes was on the screen, Fonteyn on the Covent Garden stage, Caruso at La Scala, Matthews at Wembley, Bradman at the Oval.

Perhaps I exaggerate – but, not by much – for last week we were watching a miracle of flesh and blood, a hard and hazardous art brought to the peak of perfection.

And after Saturday's race, as Mill House and Willie Robinson came back, amid scenes of enthusiasm more often associated nowadays with Beatlemania, the play, like all great plays, left one question still unanswered. For every hero needs a rival worthy of his steel and, three fences from home in the 1963 Hennessy Gold Cup, a single tragic slip had robbed us of the final confrontation, so long and eagerly awaited, between Mill House and Ireland's champion Arkle.

Seconds earlier, as Robinson let Mill House (12st) stride effortlessly away from Solimyth (10st) to turn for home in front, his fellow Irishman (and life-long friend) Pat Taaffe sent Arkle (11st 9lb) after him.

From the stands, at that moment, it seemed that all our dreams of a head-on clash were to be fulfilled – for these two had clearly got the rest well beaten and neither had, as yet, come off the bit.

Watching a film of the race that night, one got the clearest possible view of what followed. Arkle jumped the first fence in the straight perhaps three lengths behind his rival and, landing safely, Taaffe asked him to close the gap.

Anyone who ever rode could feel his satisfaction as, a moment later, Arkle surged up to Mill House's girths, and, unless the camera lied, *came back on a tight rein* before the third last fence.

At this – an open ditch – he rose almost upsides and, in the opinion of one experienced observer standing beside the fence, it was his attempt to match the leader's mighty leap that brought disaster.

However that may be, Arkle – who did not, according to Pat Taaffe, hit the fence itself – *had* fatally overreached himself and stumbled on landing with all four legs asprawl and all momentum gone.

In that split-second, although he did not fall, the race was won and lost. For Mill House, as always, had sailed on without pause or check and, before his struggling rival could recover, was ten lengths clear.

At the second last, as if to rub it in, he once again took off far back and as he landed a roar went up from the crowded stands, the like of which, *with one fence still to jump*, I have never heard on an English racecourse.

The fact is that, with Mill House, the expression 'bar a fall' means nothing. So great is his strength, so fantastic his panther-like agility, that one simply cannot imagine a man-made obstacle seriously hindering him.

Long before the last fence on Saturday we knew that he would win and cheered him home with the special warmth an English crowd reserves for the sight it loves best of all – a truly great horse winning as a great horse should.

Willie Robinson said afterwards that, between the last two fences, Mill House, who had not, after all, had a race since April, was beginning to feel the strain. No doubt he was, but it didn't show and, sweeping home on the flat eight lengths ahead of Happy Spring (10st), his stride seemed as long and effortless as it had from the beginning.

Fighting back heroically to make up for his tragic moment of fallibility, Arkle ran on to be third, only three-quarters of a length behind Happy Spring.

And so the question must be faced – what would have happened had Arkle landed safely and been there to challenge at the last?

It would, in my opinion – confirmed by both Robinson and Taaffe – have been desperately close. Robinson says that Mill House definitely felt the need of a previous race, and that being so, it is, I suppose, on the cards that Arkle, a thoroughly fit horse with a well-established turn of speed, might even have run him out of it.

The first fence in the 1963 Hennessy: left to right, Arkle, Pappageno's Cottage (blinkers), John O'Groats and Mill House (no. 1).

But the fact remains that the first and only time Arkle attempted to take the favourite on he paid the penalty – and there were two more fences to be crossed, at either of which Mill House might have forced him into a similar – or even worse – mistake.

It is perhaps the most deadly weapon in Mill House's armoury

– that, taking off beside an ordinary horse, he can, nine times out of ten, outjump him and, if the process is repeated, break his heart.

To sum up, it seems to me that Arkle, magnificent 'chaser that he undoubtedly is, may never again have another opportunity like the one he missed on Saturday. In the Cheltenham Gold Cup – barring accidents, their next meeting – he will have to take the champion on at level weights and by then in all probability Fulke Walwyn will have improved Mill House by several pounds.

But the fascination remains, and so long as it does, National Hunt racing need fear no lack of public interest or enthusiasm.

These two wonderful horses – or Mill House on his own, for that matter – will always fill any racecourse, and that, in these hard days of betting shops and television, is the measure of their greatness.

Although most of its drama was packed into the final act, Saturday's race had been a sight to remember from start to finish, made so, needless to say, by Mill House himself and the glorious exhibition he gave of how steeplechase fences should be crossed with maximum speed and minimum effort.

At the very first he gave us a taste of what was to come – taking off fourth and, with one giant, hair-raising bound, landing in front. Thereafter, with only Bill Rees and Solimyth ready to keep him company, Willie Robinson had no choice but to sail along in the lead, with Arkle (pulling hard, for the early pace was slow) never far behind and never, so far as I saw, making a mistake until the fatal one already described.

At the first open ditch, Pappageno's Cottage (10st 5lb) fell and, passing the stands riderless, nearly caused a disaster by swerving violently across Mill House's nose. Understandably put off, the favourite met the water all wrong, but 'fiddled' it brilliantly, losing not a yard of ground with a quicksilver change of legs well-nigh unbelievable in so big and long-striding a horse.

At the second fence down the back side he did the same again, apparently taking off right under the guard-rail but, according to Willie Robinson, touching not a twig of the fence itself.

These two incidents, together with a whole series of leaps in which he took off two strides away on one side and landed as far out on the other, left one, as I say, with an impression of unshakable confidence.

In fact, occasionally Mill House does hit a fence, but no mere birch can hope to withstand the terrible weight of his massive body, propelled with all the power of barn-door quarters at upwards of 30 miles an hour.

For much of the first two miles my old friend Solimyth struggled his heart out beside the champion and actually headed him for a hundred yards as they turned downhill on the final bend.

Of the others, John O'Groats (10st), fourth in the end, ran really well, always in the leading group and surviving at least one serious blunder, but despite the moderate pace (even the final time was much slower than last year), only Happy Spring had the strength to raise a gallop in the straight.

Springbok (10st 1lb), for instance, last year's winner with 8lb more on his back, was hung up to dry three fences from home, King's Nephew (10st 6lb), though fifth, patently failed to stay and Duke of York (10st 10lb), jumping too deliberately, as usual, was pulled up a long way out.

All these sad failures underline with painful clarity the awesome predicament in which English National Hunt handicappers are going to find themselves as long as Mill House stays fit and well.

There is now not one single horse in this country who can fairly be weighted within two stone of Mr Gollings's champion and if by the end of this season he has won the King George VI 'Chase (his next race) and the Cheltenham Gold Cup, we may well see a Whitbread run at Sandown with the handicap reading as follows – Mill House 12st, the rest 9st 7lb!

Fortunately, for everyone's peace of mind, Fulke Walwyn does not intend to enter him for the Grand National this year – but when he does there are going to be an awful lot of hungry jockeys!

For Walwyn, of course, the Hennessy (his fourth out of the seven races run so far) was just another, now quite unnecessary proof that Mill House has a trainer worthy in every way of his own excellence. For the second time in twelve months this enormous horse had been got ready, without a race in public, to run three and a quarter miles at top speed and beat all the best staying 'chasers there are.

Good horses may make good trainers – but Walwyn and Mill House are the perfect complement to each other.

As for Willie Robinson, I can only say that throughout Saturday's race one almost forgot he was there – so neatly and unobtrusively did he adjust himself to the big horse's effortless rhythm. They, too, are the ideal team, a perfect blend of sympathy with strength.

In the paddock at Newbury, Mill House and Arkle made a fascinating pair for comparison. Although the winner is a whole size bigger than his victim, both have the same tremendous depth through the heart and the same wide, powerful quarters.

In action, Mill House is just the better mover. Despite the sticky ground, he fairly floated down to the post on Saturday and in the race, bobbing unconcernedly along in the lead, made most of the others look like children scampering behind a grown-up man.

Bred in Ireland by Mrs B.M. Lawlor, he is a bay, six-year-old gelding, 17 hands 1in high, by King Hal out of Nas na Riogh, a mare by Cariff out of Breviary, who was by His Reverence out of Short Step by Hurry On out of Naine by Bachelor's Double.

There seems little point to me in attempting a comparison between Mill House and the great 'chasers of the past. The only one I ever saw who might – just might – have given him a race was Pas Seul at his best, but Golden Miller, of course, was before my time.

As yet Mill House has a long way to go to equal the Miller's record (five Gold Cups and a National), but given health and luck I have not much doubt he could do it.

That is in the future. For the present, let us just be thankful that nature has thrown together in one body so many outstanding qualities. A horse like this comes but once in the average lifetime – and those who see him at his prime should count themselves lucky indeed.

7 December 1963

MILL HOUSE – THE GIANT WHO NEVER GAVE UP HOPE

Once upon a time there lived a handsome giant who became a king – but lost his crown and suffered many dreadful trials thereafter.

He stayed so long in the wilderness that even his most faithful subjects began to think he would never come back. They paid homage to other, younger kings – and some of them forgot him altogether.

But the giant was brave as well as handsome – and patient as well as brave. So, although it often seemed that his strength had gone for ever, he never gave up hope . . .

And last week at Sandown Park, as Mill House galloped home, dead tired but infinitely game, the fairy tale of which those words might be the start came, unbelievably, to life.

The brave and handsome giant had come back after all to claim his kingdom, and in the tumultuous roar that welcomed him, four years of doubt, defeat and pain were gloriously swept away.

No fairy tale ever had a happier ending than Mill House's victory in the 1967 Whitbread Gold Cup and, for a horse whose fame was built on bold and fearless jumping, no victory was ever more appropriately gained.

For there's no doubt at all where Mill House won the Whitbread. He won it in the air, giving, from start to finish, a display of sustained, explosive power and agility which can seldom have been equalled and never, surely, excelled in a steeplechase of this distance.

And this, mark you, was a horse who, last time out, had turned a violent somersault. To hit an open ditch as hard as Mill House hit that one at Cheltenham must be a terrifying as well as a very painful experience. And yet last Saturday there was not one of the 24 fences in the Whitbread at which the big horse showed the slightest shadow of anxiety or caution.

Just once – at the downhill fence second time round – his judgment wavered briefly and even then, scorning to play safe, he crashed through hard and low – and gained ground in the process.

But wonderful though it was – magnificent to watch and, in the end, fatal to his opponents – Mill House's flamboyant jumping was, for David Nicholson who rode him, a major problem too.

For the stable view was that even on last week's perfect going Mill House would barely stay the three miles and five furlongs of the Whitbread. And the chosen tactics therefore were to wait behind as long as possible – at least for the first two miles.

But no one told Mill House that – or, if they did, he knew better. For the first two fences and past the stands he allowed Monarch's Thought to lead, but that was all. 'I could just about hold him on the flat,' says Nicholson, 'but every time he saw a fence, whoosh, we were gone.'

And now, down the hill, quite suddenly, it was like the good old days. With three great strides and one enormous bound, Mill House threw tactics to the winds. '*Wait?*', you could almost hear him say. 'Let *them* wait – and catch me if they can.'

But behind is not the only place to wait and, making a virtue of necessity, David Nicholson set himself to hoard the reserve of strength he knew would surely be needed before the end.

Without giving away an inch of the ground Mill House's leaps were gaining, he managed still to dictate a reasonable gallop and the others, though constantly outjumped, stayed close together, snapping at the leader's heels like jackals behind a stag.

For the huge crowd, however, all thought of tactics was soon submerged in a wave of emotion and excitement; 18,000 people were present at Sandown last week and, by the end of the first circuit, there can have been few among them who, whatever his allegiance, did not at least half hope Mill House would win.

At his wonderful best the big horse has always been an inspiration to watch and on Saturday, bounding down the long back straight, flicking fence after fence behind him, he seemed, more than ever, the spirit of steeplechasing incarnate.

Any horse jumping as he was jumping – grace, power and speed all blending in the sunshine – would have been a memorable sight. But this was more, far more, besides. This was Mill House, the hope of England, fighting back from the shadows to which fate and Arkle had so long consigned him; fighting age and injury and failure in his own inimitable style.

So past the crowded stands they cheered him – as only Arkle has been cheered before – and as he stormed down the hill, ten furlongs and 11 fences still to go, the hopes of literally millions were riding on his back.

It was here, at the downhill fence, as has been said, that Mill House made his only error. 'I was getting pretty brave by then,' says David Nicholson, 'and I asked him to stand just too far back.'

The same class of mistake brought tragedy at Cheltenham, but this time, using all his strength and weight, Mill House made very sure it was the fence that came off worst. So on he went, unchecked, still pulling hard – and here, I suppose, the other twelve deserve a mention.

Starting down the back side for the last time, Woodland Venture (12st), Kellsboro Wood (11st), San Angelo (10st 9lb), Kapeno (10st 10lb), Limeking (10st 6lb) and Rondetto (10st 10lb) were all still plenty close enough.

What A Myth (11st 11lb), labouring on the firm ground, had never really been in the hunt, and though some of the others may still have been within theoretical striking distance, they were never to get any closer.

For now, crossing the water, the race was on in deadly earnest. Johnny Haine, with Kellsboro Wood poised close behind the leader, had hoped to challenge over the Railway fences, but Mill House made the hope a forlorn one.

One, two, three – he took them in his stride without a pause and, as he stormed round the turn for home, Terry Biddlecombe had already begun to ride for dear life on Woodland Venture.

Fifth in the end, the Gold Cup winner was far from disgraced, but on this fast ground he could find no extra speed for the final half a mile.

Nor, for the moment, could Kapeno, Rondetto and Limeking, already beaten, and, going to the Pond, it was John Buckingham and San Angelo who loomed up at David Nicholson's knee, the most obvious and immediate dangers.

But Nicholson had still not called for a real effort and now, as he did so, Mill House quickened, fought San Angelo off – and jumped the second last two lengths in front.

Long before this, the stands had been exploding with excitement, but now, with only one more fence to jump and Mill House clear of Kellsboro Wood, it was as if the crowd held its collective breath.

He met the last dead right – a little close if anything – and, as the pictures show, flew it superbly at full stretch, his hind legs flung behind him like the streamers of a kite.

And, as he landed safe there detonated in the stands an ear-splitting roar in which delight and suspense were mingled.

For the suspense was still all too real. Two fences from home David Nicholson felt Mill House falter under him – and knew that there was only courage left. 'I thought something was bound to catch us,' he says – and on an exhausted horse at Sandown a jockey dies 300 separate deaths, one for every agonizing yard of the run-in.

Almost always there is a danger coming, and now it was from an unexpected, if appropriate, source. Kellsboro Wood landed second on the flat, but Kapeno had suddenly found another wind and, hurtling up from far behind, began to close the gap with every stride.

For more than three miles and 20 fences Mill House had scarcely seen a rival. He had jumped and galloped his heart out, like the cheerful, willing giant he has always been – and now, with victory so close, it seemed for one awful moment that the reward was after all to be denied him. And that, with all due respect to Kapeno, to Nick Gaselee who rode him so well and to Colonel Whitbread, without whose help this wonderful race could never have taken place, would have been an unmitigated tragedy.

But this time for a change the Fates were kind. Head down, dog-tired, with weariness in every line of his great frame, Mill

House held on. By a rapidly contracting length and a half Kapeno was second – the same distance in front of Kellsboro Wood.

Both these two covered themselves with glory – especially Kapeno, who had finished the course in the Grand National and, on Saturday, far outstripped the others who had done so. San Angelo (4th) also ran a magnificent race over a distance probably just too far for him.

But there was little time at Sandown on Saturday to feel sorry for the losers. I have met no one – not even witnesses of Brown Jack's final victory at Royal Ascot – who claims to remember a reception comparable with that which awaited Mill House.

Many an unashamed tear was shed around the winner's enclosure and, to round off a scene no script-writer would have dared concoct, Queen Elizabeth the Queen Mother, having presented the trophies, asked that Willie Robinson be called for. And as Mill House's old companion-in-arms limped across on crutches, the crowd roared yet again, this time in sympathy as well as admiration.

But throughout the professional racing world the first reaction – apart from universal pleasure – to Mill House's triumph was 'what a masterpiece of training!'

And even the word masterpiece scarcely does justice to this, the crowning feat of Fulke Walwyn's long career. Training Mill House must always have been rather like walking a tightrope – and when, last year, one of his tendons was damaged, the problems involved in getting him fit looked, for any normal man, well nigh insoluble.

There followed another injury, this time in his quarters – and then that disastrous fall in the Gold Cup. For Walwyn – and for Mill House's owner, Mr Bill Gollings – that might well have seemed the final straw, but neither gave up hope. And somehow – with the same delicate, infinitely patient skill that brought Mandarin back to win a Gold Cup at the age of twelve – Walwyn actually managed to produce Mill House at Sandown last week a better, fresher, stronger horse than he has been all season.

Obviously, on the face of his Sandown performance, Mill House 'would', bar the fall, have won the Cheltenham Gold

Cup. Probably he would, but I feel certain (and David Nicholson agrees) that he was a very different horse last week from the one we saw at Cheltenham.

Perhaps the argument will be settled next year, perhaps Arkle will be back by then, but that is for the future. At this moment Mill House need never win, or even run in, another race.

His fame is secure, his name will always be remembered – no longer just 'the horse who had the bad luck to be born in the same year as Arkle' – but a champion in his own right, a champion who, against heavy odds, exploded for ever the sad old rule that they never come back.

6 May 1967

SEA BIRD II – ONE HELL OF A HORSE!

The championship of the racing world was decided beyond all doubt or question this week when, in the Prix de l'Arc de Triomphe at Longchamp, M.J. Ternynck's Sea Bird II totally outclassed by far the most representative international field ever seen on any racecourse anywhere.

No test of greatness was ever more comprehensive, no triumph ever more complete. With the Derby winners of France, Ireland, America and Russia trailing respectfully behind him like courtiers behind a king, Sea Bird left no room for argument.

Others – Ribot, for instance – have had longer, more arduous careers, but no one who watched the Arc de Triomphe on Sunday can ever say, with any certainty, that they have seen a better three-year-old than this.

The result established, what is more, that France, this season, has not one but two outstanding Classic colts. For, though quite unable to match the unearthly brilliance of his rival, M. F. Dupré's hitherto unbeaten Reliance beat all the rest with almost equal ease.

In an atmosphere of pent-up multiracial tension that would have made the Tower of Babel sound like a village fête, Sea Bird paraded past the stands sweating freely as he has sometimes done before. Reliance, too, looked ill at ease, but if anyone took these signs as a warning of disaster they were soon shown their mistake.

According to the custom of his native land – an insulting one, I've always thought, to horse and jockey alike – the little American colt Tom Rolfe (8st 10lb) was accompanied down by a lead pony. In all the circumstances – after twelve races this season and under completely unfamiliar conditions – he acquitted himself nobly to finish sixth, which is more, I'm afraid, than can be said for any of the Anglo-Irish contingent.

Solstice, having refused his trial entry into the starting gate, was a non-runner, but otherwise, though Oncidium (9st 6lb) hesitated briefly, there was no trouble at the start.

I cannot for the life of me think why, after the St Leger, a pace-maker was considered necessary for Meadow Court (8st 10lb), and in any case Khalife (8st 10lb), entrusted with that thankless task, was never fast enough to accomplish it.

Instead the early leader – at a furious pace – was the Italian Marco Visconti (8st 10lb), hotly pursued by Anilin (9st 6lb) for Russia, with Khalife struggling in vain to reach the front. Behind these three Lester Piggott had Meadow Court well placed. Pat Glennon was content to be sixth or seventh on Sea Bird (8st 10lb) and Saint-Martin had tucked Reliance in on the heels of his most serious opponent.

Turning downhill into the straight, Marco Visconti was finished; Anilin showed briefly in front and, as Tom Rolfe appeared beside the Russian, a Cold War confrontation looked, for a moment, on the cards.

But the impression was short-lived for now, as the leaders straightened out for home, thousands in the flesh at Long-champ and millions more on television all over Europe were privileged to witness a spectacle which contained, I believe, the very essence of what flat racing is all about.

Had he looked around him, Pat Glennon could, at that moment, have run his eye over horseflesh collectively worth more than a million pounds. Instead he moved his hands on Sea Bird's neck and in three strides the horse made his opponents look worth as many shillings.

It was over far quicker than you could read those words. Reliance, ridden with Gallic fervour, did his best – far better than any of the others – but he might as well have tried to catch the tail of a whirlwind.

Not in twenty strides, not even in ten – almost, it seemed, in a single giant bound – Sea Bird catapulted clear. Six lengths in front with a furlong to go, he would have doubled that distance at the line had he not – either startled by the roar of welcome or because of his old left-handed tendency – begun to run across the course.

It made not the remotest difference. Well before the end Pat Glennon was patting Sea Bird's neck and the only really significant struggle in the race was for third prize, four lengths behind Reliance, between the stable-companions Diatome (8st 10lb) and Free Ride (9st 6lb).

Diatome got the best of it, the gallant Anilin was fifth, with Tom Rolfe sixth, Demi Deuil seventh, Carvin eighth and Meadow Court ninth.

On the last-named, Lester Piggott again blamed the going – which was indeed extremely soft – but I'm afraid that excuse wears a trifle thin when there are horses about like Sea Bird and Reliance, to whom all conditions come alike.

Nonetheless Meadow Court did at least beat all of his Anglo-Irish colleagues. Ragazzo (8st 10lb) was always outpaced and neither Soderini (9st 6lb) nor Oncidium ever showed with a ghost of a chance.

This, however, is no time for narrow jingoistic regrets. The only cause for sadness is that we shall never see Sea Bird in action again and that, at least for the next five years, he will be lost to European breeders.

Owner M. Jean Ternynck leads in Pat Glennon and Sea Bird
II after their Arc triumph.

Like Ribot before him, he is bound for Kentucky and will stand at the stud of Mr John Galbraith, an American for whom, evidently, only the best is good enough.

For Pat Glennon this triumph was a fitting end to a highly successful period in Europe.

Perhaps the strongest of all good Australian jockeys seen here in recent years, Glennon, who is returning home for family reasons, deserves a large share of credit for the understanding with which he has converted Sea Bird from a nervous, high-strung two-year-old, by no means an armchair ride, into the ruthless racing machine we saw this week.

It was noticeable at Longchamp that, though sweating when his rider mounted, Sea Bird had cooled off considerably by the time he entered the starting stall. Of the many tributes showered upon the horse after the Arc, perhaps Glennon's is the most significant – 'by far the best horse I have ever *seen*, let alone ridden.'

Coming as it does towards the end of a long season when horses busy throughout the summer are apt to be past their peak, the Arc de Triomphe is, especially, a 'trainer's race' – and this year's result merely seems to confirm that Etienne Pollet has few equals and no superiors in his difficult profession.

Refusing to be tempted by minor, but nevertheless extremely valuable prizes, Pollet had kept Sea Bird at home since the Grand Prix de St Cloud in early July. Had the colt been beaten this week there could have been no excuse.

Pollet gambled heavily on his own ability to keep a horse fresh and get him fit without a preparatory race. The gamble succeeded superlatively – and deserves superlative praise.

Sea Bird's breeding is, alas, of mostly academic interest in Europe for the next five years. By Dan Cupid, himself only narrowly beaten by Herbager in the French Derby and a son of the great Native Dancer, Sea Bird is out of Sicalade, a mare by Sicambre out of Marmelade who, by Maurepas out of Couleur, is a full-sister to the One Thousand Guineas winner Camaree.

This great horse is, then, yet another example of a combination between top-class French and American blood lines.

Though not conventionally handsome, and not absolutely without flaw as regards temperament, Sea Bird is sound and, having won the Epsom Derby, has proved his ability both to travel abroad and to adapt himself to strange conditions. He acted equally well on any going, would almost certainly have stayed beyond 1½ miles had he been asked to do so, and, more important than any of these qualities, possessed, to a degree unique among his contemporaries, the power of immediate devastating acceleration.

He is, in fact, one hell of a horse – and the sooner we get him back to Europe the better.

9 October 1965

DUNKIRK'S MACKESON – A TRIUMPH FOR MAN AND HORSE

In all the predictions, reservations and arguments (some of them fairly heated!) which preceded last Saturday's Mackeson Gold Cup (2m), no one, I think it safe to say, can have foreseen how the race would, in fact, be run and won. But although the manner of Dunkirk's victory was unexpected, about its merit and gallantry there is no doubt at all.

In all his previous triumphs – and particularly in the three most recent ones which earned him the title of champion two-mile 'chaser – Colonel W.H. Whitbread's brilliant horse had galloped and jumped the opposition off their legs. Now, up the Cheltenham hill, borne down by the 31lb he was giving Choreographer, it was his own legs that turned leaden with fatigue – and only his courage and his rider's strength that kept him going to the bitter end.

This, to an even greater degree than usual, was a triumph for man as well as horse. Bill Rees rode Dunkirk in almost all his early races, and took all the by no means inconsiderable risks involved in teaching so headstrong a tearaway to jump steeplechase fences.

Last season, at Sandown, riding to orders, he managed to hold up Dunkirk in the Stone's Ginger Wine Handicap 'Chase – tactics which, as we now know, are totally unsuited to the horse's talents.

It was after this race that, with Rees out of action through injury, Dave Dick struck up the brilliantly successful partnership which catapulted Dunkirk to the top of the two-mile tree.

Dunkirk and Bill
Rees, 1965.

Many people, myself included, jumped to the conclusion
that this was a case of the right man for the right horse –
and Colonel Whitbread, understandably reluctant to break up
a winning team, gave Dick the ride again this season.

No jockey likes to be stood down and Bill Rees would not
have been human had he not felt unkindly treated by the
Fates. And that feeling was, not unnaturally, increased when
various scribes (and again I was among them) suggested that
Dave Dick's recent accident might have damaged Dunkirk's
prospects in the Mackeson Gold Cup.

It was, then, with a double burden on his mind, that Rees rode
out at Cheltenham last week. For defeat he could expect the
blame, however undeserved, for victory no special credit.

Add to this the strain inseparable from riding any red-hot

favourite in an important race – a favourite, what's more, who pulls like the devil and was pouring with sweat on Saturday – and you may have some idea of the thoughts revolving round his jockey's head.

As Dunkirk stormed downhill past the stands to the starting gate, taking a stronger hold on the slippery reins than ever he did in the race, I for one would not have been in Rees's boots for a king's ransom.

In fact, for some reason – a slight technical hitch while saddling may have helped to upset him – Dunkirk (12st 7lb) was probably not quite himself. Setting off in front as usual, he jumped the first few fences well enough, but never built up his customary lead and was never in command of either his rider or his rivals.

These, even so, were soon strung out behind him – but the unconsidered outsider Choreographer (10st 4lb) laid up with ominous ease and, at the open ditch, four out, jumped smoothly past to take the lead.

So now, to Rees's other worries a tactical one was added. Should he press on and stay in front at any cost, or sit and suffer with the spectre of defeat too close for comfort?

Rightly – and to his undying credit – he chose the latter course and then, storming down towards the last three fences threw his heart beyond them, staking it all on three decisive leaps.

That brief respite almost certainly won the day, for now, flashing fast and low across the second last, Dunkirk snatched back the lead and, gaining a few more yards at the last, landed two lengths to the good.

It was only just enough. The weight was beginning to tell and, up the hill, Choreographer, beautifully ridden by Peter Pickford, closed the gap inexorably.

Another 20 yards would have been enough, and arguably the 3lb extra he was carrying made the difference. But Bill Rees would not be denied. Dunkirk, dog-tired but game, pulled out his last reserves and at the post there was half a length to spare.

In the applause which welcomed back the winning pair, several emotions were mixed – admiration for a good and gallant horse, delight that Colonel Whitbread, N.H. racing's most faithful and generous benefactor, should, at last, win one of the prizes sponsored by his own brewery, and, perhaps most of all, recognition of the hazards, mental and physical, which Bill Rees had so skilfully overcome.

This, for him, was a moment of truth – and the truth is that no man alive could have got one more ounce from Dunkirk last Saturday afternoon.

20 November 1965

FLYINGBOLT'S CHELTENHAM

Cheltenham last week had many heroes and at least two heroines, but when old men remember years ahead, the first name in their thoughts will surely be Flyingbolt's. For although Mr T.G. Wilkinson's great chesnut failed in his unique double bid, he failed only by three and three-quarter lengths, and had Arkle himself attempted the same impossible task, no one would have counted such a failure any discredit.

And 'impossible' is, I believe, the right word, for in Mr John Rogerson's Salmon Spray, Flyingbolt met a superb specialist hurdler at the height of his powers – perfectly trained, magnificently ridden and running under ideal conditions.

The crisis of the 1966 Champion Hurdle came four flights from home as Flyingbolt moved up to join Tamerosia and Kirriemuir in the lead.

Hitherto his jumping had been flawless – fast, accurate and only very slightly big. But now, meeting the hurdle all wrong, he got right under it, crashed through and landed asprawl, losing both impetus and at least three lengths.

But for that one error Pat Taaffe, who had chosen the longer, outside route, doubtless to minimise the risk of interference, would probably have set sail down the hill, established a lead and made full use of his mount's undoubted stamina. Perhaps the result would have been the same – but it would at least have been a great deal closer.

As things were, Flyingbolt had to spend precious energy in recovering those lengths and showed his greatness by doing so without, apparently, coming off the bit.

By the second last he was in front, pressed hard by Compton Martin, and it was here that Kirriemuir, going flat out for a narrow gap on the inside rail, misjudged his leap and paid the penalty.

A moment later, having disposed of both Compton Martin and Tamerosia, Taaffe glanced sideways and saw the sight he must have half expected. It was Salmon Spray's white face poised menacingly at his knee and, as Flyingbolt came under pressure for the first time, Johnny Haine, who had ridden the sort of cat-and-mouse waiting race at which he has no superior, threw down his final, unanswerable ace of trumps.

Salmon Spray rose at the last perhaps half a length in front and doubled that advantage by skimming the bar like a greyhound. Beside him, as the photographs show, Flyingbolt gave it a foot too much air – the tiny vital margin between the expert and the great all-rounder.

In fact, it did not matter, for jumping is not Salmon Spray's only weapon. He wielded another now – the electric burst of acceleration of which, in some of his recent races, mud had understandably robbed him.

In a dozen strides the race was over. Salmon Spray sprinted away to win by three lengths and, although Flyingbolt never gave up trying, Sempervivum, running the race of his life on ground too fast to suit him, battled through to take second place by three-quarters of a length.

The Irish mare, Talgo Abbess, was fourth, two more lengths behind. Tamerosia was a rather surprising fifth and Spartan General, for whom the dash from the top of the hill had been just too hot, an honourable sixth.

For the rest, except Kirriemuir, who might well have been placed, there were no obvious excuses. They had gone no great gallop early on and Makaldar, like Spartan General, was simply run off his legs when the race began in earnest.

Johnny Haine said afterwards that a couple of uncharacteristic mistakes had cost Salmon Spray no ground and that his only serious problem had been to find a way through the close-packed leaders two flights from home. For the coolness and style with which he solved it, no praise can be too high.

So, after twelve months of argument and doubt, those who had always considered that only a luckless fall deprived Salmon

Spray of last year's Champion Hurdle were proved correct. He won fair and square, strictly on merit and although, in defeat, Flyingbolt earned almost equal honour, that in no way detracts from the achievement of his conqueror.

The first leg of Flyingbolt's double had gone strictly according to plan when, on the Tuesday in the N.H. Two-Mile Champion 'Chase, he cantered unconcernedly round to beat Flash Bulb by 15 lengths. Sunny Weather made the early running but, as expected, jumped so violently to the right that his speed was useless.

As Flying Wild and Flash Bulb went past him after the water, Flyingbolt was still lobbing calmly along behind them – a very different sight from the headstrong tearaway he used to be – and it was only four fences from home that Pat Taaffe let him pull up to join Flash Bulb in the lead.

The latter (carrying both Salmon Spray's colours and his jockey) is usually held up for a late run, but now, understandably determined to give the favourite as hard a race as possible, Johnny Haine drove him down the hill as if for life itself.

Flash Bulb gave all he had, but it simply wasn't enough to get his relentless rival off a tight rein. By the second last Flyingbolt was clear in front and the further they went the wider the gap became.

This shattering performance (in fast time considering the total absence of effort involved), followed by his heroic failure next day, stamps the big chesnut more clearly than ever as the second-best 'chaser in the world.

Flyingbolt's more ardent admirers would dispute even that qualification, but Pat Taaffe says that if ever the twain shall meet he still wants to be on Arkle. I agree, but over two or two and a half miles there would probably be precious little in it.

26 March 1966

At one time the Irish handicapper put Flyingbolt only 2lbs behind Arkle, but Pat Taaffe, in his delightful book, My Life *– and Arkle's, wrote, 'I am sure there was at least a stone between them.'*

'Over two miles, of course, it would have been a very much closer thing,' he went on, 'but Arkle would still have won.'

Pat described, with feeling, the only time the great pair were allowed to school together: 'They took four fences neck and neck, flat out as though their lives depended on the outcome. Paddy [Woods] and I just held on to them for dear life and waited for the fires to cool down. Well, they cleared the fences all right but it was a bit too close for comfort. Mr Dreaper never allowed them to be schooled together again.'

BAULKING GREEN – A BATTERED OLD HUNTER STEALS THE LIMELIGHT

The Derby is less than three weeks off and by rights, no doubt, this page should be filled with learned talk of aristocratic and expensive three-year-olds. But they, I'm afraid, must wait – for last week their richly rewarded capers suddenly seemed almost insignificant beside the doings of an old and battered hunter.

His name, I need hardly say, is Baulking Green, and if a horse's value depended on the pleasure and excitement he provides for human beings, this one, surely, would be worth as much as any Derby winner ever bred.

In fact, of course, if – which is in the highest degree unlikely – Baulking Green was now put up for sale, he would hardly fetch the stud fee of one average Derby colt. And on Saturday at Ayr, by winning the Usher Vaux Scottish Champion Hunters' 'Chase (3m 3f) for the third successive time, he earned his owner, Mr Jim Reade, a mere £895.

There is, alas, no cash equivalent of the courage with which, at the age of fourteen, Baulking Green dragged his tired legs home to beat Cham and Sizzle-On.

Racing is not boxing where, after a good fight, spectators throw money into the ring. But if it was, the excitement generated both at Ayr and on thousands of television sets last week would surely have filled the unsaddling enclosure like a treasure chest.

I'm prejudiced, of course, but it takes two to make a fight and for this one Cham, beaten a length in the end, deserves at least a share of credit.

But he *was* beaten – fair and square – by a better horse on the day and a horse four years his senior. So let there be no mistake.

Baulking Green is the champion still – and if, in the past, I have sometimes doubted his claim to that title, well, on Saturday such doubts were hammered out of me the hard way.

Baulking Green with owner Jim Reade in 1978, shortly after the horse's twenty-fifth birthday.

After only three fences it was clear how things were going to be – not the result, of course, but that either Baulking Green or Cham would win. For we landed over the water together and from then on never saw another horse.

If that seems unfair to Sizzle-On, who after all finished a very close third, I apologise. But the fact remains that this both looked and felt a two-horse race – a duel fought out toe to toe for three exhausting miles.

Perhaps I was wrong to make it so, but at the time, counting on Cham's superlative jumping, the logical tactics seemed to take the favourite on and force him into error.

The Ayr fences, however, though superbly built, are much more formidable obstacles than those at Worcester, where Baulking Green fell last time out. And recognising this, the cunning old devil took no chances whatever early on.

It was only down the back side second time – five or six fences from home – that his judgment wavered at last. We were really going by now – with the others left far behind – and as Baulking Green crashed through beside him, Cham landed clear in front.

From the stands, I believe, it looked a decisive moment, but I felt no such confidence. For now, going into the final bend, Cham had begun to hang so badly that the effort of steering took most of my time and strength. And, in any case, Baulking Green and George Small have survived many far worse blunders than this.

As we straightened out for home they were back beside us and, at that moment, neither George nor I would have cared to name the result.

The second last at Ayr is an open ditch and this too Baulking Green hit fairly hard. Again Cham's head showed just in front – but only for half-a-dozen strides and it was in the next half-dozen that my last doubts about Baulking Green were swept away for ever.

With a great shout, George Small called for his final effort and, though desperately tired, barely able to raise a gallop, the old horse threw himself forward.

Had I been able to keep Cham straight, it would have been closer still but, almost certainly feeling his damaged legs, he was hanging violently now and on the flat we could simply do no more.

Sizzle-On, finishing like a train, was only a neck away third, but although he had certainly run the race of his life I think that, by fighting each other almost to a standstill, we may to some extent have flattered him.

This was Baulking Green's 22nd victory – and, although several others have ridden him, it is with George Small that his name and greatest feats will always be connected. If ever horse and man were made for each other, these two surely are they.

Age and hard knocks have been powerless to damp their enthusiasm and, together, tough, fearless and supremely determined, they have built up a partnership typical of all that's best in N.H. racing.

Last Saturday I wished with all my heart they had stayed at home, but if Cham had to be beaten, at least defeat in such company was no dishonour.

20 May 1967

I seem to have spent hours chasing Baulking Green round various British racecourses – and only ever managed to beat him when he fell or ejected his rider. Just once, though, on 5 May 1962 at Taunton, Major Rushton's great hunter Rosie's Cousin did have him in real trouble.

Rosie, one of the best and quickest jumpers I ever rode, was about a fence in front with only three to go. But it had just rained on firm ground and the last bend at Taunton was like black ice. It is never much fun falling on the flat and that one really hurt.

BLAZING SCENT – A HORSE TO AROUSE A FEELING OF PITY AND ANGER

Jimmy Wilde, outside the boxing ring, used to look barely able to punch his way out of a paper bag, and with horses appearances can be equally deceptive.

In the paddock at Newmarket last week, for instance, the logical reaction of any horse-lover seeing Mr Bob Capon's Blazing Scent for the first time would have been one of pity mixed with anger.

There never has been much of Blazing Scent, and on Saturday what little there is seemed likely to vanish in a pool of sweat.

He could not have looked any wetter – or more exhausted – if he had just swum the Channel, and the kind-hearted lady standing behind me could not really be blamed for saying: 'Oh look at that poor little thing – they ought to be shot for making him run a mile in such a state.'

She would, no doubt, have felt even more sympathetic had she been at Nottingham on 28 March 1961, when Blazing Scent first appeared on the racecourse.

A late foal, he was still two months short of his second birthday that afternoon but, wearing blinkers, he came storming along in the last hundred yards to win a selling race by a couple of lengths.

Doug Smith rode the favourite that day – a two-year-old trained by Geoffrey Brooke – and, as he dismounted, he told Brooke that Blazing Scent should, if possible, be bought.

Acting on this advice, Messrs Bill Ball and Bill Carter paid 700 guineas for this little chesnut and sent him to George Todd who, at first sight, took an understandably poor view of this somewhat miserable-looking addition to his string.

Needless to say it did not take George Todd long to change his opinion, and by the end of that season Blazing Scent, ridden by Doug Smith and beating the very useful Old Tom – later to win a Lincolnshire Handicap – was winning a hotly contested nursery on Manchester November Handicap day.

He has been running ever since and, but for a somewhat unlucky disqualification at Ascot last year, there would not have been a season in which he did not win at least one race.

Doug Smith was at Newmarket last week to saddle Secret Ray and, addressing his jockey on the subject of Blazing Scent, he said, with foreknowledge based on personal experience, 'If that old so and so is anywhere near you a furlong out you've got no chance at all.'

So neither he nor anyone else with a memory was surprised when, having, as usual, been last for more than half a mile, the old so and so came scampering up the wide outside to catch Secret Ray and beat him by a length.

Blazing Scent was ridden with admirable coolness and precision by Tommy Cafferty, but if ever I saw a horse who knew exactly what he was doing, this was the one.

As he passed the leaders, his wise old head was cocked sideways watching them and if a horse's face could show emotion his, I'm prepared to bet, would have worn a smug smile of unconcealed delight.

The only moral to this story is that, as I've said before, by far the most important quality in a racehorse is invisible. After 48 races, 17 seasons and 11 victories, Blazing Scent still has that priceless quality intact.

You can give it any name you please – guts, honesty, enthusiasm or just the will to win. It does not show in a sales catalogue or a parade ring.

The greatest judge alive can't spot it in advance – but when you find a horse who has it, whatever his other shortcomings, you are a lucky man indeed.

21 June 1968

PERSIAN WAR NOW STANDS WITH THE GREATEST

The 1970 National Hunt meeting was, overall, a triumph in Ireland, so I hope I may be forgiven for beginning this account of it, not with the Gold Cup, which Irish horses so completely dominated, but with a moment in which they had no part at all.

It came on the Wednesday afternoon as Mr Henry Alper's Persian War skimmed clean and low over the last flight in the Champion Hurdle. Behind him lay not only 13 of the best hurdlers in training but also ten long months of doubt, disaster and defeat.

In that period he had run and been beaten seven times, had suffered and overcome a painful splint and an infirmity of the wind – and had even been accused of giving less than his all in a finish.

But that was in the past. Ahead lay the familiar Cheltenham hill – on which no horse had ever caught him – and the welcoming roar of a crowd which values courage above any other virtue.

In front throughout the final mile, Persian War had already faced and beaten half-a-dozen challengers and now the last of them, the gallant Major Rose, was storming up behind him.

There have been only two comparable moments in the history of the Champion Hurdle and now, as Persian War thrust out his handsome, honest head in answer to Jimmy Uttley's final call, there was no longer any shadow of a doubt that he is worthy to stand with Sir Ken and Hatton's Grace – the three greatest hurdlers to run at Cheltenham since the inaugural championship held forty-three years ago.

The race, as in his other two triumphs, had been dominated from start to finish by Mr Alper's colours. Bobby Moore, his pace-maker, led for the first four flights and Persian War, who took over there, had never been farther back than third.

His jumping, which has so often let him down of late, rose superbly to the great occasion. Every single flight was measured precisely and flicked away like a tiresome fly, so that for those behind, the slightest mistake or hesitation had to be retrieved the hard way.

And in one respect this flawless exhibition may have been decisive, for although Major Rose jumped well by his standards, the obstacles, to him, have always been just that – something to be overcome or, if need be, kicked out of the way – but never the positive advantage which Persian War made them look last week.

Behind the champion as he turned downhill for home, Escalus was where he had been from the start, tucked in, close up, never more than a foot from the inside rail. Josh Gifford, a little farther back, had steered an equally economic course on Major Rose, Coral Diver was plenty close enough and, down the hill, both Solomon II and Drumikill moved up to challenge.

For Solomon this was a particularly heroic effort. Having his second hard race in five days, he may even have headed Persian War two flights from home and, sixth in the end, had done the West Country proud.

For Scotland, Drumikill, too, ran his best race of the season. On softer ground, as Barry Brogan said afterwards, it would probably have been a repeat of last year's race, but now, having made his bid, Drumikill found the others quickening too much.

Going to the last, although Persian War was by no means at full stretch, Escalus and Coral Diver looked the principal dangers. But behind them, Major Rose, slightly taken off his feet coming down the hill, was in top gear again and on the flat it was he who threw down the only real challenge.

It was brushed aside, in the end, by a length and a half, but this wonderful little horse – who on the flat would give

Persian War at least two stone – had run his best race ever over hurdles.

Persian War leading the unplaced Solomon II at the last flight of the 1970 Champion Hurdle.

He could not quite pull it off, but no horse ever tried harder, no horse was ever better ridden and this, at his last N.H. meeting, was an appropriately brilliant achievement to crown Ryan Price's career as a trainer of high-class hurdlers.

A length and a half behind Major Rose, Escalus too ran the race of his life – reversing last year's running with Coral Diver (fourth, a neck away) and leaving a real hope that he may yet do even greater things for Queen Elizabeth the Queen Mother.

So once again Colin Davies had brought Persian War to his peak on the one day that mattered most – surely the only unanswerable proof of a trainer's skill.

And quite apart from his flawless riding at Cheltenham, Jimmy Uttley deserves a large share of the credit – for there have been times this season, notably at Nottingham last month, when he has had to bear criticism rather than risk over-straining Persian War too soon. On the Wednesday afternoon it all came right and no one who was there will easily forget it.

27 March 1970

MILL REEF: A MARVEL OF GRACE, SPEED AND POWER

It is twenty years since a winner of the Gimcrack Stakes last went on to win a Classic, but no one lucky enough to be present at York last Thursday afternoon can feel the slightest confidence that this rather gloomy record will stay intact in 1971.

For the 1970 Gimcrack Stakes (6f) produced one of the most remarkable and memorable sights ever seen on the Knavesmire – or for that matter any other English flat racecourse.

It is a comparative rarity to see *any* six-furlong race won by 10 lengths, but when that race is the championship of its class and contains the winners of sixteen other races, well, *then* the horse who turns it into a hollow uncompetitive procession deserves much more than just a second glance.

That is what Mr Paul Mellon's Mill Reef did last week – and he did it, what is more, on ground so soft that for several hours on the morning of the race his trainer, Ian Balding, was in two minds whether to run at all.

If Mr Mellon had not come specially to York to see his colt, it might well have been decided to play safe – and the York crowd would have been denied the sort of treat for which any lover of horses would go a long, long way.

The race itself needs little description because, from the moment Geoff Lewis allowed Mill Reef to move up between the leaders two furlongs out, the only conceivable question was by how far he would win. And the most extraordinary feature of his performance is that, from there on, though apparently cruising on a tight rein, he drew steadily further and further away from his desperately hard-ridden rivals.

The two of them who finished closest, Green God and Grand Chaudière, had filled the same positions (second and third) half a length and two lengths behind the unbeaten Swing Easy in the Richmond Stakes at Goodwood. And it may or may not be significant that Green God's trainer, Michael Jarvis, considered him certain to have improved since the Goodwood race, before which he had been off the course for two months.

By any calculation, therefore, Mill Reef can hardly be less than $9^{1/2}$ lengths in front of Swing Easy, whose record would, in many years, make him just about the best of his age.

And the exciting possibility is that there are now in training not one but two colts of this exceptional calibre – for Mill Reef was, after all, beaten a short head by My Swallow in the Prix Robert Papin.

After that race, having seen Mill Reef beforehand (looking only a shadow of his normal self), and considering the gruelling struggle he had against the combined strengths of My Swallow, Lester Piggott and a bad draw, I seriously wondered whether he would ever be quite the same again. Now, thanks to the skill and patience of his trainer – and to his own admirable constitution – those pessimistic doubts are all exploded.

Clearly that 'failure' has had no effect whatever – either mental or physical – on Mill Reef and I for one am more than ever convinced that My Swallow, good horse though he is, was a desperately lucky winner at Maisons Laffitte. The draw alone was enough, almost certainly, to excuse a short-head defeat, but, quite apart from that, Mill Reef, who had scarcely eaten at all for two days, never showed, either before or during the race, the zest and eagerness which have been such a notable feature of all his three other appearances.

By the sound of it, he and My Swallow may not meet again until next year's Two Thousand Guineas, but then – unless something very significant has occurred in the meanwhile – I have not the slightest doubt which my money will be on.

When a racehorse shows as much sheer speed as Mill Reef showed last week, the conventional reaction is to doubt his stamina, and last week there were many who compared the Gimcrack winner with Tudor Minstrel, of whose unforgettable Two Thousand Guineas his victory was indeed reminiscent.

But Tudor Minstrel was a tearaway who lost the Derby

principally because neither his brakes nor his steering worked properly at high speed.

Mill Reef, by contrast, may pull pretty hard, but Geoff Lewis was able to hold him in behind until halfway at York and, although he has yet to race around a bend, the impression one gets is of a handy, beautifully balanced colt. The interpretation of American pedigrees with regard to stamina on English courses is neither easy nor necessarily worthwhile, but it is a fact that Berkeley Springs, a half-sister to Mill Reef's dam, ran second in both the Oaks and One Thousand Guineas. She clearly got $1^1/2$ miles adequately on Oaks day, but later failed badly at that distance and was certainly better at a mile.

But although it is anyone's guess how far Mill Reef will stay as a three-year-old, no one who saw him storming past the post the other day – after six soggy furlongs – can seriously doubt his ability to last at least another two. Anyway, whatever his future, last week at York he was a marvel of grace, speed and power, and I for one can't wait to see him in action again.

28 August 1970

A FAREWELL TO MILL REEF

Fourteen years after cheating death on the gallops and operating table, Mr Paul Mellon's Mill Reef had to give the old enemy best last week. It was only the third defeat he ever suffered and, first on the racecourse, then at stud, his exploits made him one of the best known, best loved flat racehorses of all time.

Mill Reef at the National Stud.

My first two – very different – memories of Mill Reef are of gleaming, elegant perfection in the Royal Ascot paddock before the Coventry Stakes and of his woebegone, listless appearance at Maisons Laffitte before the first and most heroic of his 'failures'.

'*Le petit*,' an old French jockey muttered that evening – '*Le petit, mon dieu, quel cheval, quel coeur.*' He had ridden Ksar, they said, and, as Mill Reef, who had not eaten properly since leaving England, fought out that desperate duel with My Swallow, the old Frenchman had recognised something very special.

The fear that Mill Reef might never recover from that battle was gloriously buried in the Knavesmire mud on Gimcrack day and thereafter only the peerless Brigadier Gerard came between him and victory.

As a three-year-old his true greatness was first established in the Eclipse, confirmed when he almost literally ran away with the King George, finally underlined in gold on that unforgettable Paris afternoon when his familiar white noseband exploded out of a packed Arc de Triomphe field.

He showed the French his excellence once more, as a four-year-old in the Ganay, but then all the other battles were fought against illness, misfortune and pain.

With the help of his devoted friends at Kingsclere, Ian Balding, John Hallum, Bill Palmer and all the rest, thanks to the surgical genius of Edwin James Roberts, and thanks, above all, to his own good sense and courage – the battles were won.

So although Mill Reef could never run again, he was able to transmit his excellence – and thanks to Mr Mellon he did it at the National Stud.

Shirley Heights, Acamas, Fairy Footsteps, Wassl, Lashkari, Glint Of Gold, Diamond Shoal, King Of Clubs, Elegant Air, Paris Royal – the list is long and has not ended yet. Mill Reef's sons are already proving themselves at stud and as long as Thoroughbreds race, his name will appear in winning pedigrees.

But those who saw him run will never forget his ease and grace and courage and power. Let his epitaph come from a poem his owner wrote to commemorate the Gimcrack Stakes:

Remember me, all men who love the horse,
If hearts and spirits flag in after days;
Though small, I gave my all. I gave my heart.

7 February 1986

CAPTAIN CHRISTY'S GOLD CUP

The romance, heartbreak and unpredictable thrill of British jumping at its best was wrapped up in one neat package on Thursday afternoon of last week and presented to the Cheltenham crowd. The emotions with which we accepted the gift varied widely according to taste and prejudice, but as Bobby Beasley and Mrs Jane Samuel's Captain Christy galloped home ahead of The Dikler and Game Spirit I cannot believe that there was a man, woman or child at Cheltenham – or for that matter in front of a television set – able to watch completely unmoved.

In many hearts, of course, the feeling uppermost was one of grief or anger. Because, for the first time in his life and through absolutely no fault of his own, Pendil was loose and riderless as Captain Christy passed the post.

A moment earlier, sailing down the hill as smooth as silk after giving as flawless an exhibition of jumping as any favourite in the Gold Cup's history, the little horse had looked ideally poised for the late challenge which was Richard Pitman's and Fred Winter's battle-plan.

Ideally, that is, except for one important detail, because the plan in question had included a resolution not at any stage to track High Ken – the one really doubtful jumper in the field. And now, as High Ken took over the lead from Charlie Potheen at the top of the hill, Ron Barry moved The Dikler up into second place on the outside. Game Spirit was on the rails and so as they raced towards the third last – which has decided more races than any other single fence at Cheltenham – Richard Pitman found himself in a straitjacket between The Dikler and Game Spirit with High Ken's quarters staring him in the face.

What followed was straight out of a jumping jockey's nightmare, for Pendil had already measured his take-off when High Ken began to fall. There was no time to swerve or check, no chance even to pick up again and jump the fallen horse.

The favourite's legs were simply swept away as he landed and with them went twelve months of hopes and dreams, hard work and skill, worry and painstaking preparation.

But all those things lie behind every fancied runner in a race like this and now, as Ron Barry drove The Dikler into the second last in front, it seemed that history would be repeated.

And, in a way, it was, for the big horse jumped the last three fences as fast and accurately as fences can be jumped.

Just as he had a year ago, The Dikler, perfectly trained and superbly ridden, threw all his heart and strength into those three fences and the final hill. And this time, with no Pendil to catch, it should, by all reasonable calculations, have been more than enough.

But 'reasonable calculations' are no part of jumping's essence – and those who rely on them must expect regular disappointments. Pendil's downfall had demonstrated the harshness of the game, The Dikler its courage and beauty. And now, from a much less predictable quarter, came proof that sport can be the framework for real human achievement.

Just four years ago, Bobby Beasley was struggling unsuccessfully and unhappily to establish himself as an insurance salesman in, of all places, Slough. A brilliant career, entirely worthy of his famous family, lay in ruins behind him and it is hardly surprising that, for a while, he looked for brief oblivion in the bottle.

But Bobby's grandfather rode in steeplechases when over seventy. There is steel in the blood and, giving himself one last slim chance, Bobby Beasley went back to Ireland.

Not everyone had forgotten. Paddy Murphy gave him his first ride at Leopardstown, Alcoholics Anonymous helped him overcome the drink and, most important of all, his old friend Pat Taaffe, only recently launched as a trainer himself, asked him to come and ride schooling.

So it was that when Pat bought Captain Christy from Major Joe Pidcock for £10,000, Bobby Beasley became his first regular professional rider. Together they won the Irish Sweeps Hurdle – and the first stage of Bobby's incredible comeback was complete.

But what Captain Christy had done he might also easily have undone, for when put to fences this season he combined brilliance with hazardous carelessness and, in his only two visits to England, succeeded in leaving his rider on the floor.

It does not require much imagination, I think, to visualise the pressure on Pat Taaffe – whether expressed or implied – to find a new jockey for Captain Christy. 'He's too old.' 'He's gone.' 'He's over the hill.' 'And anyway, they never come back.' Such sneers are common currency on the racecourse and, however stoutly he disregards them, a trainer's first responsibility is to his owner, not his jockey.

But Pat Taaffe, whose own association with Tom Dreaper was unshakably based on mutual loyalty, knew both his man and his horse.

Together he and Bobby set about curbing Captain Christy's headstrong ways. They schooled him on 'nearly every racecourse in Ireland' and slowly, with the help of a double-ringed snaffle, the horse was persuaded to settle down.

Given the choice, even then, Pat Taaffe would not have started Captain Christy in the Gold Cup but, as with Bula, the owner insisted.

It is a moving thought, in fact, that, but for Bula's injury, the Gold Cup finish might have been fought out between two novice 'chasers neither of whose trainers had wanted them to run!

That, then, was the background to the handsome bay horse and the haggard, toothless man who for nearly three miles of the Gold Cup had crept quietly round almost unnoticed behind their famous rivals.

And now, as Pendil went down and The Dikler hit the front, they came through together to keep the most vital date of both their lives.

Soothed and settled as never before, Captain Christy had not so far made a serious mistake and, jumping the second last at The Dikler's heels, he landed upsides.

Round the final bend it was Ron Barry's whip that showed; Bobby Beasley had scarcely moved, and going to the last a length ahead the Captain was clearly in control.

But fate had one more card to play, for now Captain Christy's old fallibility recurred. Taking at least half a stride too many, he hit the fence at least a foot too low – and pitched precariously on the landing side.

'If I fall off this time, I'll *streak* past the winning post,' Bobby Beasley had promised me the day before, but that interesting spectacle was never really on the cards. He sat like a rock and the only result of Captain Christy's blunder was to give one last twist to this uniquely dramatic contest. For The Dikler, hurling his heart beyond the fence, had snatched a half-length lead.

Having already proved now completely that his horsemanship has survived the years, Bobby Beasley had the chance now to show that he is still a great jockey as well.

Seizing it gratefully, he gathered Captain Christy together and drove him home to such effect that, at the line, gallantly though The Dikler struggled on, there were five lengths to spare.

That margin, and the power with which the winner finished, makes it impossible, I believe, to say with any certainty what would have happened had Pendil stood up.

Certainly he could not have been going more easily when disaster struck – but then so was Captain Christy and, except for that last fence lapse, he would have beaten The Dikler virtually without coming off the bit.

Bred by Mr George Williams at the Carricknaveen Stud in Co. Cork, Captain Christy is by Mon Capitaine out of an unraced Bowsprit mare called Christy's Bow.

Bought originally for only 290 guineas at Goff's November Sales in 1967, he won two flat races before Major Pidcock acquired him and the Major can recall with pride that he both trained and rode the Gold Cup winner to win his first race over hurdles.

22 March 1974

NIGHT NURSE
REPEATS THE DOSE

Perfect jumping ground was transformed by the Wednesday into a well-trodden quagmire – precisely the conditions, most of us believed, in which Night Nurse would find it hardest to retain his title in the Champion Hurdle.

Bird's Nest by contrast – or so the theory went – would be in his element. A flood of money made him 6 to 4 favourite and, surely for the first time in history, a reigning Champion Hurdler was allowed to start at 15 to 2.

Which just goes to show that the bookmakers, like many other supposedly well-informed people, don't know everything, because no one had told either Night Nurse or Bird's Nest about their preferences and in two entirely different ways, one glorious and one inglorious, they proceeded to prove us all absolutely and comprehensively wrong.

It was no surprise to see Night Nurse set off in front, no surprise that he jumped like a stag inspired, and no surprise that Bird's Nest, Dramatist, Beacon Light and Monksfield were able, without apparent difficulty, to keep good places close behind him.

Considering our views about Night Nurse's prospects in the going, it was not even a surprise when Beacon Light headed him at the third last, with Monksfield and Dramatist almost in line abreast on their outside. But then, suddenly, the actors began to depart dramatically from their scripts.

For one thing, Bird's Nest, close behind the leading four, came under pressure, lost his place and began to hang badly. Andy Turnell, unluckily concussed the day before, had not been allowed to ride him, but absolutely no blame attached to Steve Knight who took his place.

Unless there was some excuse unknown to me, Bird's Nest was beaten before the race began in earnest – and then showed his discontent with the situation by veering violently across the course.

But by then, as I say, the race was on, and, far from being swallowed up by his pursuers, as had seemed so likely seconds earlier, Night Nurse had quickened to hold his vital inside berth around the final turn. That first battle was, in a way, the decisive one, because if the three challengers had been able to cut him off, the champion's position would have been almost impossible.

But Paddy Broderick knew that, Night Nurse answered his call to arms – and Beacon Light was brushed aside like a leaf in an autumn gale.

There were still battles to be fought, however, because both Monksfield and Dramatist rose to the last within half a length of the champion. His answer this time was a superlative leap even by his high standards.

The photographs have not really done it justice but it gained

Night Nurse (right) taking the last in the 1977 Champion Hurdle with Monksfield (left) and Dramatist.

Night Nurse at least a length and, doggedly though the other two fought to win it back, the race was over half-way up the hill.

I have seldom seen a better exhibition of total determination than Night Nurse's over the last three flights, and as he and Paddy Broderick rode back, not even the ranks of Bird's Nest's supporters could forbear to cheer.

Quite apart from Paddy's riding and Night Nurse's courage, this, I need hardly say again, was an almost miraculous feat of training by Peter Easterby. Before Christmas he had a sick horse who had just been beaten out of sight at Newcastle. Since then, with only one race (Kempton on Boxing Day), he has coaxed Night Nurse back to the peak of health, strength and enthusiasm we saw last week.

25 March 1977

SEA PIGEON
STANDS ALONE

The only sad thing about Sea Pigeon's second Waterford Crystal Champion Hurdle was that Jonjo O'Neill could only watch it from the TV commentary box. But, as Jonjo was the first to admit, not even he could have give Sea Pigeon a cooler or more economical ride than his unflappable understudy John Francome.

It all looks so easy now in retrospect, but the fact is that Tony Carroll and Meladon (whom Stan Mellor had bought three days earlier to act as pacemaker for Pollardstown) did their job so well that at one time, with only Going Straight attempting to give chase, there was an uncomfortably wide hiatus between the leading pair and their pursuers.

As Meladon and Pollardstown (on whom Philip Blacker never made the common mistake of ignoring his pacemaker) turned uphill at the far end of the course, it looked all too possible that Sea Pigeon might have to come out of the pack on his own and conceivably waste his speed in the process. But all was well. Meladon had not after all been able to go quite fast enough and by the top of the hill the pack was baying on his heels, with Sea Pigeon cruising happily among them towards the outside.

'Happily' may be a slight exaggeration, because John Francome told us later that the old horse was always finding the going hard work. It was certainly a good deal heavier than Thursday's, but 'hard work' or not Sea Pigeon was still impatient for his head down the hill and as Daring Run challenged Pollardstown going to the last, the Champion was poised in third place only a length behind them.

But there, for a tantalising while, John Francome chose to stay. Sea Pigeon jumped the last beautifully, but so did the other two, and with Daring Run landing just in front as they set off up the hill, the cat gave the mice one more short, final breathing space.

Pollardstown used it bravely to fight off the Irish challenge, but then, without even feeling for his whip, John Francome gave the signal.

At the last flight in the 1981 Champion Hurdle, John Francome and Sea Pigeon (right) are about to bear down on Pollardstown and Daring Run, who are out of the picture to the right. Trying to keep up with Sea Pigeon is Starfen.

We scribes often talk or write about 'acceleration', 'a superlative turn of speed' and the difference made by 'a touch of class'. But now unforgettably all those boring old phrases were brought vividly to life as Sea Pigeon galloped majestically into the history books.

The oldest Champion Hurdler since Hatton's Grace in 1951, he has now won more money than any other gelding either jumping or on the flat.

Sea Pigeon is quite simply a marvel, now without any doubt the most popular racehorse in training and, like his supremely skilful trainer, an all-the-year-rounder.

Of his beaten rivals last week, Pollardstown and Daring Run

both obviously ran the races of their lives and Sea Pigeon's stable companion Starfen was a very honourable fourth.

Heighlin, who made a bad mistake at halfway, had not looked particularly full of beans in the paddock, Bird's Nest dropped himself right out at the top of the hill before changing his mind again to finish eighth and Celtic Ryde, just in front of him, had never been seen with a chance.

There is in fact no reason obvious to me why, barring accidents or the appearance of something new, Sea Pigeon should not go on to proving that among modern hurdlers he stands alone.

27 March 1981

JUST HOW DO YOU REPLACE SILVER BUCK OR THE DIKLER?

For all followers of British jumping, whether their memories are long or short, last week was an especially sad one, bringing as it did the deaths of Silver Buck and The Dikler, two of the best and most popular steeplechasers of the last twenty years.

For The Dikler, at least, death came after a happy retirement at the age of twenty-one. Mrs Boddington sadly decided that another winter would mean more suffering than pleasure. But although it seems far longer than seven years since Silver Buck won his first race in England, at Catterick in 1977, he was still only twelve last week when a sudden haemorrhage killed him while at exercise.

Mrs Dickinson had never intended to aim him at the top prizes this season, but was understandably confident of finding some suitable races in which the biggest N.H. prize money winner of all time could make a dignified and successful farewell.

And then, by rights, Silver Buck should have been able to look forward to many happy years – either comfortable idleness or, much more likely for such an intelligent, well-balanced horse, entertaining activity out hunting or in some other sphere.

Although, in the end, they became so very different, Silver Buck and The Dikler started life in much the same way. Both went out hunting. Both ran in point-to-points and both, by the sound of it, were a long way from armchair rides!

The first time Silver Buck appeared on a point-to-point course his behaviour (diving into a wire fence the moment he was mounted) caused the father of his jockey, Timmy Jones, to remark that, while he personally had no objection to giving a horse a 'school' on the course, he did feel it was a bit much to break one in there!

But though by no means an easy ride in his early days – and always apt to pull up when he hit the front – Silver Buck in his prime was, I imagine, a much more straightforward ride than The Dikler.

After winning his second point-to-point in a brilliant time, Mrs August's big bay ran out in his third and throughout his career, both at home and on the racecourse, it took strong, first-rate horsemen all their strength and skill to ride him.

So it was all the more a triumph, for The Dikler himself and for his owner's step-daughter Jackie Boddington that, in retirement, he adapted calmly to hunter trials, shows and even dressage!

On one occasion, faced with a double bank, he showed his contempt by clearing it in one and at Woburn I remember him doing his famous trick of standing, quite immovable, for ten minutes at one end (the wrong end) of an arena.

But come to think of it, that was the day Crisp so delighted everyone by refusing at a children's show jump, pitching Richard Pitman over his head!

As I wrote in the foreword to Mary Comyns Carr's delightful book, *The Dikler And His Circle*, it would be a grave exaggeration to say that The Dikler has *always* been one of my favourite horses. On at least two occasions I deeply regretted his presence in the winner's enclosure – feeling, to tell the truth, that the world in general and the racecourse in particular would be a better, happier place if he was pulling a plough or doing some other form of hard labour!

But even then – I wanted Pendil to win the 1973 Gold Cup and my feelings after Proud Tarquin's disqualification from the 1974 Whitbread are not too difficult to imagine – I have to admit that it all depended on your point of view!

I have still never seen anything to equal the ferocity with which Ron Barry and The Dikler attacked the last two fences at Cheltenham in 1973 and the truth is that throughout his career The Dikler was *never* dull.

He could occasionally infuriate, he could sometimes disappoint even those who knew and loved him best. But above all, he was *exciting*. You might never be sure just what would happen next – but you could bet your boots it would be well worth watching.

Similarly, I often seemed to be cheering for one of Silver Buck's opponents – usually Night Nurse! – and was one of those poor benighted idiots who thought he did not truly stay the Gold Cup distance. But the day he proved us all gloriously wrong was still a happy one – and so were many others spent watching him in action.

Silver Buck was in many ways a typical 'Dickinson horse' – beautifully schooled, carefully placed and admirably ridden. Father and son saddled him to win many times and it is a real tragedy that now the third member of that famous family team will never do so in her own right.

To Mrs Dickinson, to Mrs Feather and to all the lucky men who rode and had to do with him, Silver Buck's premature death must mean the loss of an old and much-loved friend. They will be very, very lucky to find another like him.

28 September 1984

DAWN RUN: SHE GAVE US SO MUCH

Only one horse has ever managed to win both a Champion Hurdle and a Cheltenham Gold Cup but that unique distinction is only one reason why the death of Dawn Run overshadowed everything last week.

Quite apart from all her various victories and defeats, Dawn Run had a place in the hearts of her admirers to which, in recent jumping history, only Arkle's can be compared. In terms of supremacy over her contemporaries, of course, she never approached the great 'chaser's lonely pre-eminence. While the serious mistakes Arkle made can be counted on one hand, there was always an unpredictable fallibility about Dawn Run's jumping, of which, alas, last week's headlong fall was a final, fatal demonstration.

Sexual egalitarians may not like it but, in the traditional world of racing, ladies are still regarded and treated rather differently from men.

Dawn Run, a stubborn, determined mare with a mind of her own, happened to be owned by an equally stubborn, determined lady. No doubt there will be some who 'blame' Mrs Charmian Hill for sending her beloved champion to France again but that is a particularly unsympathetic brand of wisdom-after-the-event.

I prefer to remember the great mare and her diminutive, well-over-sixty owner storming up Paddy Mullins's gallops with the trainer murmuring philosophically, 'Well, they both enjoy it, you see . . .'

Whatever anyone says now – and whatever your view of the

various jockey-changes – Mrs Hill's relationship with Dawn Run was one of the most remarkable features of the story, and about as far as you can get from the remote, impersonal, stocks-and-shares attitude to which so many modern owners are now reduced.

But to anyone who enjoys watching good brave horses run and jump, last week's tragedy brings, first and foremost, a selfish sense of loss. We have been cruelly deprived of something invaluable and irreplaceable – a loved, respected heroine-worshipped friend from whom we had every reason to expect more golden moments of pleasure and excitement.

Now we have only memories – but, heaven knows, they are vivid enough.

Liverpool, 1983: when, running twice in two days, Dawn Run served the first clear notice to us here in England of her special quality. After giving weight and an effortless beating all round in a handicap, she led the reigning Champion Hurdler Gaye Brief over the last and then, though outpaced on the flat, fought back with the dogged hatred of defeat which has since become her most personal trademark.

Ironically, Gaye Brief was there again last week – though only, by the sound of it, a mere unwilling shadow of his real self.

Another old rival, Buck House, is, alas, already dead – an even unluckier victim of colic while turned out at grass. I remember him trying in vain to stretch Dawn Run at Navan the first time she jumped fences in public – and those who were lucky enough to be there have a last joint memory of this great, doomed pair when they met in the controversial match which was to be Dawn Run's last victory.

But, of course, one memory stands far out above the rest and, remembering how beaten Dawn Run looked between the last two fences of the Tote Gold Cup, it is still hard to believe the form book.

But it *did* happen. With just an outside chance of second place – much more likely third – Jonjo O'Neill and Dawn Run took the race by the throat and wrestled from it an impossible victory.

Of course, the 5lb allowance helped; of course it was sad to see Wayward Lad robbed of what should have been his finest hour. But no one who saw Jonjo and Dawn Run that day will ever forget the magic of their strength and resolution.

Dawn Run wins the Champion Hurdle in 1984.

The knowledge now that we shall never see it again – and that Dawn Run will never have a chance to pass it on – is hard indeed to bear. But we can remember – and be grateful for – the thrills and joy she gave us.

The only tiny consolation at Auteuil on Friday was that when disaster struck five hurdles from home it was at least instantaneous. Dawn Run's death was no less of a shock for Mrs Hill, Paddy Mullins and his family, but it can only have caused the great mare herself a fleeting pain, if that. To her devoted trainer, who had not wanted to run in France, and to his son Tony, who had ridden Dawn Run more than any other jockey, one can only offer sympathy – useless but nonetheless heartfelt. The gap left in their lives must be larger and less fillable than any.

Lastly, it must be added that no blame of any kind can be laid on Michel Chirol, the 41-year-old Frenchman with whom, for some reason unknown and incomprehensible to me, Mrs Hill and her son had decided to replace Tony Mullins. Until the fall, Dawn Run looked perfectly happy and Chirol, heartbroken but otherwise unhurt, is confident that she would have left her rivals well behind the moment he asked.

As for the fall, the truth is that, throughout her career over hurdles, as well as fences, Dawn Run had never been a consistently accurate jumper. She has always been apt, without warning, to perpetrate sudden comprehensive blunders – either standing off too far at hurdles or, as at Liverpool, virtually ignoring a fence.

It has never made any difference who was riding. Jonjo O'Neill achieved something close to a clear round in the Gold Cup only to be ejected at Liverpool and Tony Mullins had suffered the same fate earlier at Cheltenham.

So although I still personally deplore the decision to replace Tony Mullins, it was not, of itself, the reason for Dawn Run's death. It is, in fact, pointless, invidious and cruel even to speak of 'blame'. The great mare died with no pain, doing the thing she loved best.

She had given the human race far more than we ever gave her and for that, with gratitude, she will always be honoured and remembered.

4 July 1986

WAYWARD LAD GOES
WITH GRATITUDE

Whatever your view of the current controversy about Wayward Lad's retirement, he cannot be allowed to leave the scene he has graced so memorably for seven seasons without a word of gratitude and tribute.

Bred by Mrs A.M.D. Hutchinson, Wayward Lad was originally bought at Doncaster by the Barnsley trainer Steve Norton. Steve sold him, as an unbroken three-year-old, to a partnership of three – David Ingham, in whose colours Wayward Lad ran his early races, John Garner and Gordon Thewless; Gordon bought a 60 per cent share and gave it to his wife Shirley as a birthday present.

After a couple of years, Messrs Ingham and Garner sold their shares to Les Abbott, the part-owner with whom Mrs Thewless is now in dispute about the horse's future.

When Tony Dickinson was first asked to train Wayward Lad, he sent him to be broken by Tom Corrie, then training in Shropshire. A girl working for Tom, whose name I have, regrettably, been unable to discover, seems to have been responsible for Wayward Lad's early education. She made a fine job of it because, according to Mrs Dickinson, he has almost always been a joy to ride at home.

'Just as long as you go gently with him,' she says. 'If you sit nice and quiet, he'll do anything, but at one time, if anyone tried to kick him along in a hurry, he would stand stock still, refuse to go either backwards or forwards and get in a terrible tizzy!'

It was decided not to run Wayward Lad as a three-year-old

but Mrs Dickinson remembers taking him and a few others to school at Market Rasen.

'Robert Earnshaw rode him,' she says, 'and he went so well, we came home thinking, By Gum, this might be some horse.'

No doubt it was partly that school which caused Wayward Lad to start an 85 to 40 favourite for his first novice hurdle at Leicester. Ridden, for the first and only time, by Colin Tinkler, he won hard held. In eight hurdle races that season, he was only beaten twice.

I remember one of his defeats, by John Francome and Woodford Prince in the three-mile Philip Cornes Saddle of Gold. A horse called Corbière finished third and the result was sometimes used, quite wrongly, to demonstrate that Wayward Lad 'does not stay three miles'!

Trained, in turn, by all three members of the Dickinson family, the elegant dark brown gelding, a good 16 hands 1 inch but so well proportioned that he often looks smaller, was ridden by nine different jockeys, only two of whom failed to win on him.

In 55 races over fences and hurdles, he won 28 times on 16 different courses, finished second in 12 of his races and third in six. Although twice deprived of his rider, once by a stumble after landing safe and once by a collision with the rails, Wayward Lad has never fallen in his life. Pulled up in the 1984 Gold Cup, he only ever ran six times unplaced.

So, unlike too many other horses, especially on the flat, his record total of £217,923 prize money won in this country does bear some recognisable relation to the entertainment he has provided. Only Dawn Run has won more as a jumper and, of course, her total included prizes gained in France and Ireland.

Considering how consistent he has been in the long run, it is amazing how often we so-called 'experts' have been wrong about Wayward Lad. After his novice 'chase season, for instance, *Timeform* wrote, with some reason: 'At the moment Wayward Lad's jumping lets him down far too often and his problems in that department will have to be ironed out if he is to have any chance of fulfilling the highest hopes.'

Well, they were ironed out, thanks largely to Robert Earnshaw, who took over from Tommy Carmody as stable jockey. But

Wayward Lad's only defeat in seven races that season still managed to convince some people, me among them, that he 'did not truly stay three miles'. He certainly looked to run out of something three fences from home when Lesley Ann challenged him at Cheltenham but, as we soon found out, it was not stamina.

Because, the next season – Michael Dickinson's *annus mirabilis* – Wayward Lad contributed manfully to all the stable's extraordinary records. He only supplied two victories of the 120 Michael trained but, in his first King George VI 'Chase, he was one of a unique 12 winners the trainer sent out that Boxing Day.

A happy ending to the wrangle over Wayward's Lad's retirement. After the twelve-year-old had been put up for sale to dissolve the partnership of his owners, he is reunited at Doncaster Sales with Mrs Monica Dickinson, whose husband Tony had just bought the horse for 42,000 guineas. Wayward Lad was subsequently sent to the USA to spend the rest of his days with his former trainer, the Dickinsons' son Michael.

Wayward Lad has been wonderfully sound throughout his career and the only lameness Mrs Dickinson can remember was a bruised and/or pricked foot which interrupted his preparation for the 'Michael Dickinson' Gold Cup. He still managed to finish third of the famous five and, although the 'does not stay three miles' canard has long ago been exploded, the fact is that Cheltenham is one of the very few courses on which Wayward Lad has consistently tried and failed.

Two more King George VI 'Chases were to follow and, after some comparative disappointments in the 1984–5 season, Wayward Lad, reunited with John Francome, reminded us just how good he still was in his first Whitbread Gold Label at Aintree.

That race was to give him his triumphant farewell last month, but the two memories I shall treasure as much as all the triumphs are of the prize he never won.

There were two heroes in Dawn Run's Gold Cup, for let it never be forgotten that Wayward Lad came there to win the race halfway up the Cheltenham hill. It was only the irresistible combination of Jonjo O'Neill's determination and the great mare's heart that wore him down – that and the Cheltenham hill.

He flung himself at the last fence this year too, and headed Cybrandian for one glorious moment. But then the hill intervened again and now, alas, Wayward Lad will never beat it.

16 April 1987

DESERT ORCHID'S WHITBREAD TRIUMPH CAPS DAVID ELSWORTH'S YEAR

One of life's greatest pleasures is watching something done as well as it can be done, and a huge crowd at Sandown Park last Saturday afternoon was lucky enough to have that pleasure twice over.

No horse can ever have jumped 24 consecutive steeplechase fences much better or more boldly than Desert Orchid did to win the 32nd Whitbread Gold Cup and I honestly do not believe that a Whitbread winner has ever been given a cooler or more stylish ride.

Until a few strides before the last fence, Simon Sherwood did not visibly move a muscle and, having scarcely changed his hands from start to finish, the first time he took either off the reins was to give Desert Orchid a triumphant left-handed slap of congratulations as they passed the post.

With no fallers, no apparent injuries and only a few not inexplicable disappointments, this was, in fact, as near 'perfect' a steeplechase as you could hope to find. I have had the good fortune to see all 32 Whitbread Gold Cups and my guess is that only Mill House (1967) and Queen Elizabeth the Queen Mother's Special Cargo (1984) have given comparable pleasure to their audience.

But at Whitsbury, where David Elsworth trains Desert Orchid for Richard Burridge and his father, all this, for most of the previous week, had seemed an extremely improbable dream.

This time last year, if you remember, Desert Orchid had been plagued by corns before the Whitbread and, when the race itself was run on firm ground, the nation's most popular grey found jumping so uncomfortable that Colin Brown had to pull him up.

Last Monday morning Rodney Boult, who is both Elsworth's head lad and Desert Orchid's regular rider at home, came back with a gloomy report from their morning canter. When the nine-year-old's shoes were removed, a small corn was discovered and history seemed to be on the verge of painful repetition.

Despite twice-daily laser treatment and constant poulticing, Desert Orchid was still lame on Wednesday morning. The shoes came off again and from that moment, until he was finally plated for Sandown with special rubber pads under the shoes, his precious feet were either on grass or in a horsebox.

Luckily, the grass at Whitsbury was plentiful and the stable's star was carried up to the gallops in style to work barefoot.

Needless to say, Elsworth's vet, Jan Puzio, his blacksmith, Paul Henderson, Desert Orchid's devoted stable lass, Janice Coyle, and the rest of the Whitsbury staff all played their part in the battle.

Like most racing triumphs, in fact, this was a matter of teamwork – and, since the result was a joy for so many of us, the whole team deserves both credit and our gratitude.

After only two fences on Saturday, it was clear that their hard work had been worthwhile. No horse whose feet were hurting ever skipped quite so high, wide and handsome over Sandown's first fence and open ditch.

A bundle of eager, grey muscle in the paddock, Desert Orchid had sweated up rather less than usual.

'Rarin' to go' is a weak understatement of how he looked and, although I know it cannot be entirely true, his ears seem, in my mind's eye, to have been cheerfully pricked throughout the day!

To Simon Sherwood's surprise and relief, there was never any argument over who was going to make the running. Like the rest of us, he had rather expected either Run And Skip or Lean Ar Aghaidh to take Desert Orchid on and being left to his own devices was an unexpected bonus.

That suited the leader fine and Simon confirms my memory (and the message of the video) that Desert Orchid's jumping was quicksilver-fast and accurate throughout.

Just occasionally he stood back what for other, lesser horses, might have been dangerously far – and always landed safely, far out the other side.

As a result, never seriously challenged, scarcely taking hold of the bit, he was a perfect picture of relaxation, lobbing calmly along without a care in the world.

Behind him Run And Skip, the horse who matched strides with Dawn Run for so much of that other great steeplechasing occasion, the 1986 Gold Cup, was always close up and Memberson ran a fine race for much further than might have been expected.

Lean Ar Aghaidh, last year's hero, looked extremely well, went down with noticeable zest and held a good position during the first circuit. But this time, with only a two-week gap, the strain of his much less happy experience round Aintree had, after all, left its mark. Halfway down the Railway second time, a sad Guy Landau began to pull him up – at just about the same place where Desert Orchid opted out a year ago.

Now, by contrast, the grey marvel was up there cruising in the lead and it was now, after jumping the three close fences, that Simon Sherwood took the calculated risk of giving him a breather. Calmly allowing Run And Skip through inside to take the lead, he might, for all the notice he took, have been hacking to some unimportant October meet. Yet hard on his heels as they galloped across to the Pond sat two even more serious dangers – Peter Scudamore on Strands Of Gold and Jimmy Frost, longing to make the most of his first public appearance on Kildimo.

Both these jockeys had ridden flawless tactical races and Strands Of Gold, who gave Peter that dreadful fall at Becher's, had repaid him now by jumping well, bidding to follow in the footsteps of Andy Pandy, who also fell at Becher's in 1977 before coming up to win the Whitbread.

But turning up the hill, Strands Of Gold could do no more and it was another bit of history which looked like being repeated. For Kildimo had beaten Desert Orchid when they met at Wincanton and now, ominously, his head showed in front between the last two fences.

At such a moment, 99 jockeys out of 100 would have gone for the whip but Simon Sherwood did not even pick his up.

'The last thing Desert Orchid wants is to be bullied,' he says. 'The only time I even squeezed was going to the last and just after. He did it all himself.'

Desert Orchid and Kildimo almost inseparable at the last fence of the 1988 Whitbread.

Both horses met the last dead right and jumped it well but, somehow, as they landed, you knew it was all over. In the stands we were doing our best to let them hear the news back in Whitsbury and all three jockeys agree that the noise – which you seldom hear at all in a finish – was something entirely new in their experience.

So, still without even being shown the whip, Desert Orchid galloped the last furlong of much the longest race he has ever completed. He did it cheerfully, as if quite prepared to go round again, and for quite a while afterwards many of his admirers found it hard to see very clearly and difficult to speak at all!

I remember when Mill House won, how the crowd ran up past the rhododendrons to be there to welcome him and it happened again now. The noise and atmosphere in the winner's circle was such that almost any horse would have regarded it with some suspicion. But not Desert Orchid. Ears pricked, he walked straight in.

As Lady Thomson, formerly Mrs Tom Dreaper, said next day, 'He *is* like Arkle. He knows they are *his* public and he loves it.'

Kildimo, beautifully ridden by Jimmy Frost, was beaten 2¹/₂ lengths in the end, with Strands Of Gold third and the comparatively inexperienced Proud Pilgrim a highly respectable fourth. He had fallen three times in his last six races and to get round so well in this company was a triumph.

Apart from Lean Ar Aghaidh, the only other 'disappointment' was Gee-A.

'I had to drop him out to get the trip,' Gee Armytage said. 'But he hated being behind and when I said, "Let's go" he said, "Not on your life!"'

Desert Orchid's 21st victory guaranteed David Elsworth a richly deserved first trainer's championship. Indeed, his prize money total is now only £3,000 behind Michael Dickinson's all-time record.

But the 32nd Whitbread was not a matter of records, figures or money. It was simply a demonstration that, given the right horse, the right course and a sunny day, British racing in general, and British steeplechasing in particular, does still have the power to lift your heart above the gloom and violence of the 'normal' world.

The wonderful thing about Desert Orchid is, touch wood, that he is only nine. As he goes back to enjoy a summer holiday with several of his sisters at the Burridge farm, we can look forward to seeing him again.

'I am glad he did not run in the Gold Cup,' Charter Party's trainer David Nicholson said with feeling, and, who knows? Now that the left-handed bogey has been beaten once at Liverpool, it would be a brave man who laid long odds against Desert Orchid winning a Gold Cup one day. I hated the thought of seeing him stagger exhausted up the Sandown hill last week and no fear was ever made more gloriously redundant.

28 April 1988

TRIPTYCH CHANGES HER MIND

Triptych, bought by Peter Brant for $3.4 million at Alan Clore's dispersal sale, had one of her rare non-going days in the Prix Ganay. Steve Cauthen tended to blame himself but there did seem a possibility that the great mare might have opted for an easy life.

So it was with sinking hearts that we watched the early stages of the Hanson Coronation Cup last week.

Triptych only had three opponents but they were not just any old three – the St Leger winner Moon Madness, last year's Vermeille winner Bint Pasha and Kahyasi's distinguished tail-swishing stable-companion Infamy, who won five of her six races in the second half of last season.

The trouble was that, for the first mile last Thursday, Triptych showed no sign whatever of wanting to take any active part. The ground was probably firmer than she likes these days and, sulking along at the back, she looked like a member of some radical teaching union refusing, on grounds of principle, to supervise a children's game of Follow My Leader.

To his eternal credit, Steve Cauthen sat like a mouse, humouring Triptych's every whim. He must have been starting to despair when, suddenly, for no recognisable reason, the great mare changed her mind.

From last place, four or five lengths behind her nearest rival, she suddenly switched on such an effortless burst of power that Cauthen, who had been half expecting to finish tailed off, found himself in serious danger of hitting the front too soon.

In fact he did so, and the moment Triptych overhauled

Infamy and Moon Madness, she immediately began to pull up. 'That's enough, young man,' you could hear her saying – and, luckily, it was.

9 June 1988

Triptych (Steve Cauthen) going to the start of the 1988 Coronation Cup.

Over five seasons Triptych ran in 41 races. She won 14, of which 12 were Pattern events, nine of them Group 1. She reached the first four in 19 further races, of which 18 were Group 1.

Racing in six different countries, she was ridden by 15 different jockeys and won the equivalent of more than £1,500,000.

Poor Triptych. She had one last slice of racecourse luck when Lesotho's jockey failed to make the weight after beating her in the Prix du Prince d'Orange. But that was all.

Taken to Kentucky to be covered by Mr Prospector, the great mare was killed in a horrible freakish accident. A truck had been driven into her paddock one night and, for some unknown reason, Triptych galloped headlong into it, suffering fatal injuries.

People

Terry Biddlecombe's farewell to race-riding. In the unsaddling enclosure at Cheltenham on 14 March 1974 are (left to right): Johnny Haine, Vic Soane, Tommy Carberry, Terry Biddlecombe, Taffy Salaman, Richard Pitman, David Nicholson (obscured) and Ron Barry.

Most of the fun that this book describes has come from horses, so it is not surprising that they and their exploits have taken up most of the first four chapters. But racing depends on people too and, to tell the truth, if I had to take just one chapter to keep me happy on a desert island, I fancy this might be the one. Brief and inadequate though they are, these twenty sketches bring me back enough memories to fill a dozen books.

Can it really be thirty-three years since I first met Jimmy Snow in that Redcar press room – or twenty-eight since Edward Courage dreamed up the Farrell Brookshaw Fund from the depths of his own wheelchair? It grew, steadily, into the Injured Jockeys' Fund – and the best decision that fund's trustees ever made was to ask Queen Elizabeth the Queen Mother to be our Patron.

How could I have the nerve to write such a condescending review of Dick Francis's first novel, Dead Cert – especially since (as the note admits) I was so much involved in Tony Richardson's unsuccessful attempt to film it! Who knows how many more millions Dick would have made from his twenty-nine bestsellers if we had done Dead Cert a bit better? Twenty-nine books – can you believe it? Every one produced dead on time and their author still exactly the same modest, unspoiled man he was the day Devon Loch collapsed. If, as I imagine, it was that disaster which prompted Michael Joseph to ask Dick for an autobiography (The Sport of Queens), then Devon Loch's fall must have been one of the luckiest bits of 'bad luck' you ever heard of.

Although eight of its subjects are dead, this is not meant to be a sad chapter. Jayne Thompson's death was indeed a tragedy and so was Brian Taylor's. But it is difficult to remember Brian without a smile – and impossible to feel sad for very long about Bill Tellwright and John Thorne, men who died doing their favourite thing.

As for the two rather introspective pieces about Lester Piggott, at least they end with a bet 'that he will one day be back where he belongs, in the winner's enclosure'. I certainly do not claim to have anticipated those happy Breeders' Cup scenes at Belmont Park – but the eleven-times champion has never been all that easy a man to predict!

QUEEN ELIZABETH
THE QUEEN MOTHER

British National Hunt racing could not survive in anything like its present form without enthusiasm. It needs a regular supply of men and women who, while hoping for the best, are quite prepared to put up with the worst. Only fools start owning jumpers with the idea of making money and no one goes on riding them for long without recognising that, unless you love it, the kicks are seldom worth the halfpence.

But, 'unless you love it' – that is the point – and at that momentous Windsor Castle dinner party in 1949 it was, I am pretty sure, the point which caught Queen Elizabeth's imagination as she listened to the late Lord Mildmay.

No man ever had more right to tell a Queen about the triumphs and disasters of the game and sadly, one of those disasters – the neck injury which had already spoilt his and Cromwell's chance in the 1948 Grand National – almost certainly caused Lord Mildmay's death by drowning the following year. But when he died, the greatest and most valuable legacy he left to his beloved sport was without any doubt the infectious enthusiasm which he had passed to his listeners that night.

Since then, of course, the Queen Mother's many successes as an owner have given us who watch and cheer them untold pleasure and excitement. But they are only half the story – and less than half the reason why she is so deeply loved and respected in the jumping world.

With luck, perseverance and a bit of money, anyone can win 300 races but, almost from the beginning, the Queen Mother also knew the other, bitter side of jumping.

It is true that both her first two horses, Monaveen and Manicou, had fairy-tale successes, one in the Queen Elizabeth 'Chase, the other in the King George VI. But not long after Lord Mildmay's death, Monaveen himself was killed at the Hurst Park water jump and, after that brilliant Kempton victory as a five-year-old, Manicou never won again.

So, long before Devon Loch, the Queen Mother had proved to the jumping world the extraordinary resilience of her spirit. As a nation we knew it already from the war, but in racing, while good winners are two-a-penny, good losers are very rare indeed.

Birth, wealth and eminence are no guarantee and horses who run below expectations can, and do, cause dukes and millionaires, as well as punters, to behave like spoilt schoolboys.

The Queen Mother's smiling, philosophical acceptance of that inexplicable tragedy at Aintree is too well remembered to need fresh description. Then, as always in black moments of disaster or defeat, her first feelings were for those most closely involved with the horse – for Dick Francis and Peter Cazalet, and all the lads at Fairlawne.

As Bill Curling records in his fine and beautifully produced book, *Royal Champion*, the Queen Mother wrote as follows to Peter Cazalet: 'I am beginning to learn more of the immense amount of thought and work that goes into the preparation of a horse for racing and I understand a little of the anguish you must have felt at such a cruel blow. We will not be done in by this and will just keep on trying.'

That brand of sympathy with the men and women who do the real work has warmed and brightened all the stables with which the Queen Mother has been involved. No one is ever forgotten or passed by when she goes to see her horses, and while trainers are apt to regard the arrival of some owners with resignation, if not dread, a visit from the Queen Mother is looked forward to unreservedly by the whole yard, trainers and stable lads alike.

For her jockeys, indeed for all jockeys, she has long had a special fondness and concern. The hard side of their lives had been demonstrated early on when Dick Francis was forced to give up by a recurring dislocation of the shoulder. It was rubbed in even more painfully by the misfortunes of Bill Rees, who broke a thigh in Dunkirk's tragic, fatal fall – and then, with the bone not properly healed, broke it again next year just after riding his fifty-first, and last, royal winner.

For some years now the Queen Mother has been an enthusiastic patron of the Injured Jockeys' Fund. She supports its work in many invaluable ways, but I think I can speak for all the fund's trustees when I say that of our various 'duties', by far the most pleasant have been the occasional lunches which we give our patron.

Twenty-seven lucky men, all but one of them still alive, have ridden a winner in the famous blue and buff colours.

One of the most bitter memories of my own riding years is letting Sunbridge jump his way to the front about a mile too soon in the National Hunt 'Chase at Cheltenham – only to tire, understandably, and finish third instead of first, as he would have done, given half a ride. But, like many far more important disasters, my crestfallen apologies that day were met with kind words and the marvellous smile which has been winning the hearts of men (and women) for the best part of eighty years.

All who love and value National Hunt racing could give heartfelt thanks on the Queen Mother's eightieth birthday that, for some of these years, our sport has given her pleasure and got in return the enormous and disproportionate reward of her enthusiasm and support.

1 August 1980

THE PRINCE OF WALES

'The best way to understand something properly is to have a serious cut at it yourself.' That is demonstrably H.R.H. The Prince of Wales's chosen attitude to his many-sided life and, putting it into practice last Friday afternoon at Sandown, he brought the *Horse and Hound* Grand Military Gold Cup closer to the centre of public interest than ever before in its long honourable history.

To this particular chapter of that history there was not, as it turned out, to be a 'happy' ending – but that depends on what you mean by happy.

The Prince, having only his third ride in a steeplechase and his first in public on a new, comparatively unfamiliar horse, had gone out primarily in search of experience. The actual experience he got has been shared at one time or another by every single man or woman who ever rode at all regularly over fences.

I don't suppose he enjoyed it any more than the rest of us have, but as he and Good Prospect trotted back unscathed, there was a broad smile as well as a good deal of blood on the Royal countenance.

But, quite apart from the honour done to 'our' race, by far the most important and delightful feature of last week's events was the hold which cross-country riding in general and steeplechasing in particular has now evidently taken on Prince Charles's imagination.

Interviewed by Brough Scott before and after the race, he made that very clear. 'None of the other sports I have done bears any comparison,' were his actual words and, from a man who skis behind Charlie Palmer-Tomkinson (the rough equivalent of following Pat Hogan across Co. Limerick), that is a very considerable statement.

H.R.H. The Prince of Wales, complete with bloody nose, riding back on Good Prospect after their fall at Sandown Park in 1981.

'I have this awful thing of wanting to do things well,' the Prince told Brough – and he has no illusions whatever about the difficulties involved in mastering even the basics of his latest chosen 'challenge'.

Given the time, I have no doubt that he would master them with ease, but his time is at a premium and, as his trainer Nick Gaselee confirms, it has required a masterpiece of careful planning and rapid travel to fit in even the 'two mornings a week or thereabouts' which led up to last week's ride.

The actual misfortune which ended it at one of the Railway fences was all too familiar – painfully so if you have fallen off often enough yourself.

Unlike the sadly ill-fated Allibar, Good Prospect is not a big horse and, sitting on him, I imagine there would be very little in front of you. He has never actually fallen in a race, but Prince Charles is not the first jockey to find him absent from that all-important location between you and the ground.

Like all good, experienced jumpers, this one is, I am sure, as clever as a cat and probably rather more opinionated. In fact, I bet he reckons to know more than any jockey, Royal or otherwise, about the best place to take off at any given obstacle.

On Friday, having lost his position a bit as they turned down the back second time, Prince Charles was just working his way back into contention when, with perfectly understandable eagerness, he saw, or thought he saw, a longish stride at what turned out to be the fatal fence.

Possibly he did not 'ask' quite firmly enough – and then again, equally possible, Good Prospect would still have ignored the request if John Francome and Jeff King had made it together.

Anyway, he fiddled half an extra stride, brushed through the top and, worst of all, landed slightly off a true line.

It does not sound much – and might not have been much to Messrs Francome or King. But Prince Charles had followed his own instructions about the take-off and as he came down Good Prospect had somehow wriggled out from under.

It happens to everyone and the only thing which varies is the time you take to learn how to avoid it by reacting differently. As far as I can remember it took me about fifteen years, but my own guess is that the Prince will be a whole lot quicker. Anyway, all was well and jumping is fortunate indeed to have acquired such a heartfelt enthusiast.

20 March 1981

THE PRINCESS ROYAL

Heaven known how many bits of history, sporting and other-wise, were made at Epsom last week when Princess Anne finished fourth on Against The Grain in the Farriers Invitation Private Sweepstakes.

Since King Charles II disported himself on Newmarket Heath, the point-to-points in which the Duke of Windsor rode as a Prince and the steeplechasing exploits of the present Prince of Wales have been the Royal family's only known ventures into race-riding.

Prince Charles did finish second in a Private Sweepstakes on the flat at Plumpton (beaten by ITV's Derek Thompson on Classified), but there is not much doubt that, by riding the Epsom Derby course and distance, Princess Anne was breaking brand-new ground for the Royal family.

It seems equally certain that Elain Mellor, who won last week's race on No-U-Turn, was the first lady ever to ride a winner over flat-racing's most hallowed and historic course and distance.

'Just to be in that winner's enclosure was the thrill of my riding life,' she said – and added, after being presented with the trophy by Lester Piggott, that for her, as for the eleven-times champion, this will almost certainly be a final active season.

Sadly, much as she enjoyed herself, Princess Anne did not hold out much hope that we may see her in action again on the racecourse. 'I hardly had time to enjoy it,' she said, 'but although it has all been tremendous fun, I think I'll put it down to experience.'

The Princess, a former European three-day event champion and member of our 1976 Olympic team, had, characteristically, taken pains to achieve the far from easy transformation from all-round horsemanship to flat race-riding.

She wisely enlisted the help and advice of Against The Grain's trainer David Nicholson and over the past six weeks rode out at his Condicote yard whenever her arduous schedule allowed it.

'Five to seven on the dot – she was never late once,' says 'the Duke' – 'and then quite often you would find she had come from Scotland or somewhere abroad the night before.'

To anyone who has ever walked round a top-class cross-country course like Badminton, it came as no surprise to find that the hills and bends of Epsom gave Princess Anne no problems.

But the speed and elegance with which she adapted to riding at a racing length did surprise quite a few people, notably those of us who found it far from easy after twenty years!

Against The Grain did his level best to provide the perfect happy ending, but, perhaps not unnaturally, found himself at one stage short of the necessary yard or two of extra speed.

The crucial moment came about three furlongs out when, having smoothly negotiated Tattenham Hill and Corner, Princess Anne found herself alongside Mrs Mellor, about six lengths behind the leaders.

The difference, in the next 20 seconds or so, was that No-U-Turn quickened while Against The Grain did not. In the last furlong, still perfectly balanced, he was staying on again, but by that time the race was over.

Thanks to sponsorship of all 16 runners and a generous extra donation from Sheikh Maktoum Al Maktoum, the original objective of the Farriers Company was brilliantly achieved – a handsome sum for Riding for the Disabled, of which Princess Anne is President.

The RDA is lucky to have at its head a whole-hearted enthusiast who happens also to be a horsewoman of the highest class. I just hope she reconsiders her decision not to ride in a race again.

3 May 1985

H.R.H. Princess Anne rides Against The Grain into fourth
place at Epsom.

*Happily, Princess Anne's decision to 'put Epsom down to experience'
was very soon reconsidered. As I write in March 1991, she has had a
total of eighty rides with three winners on the flat and one, Cnoc Na
Cuille at Worcester, over fences (see below).*

*Gulfland and Ten No Trumps gave her victories in two of the
year's most important Ladies' Races – notably Ten No Trumps's
Dresden Diamond Stakes at Ascot on the day of Reference Point's
King George VI and Queen Elizabeth Diamond Stakes.*

On ground as hard as Worcester was last week, any steeplechase, even a modest one like the Droitwich Handicap 'Chase,
is run at speeds between 25 and 35 m.p.h. Round the bends the
ground is apt to feel like an icy road and, if you fall, about as
welcoming as a motorway.

The Princess Royal, a 37-year-old mother of two (both her
children were eager spectators at Worcester), was having, on
Cnoc Na Cuille, her eighth ride over steeplechase fences. Her
four opponents were all ridden by experienced professional
jockeys and the form book said that one of them was almost
sure to beat her.

'I have never been so frightened in my life,' the Princess said later, and, who knows, maybe even after travelling all over the world, winning a European three-day event championship and riding, repeatedly and successfully, round Badminton, she was not exaggerating all that much.

Even for young men without a care in the world, jumping at speed with other horses round you takes a bit of getting used to. And even with only five runners, the first two fences of this contest did look distinctly hairy.

The favourite, Tiger Ted, did his best to refuse at the first and although Cnoc Na Cuille, who had set off last of the four, jumped past him safely enough, there was a good deal of undesirable body contact.

'All five horses seemed to touch each other at least once,' the Princess said, 'but Cnoc Na Cuille is like me. He prefers fresh air and open spaces to a crowd.'

So off they very reasonably went in front and, Brendan Powell having persuaded Tiger Ted to take a bit more interest, these two went clear of the other three. The body contact was not over, though, because, turning into the back straight for the last time (a notoriously sharp and tricky bend), Cnoc Na Cuille received a fairly violent shoulder charge from his opponent!

'For one nasty moment I thought I must be going the wrong way,' the Princess said later, but Brendan Powell is emphatic that there was no risk of any such disaster.

'Do you think I want to be deported back to Ireland?' he enquired. 'It was just that mine is an awkward old boat. He was having trouble getting round the bend and she came in a bit just as we were going out!'

When the Princess asked him, a little later on, 'Are we going fast enough?' Brendan's answer was, 'A good bit too fast for me,' and, as they jumped the first in the straight, he had to pick up his whip on Tiger Ted.

There was still nothing in it at the second last, and here Cnoc Na Cuille got a yard or so too close. 'I thought we had lost it,' the Princess said, and Brendan feels that if Tiger Ted had really jumped the last and 'landed running' they might just about have held on. 'But there seemed to be 80,000 people cheering for her and only one for me,' he said. 'And that was me mother in Ireland!'

Wherever they came from, the cheers were heartfelt – and they had the desired effect. The Princess Royal would not claim – and wisely does not try – to emulate John Francome in a finish. But she keeps strictly in time, sits admirably still and horses have always gone for her. Last week, Cnoc Na Cuille ran home like a hero and all Brendan Powell's best efforts were foiled by half a length.

So, to her two wins on the flat Princess Anne has added a steeplechase, without question the first member of the Royal Family ever to complete that famous sporting double, quite apart from all her earlier eventing triumphs.

Her great-uncle, the late Duke of Gloucester, won over fences at *bona fide* Hunt meetings before the war but, besides Prince Charles, no other close relative seems even to have competed under National Hunt Rules.

The Princess has no ambition whatever to ride over hurdles and plans to qualify Cnoc Na Cuille during the winter for hunter chases. He spent the summer at Gatcombe and is, she says, 'A gentleman. He loves the children and the dogs and you can open gates off him easily.' What more could anyone ask?

10 September 1987

TERRY BIDDLECOMBE

No one present at Cheltenham racecourse around 5.15 p.m. on 14 March 1974 could doubt that he was witnessing a very special occasion. For when the runners appeared for the Cathcart Challenge Cup, six of the seven held back and, as the seventh cantered past the crowded stands, the commentator's words identifying him were drowned in a tidal wave of cheers.

It did not matter, though, for to most of that huge crowd the tall figure perched above Amarind's withers was entirely unmistakable.

Over the past sixteen years that crouch, together with a mop of straw-coloured hair and a wide, slightly battered grin, has etched itself indelibly on the consciousness of every man, woman or child who takes even a passing interest in British National Hunt racing. And although in that period the sport has had other heroes, none has better personified the mixture of courage and humour which lies at its heart than Terry Biddlecombe.

So now, as they cheered him for the last time, the Cheltenham crowd was acknowledging a debt, saying thank you as well as goodbye; and while their gratitude was very real it was also infinitely well deserved – earned the hard way a thousand times over.

Terry Biddlecombe was, to begin with, a very great jockey indeed – a natural who developed and perfected his own unique style until, in the considered opinion of far better judges than I, he ranked with the greatest of all time.

For a tall man brought up not in a flat-race stable but in the hunting field, it was the last style you would expect – based on very short leathers and a shortish rein.

Terry Biddlecombe on the 1983 Grand National winner Corbiere (left) with the Vine and Craven Foxhounds in December 1984.

No one had ever ridden quite like that over fences before, no one has since – not successfully, at least – and I doubt whether anyone ever will again. Because without superlative balance, perfect timing, great strength, a natural instinctive sympathy for horses and a flawless nerve, Terry's style might so easily have been both ugly and ineffective. But he had all those qualities – and kept them to the very end, untouched by falls and injuries and pain.

He also had, to at least as high a degree as any jockey in my memory, a tactical instinct which bordered on genius.

On bad horses as well as good ones, and in small races as

well as great, you very, very seldom saw Terry Biddlecombe in the wrong place at the wrong time.

I remember, for instance, a day at Hereford not long ago when he rode in every race and won four of them. Three times I followed him round, the other three I watched him all the way – and throughout that long afternoon no horse he rode went one yard farther than the shortest route.

Around them all there seemed to be a magic shield and as Terry sat within it, calmly following his plan, the rest of us jostled and barged like minnows round a shark.

The statistics of Terry's career are well known, but apart from his three championships (one shared with Bob Davies), he came desperately close to the title in three other seasons. So close that if only God had constructed him on a slightly smaller scale, or given him slightly fewer injuries, he would, without much doubt, have been champion six times instead of three.

The sheer physical endurance involved in that record would be – and was in Stan Mellor for instance – remarkable in a natural lightweight. But there was scarcely a day in all those sixteen seasons when Terry did not have to think about his weight.

The Turkish baths became his second home and no sketch of his career would be complete without a picture of him streaming sweat, encased in a rubber suit – and admittedly, as like as not, with a glass of champagne in his hand.

That last was typical because Terry never allowed either broken bones or unwanted pounds to diminish his voracious appetite for life. Confronted with a candle, his instinct was always to light it at both ends – and then go cheerfully back to the baths and sweat out the results in time for another day.

The combination of constant wasting and the falls that are a regular unavoidable part of any leading professional's life took their toll in the end even on Terry's iron constitution. His kidneys, alternately battered and dehydrated, often gave him hell and on more than one occasion, after riding a race of which any fit, healthy man would have been proud, he came back ashen-faced, in obvious pain, having cashed one cheque too many on the bank account of his energy and strength.

Such was the man to whom we said thank you the other

day and, if asked to sum up the reasons for our gratitude and respect, my answer would be this.

In an age when more and more sports are becoming grim, heartless, money-grubbing businesses, Terry Biddlecombe brought to his hazardous profession the outlook and philosophy of a Laughing Cavalier.

He not only did something very difficult supremely well but, even more important, he played the game as all games should be played, hard and fair, but above all because he enjoyed it.

There was nothing, to the very end, at which he could not smile and that is why, when Amarind jumped the last fence at Cheltenham the other day – and galloped wearily up the hill in fading light – so many of us felt that the sport we love had lost something which may never be replaced.

29 March 1974

SCOBIE BREASLEY

Scobie Breasley in 1950.

More than one landmark was passed last week – Miss Norah Wilmot became the first English lady to be officially recognised as the trainer of a winner, Lester Piggott reached his century for the tenth time, Sandy Barclay got halfway towards the total (a notable achievement for an apprentice) and Harry Wragg won his umpteenth valuable handicap.

But none of these quite matched the memorable and happy moment when, on Saturday afternoon, a smiling grandfather stood in front of the Windsor weighing room cradling in his arms an enormous bottle of wine.

His name, of course, was Arthur 'Scobie' Breasley, the wine

– a rheoboam of champagne – was a gift from the Windsor executive, and the applause was from us all.

For Breasley had just become the first Australian to ride 2,000 winners in this country, and if the shades of Fred Archer and George Fordham were looking down at Windsor, they must, I'm sure, have been proud to welcome him to their select and honourable company.

So, no doubt, are its surviving members, Willie Nevett, the brothers Eph and Douglas Smith and, perhaps most of all, Sir Gordon Richards. For when Sir Gordon hung up his boots it did not take him long to decide that Breasley was the man for him.

It was, in a way, a strange decision, for no two great jockeys ever had more totally different styles and just occasionally down the years Sir Gordon, though I've never heard him say so, may well have longed, in a desperate finish, for his own dynamic strength in place of the Australian's gentle, sympathetic touch.

But far more often than not – as he would be the first to say – it would have made no difference, and for every such moment there have been hundreds more when Sir Gordon and many other trainers have thanked their stars for the Fate which brought Scobie Breasley from Wagga Wagga to the English racecourse.

I wonder what Archer would have made of the extraordinary, ageless man who is the latest member of 'the Two Thousand Club'.

His style, of course, would have astounded him – for when in despair he fired that fatal pistol-shot, Tod Sloan had still not brought the short-legged 'American' crouch to England.

At first sight, Archer – like so many English observers since – would probably have considered Breasley weak, but, like Sir Gordon, he would very soon have realised the truth. For The Tinman was a horseman, too, and could not long have failed to notice the superlative horsemanship which is the solid foundation of Scobie Breasley's art.

He would have seen how, 99 times in 100, the horses the great Australian rides are *enjoying themselves* throughout a race. He would have appreciated the silken hands which calm the hardest puller, the almost flawless judgment of pace and, above all, the uncanny skill with which an ounce or two is saved for the only place that counts.

He, whose whip one suspects was sometimes used without

much regard for the horse's feelings, might not at first have understood this facet of the Breasley method.

But here, too, he would soon have seen the light – seen how, waved rhythmically beside a horse's eye, the whip becomes not a hated weapon but a magic wand to supplement the urge of arms and legs.

He would have admired the lightning speed with which it is switched from hand to hand and he would, if he talked to many trainers, have realised how seldom a horse ridden by Breasley comes back with a mark on either his skin or his enthusiasm.

He, who wasted himself into the grave, would doubtless have envied the Australian's build – his ideal weight, his ability to eat more or less what he wants.

But he would also have admired the tireless energy of a man nearly twice his age and the nerveless determination with which, at 52, after dozens of crashing falls, Breasley still goes for a gap on the rails as if the ground was a feather mattress and a horse's hoof a powder puff.

Fred Archer would, in short, have acknowledged an equal. He would, as we all do, have raised his glass to toast a master of the art, a genius who, like all true geniuses, is in his way unique.

And I, who have criticised Scobie Breasley on these pages and elsewhere as often as anyone, am proud to acknowledge that far more often than not those criticisms were undeserved.

The great Australian is, in fact, his own severest critic and, when he makes a mistake, acknowledges it with a smile that disarms the angriest trainer. Next day or the day after that he will make up for it – and how many horses can you think of who, after being ridden by Breasley, win or lose, do any better for another jockey?

The forerunner and pathfinder for the great post-war Australian invasion of Europe, Breasley is still, in the evening of a long career, head and shoulders above his many skilful compatriots.

We may sometimes wish they were not needed – that we could grow our own – and that day, I believe, may not be too far distant.

But to any such patriotic hope, Breasley is the exception. He long ago became an essential part of the British racing scene and long may he continue to adorn it.

31 August 1966

STEVE CAUTHEN

Steve Cauthen has been riding since he was two years old and is not far off his 1,000th winner. But I very much doubt if even his unique and rocket-like career has ever hitherto included anything quite like the hilarious mixture of triumph, farce and extreme physical discomfort with which British racing greeted him for the first time, at Salisbury last week.

They have so many ponies on American racecourses that Steve has no doubt seen the occasional loose one. But nothing, I suspect, half as shaggy, unkempt and unexpected as the splendid character who, having escaped from a nearby field last Saturday, lolloped calmly past the stands halfway through the rain-swept afternoon.

Then again, no sensible jockey is ever surprised when the stewards who are appointed to control his destiny behave in an odd or unpredictable manner. But I wonder when Steve – or anyone else for that matter – last saw two of these august officials drive down to see whether the course was fit for racing – and get their car so badly bogged that they (or rather the obliging Clerk of the Course, 'Washy' Hibberd) had to get out and push!

Even in America the electricity sometimes must go wrong, so silent commentators and darkened weighing rooms are no doubt nothing new in Cauthen's life, but I wonder how many races he has ridden in where the first time the winning trainer even knew that they had started was when someone slapped him on the back and said, 'Well done, you've hacked up.'

That is what happened to Ryan Price as his Lake City won

the Two Thousand Guineas Trial and there were several other little local difficulties at Salisbury – like a number board which would not work and two horses (Lord Rochford and The Sandford), whom several bookmakers believed to be non-runners until some sharp-eyed punter pointed out that they were cantering down to the start.

All this, together with the cold, incessant rain, was cruel bad luck for Salisbury – where only a reasonable day would have been needed to break all recent records for attendance.

Steve Cauthen in 1987.

Even in the foulest conditions you could imagine for an April afternoon, Steve Cauthen still proved his crowd-pulling potential value by persuading nearly 8,000 to brave the elements.

He sent them home more or less happy too – by winning on his very first ride and in general by looking, in the words of his famous countryman Eddie Arcaro, 'the best advertisement American racing could hope to send across the Atlantic'.

I am afraid you could hardly say the same on behalf of British racing for the TV film which Arcaro and the ABC cameras took home of Saturday's proceedings. But whatever they think in Kentucky, their most famous 18-year-old was more than happy with his start in England.

He began, as I've said, triumphantly on Mr K. Hsu's Marquee

Universal, a nice, strong colt by Thatch who had won his only race last season. He was, without much doubt, quite easily the best horse in the Grand Foods Handicap, but Steve Cauthen could not possibly have given him a smoother or more stylish ride.

By modern European standards he rides a pretty reasonable length – made to look shorter than it is by the fact that only the tip of his toe is lodged in the stirrup.

This almost universal American habit always looks horribly precarious to me, but in Cauthen's case it is part of a beautifully poised and streamlined seat – so streamlined that, from head on you can hardly see him tucked away behind the horse's neck.

Marquee Universal would no doubt prefer faster, less abnormal conditions, but he kept his balance well in the heavy ground and, after waiting behind the leader, Twickenham, Cauthen came up the middle to win decisively going away.

A couple of taps was all the encouragement Marquee Universal needed and the whole operation was carried through with an admirable maximum economy of effort.

Of course, one day and three rides is pathetically inadequate evidence on which to judge, but nothing we saw at Salisbury last week has altered my conviction that watching Steve Cauthen ride this season is going to be not only a regular source of interest and discussion but also, for anyone who likes to see a job well done, a constant and abiding pleasure.

13 April 1979

EDWARD COURAGE

Edward Courage in 1969.

Edward Courage, who spent over half his life in a wheelchair, still managed to pack far more into 75 years than most completely able-bodied men. His disability, caused by an attack of polio in 1928, seemed to increase rather than diminish his energy and appetite for life.

It certainly increased his compassion for others suffering similar afflictions. He was one of the original trustees of the Injured Jockeys' Fund and was also a founding member of the society for Research into Crippling Diseases.

Before the war, Mr Courage was not only a hard-working director of his family brewery, but also an indefatigable all-round sportsman. Real tennis, point-to-pointing, hunting, shooting and fishing were among his pastimes and he remained devoted to the last two even after becoming a paraplegic.

It was only after the war that Edward Courage and his new wife Hermione turned their attention seriously to National Hunt racing. Then, for a change, he had a slice of real good luck in the shape of a mare called Drumrora. She herself came from the same family as the 1903 Grand National winner Drumcree and it was from her that almost all Edward Courage's jumpers were descended.

He never won the Grand National but Tiberetta finished third, second and fourth in three consecutive years and won twice over the big Aintree fences. Spanish Steps, her son, was also third and fourth in the National.

Apart from the fact that he twice kindly allowed me to ride the great Royal Relief in the National, my own friendship with Edward started with the foundation of the Farrell Brookshaw Fund, partly inspired by the injuries Paddy Farrell suffered when Edward's Border Flight fell with him at the Chair in the 1964 Grand National.

From that time until the day before he suffered his final stroke, Edward Courage practically never missed a meeting of the Injured Jockeys' Fund trustees. His great knowledge of disabled people's problems blended with his compassion and knowledge of the world to make him an infinitely valuable trustee.

There are literally hundreds of injured jockeys and their dependants who, whether they know it or not, owe him a deep debt of gratitude.

9 July 1982

DICK FRANCIS

I should like to call the attention of anyone who enjoys a good story to what must surely be the first novel ever written by an ex-champion steeplechase jockey.

The day after you have had a part of your insides (however unimportant) forcibly removed is probably not the best time to attempt literary criticism – but it was in this condition, a fortnight ago, that I received and read Dick Francis's recently published book *Dead Cert*.

Dick Francis with the winner Mac Vidi and owner-trainer
Miss Pamela Neal after the Dick Francis Handicap Chase at
Lingfield Park on 8 December 1979.

Just as comedians want to play Hamlet, humble journalists often yearn to write books and it has always been one of my ambitions to produce a racing novel.

Unfortunately an incurable tendency to idleness, together with inability to think up a worthwhile plot, have always so far forestalled me, but evidently neither of these handicaps afflicts Dick Francis.

I do not pretend – and nor would he – that his book is a work of art but if, as Ian Fleming says, the novelist's job is to make ordinary people, in beds, trains and aeroplanes, *turn the page* then, for one reader at least, Francis has succeeded. His story is of an amateur rider who, after seeing his best friend killed in a fall, discovers that the fall was no accident, and, by a process of mixed luck, determination and coincidence goes on to detect and destroy the villainous collection of crooked jockeys and cosh-carrying taxi-drivers who were responsible.

Some of the incidents described admittedly stretch probability a trifle far, but the book is perhaps no worse for that and Dick Francis, after all, had at least one experience in his riding life that was far, far stranger than fiction!

In one climactic sequence the hero, riding bareback on 'the best hunter-'chaser in England' is pursued across country by a hostile horde of radio-controlled taxis – and finally escapes by jumping the bonnet of one of them. I would not personally have liked to try this on Colledge Master but Laurie Morgan would almost certainly take it in his stride!

Two minor – perhaps quibbling – criticisms occur to me. One jockey is described as taking his whip with him when he goes to weigh *out* before a race – something I have never seen anyone do – and another (one of the villains) is had up for not trying because the 'senior steward's tale-bearing son' had ridden in the race, seen what happened and sneaked to Dad.

I can't remember ever riding with a senior steward's son, but if one did behave in this deplorable fashion neither he nor his father would last long in N.H. racing. The incident is not vital to the plot and to drag in such an unlikely state of affairs seemed to me a mistake.

But these, as I say, are quibbles. *Dead Cert* is an exciting, imaginative book of which many professional thriller writers would be proud. And not many of *them*, I think, could get anywhere near as close to winning the Grand National for a Queen as Dick Francis did that tragic day on Devon Loch . . .

13 January 1962

The fact that I had just had my spleen taken out after a fall at Cheltenham is no excuse for this grudging review. 'Not a work of art', indeed!

To make matters worse, I was approached in the early 1970s by Tony Richardson. Fresh from an extremely profitable triumph with Tom Jones, *he had bought the film rights to* Dead Cert *but was finding it difficult to obtain a filmable script.*

Tackling the job with quite unjustifiable confidence, I borrowed Mary Gordon Watson's great double Gold Medal-winning eventer Cornishman V to play the taxi-jumping hero-horse, enrolled a lot of jockeys as extras – and set about filming at Fontwell Park, Findon and Aintree.

The result, though tremendous fun to make and, pictorially, fair in parts, was a miscast, badly written botch-up of Dick's book. Its only 'triumph' came on the first night, attended by Princess Anne in aid of the Injured Jockeys' Fund and played in front of an almost entirely racing audience. Dead Cert *was not meant to be a comedy – but how they roared at the antics of their all too easily recognisable friends!*

Doubling for the hero on Cornishman, I had to wear a wig which made me look like a geriatric Beatle. Another day the actor supposed to play the vet did not turn up, so I achieved my first and only dramatic line: 'This urine sample is no good.' Nor, alas, was the film . . .

JOHN FRANCOME

'The best jumping jockey of all time' is a 'title' the award of
which can never be more than a matter of opinion – and
that opinion could never be founded solely on records or
statistics.

But the fact remains that when Don't Touch became the
1,036th winner of John Francome's unique career at Fontwell
Park last week, there was no longer any doubt that, statisti-
cally, for sheer sustained, consistent excellence, the present
champion's record stands alone.

Only nine men have ridden 100 winners in one season and,
of those nine, of course, only two have reached the thousand.
But before he passed Stan Mellor's lifetime total, John Francome
had already become the only man ever to ride *four* 'centuries' –
one after another in the last four seasons.

Champion now for the fifth time (including one title shared,
voluntarily, with Peter Scudamore), he had, in this latest season, the incredible winning ratio of 24.77 per cent, very nearly
one winner from every four rides.

Well, needless to say, those are just figures. They do not begin
to convey the magical, largely invisible mixture of strength,
balance, timing, sympathy and skill on which John has built
and developed his method. They certainly do not convey the
pleasure which watching him gives to anyone with half an eye
who likes to see something extremely difficult done supremely
well.

Thank heaven he intends to ride again next season – so our
debt of gratitude will grow, not just for the fun of watching

but also for the example he sets to younger would-be jockeys. Because, in sharp contrast with the quite literally inimitable Lester Piggott, John Francome *can* and should be copied.

John Francome in characteristic pose on Gratification.

No one, unless lucky enough to be born with it, can hope to reproduce his matchless eye-for-a-stride – but the rest is all based on perfectly sound conventional principles.

John (who, I'm sure, will appreciate being described as 'sound and conventional'!) just happens to have put the methods together better than most, but the only exaggerated thing about him is his success.

From almost every point of view it would have been nicer and more appropriate for the historic 'record' winner to be trained by John's greatest supporter (and admirer) Fred Winter. But John Jenkins, who does train Don't Touch, has played a big part in the champion's success throughout this season and it *was*, in a way, appropriate that Don't Touch should go to the start of the Lavington Handicap 'Chase with the ominous legend P.P.P.F.U. in front of his name!

'All the way here in the car I kept asking myself what on earth I was thinking of to take the ride,' John Francome said afterwards. But he has often also said in the past that teaching young horses to jump – and solving the problems of older ones who don't – is the part of his job he most enjoys.

It is also one of the parts he does best and, in his sympathetic hands (fitted, admittedly, with a helpful first-time pair of blinkers), Don't Touch produced a faultless clear round at Fontwell.

A long way from the last fence it was clear that John Francome knew precisely where he was going to take off and sure enough, he did. So Stan Mellor's twelve-year-old record was broken and a bit of racing history made.

I never expected to acknowledge the existence of a better jockey than Fred Winter – and am still convinced that, if the pair arrived at the last fence together on two tired horses of exactly identical ability, Fred would, just, come off best.

'Yes, but even if you are right, how many lengths would John have taken off me out in the country?' is the great trainer's modest reply – and, who knows, perhaps he is right. The comparison is both odious and unnecessary. What matters is that these two, Fred Winter and John Francome, have ridden as well as men can ride. We are both lucky and privileged to have watched them.

8 June 1984

STAN MELLOR

By far the nicest, most important and most welcome event on the British racing scene last week was the appearance of Stan Mellor's name in the Birthday Honours list. Because, of all the distinguished men and women on that list, I honestly doubt if a single one had a better right to be there.

That may sound a ridiculously prejudiced statement to someone outside the jumping world and, if Stan Mellor was just a very good, very brave and very successful jockey, perhaps it would be. There have, after all, been a lot of good, brave, jumping jockeys in the past, and only one of them, Fred Winter, CBE, has ever previously been honoured.

But behind the decoration Stan will shortly be receiving there lies far more than seventeen years' hard, dangerous work, 889 winners (in Britain alone), one really dreadful injury overcome and a dozen only slightly lesser ones shrugged carelessly aside. Though heaven knows that record alone would, by the standards of the normal world, cry out for recognition.

Back in 1951, fourteen years old and with neither racing nor anything much else in his background, Stan Mellor left school to join George Owen's Cheshire stable.

All he knew was that he wanted to ride – and it didn't take George (who had already given Dick Francis and Tim Brookshaw the chances that set them on the road to the N.H. jockeys' championship) very long to realise that in this small, insignificant-looking boy there was something worth encouragement.

It must have taken a bit of recognising – and, from the first, there were plenty who said Stan would always be too small to make a jumping jockey.

Stan Mellor in 1961.

'They told me that *then*,' he says cheerfully '*now* they tell me how lucky I am not to have to worry about my weight!'

Too small or not, the winners soon began to come and in 1959, only seven years after having his first ride as an amateur, Stan Mellor succeeded Tim Brookshaw as champion jockey. He kept the title for three seasons – and looked like winning it again, when a horse called Eastern Harvest threw him beneath the crowded, crashing hooves of the field for the 1963 Schweppes Gold Trophy.

It was that Liverpool meeting at which Carrickbeg did *not* win the Grand National, and, feeling pretty sorry for myself, I went with a couple of others to visit Stan in hospital the Sunday morning after.

With his jaws and cheekbones smashed in fourteen places he was, quite literally, unrecognisable – and I have never seen a racing injury more calculated to shatter the nerve and/or the enthusiasm of its victim. On Stan Mellor it had no effect whatever.

He got married that summer – making, as usual, the right decision – and calmly set about picking up the pieces of a career which, for most men, would have been shattered as completely as his face.

No one who in the past six seasons has seen a horse lifted into and over the last few fences of a steeplechase (by what looks, at such moments, more like a small round-shouldered demon than a jockey!) needs telling how brilliantly that career has flourished since.

At Stratford the other day Stan came desperately close to a fourth championship and now only sheer bad luck (I am touching wood as I write) can rob him of the 111 winners which will make him the first man ever to ride a thousand over fences and hurdles in this country.

Such is his story (so far) as a jockey – but there is, as I've said, much more besides. For it is absolutely no exaggeration to say that Stan Mellor, whose formal 'education' ended when he was thirteen, has done more to improve the status of his profession and its relationship with the Turf authorities than any other jockey in the history of racing.

When the N.H. Jockeys Association was formed in 1964, Stan became its first chairman and when it was amalgamated with the flat-race jockeys association he remained as vice-chairman until last year.

Those are just words – which could easily mean nothing – but as Lord Wigg, Sir Randle Feilden and all the others who have shared the control of racing during that period could tell you, Stan Mellor has made them mean a very great deal.

For in the past seven years or so the whole life and living of a British professional jockey – his rewards, his compensation for injury, the hearing of his grievances and the hearing of complaints against him – has been transformed and improved beyond recognition.

And although the credit for this transformation must, of course, be shared between many people, a major factor in it has been the character, charm, common sense and sheer hard work of one small, infinitely determined man.

During the same period – ever since 1964 – Stan Mellor has put the same qualities at the disposal of the Injured N.H. Jockeys' Fund, whose trustees would often have been lost without his knowledge and judgment.

All this adds up to a formidable total of hours spent working unpaid and almost entirely for the benefit of others. From any man it would be admirable – from a professional jumping jockey dedicated to his job and pursuing it day in, day out for eleven months of the year, it is and has been downright miraculous.

So if anyone ever tells you that the British Empire's dead and that the MBE means nothing, just tell *them* about Stan Mellor.

Tell them that, to those who know this man and his achievements, *no* honour could have been too great. The letters may be irrelevant, but the whole racing world feels honoured by what they represent – recognition for a man of whom that world is deeply proud.

19 June 1970

LESTER PIGGOTT

When I started writing for *Horse and Hound* in 1959, Lester Piggott had been riding winners for eleven years – 542 of them on the flat and 20 over hurdles. He had already won two Epsom Derbys and the next season, in 1960, was champion jockey for the first of eleven times.

Almost all his best-known exploits have been described on these pages since, mostly with heartfelt admiration, often with amazement and, just occasionally, with disapproval. But all that time, throughout his unique career, in fact, this extraordinary man has provided many more questions than answers.

That is how it will remain when he retires and anyone who pretends to have all the answers – or even most of them – is living in cloud cuckoo-land.

My own first memory of Lester is in 1950 or thereabouts. He had just ridden a winner at Windsor and, as he rode across the unsaddling enclosure, Fulke Walwyn called up, 'Well done, Lester.'

There was no answer or acknowledgement of any kind, no flicker on the round, almost chubby but even then expressionless face. Seeing what had happened, Keith Piggott ran down the weighing-room steps. 'He didn't hear you, Fulke. He didn't hear you,' Lester's father shouted, determined that the great trainer should not think his words of congratulation had been churlishly ignored.

Lester's slight but real deafness has since become the raw material for countless apocryphal Piggott jokes – 'Go back round to the one pound ear' and all that – and its actual effect on the man is one of those unanswered questions. But that Windsor scene stayed in my mind, touching evidence of Keith Piggott's affection and anxiety for his son.

I remembered it with sympathy four years later when, suspending Lester for six months after the Never Say Die incident in the King Edward VII Stakes at Royal Ascot, the stewards of the Jockey Club ordered that he be apprenticed to some trainer other than his father.

Right or wrong, it must have seemed a gratuitous insult at the time and Lester has always given Keith – himself an iron-hard and extremely successful jumping jockey – full credit for his early education as a rider.

'He knew his stuff and I tried to please him because I knew he knew his stuff . . .' is one of several quotations I have borrowed from Julian Wilson's elegantly produced and crisply written *Lester Piggott – The Pictorial Biography.*

From all I have heard of Keith Piggott's riding, it seems unlikely that the tactical advice he gave Lester involved the use of many kid gloves and that, presumably, was one of the assumptions on which the stewards' 1954 directive was based.

But the lessons had been learnt by then and, while no one in his senses has ever expected Lester to do them any favours in a race, it is equally unthinkable that he should whinge or complain afterwards about measures taken against him.

That, of course, does not mean he would not remember and repay them. 'Do as you would be done by' is the basis of all jockeys' conduct and is, incidentally, the reason why most experienced professionals believe that the stewards worry too much about the supposed dangers of 'careless' riding.

'No one goes on taking unjustifiable risks for long,' Sir Gordon Richards has said, 'the other jockeys just won't let him get away with it.'

One of the reasons why Lester may have taken a bit longer than most to learn that particular lesson is, undoubtedly, the courage, lack of fear or ability to overcome it, which, of all his many qualities, is the one I personally most admire.

Even in thirty-six years his list of falls and injuries does not, of course, approach those of a jumping jockey like, for instance, Terry Biddlecombe – though I have absolutely no doubt that if weight had forced Lester to stick to jumping he would still have reached the top.

Sadly, I never had the honour of riding against him – but he was at Aintree to help his father saddle Ayala, who beat Carrickbeg in the 1963 Grand National.

Lester, in fact, had schooled Ayala over fences and some years earlier I remember watching him sit like a limpet on a horse called Prince Charlemagne who won the Triumph Hurdle at Hurst Park, despite ignoring and flattening every one of the eight flights!

But even if flat-race falls and disasters are much less frequent, they also come much faster, much less predictably and, all too often, take the jockey involved much closer to death's door.

That has certainly been the case with Lester but again and again he has bounced back and, now at 50, no one has ever even bothered to suggest that his nerve has been affected by the years.

Of all his falls and escapes the narrowest, most frightening and most miraculous was surely from Durtal before the 1977 Oaks. Taking a fierce hold on the way down, Robert Sangster's filly pulled the saddle right forward and as she tore into the Epsom paddock area the elastic girths slipped, throwing Lester sideways.

One foot – the worst of any jockey's nightmares – remained stuck in the stirrup and, as Durtal half attempted to jump the rail, Lester was seconds away from virtually certain death.

But although two of his worst moments have been at Epsom, the resident Fates must love him. Now, unbelievably, they intervened by smashing the aluminium of the stirrup against an upright and, so miraculously, freeing his imprisoned foot. Mercifully dragged only a few yards, Lester came back looking just a trifle shaken – but rode in two more races that day and won the last . . .

In 1981, dragged under the starting stalls with one ear half torn off, he had another near magical escape at Epsom – and won the One Thousand Guineas on Fairy Footsteps one week later. Then last year one foot did get stuck at Leicester – towing Lester for 50 violent, terrifying yards. Five weeks later he was back – for his 28th Classic on Commanche Run.

That ride, like many others, was, of course, ruthlessly obtained at another man's expense. Heroes are not often saints and Lester Piggott's character is a coin with at least two sides. It would be a grave exaggeration to say that he has invariably set a flawless example – and pointless, now, to argue the pluses and minuses of his contribution to racing.

Much as we shall miss him, for instance, it will not be a total disadvantage, at least for us media hacks, to have a champion jockey who does not use words as though they were £5 notes.

Public relations have never been Lester's strongest point – probably for the first-rate reason that there are only a tiny handful of people in the world about whose opinion of him he gives a damn.

In much the same way it is sad that Lester Piggott's style and method should be so unique as to be almost impossible to imitate.

If you look at Julian Wilson's picture of him aged 15 the seat is a model – knees just reaching the horse's withers and lower leg almost perpendicular. But then turn to the present day. The knees have risen six inches, the bottom is poised at the high port and, in a finish, the whole zig-zag has to be compressed – with bent legs flapping in and out and contact between horse and man apparently a matter of disorganised, unrhythmic chance. Well, of course, it is nothing of the kind.

'You've got to be holding yourself as still as you can while you're making the right movements.' Lester told the *Observer*'s Kenneth Harris in a uniquely articulate interview which, again, I have plundered from Wilson.

> The more control you have of your body, the fewer movements you have to make – but the more muscular effort you need; you need more strength to stand still on one leg than to walk down the street.
>   In the finish of a race, as well as keeping your horse balanced, you've got to be doing things with him.
> You've got to be encouraging the horse – moving your hands forward when his head goes forward, squeezing him with your knees, urging him with your heels, flourishing your whip, maybe giving him a crack, and all this without throwing him off balance – which

means not letting yourself be thrown around in the
saddle.

I make no apology for quoting that passage at length because
it describes as well as possible *one* of the things Lester Piggott
has been doing for thirty years better than anyone else in the
world.

To do it, he has needed to teach himself the Spartan self-
control of a fasting hermit. He has needed to acquire and
maintain, at the age of 50, the muscular strength and fitness
of an Olympic gymnast – and he had, to begin with, a massive
will to win, connected with, but never affecting, an ice-cool
tactical brain.

The result has sometimes been beautiful, almost always exciting and quite often unforgettable. Just occasionally, for the
pleasure of enjoying it, the racing world has had to pay a
price. But over more than thirty years that price would have
been worth paying many thousand times – and every penny of
Lester Piggott's not inconsiderable fortune has been earned.

He has also earned our grateful best wishes for a long,
happy retirement and, if he is rash enough to embark on it,
a successful career as a trainer.

25 October 1985

Boos as well as cheers have always been part of Lester Piggott's
life and for all the countless admirers who rightly praised his
genius there were always critics eager to underline his equally
real faults.

But as the doors of Norwich Gaol shut behind him last week,
I don't believe that anyone who has ever gone racing, entered a
betting shop or taken the tiniest interest in the sport can have
felt completely unmoved or unaffected.

Sympathy, no doubt, will not be universal but in all our
reactions, however stern, there must surely be a real element
of sadness.

Bred on both sides of his pedigree to be a jockey, Lester was
taken away from school soon after he rode his first winner at
the age of twelve. His hearing was never good and, partly

because of that, his quiet, nasal speaking voice has always been sparingly used.

A 'private' education never seems to have given him much interest in anything outside racing and, from early childhood, he was brought up by his parents to beware at all costs of the cadgers and hangers-on who, in racing, have always swarmed around successful jockeys.

The young Piggott soon found himself succeeding hugely in that very world – one where the traditional way of rewarding success has always been in 'readies', or ready money. Both winning bets and prize money are tax-free and until the rules of racing were revised to deduct percentages for trainers, jockeys and stable staff at source, few owners saw any reason why a winning jockey should be expected to pay tax on his present.

Lester's career coincided, moreover, with a boom in the value of bloodstock and the syndication of successful colts as stallions for millions of pounds or dollars. Often it was his skill, strength and will to win which conjured the inches that made those colts' reputations in the first place and nothing was more natural than that he should be given a share in the stallion value he had helped to create.

That explains, in part, the temptation. Of course, it neither explains nor excuses the disastrous way in which this easy-going, ready-money atmosphere combined with Lester's inbred parsimony and, let's face it, greed.

Together, they turned him into an international hoarder on a massive scale – and no one, least of all his unfortunate family, has yet been able to work out what on earth he thought he was ever going to spend it on.

Lester, of course, had from the first another much older, stronger and more desirable obsession. In the last two pages of his autobiography, Sir Gordon Richards attempts to describe the mainspring of his success. 'The will to win', he wrote, 'that was my secret' – and even if he might use different words, I am pretty sure Lester would feel the same.

Neither of these two great jockeys was a conventionally stylish rider but each developed an individual, inimitable method of communicating to a horse his own overpowering will to win.

The difference was that when Lester's will to win – his

obsession for victory – came up against the rules or sporting traditions of racing, it was, more often than not, the rules and traditions which came off second best.

Sometimes the stewards disqualified him for taking what they and the rules called too big a risk and just occasionally the crowds booed him for pinching other jockeys' rides.

But winning always meant far more to Lester Piggott than public opinion or official disapproval and, sadly, it is all too evident now that when his other obsession – for money – came up against another less flexible set of rules, he mistakenly supposed that the outcome would be the same. So, having admired and cheered him for one brand of piracy we must surely admit some complicity in the other.

Especially since it was to satisfy the demands of our 'sport' that Lester Piggott fought his long and agonising battle with the scales. Solitary by nature, and never much of a communicator, he fought it alone and uncomplaining and neither his strength nor courage was ever affected by what, to most of us, would be an unbearably Spartan lifestyle.

Even counting his jumping colleagues there has never, in my time, been a braver jockey and although, no doubt, Lester started out, as many do, naturally fearless, his nerve survived intact, despite thirty years on a concentration-camp diet and numerous hair-raising experiences, many of them involving painful injuries.

I had never heard before Mr Mathew's plea of mitigation that those injuries included damage to Lester's brain and, although that may well be true, no one who has had even my fleeting acquaintance with the eleven-times champion will readily accept that he is 'of low intellectual capacity in the low average range'.

But whatever your view about that, Mr Mathew's plea is well worth reading, especially where he deals with the letter from Henry Cecil which started the Inland Revenue investigation.

It was a letter 'circulated openly to owners of standing in the racing world including at least one steward of the Jockey Club' and although Cecil was later fined £2,000 for breaking the rule which requires registration of agreements between jockeys and trainers, no one, at the time, seems to have advised Lester Piggott against the disastrous course he was taking.

We can only hope that the stewards of the Jockey Club will take the whole incident into very serious consideration indeed when they or their successors are pondering the restoration of Lester Piggott's licence to train.

Lester Piggott with Henry Cecil, Ascot, 1982.

The one consolation I can see in the comparative severity of last week's sentence is that it may eventually make it easier for the stewards to restore that licence when Lester comes out of prison – on the principle that one offence deserves only one punishment, that he will, by then, have paid in full for his offence and that neither the Jockey Club nor the racing world as a whole can look back on this case with any pride or satisfaction.

The only other redeeming feature of the whole sad episode is the characteristic dignity with which Lester Piggott accepted his fate. Throughout the long ordeal and official inquisition, he has never once complained and you can bet your boots he never will: I would also like to bet that, given even reasonable luck, he will, one day, be back where he belongs, in the winner's enclosure.

29 October 1987

RYAN PRICE

Ryan Price, who died last Saturday, had been fighting his last battle for a long time and at least when, finally, it was lost on his 74th birthday, he had three careers behind him, all carried through with the same panache and devil-may-care confidence.

A brilliant point-to-point rider before the war, he served through it in the Commandos, winning an MC and, from the moment he set up as a trainer, in Lavant first and on a shoestring, the world of jumping was never quite the same.

The statistics and sensations, real or imagined, would fill a book. They have, in fact: Peter Bromley's admirable biography *The Price of Success*.

But it is the style of the man that we shall remember even more clearly than Kilmore's Grand National, the Champion Hurdles of Clair Soleil and Eborneezer, What A Myth's Gold Cup, those four Schweppes and, when Ryan concentrated on the flat, Ginevra's Oaks, Bruni's St Leger and Giacometti's Champion Stakes.

Every one of them, you can bet your boots, was led out of the paddock, not by their lad but by the trainer himself. Or rather by a twentieth-century reincarnation of Captain Kidd, with that brown hat tilted above narrowed, miss-nothing eyes in a lived-in, deeply lined face.

In the early days, when Ryan first spotted an almost unknown Fred Winter and began their unbroken seventeen-year partnership, the horses had probably been driven from Lavant and led round the paddock by Dorothy Price.

Then, and for ever after, she was a vital part of the team, an indispensable one in fact, the unshakeable rock to which Ryan could always sail back when the seas got stormy outside.

Ryan Price in 1982.

And besides all that, Dorothy contributed her own miracle to the story. Because she could not have a baby, she and Ryan adopted two children and were happily bringing them up when, unbelievably, against all medical prediction, Dorothy found herself pregnant. So she has a family of three to remember, with her, their extraordinary father.

The more public part of those memories many of us can share and my own outstanding impression of Ryan Price, either at home or on the racecourse, was the deep affection, even love, he felt for the horses in his charge.

In the paddock or winner's enclosure you saw, or rather heard it expressed and exaggerated in that unmistakeable grating voice, 'A CHARMING filly, my boy, CHARMING.' 'WIN? What do you mean? OF COURSE he will bloody well win. This is an ATHLETE, a CHAMPION . . .'

You saw it, a little quieter but just as heartfelt, every time the Captain entered a box at Findon – and you saw it clearest of all in the paddock high on the Downs where his beloved heroes, Kilmore, Clair Soleil, Persian Lancer and many more lived out the carefully tended, well-fed evenings of their lives.

Of course, there will be some for whom the name Ryan Price means scandal, sensations – and the Schweppes Gold Trophy. The Rosyth suspension, that dreadful day when Hill House was booed home at Newbury and the interminable wrangling inquiry which followed his 'positive' dope sample.

As an uninformed but fascinated observer, it always seemed to me that Ryan was sometimes his own worst enemy in these affairs – and, racing being what it is, he had a few. He scarcely ever spoke a word without exaggerating slightly and was never odds-on to let absolute accuracy stand in the way of a good story.

Heard on a racecourse and repeated out of context, some of his more outrageous claims and statements, dismissed or watered down immediately by the friends to whom they were made, could be and were magnified into dreadful and damning 'evidence' by less well-meaning hearers.

But none of that matters now. Ryan Price will be remembered for his bravery, for the sympathetic skill with which he schooled and trained good horses, good jockeys and, as we know now, good trainers.

Guy Harwood started his education at Findon and it is no coincidence that Fred Winter, Josh Gifford and Paul Kelleway, all stable jockeys there, have all gone on to use lessons learnt by watching and hearing the great trainer for whom they rode.

They have good reason to remember Ryan Price with gratitude and so does the rest of the racing world. He added life and colour and excitement to it, and since he left, the racecourse has been a drabber place.

22 August 1986

JIMMY SNOW

Jimmy Snow, who covered Northern racing for many years in *Horse and Hound* as Herod, died in Richmond, Yorks, on Monday, aged 73.

My first assignment for the *Daily Telegraph* was to Redcar in 1957 and Jimmy was the first person who ever spoke to me in a racing press room. We had never met before and certainly did not know each other's names.

But, out of utterly distinterested kindness, simply because he could see that I was lost and clueless, Jimmy guided me to the weighing room, showed me the telephone, introduced me, can you believe it, to Captain Charles Elsey and, in general, held my hand. We have, I am proud to say, been friends ever since.

Born in 1913, Jimmy Snow went to Shrewsbury and joined the Sherwood Foresters in 1939. For most of the war he was a brother officer and boon companion of Clive Graham, then already a racing correspondent for the *Daily Express*.

It was partly due to their friendship, and, of course, to his own lifelong passion for racing, that Jimmy joined the *News Chronicle* and then the *Sporting Chronicle* in the first post-war decade.

When I first met him he was already Northern correspondent to *The Times*, a job which, since his senior partner Francis Byrne seldom ventured far north of Newmarket, involved the coverage of a considerable area!

For years, we happily shared the racing pages of this paper and our Sunday telephone conferences would, if printed verbatim, have kept the lawyers working overtime.

Highly intelligent, widely read and blessed with a well-developed sense of humour, Jimmy knew, loved and was liked and trusted by all the great characters of Northern racing. He wrote a fine biography of Harry Carr and men like Matt Peacock, Captain Elsey, Neville Crump, Bobby Renton and Billy Nevett were his heroes and friends.

They will all remember Jimmy Snow first and foremost as a happy man. I can see him and Clive Graham now, sitting with a bottle of gin and their form books at the far end of the press room at York.

'We may not get paid much but at least we are paid to do something we enjoy,' was their philosophy, and if there's a press room in heaven you can bet your boots the glasses were out on Monday night.

30 January 1987

BRIAN TAYLOR

On Saturday, the luck ran out on the other side of the world for Brian Taylor, one of the nicest, friendliest flat-race jockeys of the post-war era.

Hard to bear at any time, such tragedies seem even worse, even more unnecessary, on the flat. The fact that the horse Brian Taylor was riding at Sha Tin, Hong Kong, had fallen before is neither here nor there. He simply stumbled and for some reason fell – and if any excuse was needed for the strict safety measures and discipline which the Jockey Club enforces nowadays, the unpredictable, unavoidable violence of such disasters would provide it.

Brian Taylor, who rounded off his distinguished riding career in this country with a winner, had gone back to Hong Kong to fulfil the last few months of his contract there. He had already started to build up his own breeding and farming operation at Newmarket and had richly deserved the long, happy and useful retirement to which with every reason he was looking forward.

An all-round athlete and high-class golfer, he was, I believe, the only jockey who imitated, even with partial success, the inimitable Lester Piggott. Brian would have been the last to claim any sort of 'equality' with his old friend and rival but sometimes, in a finish, it was not easy to distinguish between them. No one else, in my memory, has deserved that compliment.

But more even than his skill and success in the saddle, Brian's friends will remember and mourn the loss of his cheerfulness and humour. During 1984 he emerged unscathed and with dignity from a long, worrying disciplinary ordeal and I have no doubt at all that, given the chance, he would have repaid racing for the good years it has given him. But now that chance has gone.

14 December 1984

BILL TELLWRIGHT

Out hunting, on the racecourse, or just larking about at home, riding across country always ranked very high among the joys of Bill Tellwright's life.

So at least we can be pretty sure that he died a happy man last week when his neck was broken in a freakish accident while schooling a hunter near his home.

The trouble, needless to say, about such 'good, quick ways to go' is the horrid, abrupt and unexpected shock they bring to those who are left behind.

The manner of Bill's death may, in a way, be a consolation to his countless friends, especially to those who shared his pleasures. But that only increases our sympathy for Jane and their four children.

In an age when the genuine amateur is very definitely an endangered species, Bill was a prime example of the breed. Tough, cheerfully resolute and extremely difficult to dislodge, he rode over a hundred winners under Rules and in point-to-points. His triumphant farewell came only three years ago, on Rathlek in his own North Staffs members' race.

I cannot speak from experience of his time as an MFH, but would be very surprised to hear that hunting with him – if you could stand the nervous strain – was anything but fun.

On the racecourse his finest hours were the Royal Artillery Gold Cup and Nicolaus Silver's Kim Muir at Cheltenham, and it was on the same course in the 1960s that I inadvertently presented him with victory in an amateur riders' 'chase.

The new course had only just been built and we were the

only two survivors from a nine-horse field. Turning downhill over the second last I was well clear on Pioneer Spirit when, to my horror, a hurdle appeared on the horizon.

I shall never forget the look of surprise, followed by pity, followed by delight, with which Bill ignored my warning cries, swept past, round the bend which concealed the last fence – and on to victory!*

He bought me a large consoling drink after the stewards had fined me £25 – and we have enjoyed several more since to celebrate the memory.

It is only one of many I share with all who knew Bill Tellwright, a sportsman in the best sense of the word.

31 October 1986

---

* See pages 336–7

JAYNE THOMPSON

Jayne Thompson's death made everything else that happened on England's racecourses last week seem pointless and unimportant.

It is only a luckless few who pay the ultimate price for all our pleasure but when it happens the rest of us ought surely to ask ourselves whether any mere game can be worth so much.

Without any doubt Jayne herself would have laughed at the question. Ever since she first got on a pony, riding was what she wanted to do and she was very good at it.

Leading lady rider two years ago, she thrived on the competitive side of racing and her pretty, smiling face made the weighing room and the racecourse in general warmer, happier places.

When the jockeys at Newcastle last Saturday decided to wear black arm-bands in her honour, it was no mere empty gesture but a message from friends sincerely sent.

Anger at the waste is the first and most natural reaction and it is little if any consolation that the accident and the injuries it caused were both sheer unavoidable bad luck.

Hot Betty had never fallen in six previous races over hurdles and in two of those Jayne rode her into a place close behind the winner. They started joint second-favourites at Catterick and seemed to have an excellent chance of winning. So is it worth it? I honestly do not know. Of course, when things go even halfway right the thrill seems worth anything and last week the price seemed immeasurably too high. The only certainty is that, for the foreseeable future, racing will go on and jockeys will go on getting hurt and sometimes killed. All we can do is rule out as many avoidable risks as possible, pray for luck and sympathise with those whose luck runs out.

Jayne Thompson winning on Roseman at Market Rasen in 1985.

Hot Betty was trained near Doncaster by Jayne's ex-coalminer father Ron, so it was into a happy family team that this tragic thunderbolt fell at Catterick. Jayne's boyfriend, Geoff Harker, rode two winners that very day and, after spending the worst week of his life waiting in vain at Jayne's bedside, rode another at Newcastle on Saturday.

For Ron Thompson, for his wife, their son and Geoff Harker, racing, no doubt, will never be the same. I only hope that, one day, they may find it once again giving them some of the thrills and pleasure Jayne enjoyed so much.

21 November 1986

JOHN THORNE

For anyone who loved National Hunt racing as much as the late John Thorne, Cheltenham in March has always meant, quite simply, the three most exciting, fascinating days of the whole year. The last thing John would want is for his death to cast a shadow over the annual festival of his beloved sport.

But the fact remains that neither he nor Spartan Missile will be there and for many of us there will be moments – as the amateurs ride out for the National Hunt 'Chase and the Christie's Foxhunters, for instance – when memories of that cheerful, indomitable figure in the familiar green and grey will bring painfully home again the dreadful loss which was suffered last week by John's happy, devoted family and the jumping world as a whole.

John Thorne was part of that world for thirty-three years – ever since he came out of the Army, rented some land in Warwickshire from Lord Willoughby de Broke and started developing the supremely effective, efficient and productive establishment which became the Chesterton Stud.

Spartan Missile – who came so heartbreakingly close last year to fulfilling John's greatest racing ambition – is in so many ways typical of his master, a perfect, all-round examplar, in fact, of John's unique contribution to the world he loved.

John not only had bred his dam, Polaris Missile – and won the N.H. 'Chase on her – but also discovered and developed at Chesterton the enormous potential of his sire, Spartan General. Their son, like his master, was big, tough, brave and occasionally stubborn.

John Thorne and Spartan Missile, 1979.

Like his master, he learnt his trade over the formidable Warwickshire country – and to the end, trying to follow John Thorne across that country was about as easy, safe and good for the nerves as chasing Spartan Missile round Cheltenham, Aintree or Auteuil on an indifferent jumper.

I never tried it myself but Brough Scott has a vivid memory of five hectic hours of on-the-spot journalistic research last winter! With more than a stone still to lose, Spartan Missile's owner-rider spent those hours wearing a rubber sweat suit under the full pink coat regalia of a Joint Master.

He led the field through two fine hunts, pausing only to gallop down a precipice, at the bottom of which his amazingly patient, long-suffering wife was waiting with the second horses. Then off again, up the precipice this time – and on, quite tireless, to the end of a day designed to cripple a man half his age.

That was John Thorne at fifty-four. At the age of seventeen, too young, they told him, to parachute, he crossed the Rhine by glider instead – and landed nine miles beyond the German lines. In the considered opinion of friends who knew him better than I did, it was the horrific battlefield experiences of those days in 1945 which left John so totally devoid of nerves or fear out hunting or on the racecourse.

Particularly after the tragic death in a motor accident of his eighteen-year-old son Nigel, he rode all or nearly all the family horses in the earliest, least predictable races. The falls and injuries he suffered were legion and, in at least one case, came near to crippling him. But they made not the slightest difference.

Last November, larking around the farm, he broke a leg (again) and had, as usual, given it less than the normal minimum time to heal when he got up at the Bicester point-to-point last week.

His eldest daughter, Diana (herself the first woman to ride a winner under Rules), told me he came back delighted after his first ride of the day.

So, for this unique, extraordinary man there could be no better end than a final, crashing, fatal fall.

But there is, alas, more than one side to that kind of death – and in John Thorne's story there was more than one hero.

For more than thirty years his devoted wife Wendy has had to watch and wait and worry while those she loved best risked their necks and enjoyed themselves. No sooner had she suffered the desolation of Nigel's death than the girls began to ride, and all this time she provided the steady, calm, reliable background against which John could act out his hectic, sometimes dangerous life.

She was the harbour to which he could return, however battered, for some sympathetic care and comfort. She is the real heroine of this tale and from all who loved and admired her husband, she has both sympathy and heartfelt admiration.

21 March 1982

FULKE WALWYN

Although Fulke Walwyn was twice leading amateur rider while serving in the 9th Lancers, he never actually rode a winner of the Grand Military Gold Cup. As a trainer, on the other hand, his record in the race is second to none – something, of course, which can be said with equal truth about most of National Hunt racing's greatest prizes.

Seven Whitbread Gold Cups, seven Hennessys, four winners of the Gold Cup proper, five of the King George VI Steeplechase and two of the Champion Hurdle – the full list has never been equalled, let alone surpassed and although, as a trainer, there is only one Grand National on it, Fulke Walwyn and Fred Winter are the only two men living who have both ridden and trained a National winner at Aintree.

Yet the second part of Fulke's unique career began in distinctly unpromising circumstances at the worst imaginable moment. Four months before he applied for his first licence to train in 1939, a crashing fall at Ludlow put paid to his life as a jockey and left him unconscious with a fractured skull.

He recovered sufficiently to saddle his first winner on 26 August of that momentous year – just five days before Hitler's tanks rolled over the Polish border.

Except that he is convinced his old friend Frank Furlong's Grosvenor Bridge was about to win, Fulke has no memory of the Ludlow fall. His twin sister Helen Johnson Houghton remembers it only too well. 'We heard Fulke had had a fall. There was nothing new about that. But then I woke up in the middle of the night and suddenly I knew he had fractured his skull. It was just about the only "twinny" thing that ever happened to us.'

Commandeering her trainer-husband's car, Mrs Johnson Houghton arrived in Ludlow to find Fulke's first wife Diana being allowed to drive him home. The little local hospital had no X-rays but when, on his sister's insistence, he was taken by ambulance to the John Radcliffe in Oxford, a severe fracture (the second of his career) was immediately diagnosed.

Unconscious for over a week, the former 9th Lancer applied for a Medical after the outbreak of war and was promptly sent on six months' sick leave.

There could be no question of any very 'active' service, but two years later, Fulke, now serving, much to the amusement of his friends, in the Military Police, had an even narrower escape.

Before jumping was stopped altogether in 1942, he sent out a total of eight winners and it may have been to celebrate one of them that Fulke and Diana went with some friends to listen and dance to 'Snakehips' Johnson at the Café de Paris on 8 March 1941.

'We had this table in the balcony we all thought lucky,' recalls Fulke, 'but that night the balcony was full. They put us down near the band, which almost certainly saved our lives.' After the direct hit which killed eighty-four people, it still took him a nerve-wracking hour to find his wife, who had been dancing when the bomb fell. 'Di had a broken arm but much the worse thing I remember is people coming in from the street and pulling jewels off the dead.'

So Mandarin, Mill House, Special Cargo and all the other good horses which have passed through Saxon House were doubly lucky. If Gordon Johnson Houghton had been a little less unselfish – or if 'Snakehips' Johnson had played a different tune, who knows? Their careers would certainly not have been the same and you can have odds from me against them winning more or better races.

In any occupation as chancy as training steeplechasers, the first bit of luck any trainer needs is owners able to supply the raw material of his trade. On the long distinguished list of Fulke's patrons, the names of two remarkable but totally dissimilar ladies stand out.

Fulke Walwyn in 1988.

Apart from their interest in horses and the fact that Fulke Walwyn trained for them, it would be very hard indeed to think of two human beings with less in common than Queen Elizabeth the Queen Mother and Dorothy Paget. But while the transfer of the royal jumpers to Lambourn after the death of Peter Cazalet in 1973 set a seal on Fulke Walwyn's place at the top of his profession, it was unquestionably the appearance there of Miss Paget's string in 1946 which sent him into orbit.

At first it seemed an alarming offer. 'Take all twenty or nothing,' were the terms, and Fulke spent anxious hours billeting horses all over Lambourn. But in the next eight stormy, argumentative years he trained 365 winners for the eccentric millionairess – and is especially proud that, when he and Miss Paget parted, it was on friendly terms by mutual consent.

Fulke won his first Gold Cup with Dave Dick wearing the famous Paget colours on Mont Tremblant but, perhaps because my memory does not go back that far, the three most dramatic moments of his career came later for other owners.

They are Mandarin's Grand Steeplechase de Paris (pages 115–19), Mill House's Whitbread Gold Cup (pages 188–91) and the unforgettable finish to the same race in 1984 when the Queen Mother's Special Cargo got up on the line with his thirteen-year-old stable-companion Diamond Edge only inches away in third place (pages 155–61).

Mandarin's – and Fred Winter's – Paris triumph without brakes or steering has often been described and I never remember more emotion being felt and shown on a racecourse than the day when Mill House came back at Sandown to claim his long-lost crown.

However, I remember writing at the time that Special Cargo's Whitbread came about as close to 'the perfect race' as we are ever likely to get.

The running of Special Cargo and Diamond Edge, two patched-up veterans who rose above themselves that day, certainly represented a perfect masterpiece of training. But it was only one of the many with which, for half a century, Fulke Walwyn has earned the gratitude and admiration of the racing world.

22 February 1990

This piece was written after I had given up the Audax column, apropos the Horse and Hound *Grand Military Gold Cup. Now, with Fulke Walwyn's life and unique career both over, I am struggling to do him justice in a book. Anyone who has a memory or story about the Master of Saxon House would do me a great favour by communicating it.*

BILL WHITBREAD

Last week's Whitbread Gold Cup had one especially sad feature. It was the first in thirty years which Colonel W.H. 'Bill' Whitbread was unable to attend.

In 1957 England had never seen a commercially sponsored steeplechase – or, for that matter, a race of any kind linked with and subsidised by the makers of a product like beer. What is more, the National Hunt season was still almost completely dominated by the Grand National.

In 1956, the year of Devon Loch's unexplained collapse, ESB, the chief beneficiary, earned Mrs Carver £8,695. Two weeks earlier Limber Hill's Gold Cup at Cheltenham had been worth a mere £3,750 and, with a few exceptions, any decent staying 'chaser was trained, throughout the season, with Grand National day in mind. After it, the rest of the jumping season was an unimportant anti-climax, dwarfed by the flat.

Colonel Whitbread, then fifty-six and chairman of the brewery which his ancestor Samuel founded in 1742, knew all about the lure of Aintree. He rode his own Ben Cruchan in two Grand Nationals (1925 and 1926) and got round both times, despite having to remount.

I have always thought this a glowing exception to the sound old jockeys' rule that 'there are fools, *bloody* fools – and people who remount in a steeplechase!' Bill Whitbread, who also rode fifteen winners, remounted both times at one of the last three fences – and had proved long before 1956 that he has never been anybody's fool.

His brainwave in that year was to propose to the National

Hunt Committee (not then amalgamated with the Jockey Club) that Whitbreads should put up the prize money – or a large part thereof – for a 3m 5f handicap 'chase at Sandown in April, two or three weeks *after* the Grand National.

As it happens, Much Obliged, the first Whitbread winner (in a tremendous finish with Mandarin) had fallen in the National. In fact, he fell at the Canal Turn – but it has been much more the exception than the rule for Aintree 'failures' to gain compensation at Sandown.

Anyway, the Whitbread was always far more than a consolation prize. It not only set the fashion for commercial sponsorship, but also combined with its immediate successor, the Hennessy Gold Cup, to change the whole shape and balance of the National Hunt season.

The man responsible for this sporting revolution is himself a many-sided sportsman and lover of horses and horsemanship in all their forms.

The Badminton Three-Day event, held near Colonel Whitbread's country home, is just one of many trials of sporting strength to which Whitbreads give their support, and the Colonel himself, an experienced 'whip' and President of the Shire Horse Society, played an important part in the post-war rescue and revival of heavy horses.

In August 1936, when something went wrong with Whitbreads' beer, the eminent scientist called in to investigate blamed the proximity, at Chiswell Street, of the horses and/or their fodder! The Colonel has never accepted his verdict – but it was the height of the beer-drinking season and the horses were, very reluctantly, moved to different stables!

No one has ever suggested doing without them altogether – not in Bill Whitbread's hearing anyway. Although Whitbreads, unlike most of the other horse-employing breweries, do not compete at shows, their famous Shires have, for many years, pulled both the Speaker's and Lord Mayor's coaches in all their ceremonial processions.

Before the war, when first asked to supply horses for the Speaker's Coach, Bill Whitbread learnt that the vehicle had no brakes and, since the procession was to go *down* St James's Street (not in those days, a one-way street uphill), he decided on an early morning dress rehearsal!

It very nearly ended in disaster, for the Whitbread Shires, accustomed to brakes, took three-quarters of St James's Street to learn how to take the weight of the heavy coach on their quarter breechings. 'For a moment,' the Colonel remembers, 'we looked very like making a big hole in St James's Palace!'

Sadly, although Colonel Whitbread has owned good jumpers nearly all his adult life, victory in his own race has always eluded him. Probably his best horse, Dunkirk, was basically a flamboyant two-mile 'chaser, and although Mariner's Dance, Kapeno and Barona (who won two Scottish Grand Nationals) were all, in theory, possible Whitbread winners, it never went right on the day.

Any disappointment the race's inventor might feel at never (so far) winning it was much more than wiped away when, after the unforgettable four-horse finish of 1984, Colonel Whitbread had the honour and pleasure of presenting his own Gold Cup to Special Cargo's owner, Queen Elizabeth the Queen Mother.

Often rivals on the course, Her Majesty and he have each done British National Hunt racing indispensable service. Each, in a different way, has transformed the sport.

Once, in the early years of Colonel Whitbread's chairmanship, the Canadian millionaire businessman E.P. Taylor – later to breed Northern Dancer and Nijinsky – came to Chiswell Street with a vast and, on the face of it, attractive offer to take the brewery over.

As luck would have it, Bill Whitbread had met E.P. Taylor before – when both, as young men, were doing the best they could to learn about life in Canada.

'I think he was a bit surprised to see me,' Bill Whitbread remembers. 'I said, "thank you, but no" – and told the butler to count the silver after he had shown him out!'

It is a thought calculated to send a chill down any jumping enthusiast's spine that, if things had gone a little differently that day, the great steeplechase we watched last week might have been just another mammoth mile-and-a-quarter flat-race prize!

But they didn't, it isn't – and for that we all owe Colonel Bill Whitbread an unpayable debt of gratitude.

2 May 1986

FRED WINTER

A long and glorious story ended last Saturday afternoon when, after seventeen years as a National Hunt jockey, Fred Winter, CBE, sat for the last time in his own particular corner of the Cheltenham weighing room. Champagne corks were popping as, to celebrate his many triumphs on the course, they had so often popped before. But now, mixed with the jokes and laughter, there was sadness too – the sadness of a sport which, flourishing and growing as it is, can never, for many of us, be quite the same without him.

The facts and figures of Fred Winter's record are, I think, too widely known to need re-telling here and, on Saturday, for me at least, it wasn't just the well-remembered highlights that came flooding back – it was the memory, rather, of countless moments when, in grandstands great and small, I, like thousands of others, have stood and cheered and wondered, warmed by the magic of his skill.

Jumping is not only Cheltenham or Liverpool or Auteuil and Fred has not been just a 'great occasion' jockey. A race worth £180 at some humble, ill-attended meeting was, to him, as much a challenge as the Cheltenham Gold Cup – or almost, anyway.

It was this unswerving determination to give his best which, in the past decade, has done as much for N.H. racing as any other single factor – and if he needed a memorial there could be none more fitting than the present standard of N.H. jockeyship – higher, in my opinion, than at any time since the war.

No one can say how much of this is due to Fred's example but he, for years, has been the mark at which young jockeys aimed and it is the measure of his undisputed greatness that none of them, as yet, has been put forward as his equal.

Fred Winter being led in after winning the Grand National
on Kilmore in 1962.

Now he is gone, retiring, thank heaven, without any serious
scars to show for his long, arduous career – retiring, as a
champion should, at the top, without the slightest sign that
his powers might be on the wane.

That in itself is something for which we should give thanks
– and on Saturday, Tim Brookshaw's presence at Cheltenham,
cheerful as ever but still in his wheelchair, was a painful
reminder that others have not been so fortunate.

But Fred, for seventeen years, took the same risks, and also
suffered, in his time, injuries and setbacks which might well
have been the end. He hit the ground, in fact, more than 300 times
and broke his back in only his twelfth ride under N.H. rules. His
courage was never of the sort which knows no fear but rather that
far finer brand which *knows* – and overcomes the knowledge.

So here, for the last time, let me express, on behalf, I believe,
of all who love the jumping game, our heartfelt gratitude to a
great jockey and a great character.

Perhaps the yawning gap he leaves behind *will* one day be
filled. Personally, I doubt it, but we can hope and, hoping, keep
alive our memory of the best we ever saw.

18 April 1964

Bumping . . .

Graham Thorner and Precipitate (left) and Lord Oaksey and
Flyervale in a similar predicament at Windsor, 1975.

The best name ever given to a racing autobiography was unquestionably Jack Leach's Sods I have Cut on the Turf. *But Jakie Astor once suggested that if I ever put pen to paper in that way,* Bumping and Boring *would be the only appropriate title. Hence the headings of the last two chapters in this book.*

As the kind provider of many wonderful rides, and as an even kinder host at Hatley, Jakie has not only had to put up with my efforts as a Bumper but also, in our many happy arguments, as a Bore. On the understanding that he certainly need not read them, these two chapters are, with love and gratitude, dedicated to him.

FOR PURE JOY,
JUMPING'S THE GAME

I was about six when I backed my first winner, sixpence on the nose of a horse called Nettlebed whose jockey had red hair. I know he had red hair because, nearly thirty years before anyone thought of chinstraps, his hat came off at the first fence. But the leader fell at the last, my hero rode Nettlebed safely home and I was five bob richer.

My father and his before him were lifelong supporters of the Pegasus (Bar) point-to-point and when the first post-war meeting was threatened by an understandable dearth of legal runners, my sister's beloved twenty-year-old hunter was called upon for his first and only racecourse appearance.

A small, elegant chesnut called Lohengrin, he had never been known to turn his head out hunting and, since my sister had only a half-bred heavyweight to gallop with, Lohengrin's speed seemed more than adequate to us.

You have to be at least a would-be barrister to ride in the Bar point-to-point, so, having not left school, I was not even offered the ride. The invitation went instead to Gerald Ponsonby (now Lord de Mauley), who, very honestly, warned Lohengrin's trainer that he had just been struggling with his Bar exams and was far from certain to stay three miles!

Nine ran, including at least one judge, in the Bar Light-weight Race and, although they hardly looked a Gold Cup field, Lohengrin started at 20 to 1. A kindly godfather gave me a pound to put on, so there I was, proud possessor of a bookies' ticket representing by far the biggest wager of my life that far.

But not for the first or last time, alas, home gallops turned out to be misleading. Lohengrin's rivals might not have been flying machines, but they went a whole lot faster than the trees past which he had flashed so impressively at Oaksey. After the first fence he and Gerald Ponsonby were fully a fence behind.

But, as John Buckingham learnt on Foinavon some years later, you must never give up in a steeplechase. By the time they passed us first time round, two had fallen, and the fifth from home at Kimble is (or was in those days) an open ditch.

Pausing to take a cautious look at it, the riderless leader transmitted his misgivings to the five survivors and in a trice all five had come to a grinding, muddled halt and were milling round to try again.

It was into this chaotic jumble of blaspheming barristers and gesticulating judges that Lohengrin cantered sedately like a duchess at a noisy children's party. Without a glance to right or left, he popped over the offending ditch and suddenly the impossible was on the cards again.

There were, however, four fences still to jump and for different reasons both Gerald and his mount were beginning to feel the strain. They came apart twice at the last two fences, but each time the breathless jockey held on like a hero. As he and Lohengrin set off up the run-in, the first of their opponents had only just got over the ditch – so my £20 were safe and the seeds of my passion for racing more deeply implanted than ever.

It was only a few years later that the same race, the Bar Lightweight, caused them to take permanent root and deprived the legal profession of my services. By then, as a law student, I was qualified to ride – and had, in fact, done so with notable lack of success in about five other point-to-points.

My steed at Kimble was a sharp-looking mare called Next Of Kin, whose previous form did not give obvious grounds for confidence. Moreover, she did her best to live up to her name by rearing and falling over backwards not once but twice in the paddock.

In the race, by contrast, it was the others who fell over. Next Of Kin jumped round like a stag inspired and, for the first time, I learnt how it feels when things go right – when you see a stride and ask and the horse comes up and lands far out the other side to flick away as smooth as silk.

It is a sensation which comes in a million different varieties, but I have never found anything in sport to match it and, for that first lesson, I owe Next Of Kin an unpayable debt.

Before she came on the scene, most of my tiny point-to-point experience was in the Oxford and Bullingdon grinds. The University Drag was generally presided over in those days by Gay Kindersley and early almost every morning we used to chug together down the long straight road to Bicester in his geriatric Wolsey Hornet to ride out with that great sportsman and stableman Cecil Bonner.

Then, and for many years before and after, Cecil was the centre-point round which the riding section of Oxford life revolved.

With infinite patience and forbearance he organised our gallops (round Bicester Aerodrome), supervised the mutual schooling of both horses and riders, trained our point-to-pointers, found hirelings when they were needed and repeatedly put up with our incompetence.

It was Cecil, I think, who stage-managed what was meant to be the triumphant final racing bow of Gay's father Philip Kindersley, himself a past Master of the Drag, president of the Bullingdon and founder of the still thriving Mid-Surrey Farmers' Drag.

Philip Kindersley was also by that time an extremely senior and important figure in the City, well past the usual age for 'bumping round' in point-to-points. So a reliable first-rate conveyance was called for and, since victory was also very much the aim, Cecil secured on our behalf one of the best hunter 'chasers then in training.

Even with four or five motley opponents in the Bullingdon Past and Present Race, he represented one of the most cast-iron good things in 'chasing history, but, not for the first time in the chequered saga of the Bullingdon, things did not go quite according to plan.

Besides Gay and myself, the field contained an intrepid sportsman called Robin Higgin. As an undergraduate his sporting enthusiasm knew few bounds – but was limited by extreme short-sightedness and a pair of spectacles made of what looked like bullet-proof glass.

I cannot remember now whether Robin removed these specs

before he started or whether they came adrift later. But the result in any case was the same – almost total blindness.

The Higgin steed was not easy to control at the best of times and, having nearly missed the first fence through faulty steering, he approached the second at an angle of 45 degrees and took poor Philip amidships in mid-air.

I am not sure, on reflection, that what followed was altogether in keeping with rule 151 (ii) – the one about taking 'all reasonable and permissible measures throughout the race to . . . obtain the best possible placing'. From a field of six, two were riderless and the other four riders were taking all reasonable and permissible measures to recapture one of the loose ones.

Heaven knows what the crowd made of it, let alone the stewards – but Cecil Bonner's judgment had been sound. His carefully selected hunter 'chaser was, as he said, much the fastest horse in the field, and our strenuous efforts to apprehend him were in vain. Even by Bullingdon standards that race took an exceptionally long time to complete.

But as many will find, beginners and more experienced riders alike, you do not need victory or the success of devious schemes to make point-to-points exciting. When a horse jumps well and does his best and still gets beat, he can even then make you feel a king – always provided, of course, that you are not blaming yourself for letting him and his connections down.

As often as not, if you are honest, that, to begin with, will be the case. I certainly used to fall off far too frequently for comfort, made almost every known tactical error, and, even after twenty years, still used to get run away with regularly at home.

For the beginner, mind you, falling off, or at least 'going out the front door' when a horse hits a fence or pecks badly on landing, is nothing much to worry about. Within reason, in fact, I believe it may be a good sign. You learn soon enough by painful experience to take the necessary safety measures – sitting up with your feet thrust forward as shock absorbers against the stirrup irons and slipping the reins to give your horse his head and avoid being pulled clean over it yourself.

At least those early 'forward' ejections show you are going in the right direction – *with* your horse in search of victory rather than backwards in search of survival.

For a clear explanation of the quickest, safest and most effective method of crossing a fence without falling off – and for all the other skills and techniques you need to become a half-way competent rider, John Hislop's *Steeplechasing* remains by far and away the best, indeed so far as I know the only, worthwhile *vade mecum*.

The late John Skeaping's line drawings illustrate more clearly than any words the sort of avoiding action I just attempted to describe, and on every facet of cross-country riding and jockeyship John Hislop's advice is as sound now as when he wrote it thirty years ago.

He has, incidentally, also just produced some equally admirable guidelines on the proper and improper use of the whip. They now represent official Jockey Club policy and should be required reading in every changing room for senior jockeys, as well as apprentices and amateurs.

Apart from falling off or making major tactical nonsenses, the most common reason for self-criticism is – or used to be in my experience – exhaustion caused by lack of fitness. Riding for three miles over fences is quite hard work on the easiest, most cooperative horse and if, as almost always happens, he needs at least some encouragement along the way, you can very soon find yourself just as tired as if you had been running the race yourself.

My own whole attitude to the question of fitness changed when, long before Jane Fonda and Sophia Loren made the word fashionable, an American called Kenneth Cooper published his *Aerobics*. In the clearest possible language, Dr Cooper explains how your heart and lungs work, and how their operation and endurance can be improved.

He then gives a value in points to a whole wide range of alternative forms of exercise from straightforward running and walking to swimming, bicycling and even running on the spot. Thirty points a week, he says, is enough to maintain a minimum level of fitness, but I suspect he would recommend at least three times that for anyone planning to ride at all seriously over fences.

I know it sounds dull and am fully aware of having long ago

become a bore upon the subject. But it works. And if you have anyone you are fond of who plans to ride in point-to-points or any steeplechase this year, the two best presents you could give him or her are John Hislop's *Steeplechasing* and a paperback of Dr Kenneth Cooper's *The New Aerobics*.

25 January 1985

A couple of 'Veterans'' races at Ascot have reminded me painfully how good this advice remains. If only I had kept somewhere near Dr Cooper's thirty points a week!

Unless you can actually ride to work, or, better still, take part in an actual race, the best way to exercise the right muscles is, I find, riding a bicycle. The longer you can keep your bottom off the saddle, the less likely you will be to 'bump' disgracefully through sheer exhaustion in the last two furlongs.

CAUTIONARY TALES
FROM AROUND THOSE
LOVELY GAFFS

At the start of the Second World War, National Hunt racing was taking place on 79 different courses in the British Isles. Now there are only 44 – but the almost infinite variety of background against which the winter game can be watched and played is still one of its most powerful drawing cards.

Looking down the list the other day I found that Perth, which is, by all accounts, a lovely course, set in the grounds of a stately Scottish palace, is the only one I have never visited.

Well, there may be time to put that right but in the meanwhile please forgive a few fleeting reminiscences – memories which some of the less famous stages conjure up for an aged and forgetful one-time bumper.

They are in no special order – except the first. Let's get the bad news over early. I honestly can't remember Folkestone, having left it in an ambulance.

Clover Prince, an otherwise blameless animal belonging to Andrew Wates, started favourite and was still in front when he fell three fences out. That gave the others the chance to treat me like a welcome mat and one of them rearranged my jaw.

The famous East Grinstead hospital (where the great McIndoe worked his wartime miracles) soon put that straight but the general view was that, if intending to make any further use of my head, I had better stop falling on it.

'Don't read, don't even *think* too much' were, I believe, the immediate orders, and, moving home by gentle stages, we stayed a night with that prince of hosts, the late Frankie More O'Ferrall at Rudgwick.

The spring meeting was on at Chester and, demanding a *Sporting Life* and telephone, I insisted on ringing through to Ladbrokes a £10 each-way yankee. That meant a stake of £220 compared with my usual maximum of a fiver! Three of the four went in – two of Dick Hern's and one of Bernard Van Cutsem's.

If only Lester had woken his ideas up on John Cherry in the Cup, I would have won a fortune and even without him the winnings were well into four figures. Moral, I suppose: if you want to tip winners, keep getting concussed.

It has never been absolutely clear to me whether the recently publicised rule against jockeys betting applies to amateur riders. I sincerely hope not, although not many of these memories concern successful punting.

One of the few that does reflects no credit whatever on your correspondent but presumably the Statute of Limitations applies to offences committed in 1957!

At the start of that season, having laboriously compiled a lifetime total of three winners, I was riding out for Bob Turnell and fell deeply in love, on the Ogbourne gallops, with a six-year-old mare called Cautious.

The £600 she cost came from a kindly bank manager – and Bob was always well aware that his training fees would only materialise if Cautious not only reproduced her home form on the racecourse but also, even less likely, managed to stay between her owner and the ground.

The rent of the flat which Bob McCreery and I were sharing at the time was equally dependent on her efforts.

So things looked black, or, in the bank's eyes, red when, with our money down at fancy prices, Cautious ran like a hairy sheep at Wincanton and Warwick. By April we were in despair and there were calls (from McCreery) for a change of jockey.

But, as it turned out, even more important, the ground had dried up when, completely unbacked and in disgrace, we reappeared together at Wincanton.

Suddenly, before half-way, it became clear even to me that this was an entirely different Cautious – the one we had staked our all on the previous autumn and, in heavy winter going, waited for so expensively in vain!

So what to do? Not a penny on, the mare pulling double, jumping like a stag inspired – and me with even less idea how to stop a horse winning than I had how to get one home in front!

A veil had better be drawn over the next few seconds but Cautious somehow finished fourth and *Chaseform* says: 'Never placed to challenge.'

Worse was to come because, scurrying shamefacedly towards the weighing room, I met my mother, a mad-keen but not, in those days, a particularly expert race-reader.

'How wonderful to finish fourth,' she cried. 'The silly thing is I forgot my race glasses but luckily I was standing with General McCreery so I *asked him to watch you for me.*' The only snag was that the General was senior steward at Wincanton!

But he was also one of the nicest, most understanding men I have ever known, quite apart from being among the last war's greatest and best-loved commanders in the field.

'Ran well, John,' was all he said that day – and when, three weeks later, the heavenly Cautious came home at 6 to 1 in a Chepstow novice hurdle, retrieving all our bacon, the General wrote me a letter of congratulations which will always be one of my most treasured possessions.

So you can see why Wincanton and Chepstow come rather higher on my list than Folkestone!

Both are, in fact, cheerful, welcoming places, where the crowds love to see good horses as well as back them. It was not betting, half as much as the simple *presence* of Desert Orchid which overflowed the Wincanton car parks when he reappeared there (starting at 7 to 1 on) in October.

Nor do you need to back, or ride, winners to appreciate the merits of any racecourse. Even making an idiot of yourself does not necessarily turn you against it. I was once fined for not weighing-in at Fontwell but still rate it the best place in England for a first-time racegoer to see and feel and appreciate the thrills, speed and violent action of a steeplechase.

After standing by the downhill first fence in a 2m 2½f or 3m 2½f 'chase, you have only 100 yards to walk to be by the last before they come round again. And don't worry if you lose count of the circuits. Many a jockey has ridden a stylish finish up the Fontwell hill, only to find that he must go round again!

On some courses, admittedly, you do need things to go right. A bad day at Wolverhampton, where that grimy viaduct looms above you and even the grass looks grubby, can be very hard to take when you have fallen off or spent a week wasting to ride a loser.

But Barbizon won there, the horse my father-in-law Ginger Dennistoun bought for 120 guineas as a yearling. He won a seller at Kempton first time out by eight lengths, opening at 100 to 7, starting 11 to 4 favourite – and I can still remember how lovely those crinkly old white fivers felt.

Then later, when allowed to win on Barbizon at Wolverhampton, I knew how little help I had been to this big strong four-year-old, at that time badly in need of a real jockey to hold him together.

Did I get off, was I pushed – or, just possibly, injured? Cannot remember now, and who cares? What matters is that Fred Winter rode Barbizon in the Grey Talk Hurdle at Hurst Park and, for the second time in that good horse's life, I really *did* know something the bookies didn't.

For Fred, as I knew he would, improved Barbizon by at least a stone and in they went at 8 to 1.

Oh, happy Hurst Park. Why did they have to turn a great racecourse into a riverside clutch of unattractive housing?

There is a river at Windsor, too, and, towards the end of his distinguished career, my beloved Taxidermist very nearly went into it – carrying with him Taff Jenkins and a horse whose name I forget.

'What chance have I got against you with two lords sitting as stewards?' Taffy enquired as we stood waiting for their decision. But he underestimated the judicial impartiality of the Windsor panel and Ron Barry made a similar mistake at Sandown after the 1974 Whitbread Gold Cup.

Unlike Taxi, who richly deserved to be disqualified, Proud Tarquin was, in my prejudiced opinion, robbed of a prize he won on merit.

'How can you win, a poor old bogman against a barrister?' Monty Court, now Editor of the *Sporting Life*, asked Ron outside the weighing room.

But he was wrong three ways. Ron Barry, though unquestionably Irish, is neither poor nor old, I never made it to the bar, and the Sandown stewards disqualified Proud Tarquin. Which either proves their balanced wisdom – or, as I believe, suggests that they ought to be tapping their way down Piccadilly with white sticks . . .

Don't get me started on Sandown, though. This is supposed to be about the lesser tracks. Like Catterick, the only place I ever had a bandage come undone – nervy work in a 20-horse novice hurdle.

Or Towcester, where Frank Pullen, that amazing patcher-up of bad-legged horses, was once kind enough to let me ride a good old selling 'chaser. After weighing in I hurried out to find the trainer.

'Did you buy him back all right?' I asked anxiously, and shall never forget Frank's scornful answer.

'Buy him back?' the old trainer said. 'Buy him *back*? Why, when I took the bandages off, they were fainting all round the ring!'

31 December 1987

HUNT RACING HEROES ADORN FINAL'S ROLL OF HONOUR

I cannot, alas, claim to have seen all twenty-nine *Horse and Hound* Cups but a glance down the roll of honour brings back all sorts of memories. There are not many heroes of the hunter 'chasing world, equine or human, who do not figure somewhere on the list.

Spartan Missile, Baulking Green, Credit Call and Otter Way would form the nucleus of a pretty competitive contest if they could be brought together at their best and, one way and another, names like Thorne, Gifford, Collins, Easterby, Henderson and Sherwood have figured in quite a few jumping headlines since Walter Case and Gay Sheppard had their original brainwave.

It cuts away the years a bit to remember that in the very first race of the series, J'Arrive, on whom Gay Kindersley finished second to Speylove, had been *ridden* to victory in five hunter 'chases by Arthur Stephenson!

I once had the honour of riding in a hunter 'chase (at Catterick, I think) in which Arthur, Danny Moralee and Guy Cunard were all involved. It was quite an experience for an innocent beginner.

J'Arrive was worth every penny of the £4,000 Gay Kindersley paid for him. They won numerous hunter 'chases and point-to-points together, notably six races in the 1959–60 season when J'Arrive played a major part in his owner's heroic arrival at the top of the amateurs' table.

The old horse was also a formidable hunter, stabled with the late Cecil Bonner at Bicester and hard to catch across that country.

The sad thing about the first *Horse and Hound* was that Happy Morn II should certainly have won it. She was a wonderfully tough little mare and Tony Biddlecombe had just taken over the lead when, through no fault of his, a loose horse barged poor Happy Morn inside the wing.

Tony's elder brother Terry, still an amateur in those days, was fourth on Danny Boy in 1959 and Merryman II, who was third, had won that year's Scottish National. He was, of course, to go on and win the real thing at Aintree – so our 'inaugural', then called 'The Final Hunters' 'Chase', was in several ways a seriously distinguished contest!

Colledge Master, on whom Laurie Morgan was practically invincible, would certainly have won easily in 1961 if Laurie's place had not been taken by his son.

But I have every sympathy with the inexperienced seventeen-year-old. Colledge Master was making a comeback in 1961 but three years earlier, as a seven-year-old, he and Laurie Morgan were only beaten once – by that great Scottish hunter The Callant – and won the Foxhunters' at Liverpool.

But a couple of years later, when Laurie had to go back to Australia, he sent Colledge Master to Bob Turnell and kindly said that I could ride him.

The result, considering the horse's record, was an undignified disaster.

Although we did win one minor race together, the fact is that I could not ride one side of Colledge Master – and it was not until his master returned that he began winning again.

There followed (with all due respect to the dual winner Bantry Bay) what will always seem to me the era of Baulking Green.

The great Berkshire hunter won our race three times and would, I am bound to admit, have won a fourth but for ignoring the second last in 1967.

It was, I believe, the only time Baulking Green actually ended up on the floor, but, from my position, two lengths behind on Cham, I regret to say that his and George Small's departure was an extremely welcome sight.

A few weeks before, meeting in a valuable hunter 'chase up at Ayr, George and I got thoroughly over-excited and took each other on like madmen from the start. My unfriendly and, as it turned out, quite unsuccessful theory was that Cham, a superlative jumper, might hurry the often careless Baulking Green into making a mistake!

Instead we inspired the old devil and, I am told, gave quite an exhibition of jumping down the back side at Ayr.

There is no fool like an old one and both George and I would have looked extremely silly if, as very nearly happened, we had cut each others throats and been caught!

In fact George came off best in both the duel and the race – winning by a hard-fought length. But a wily unknown Irish amateur by the name of Thomas Stack flew up from the back on Sizzle-On and failed by only a neck to deprive me of second place!

So there was a bit more at stake than just another race at Stratford and, until he fell, Baulking Green was going ominously well. But so was Royal Phoebe, ridden, in his amateur pre-television prime, by Mr B. Scott.

Brough Scott on Royal Phoebe (left) with John Lawrence on Cham at the last fence of the 1967 Horse and Hound Cup at Stratford.

Brough has a picture of the last fence on his study wall in which, I have to admit, his position resembles J. Francome's marginally closer than mine.

But it just shows that style isn't everything – because Royal

Phoebe made a hash of the fence and Cham, God bless him, beat her by a length and a half.

The production of this rambling memoir has had one worthwhile side-effect – causing me to look again at Ron Liddiard's splendid biography of Baulking Green.

This, surely, is the only hunter 'chaser ever to have had a book written about him – and how well he deserved it.

Of all the many good stories, the one which brings me closest to tears is Ron's account of Baulking Green's last race at Cheltenham, the 1968 United Hunts when, at the age of fifteen, he failed by a rapidly vanishing short-head to catch Snowdra Queen.

The other sad memory I have of Baulking Green is that I never managed to beat him on Major Rushton's Rosie's Cousin, who may well be the best hunter 'chaser never to win our race.

He was certainly, bar none, the most brilliant spring-heeled jumper of steeplechase fences I ever rode – but only just got three miles, preferably on fast ground and a nice flat course.

We had precisely that at Taunton one day when Rosie and I were a fence clear of Baulking Green turning out of the back straight. I was just thinking, 'Got you at last,' when all four feet went whoosh and there we were on the floor!

When ridden by Major Rushton's daughter, Mrs Tollitt, Rosie's Cousin was never beaten in ladies' point-to-points. He died happy, too, walking back to scale with her after winning yet again.

Fine though Baulking Green's Stratford record was, it does not quite match that of Credit Call, who not only won the Cup outright but came back two years later to win it again for eighteen-year-old Joey Newton.

But it is Credit Call's first win that I remember best: the day in 1971 when he was ridden not by his owner, Chris Collins, but by Graham MacMillan.

No doubt missing the ride through injury was a bitter blow for Chris Collins, but the resulting change of jockey was an even worse one for me.

Graham MacMillan and I had been neck and neck for some time in the race for the amateurs' Bollinger Trophy and I came to Stratford with a fragile lead of one!

I watched from a long way behind on a horse called Jedheads

as Credit Call sailed home – and there we were, tied in the lead with Graham on another ride that evening at Market Rasen!

Things looked black – but wait, perhaps there was just one other chance?

Terry Biddlecombe and his brother-in-law Bob Davies had been fighting out an equally close battle for the professional title and, leaving no stone unturned, Terry had hired a helicopter to fly him from Stratford to Market Rasen. But he was two behind and had only two rides booked.

So, 'Come on,' this great and good man said. 'If the first of them doesn't win I'll see if I can get you the ride on the second.'

It didn't sound one of those gilt-edged certainties you hear about – but desperate measures seemed called for, so off we flew.

The first good news at Market Rasen was that Graham got beaten in the 7 p.m. – and the second, though not for him, of course, was that Terry never looked like winning the 7.30.

So far so good – but then a snag arose. His second and last ride was a horse called Arrow Trout in the aptly named Final Fling Novice 'Chase and, when asked whether she would like an ageing amateur to ride it, the trainer, Mrs Barbara Lockhart Smith, issued an entirely understandable – and unprintable – veto on the plan!

Well, we may never know what Terry promised her but the famous Biddlecombe charm won through in the nick of time.

So, just a trifle apprehensive, I found myself approaching the first fence alongside Graham Thorner – going quite a bit faster than either of us intended. But all was well. The admirable Arrow Trout 'guessed' a little here and there but never threatened to get out from under me. The others went even slower and, in a haze of incredulous pleasure, we sailed home 12 lengths clear.

Not everyone cheered, of course, and, the following winter, answering questions one night from the floor at some horsey gathering in the North I was assailed by a Scotsman with the furious enquiry: 'Do you think it was very sporting to beat a fine man like Graham MacMillan by taking a professional's ride?'

Well, I had not really thought of it like that and was making a stumbling, somewhat apologetic reply when a lady with fair hair stood up at the back of the hall.

'It wasn't exactly a spare ride on Arkle, you know,' she said firmly. 'It was a five-year-old having its first run over fences.'

They were some of the kindest words I have ever heard and it was only later, when I went to thank her, that I found out the lady's name. It was Mrs Dickinson and I have been in love with her ever since.

2 June 1988

TAKING THE REINS
IN SPAIN

In 1958, inspired by the Duke of Albuquerque, the Hippodromo di Madrid invited a team of English horses and riders (with all expenses paid for both them, their trainers and, I think, their owners) to come for two races, one Flat and one over hurdles, on the Sunday of Madrid's great Spring Festival of San Isidro.

Bob McCreery won the hurdle race easily on Gold Wire, the marvellous little all-rounder who won races in five different countries. He was partly owned by the great Chesney Allen and I shall never forget the night we delivered Gold Wire's Cup at the Victoria Palace, then, of course, home of the immortal Crazy Gang.

After the cup had been filled and emptied several times, Bob, Ryan Price and I were installed in a box. No doubt someone warned us – though for some reason, we took no notice at the time – that this was 'the gag box', and that if the door at the back opened we should at all costs keep our heads down.

Well, we soon learned – because whenever a member of the Gang appeared behind us he was pelted, by his colleagues on the stage, with everything from eggs to plastic (break-able) bags of coloured water! I have often wondered what the paying customers thought of a performance crammed with references to Gold Wire, his rider, trainer and personal habits, to Hippodromos, Spanish racing and Spanish Dukes – with countless other ad-libbed, ad hoc embroideries.

Needless to say, whether they understood or not, the audience loved every moment.

The only slight disaster of our Spanish venture came in the

flat race, which seemed to the whole British contingent – including Ryan Price, Tom Masson, Fred Rimell, Don Butchers and Doug Marks – at the mercy of Gama IV, a four-year-old with high-class form in France whom Gay Kindersley had recently bought to go hurdling.

I was riding a selling hurdler trained by Doug Marks called Duet Leader and, since neither he nor any of the other invaders seemed to have the remotest chance of getting anywhere near Gama, the Spanish Tote was inundated with a flood of confident British pesetas!

To begin with everything seemed to be going by the book but then, as Gay sent Gama ahead on the turn for home, I found myself on his tail – with Duet Leader pulling double! No one will ever know what inspired him but, pesetas or no pesetas, there was no choice. As though stung by some Spanish bee, Duet Leader sprinted clear – and our kindly hosts could not understand why the second English winner of the day got such a piano reception!

28 December 1984

QUITE A DAY . . .

I suppose I had better – reluctantly – describe the somewhat sensational events which led up to the victory of Bill Tellwright and French Cottage in the Whaddon Amateurs' Handicap 'Chase (3m) on the Saturday at Cheltenham. In fact, Terry Biddlecombe kindly offered to write this part of my article for me, but on reflection it seemed safer to decline!

Well, anyway, what happened was that, after only four fences of Saturday's race, Mrs R.C. Wimbush's Pioneer Spirit had, by virtue of some spectacular jumping, left all his rivals well behind and, though I did not know it till much later, only one of them, French Cottage, had survived the first circuit.

When, therefore, we jumped the second last – nearly a fence ahead – you could hardly blame the bookmaker who asked for 25 to 1 on Pioneer Spirit, with, I sincerely hope, no takers!

The thought of what followed still brings me out in a cold sweat – and I still find it hard to explain, let alone excuse.

But on the new course in use last week it's a long way, perhaps three furlongs, between the last two jumps. First time round in a three-mile 'chase you have *two* fences to jump at this point before turning left away from the stand. But *second* time, on the same bend, you can't see any fence at all until you're in the straight.

What you *can* see is a flight of hurdles – and it was these which, on Saturday, convinced my addled brain that I had somehow lost my way.

To do so is, in fact, impossible. If you follow the rails you *can't* go wrong – but the rails here are only a stretch of temporary tape and a doubtless well-meant cry of encouragement from a man standing by them on Saturday sounded to me like a shout of warning.

So I pulled up. And, turning poor Pioneer Spirit, met a somewhat bewildered Bill Tellwright (who, as he told me later, had very nearly abandoned the 'chase some time before!).

Well, there it is. I can't explain it and have absolutely no excuse to offer. It is an elementary part of any jockey's duty to learn the course, and I simply hadn't done so. I'm never likely to make the same mistake again and only hope that my cretinous example may perhaps help others to avoid it.

In the meanwhile, to Mrs Wimbush, to Pioneer Spirit's trainer, Roddy Armytage, and to anyone luckless enough to have backed the horse I can only offer my sincere apologies.

The welcome we received on Saturday was richly deserved and, in fact, did credit to the crowd's good nature. No bottles were thrown and only a small minority seemed to take the view that my action had been inspired by evil motives.

To them I can only say that, in the extremely unlikely event of my ever wanting to pass up a winning ride (they don't exactly grow on trees), I shall adopt some slightly less public method!

And anyone who thinks (as well they might) that a £25 fine was not a severe enough penalty for so unforgivable an error, will doubtless he glad to hear that, getting home on Saturday night, I ran a hot bath, neglected to turn the taps off – and brought down a dozen square yards of ceiling in the room beneath. All in all it was quite a day . . .

19 December 1964

THE GREATEST GAME
OF ALL

There will, no doubt, be better, more exciting races this season than the National Hunt Centenary 'Chase at Newbury (2¹/₂m) but almost certainly I'll be watching them on foot. By contrast, Mr John Bairstow's Master Mascus (12st) gave me the sort of grandstand no Levy Board subsidy could ever build – a priceless vantage point from which the few decisive moments of the race stand out in one's mind like mountains in a plain.

The first two fences and, because Master Mascus is pulling hard, you guess the pace is slow. Then, suddenly, he drops the bit. They've speeded up and from that moment any ground you make has to be fought for. Gort (11st 7lb) is in front, but jumping, by his usual standards, moderately.

You can see from the angle of David Mould's back as he takes off that things aren't going quite right. But on they sail with Fort Leney (11st 7lb) up there now and, as you land safely over the water, Willie Robinson on Woodlawn (10st 7lb) says, in a voice of mock surprise, 'You *made* it!'

Just ahead, round the grandstand bend, Jeff King on Jomsviking (11st) gets 'done' by a horse outside him hanging inwards. He snatches up, saves Jomsviking from a painful collision with the rails, and, as you pass him by, a few incandescent words describe his feelings.

Then the long back straight and, easing out to get more daylight, you wonder whether you are cowardly or wise. But Master Mascus likes to see his fences, jumps them flawlessly when he can do so and as you turn downhill there are only three horses in front.

One of them, Limeking (10st 7lb), hits the downhill fence a dreadful clout and, as he and Gerry Scott struggle to recover, you swerve around them, losing half a length or so. It seems unimportant then – but afterwards, who knows?

Now, in the straight, Kapeno (11st) has moved up to Gort who, beforehand, you weighed up the biggest danger (Fort Leney you discarded because of his long lay-off and, for a change, you were right).

But Gort's no danger either. Suddenly you're past him and it's Kapeno four lengths clear – a horse you know too well and one than whom, in theory, Master Mascus ought to have far greater speed.

All this goes through your head but preconceived notions of that sort are strictly for the grandstand. *Here* the form book doesn't count. What counts is that Kapeno's on the bit and Master Mascus isn't.

One more to jump – and you're meeting it all wrong. A Winter, a Molony or a Mellor would, you know, extract that extra half a stride, make him stand back and fly.

It looks so easy when you're on the ground, but now you're tired and so's the horse, so he 'fiddles' – safe but slow. You're on the flat in one piece – but Kapeno is three lengths clear.

But Master Mascus is a *real* horse – a fighter and now, dog-tired, giving a stone away, he starts to fight. You help as best you can – not nearly well enough – but there, halfway up the run-in, the gap begins to shrink.

You can hear the crowd now and, looking across at Kapeno, a lightning memory flashes back of leading on him halfway from the last one day at Wolverhampton. You got caught then so there's still hope now. Perhaps he'll stop – he is stopping; he's tired, he's faltering.

But it's too late. Nick Gaselee on Kapeno has done his job too well. There's half a length to spare as you pass the post, but somehow, pulling up, you feel no bitterness.

Later there come the sad dark thoughts of what you should have done – of how a stronger jockey would have won. But that is later. Now, gasping, suddenly exhausted but almost completely happy, you only know how lucky you are.

You thank God for the luck and the kindness that gave you this wonderful horse to ride; you thank *him* for carrying you so well and, perhaps, in the Centenary year of N.H. racing, you even spare a thought for the endless hard work that goes into keeping alive what, for you and for so many others, is and will always be the greatest game of all.

29 October 1966

Kapeno was, through no fault of his own, the horse who caused the removal of my spleen – by putting his foot in it at the Cheltenham water jump in 1965. Peter Cazalet had kindly asked me to ride him in the National but, sadly, I was never able to do so.

I did ride Master Mascus (unsuccessfully) in a Grand National and was later due to ride him in the King George VI Steeplechase at Kempton on Boxing Day. But the frost came and, with racing clearly impossible, the BBC staged a 'Computer' King George at Broadcasting House. All the jockeys involved were invited to lunch and, in a well-lubricated discussion of the likely outcome, Julian Wilson laid me 500 to 1 against Master Mascus!

Ten shillings was the stake – off went the computer and, wonder of wonders, horse after horse fell by the wayside. Master Mascus was one of the few survivors – and, to Julian's horror, ran out a handsome winner! To his eternal credit, the BBC's commentator paid up like a man.

But, foolishly seeing this as the perfect opportunity to abandon my usual (rather repulsive) false modesty, I wrote a glowing account of the superlative jockeyship to which (alone) Master Mascus owed his surprising victory. It did not, I'm afraid, reflect much credit on either the common sense of the computer or the ability of the horse!

Well, it only goes to confirm what I should have known in the first place. Making jokes about people's wives may be foolish – making jokes about their horses is fatal. *I was never asked to ride Master Mascus again and, instead of the hoped-for present, got a blistering and reproachful rocket for my pains.*

A SAD END
TO A MEMORABLE
WHITBREAD GOLD CUP

For the second time in seven days last week, Sir John Thomson's Proud Tarquin came to the last fence of a great steeplechase with a great steeplechaser beside him. Once again he failed to carry off the prize but 'failure' is no more the right description of his achievement in the Whitbread Gold Cup than it was of his defeat by Red Rum in the Scottish Grand National.

Far less, in fact – for this time, gritting his teeth and battling dourly up the Sandown hill, he thrust his head across the line in front. What followed was no fault of his, and when men talk of the Whitbread Gold Cup in years to come his name will surely be remembered with the winners.

But the name in the record books will be that of another equally courageous eleven-year-old and nothing written on these pages in meant to detract in the slightest from his triumph. Since he first appeared at Cheltenham in November 1969, Mrs D. August's The Dikler has been a constant source of entertainment, excitement, inspiration and occasionally exasperation to the jumping world.

In defeat and victory alike he has always been spectacular, but with the possible exception of the 1973 Gold Cup I doubt if he has ever run a finer race than he did last week, giving Proud Tarquin 24lb and 'failing' only by a head.

The incident which turned his failure into victory is not an easy one for me to describe impartially. It happened about two strides after the last fence – over which Proud Tarquin (10st 3lb) had landed half a length in front of The Dikler (11st 13lb).

As anyone who saw him lose a race at Lingfield in March will remember, Proud Tarquin has long had a tendency to hang to his left unless guided by a running rail. There is, of course, no rail from the last at Sandown and, forewarned by the Lingfield *débâcle*, I had manoeuvred the whip to my left hand as we came round the final bend.

Perhaps I should have used it before the last – or immediately after landing – but at the time there seemed no need.

We met the fence dead right and landed running – but then the cock-eyed compass in my old friend's head came into play and, for two strides, before I could lift the whip to straighten him, he hung across towards The Dikler.

There was no contact, let alone a bump, but The Dikler presumably saw his rival coming and undoubtedly veered away. It is an interesting and highly relevant question whether, had he kept straight, the two horses *would* have collided. But to that, as far as I could see, the head-on patrol film gave no answer.

What it did show was that Proud Tarquin responded immediately to a slap down the neck and, thereafter, ran home as if on rails. The run-in is 300 yards long at Sandown and, in the 200 plus that remained, The Dikler, though gaining very gradually, was always just being held.

In the end, however, there *was* only a head to spare and Ron Barry's first words as we rode back were ominous – 'Well done – but you came over a bit at the last.'

I don't believe Ron enjoyed the next 20 minutes any more than I did and his evidence to the stewards was scrupulously fair. Outside, apparently, the bookies were laying three and four to one on Proud Tarquin and in the crowd of experienced trainers and jockeys around the weighing room the general opinion was that we should keep it.

But they had not seen the head-on patrol film and, watching it flicker back and forth half-a-dozen times, I felt no such confidence. I have only been involved in two inquiries after important races and in both, oddly enough, the patrol film made the 'interference' look far worse than it felt at the time.

In the Cheltenham, Foxhunters' last year the camera came down heavily on the side of Bullock's Horn, so now, with the boot on the other foot, I am in no position to complain. But there is not much doubt, I believe, that if these cases had been decided with the naked eye both results would have been allowed to stand.

That is not meant to suggest that the patrol camera is anything but a blessing. It avoids far more injustice than it causes and is an invaluable aid to local stewards. But it does require a skilled interpretation and it may, on occasion, 'exaggerate' incidents which, when they happened, were part of the unavoidable cut and thrust of racing.

And this danger, in my prejudiced opinion, is particularly to be guarded against when large, tired horses are fighting out the finish of a long-distance steeplechase.

Last week, however, the Sandown stewards had their job to do and no one can envy them. They were no doubt influenced by the fact that Proud Tarquin won by only a head and may well have taken the view that the interference, however slight, might have made that much difference.

On that reasoning, as the Rules of Racing stand, they were entitled to reverse the placings – and, after long and no doubt painful deliberation, that is what they did.

There is nothing much else to say except that, whichever side you take, it was a sad end to a memorable horse-race.

Half an hour earlier – though, looking back, it seems more like half a year – Credo's Daughter (10st 1lb) and Cuckolder (10st 3lb) had shared the lead after the first two fences and, on rock-hard ground, they set a gallop distinctly faster than that at which the Scottish Grand National had been run.

Proud Tarquin was only just able to keep his place behind these two, but he soldiered doggedly on and, swinging into the back straight for the last time moved up to join Credo's Daughter in the lead.

The little mare had run a fine race, but now sheer grinding stamina came into play and over the last of the three close Railway fences Proud Tarquin forged ahead. At the time I dared not look behind, and perhaps it was just as well. For as I know now, Inkslinger, Cuckolder and The Dikler were all poised on Proud Tarquin's heels, going so easily that, as we jumped the Pond, he looked sure to be passed by one if not all three.

But Leney Princess's sons have not compiled their record (68 victories to date between them) by tame surrender. Round the bend to the second last, Proud Tarquin defiantly lengthened his stride and, as he landed over it, both Inkslinger and Cuckolder had shot their bolts.

At the last in the 1974 Whitbread: Proud Tarquin (left) and
The Dikler.

That left The Dikler and Ron Barry – and that big white face appearing at my knee was not a welcome sight. With his left hand encased in plaster of Paris, the champion jockey had, as always, controlled and directed The Dikler's explosive strength to perfection and now, launching it up the hill he won (as it turned out) his third Whitbread Gold Cup in the last four years.

No jockey has ever equalled that – nor has any trainer approached Fulke Walwyn's record of four Whitbreads to go with his five Hennessy Gold Cups. I have said before and say again without fear of contradiction that no man has ever brought to a higher point the art of training high-class staying steeplechasers.

But when that art is being discussed, not many better examples of it have been seen this season than Roddy Armytage's handling of Proud Tarquin. It was only after long and anxious pondering that Sir John and Lady Thomson, owners to whom the well-being of their beloved horses far outweighs any other consideration, decided to pull the old horse out again so soon.

In persuading them to do so, Roddy laid his judgment and skill squarely on the line, knowing how easily and painfully he could be shot to pieces. In the paddock last week he told me, 'You are riding the fittest horse in the race' – and Proud Tarquin proved him gloriously right.

As for the horse himself, in ten days he had travelled more than a thousand miles and galloped his heart out for nearly eight against most of the best staying 'chasers in training. Yet on Saturday night, when I last saw him, he was cheerfully demolishing a large dinner – with only a few minor scrapes and scratches to show for his exertions.

In his ears, I sincerely hope, a winner's welcome was still ringing and for him the bitter aftermath means nothing. I have never ridden a tougher or braver horse and never expect to.

3 May 1974

What I refrained from saying at the time is that two of the Sandown stewards were young enough to be my sons! Any racing experience they had was of the flat, whereas John Hislop, who, since he was acting that day was fully entitled to sit, refused to do so 'because he had not seen enough steeplechasing lately'!

Much as I love and admire Sir Martin Gilliatt, who presided (hating the job), John would have forgotten at least a thousand times more about long-distance steeplechasing than those on the panel which disqualified Proud Tarquin are ever likely to know.

GIVING UP

After twenty happy, exciting and comparatively uninjured years, it is, I suppose, ridiculous to feel miserable about giving up riding over fences. But I do feel miserable nevertheless and cannot, at present, think of anything likely to replace the pleasure, thrill and satisfaction with which race-riding has so long filled my life.

It would be much more sensible, of course, to feel grateful for the fabulous good luck which converted an unsuccessful 25-year-old law student into a sort of racing correspondent and would-be amateur rider.

'There's a fellow coming tomorrow who wants to be an amateur,' Bob Turnell said one night to his wife Betty. 'But if you ask me he has left it a bit late!'

Bob's suspicions were confirmed next day when, hopelessly out of control, I careered past the whole string in a thick fog and ended up entangled with a flock of sheep. But all he said was, 'Be here tomorrow,' and perhaps the most important of all the many dice which rolled my way was getting the help, advice and support of such a man.

But there have been many more – my father-in-law, Ginger Dennistoun, whose advice, though more colourful, was often just as good. Fulke Walwyn, who with his wife Cath and Priscilla Hastings gave me a chance beyond my wildest dreams on Taxidermist, and Roddy Armytage, who forgave me for Pioneer Spirit and, with Proud Tarquin and many others, gave me the happiest years of all towards the end.

One day, maybe I will have space and time to thank them all

– the men, the women and the horses. But for the moment, all I can say is that, without them, the future looks a little bleak.

John Lawrence and
Happy Medium
at Sandown Park
in 1971.

And if, by chance, I ever find myself owner of a horse with Taxidermist's final speed, Proud Tarquin's stamina and the agility of Carrickbeg or Happy Medium – well, then you may see the quickest comeback there has ever been.

21 November 1975

THE VETERANS' RACE

The question of premature fatigue must have been in many minds last week when what was, so far as I know, a unique race took place at Navan. Entitled the Veterans' Private Sweep-stakes, it was, to the relief of all concerned, a flat race run over one and three-quarter miles and its peculiar conditions were as follows.

First of all none could ride who was not forty years old or more. Ex-professionals had to have been retired for at least five years and (a condition which caused a good deal of argument but, alas, had no effect on the result) they had, as compared with ex-amateurs, to carry a 7lb penalty.

As for the horses, they must never have won a flat race at any distance shorter than 1m 6f – and had to carry a 5lb penalty for each race, flat or jumping, they had won.

With a basic weight of 12st for professionals, this caused one unhappy animal to carry over thirteen stone, but not altogether surprisingly he was not concerned in the finish.

What on earth was the point, you may well ask, of all this rigmarole – was it merely designed to give a few silly old men a chance to make idiots of themselves in public?

Well, of course, it did provide just such an opportunity and, speaking for myself, I am glad there was no patrol camera to cover the last two exhausting furlongs.

But the fact remains that, with a few exceptions, the Veterans' Private Sweepstake was neither farcical nor ridiculous. For one thing its objective, thought up by Ned Mahon and some friends in Kilkenny, was the wholly admirable one of raising money for the Kilkenny Sheltered Workshops for mentally handicapped people, and, for another, it collected together almost certainly the most distinguished group of jumping jockeys ever to ride together in one race.

The list, in no order (except that the winner, blast him, comes first) is worth repeating: Fred Winter, Martin Molony, Aubrey Brabazon, Tim Brookshaw, Phil Canty, Eddy Kennedy, Pat and Tos Taaffe, Christy McCartan, Vic Speck, Jack Dowdeswell, Frankie Shortt, Mick Curran, Tom Walsh, Paddy Woods, Frankie Carroll, P. J. Doyle, Christy Kinane, Willie Robinson, Bunny Cox, Hubert Harty, Eddie Newman and Georgie Wells.

Pat Hogan, the best man to hounds I have ever seen, would have been in the field but for a muddle over declarations. And I was proud to claim the 7lb allowance on an aptly named horse called The Guilty One.

His was not the only appropriate name, because Vic Speck rode Chance Your Arm and after Fred Winter had won on a horse called Stopped (trained by his ex-stable jockey Eddie Harty) there were slanderous whispers that he had been living up to his name with just this victory in mind! I need hardly say that since there was no prize money these unworthy accusations were totally unfounded!

Nevertheless, to almost everyone's delight, Fred and Stopped came home in front. I say almost everyone's because Georgie Wells, who finished second (aged sixty), had backed himself at long odds, and although Martin Molony accepted third place with typical good grace, the rider of The Guilty One (who had started favourite) was far from content with fourth.

But apart from Fred – who had four runners and two winners at Ascot that same day – the race's real hero was the unbelievable Tim Brookshaw. Tim, who walked out to the paddock with a stick, has no strength or feeling whatever in his paralysed legs, but he still came into the straight alongside Fred Winter – sitting as calm and poised as he did that famous National day riding Wyndburgh home from Becher's with no stirrups.

I do not know if a paraplegic has ever ridden in a 1m 6f flat race before, but am inclined to doubt it. But then Tim Brookshaw has never paid much attention to medical precedent. He makes his own rules – just as the Irish stewards did last week to allow this unique contest. Both he and they have every reason to take pride in the result.

15 April 1977

A HAZE OF
GOLDEN BUBBLES

I am sure your heart often bleeds for us hard-working racing correspondents, slogging to and fro from one course to another. But the life does have its occasional compensations and I have to admit there were times last week when some might have even called it enviable.

It is twenty years since the late Tim Brumell, who was then chairman of Mentzendorffs, the English agents for Bollinger champagne, dreamed up the idea of the Bollinger trophies. They have been given ever since, along with a large amount of delicious wine, to the leading professional and amateur jumping jockeys.

At least for the professional, what's more, they were the forerunners and pace-setters for a whole selection of awards from other sources.

In search of a suitable way to celebrate this 20th anniversary, Tim Brumell's successor, Anthony Leschallas, hit on the kind and hospitable idea of holding the latest 'Bollinger' not, as usual, in London or Newcastle but in France, at the home of the great wine whose name the trophy bears.

So it was that a motley cross-section of the jumping world, nearly 100 strong, found themselves wafted across to Rheims last Wednesday morning to be royally entertained all day by M. and Mme Christian Bizot, who have inherited control of what is still very much a family firm from their aunt, the late Mme Lily Bollinger.

Since this is supposed to be about horses, not wine, I will resist the temptation to describe at length the fascinating tour

M. Bizot gave us of the Bollinger vineyards and cellars. The former included one small patch of the only pre-phylloxera vines in France and the latter, believe it or not, contain, at this moment, four million bottles.

In fact, recent grape harvests have been so sparse in quantity that none of the great champagne houses has been able to produce enough wine to satisfy demand. This year, by contrast, ample quantity is guaranteed – and all they need now is the hot, sunny August which adds to the vintage's quality.

Although John Francome could not be there last week, this year's championship was represented by Peter Scudamore, and many previous winners, professional and amateur alike, had come to remember past glories in a happy haze of golden bubbles.

George Sloan had flown specially from America and was neither surprised nor affronted by M. Bizot's description of Bollinger's wartime tribulations: 'First we had the Germans, who took the wine and paid for it; then we had the Americans, who just took it.'

All in all it was a marvellous, unforgettable day. Champagne has always been most jockeys' favourite drink – partly because it is supposed to put on less weight than any other form of alcohol, but also because it lifts your heart so well, either when you are celebrating or when everything looks black.

The jumping world already owes Bollinger and Mentzendorffs a huge debt for setting an example which so many others have followed by giving jumping jockeys the recognition they deserve. Now, for some of us, the debt is even bigger – and there is less doubt than ever about our first choice of champagne.

Only Tim Thomson Jones of the proper jockeys who wined and dined themselves in France had to worry about riding the next day – and Tim duly won at Salisbury on Bombalini despite having 'to do light'. But for two aged TV hacks – Brough Scott and myself – hangovers were of more concern than they had been for Tim. We had rashly accepted an invitation from the Jersey Race Club to ride there in a match on Thursday, sponsored by the Rank Leisure Group in aid of the Injured Jockeys' Fund.

It seemed a good idea at the time, but by Thursday morning the prospect of riding an unknown horse for $1^1/4$ miles – let alone trying to help it go faster – caused us both to feel like the jockey in Snaffles's famous picture 'The Worst View in Europe' – '*Oh Murther! The dhrink died out of me and the wrong side of Becher's.*'

This terrifying contest was entitled the 'Chariots of Fire' match – not, as you may imagine, because Scott or I have anything in common with the great Harold Abrahams or Eric Liddell, but because Rank were showing the great film of that name at their local Odeon!

Modesty forbids too detailed an account of the race, so I will only say that, thanks partly to brilliant tactical advice from local expert Ron Vibert, partly to Scott's unselfish intention to make it a close race, and partly to having much the best horse, I came home a length in front. If, as seems all too probable, Light Of Sion was my last winner, I can only say that it is still every bit as much fun as it was twenty-six years ago.

They only have about fifty-five horses in Jersey and the race-course at Les Landes is run entirely by unpaid volunteers. But the course, though perched on a cliff top and definitely on the sharp side, is perfectly fair and the going last week would have made some English clerks of courses green with envy.

At several summer meetings travel allowances are paid to runners from England and, although the prize money is not of Royal Ascot proportions, it is almost certainly a good deal easier to win.

If I was a Southern trainer with a few moderate horses in search of a prize (heaven knows, there are plenty about), I could think of a lot less enjoyable ways to spend August Bank Holiday.

2 July 1982

. . . And Boring

John Oaksey adjusting his clothing before taking a ride for
Colonel Sir John Thomson (left).

You might have guessed that sooner or later some of the bees which have buzzed so long in my bonnet would be bound to make an appearance. Here, with apologies to those who have heard it all before, are a few old friends.

Rule 153, the whip, short leathers, racing journalists, stable-lads' pay and foxhunting – nothing very new about those.

But I wish we could find a few politicians as keen about horses and racing as Sir Winston Churchill. He won't mind keeping them company on these pages. Nor would my grandfather – and both would have firm views on the merits of jockeys old and new.

Last – and you may well think least – my only attempt so far at a short story. Dick Francis is clearly in no more danger of serious competition than was Joe Mercer . . .

THE OSTRICH-LIKE BBC

Sandown in November – blue skies, perfect going and the best horses in England – what more could any man ask? For many reasons, some personal, some objective, Sandown Park is my favourite English racecourse and for two days last week it was at its superb and spectacular best. The sooty hand of the suburbs may in time smother into extinction this sporting Shangri-La but, for the moment, its position on the outskirts of London brings nothing but big attendances and prosperity. The Executive got the huge crowd it deserved on Saturday and both sandwiches and racecards were soon as hard to find as 20 to 1 winners.

No one who was there could possibly have been left in any doubt as to the present popularity of N.H. racing. Indeed, I had thought, until a few days ago, that the ancient canard that interest in racing dies with the end of the flat was nowadays only believed in parts of Newmarket and other prejudiced areas.

It seems, however, that I was wrong. For a correspondent of mine, writing recently to the BBC to inquire why the 4.45 p.m. broadcast of racing results had been discontinued for the jumping season, received the following reply. The italics are my own.

With regard to your inquiry, we have found that, with the exception of the Grand National, there is *very little interest in National Hunt events* and, after very careful discussion, it was decided to limit the broadcasts of National Hunt results.

Very careful discussion with *whom*, I should like to know? Not, presumably, with those in charge of BBC Television's outside broadcasts. For I suppose that Mr Peter Dimmock and company would be more than a little surprised to hear that the many jumping meetings they relay so brilliantly throughout the winter are 'of very little interest' to the viewing public.

I have never considered the BBC to be the most infallible mirror of public opinion, but in this case surely it is quite unusually wide of the mark. There are still people, of course, who keep themselves alive during the winter by dreaming of the halcyon joys of Lincoln, but they are either men professionally tied to flat-racing, hardened gamblers who will not bet on jumping or just plain fair-weather sportsmen. And for each one of them I can produce several genuine lovers of horses who would far rather watch, read about or hear the result of the lowest novice 'chase than the greatest flat race ever run.

The BBC, of course, is not the only body who, ostrich-like, has ignored the obvious rise in the popularity of N.H. racing which has taken place since the war. The national press is equally to blame, slavishly covering, as it does, the gloomy closing weeks of the flat and then switching prematurely back to the early mediocrities of March and April – when the jumpers are, or should be, still at the height of their season.

By its excellent television coverage, the BBC has brought jumping to many who never visit a racecourse. It must now face the fact that countless men and women all over the country follow the winter game in all its varied phases. So let us, in the name of common sense, have no more eyewash about 'very little public interest'.

28 November 1959

HOW TO GO
OVER THE TOP
'DOWN UNDER'

There were 86,841 people of every conceivable shape and size celebrating the first Tuesday in November at Flemington last week and it is, admittedly, anyone's guess how many of them actually saw Sheikh Hamdan Al Maktoum's At Talaq win the $1 million Foster's Melbourne Cup.

But you can have good odds from me that well over 80,000 thoroughly enjoyed their day.

Australia really does come to a standstill for the Cup. Politicians stop talking in Parliament, a jury pondering charges for which a man is now serving forty years suspended its deliberations, and a friend of mine who had foolishly sent his only suit to the cleaners had to go racing without it. He was still a good deal more conventionally dressed than most!

'Standstill' is definitely not the right word to describe Flemington racecourse on Melbourne Cup day. Apart from dedicated sunbathers, a few mutually obsessed amorous couples and prostrate 'tired and emotional' bodies whose number grows as the day goes on, the one thing practically no one does is stay still.

With a few exceptions, you can tell at a glance how seriously they are taking the Sport of Kings. In the poshest enclosure, you could easily mistake it for Royal Ascot – but just over the fence there are sights which would give Her Majesty's Representative apoplexy. Tail coats are still quite popular but it is what goes with them that makes the difference.

You would not, I think, get past the gates in football stockings on Gold Cup day – and although suspender belts are doubtless still worn in the Royal enclosure you do not see many gentlemen wearing one under a tail coat and virtually nothing else.

Mind you, it was extremely hot and those who went for 'le *minimum vitale*' had comfort as their argument. They certainly suffered less than the gorillas and mobile two-man horses – or, for that matter, than the allegedly fashion-conscious lady who was clad from head to toe in crocodile.

Having selected At Talaq as the nearest thing we could find to an 'English' representative in the Cup, it was good to find that, in terms of quality, he made most of his rivals look quite plain. Like several of the 22-horse field, At Talaq had run just three days earlier, winning for the first time in Australia, though only over a mile and a quarter.

But he did beat the very much fancied Mr Lomondy – who was nevertheless made favourite on the day. Apparently Australian trainers often use this particular 10-furlong race as a final tune-up, and it had, evidently, done At Talaq no harm whatever.

Fourth in Secreto's Derby, he went on to win the Grand Prix de Paris as a three-year-old but that, and one minor victory at Newmarket, were the sum of his achievements. It was clearly not enough for a Roberto colt who cost $800,000 as a yearling and, meeting Colin Hayes at the Keeneland sales, Tom Jones, who trained At Talaq in England, suggested that he might find more scope Down Under.

Time is the secret and At Talaq was given plenty of it – partly, no doubt, because getting used to another side of the world was not his only problem. Hayes also had to deal with a damaged foot and an arthritic tendency so it was not really surprising that At Talaq did not win at all last season. No doubt that lack of success also helped to fix him quite low in the handicap considering that he is a Grand Prix winner.

Colin Hayes was by no means convinced that the six-year-old would stay two miles – but felt hopeful enough to arrange a special satellite telecast to Dubai. In fact, the same government meeting which stopped Sheikh Hamdan coming to Melbourne kept him busy during the race. But, like his equally enthusiastic brothers, he is quite accustomed to following the exploits of his horses on a video recorder.

Apart from what seems (to an old-fashioned English TV hack) the somewhat questionable Australian practice of panning back, quite slowly, through the whole field, Sheikh Hamdan would have been able to keep his colours under observation all the way. For despite a slowish start, Michael Clarke soon had At Talaq up in second place, tracking the leader Fil de Roi.

At the first bend in the 1986 Melbourne Cup.

The only question, in the first few furlongs, was would he be able to stay there – because At Talaq was not by any means fast asleep. In fact he was pulling pretty hard and while the modest pace Fil de Roi was setting seemed in his favour, it was not going to help if he wasted too much energy.

It is ten years since Bob Skelton won the Cup on Van Der Hum and last week, at fifty-one, he was the oldest jockey in the race. The clock in his experienced head told him that the pace was too slow for his mount Rising Fear and so, moving up outside At Talaq, he joined Fil de Roi in the lead.

Being overtaken like that might easily have made At Talaq pull even harder but, luckily for Clarke, it had just the opposite effect. 'The moment Bob came past, my horse relaxed completely,' the jockey told us afterwards. He was still beautifully placed on the heels of the two leaders and now the question was how long to wait.

'Don't go until the last furlong,' had been Colin Hayes's instruction, and now his 22-year-old stable jockey only disobeyed it by about a hundred yards.

The trainer knew he had plenty of speed in this company and now, sure enough, it swept him past Rising Fear and the weakening Fil de Roi. For a moment, as he went clear, the race looked over – but I understand that a lot of Melbourne Cups have 'looked over' only to come surprisingly back to life.

When, for example, the New Zealander Kiwi won in 1983, he came from impossibly far back at an impossible speed. The Australians have never forgotten that and all day long, last week, whenever Kiwi's name was mentioned, for whatever reason, a special cheer went up. Now nine years old, he was almost certainly having his last try and, after lying a long way back as usual, he appeared on the outside, passing horse after horse as though they were marking time.

'Two hundred metres out, I thought, this is it,' jockey Noel Harris said afterwards – and many of Kiwi's shrieking admirers felt the same. But the ground was hard at Flemington and the old horse's legs have seen a lot of service. From the way he pulled up they must have been hurting and, with a few lengths still to win back, his great charge faltered and died.

Fourth place was, in itself, an achievement, but when Noel Harris hurriedly dismounted it seemed all too probable that the price had been too high. Happily, both vet and Kiwi's trainer could find nothing seriously wrong. Kiwi walked away pretty sound and there was talk of running again within the week.

The New Zealand veteran had not been At Talaq's only challenger and, for those of his backers who had not noticed where the winning post was, the next few seconds were distinctly fraught.

To his great credit – and, it must be said, in contrast to the general policy of modern Australian jockeys – Michael Clarke rode the last hundred yards with hands and heels. He deserved a medal for that in my opinion – and, instead, was fined $200 for giving his whip a triumphant flourish after passing the post. It had come only just in time because Rising Fear and Bob Skelton were gaining relentlessly. They were beaten a 'long neck' in the end with Sea Legend coming from much further back to be third.

As the Australians are the first to admit, the Melbourne Cup is, by European standards, a strange race to choose as the summit of your racing year – a two-mile handicap, just as likely to be won by a well handicapped lightweight as by the best horse in the field. But the same can, of course, be said of our Grand National.

The fact is that Australian racing depends on betting – and is lucky enough to have its dependence far better organised than ours. The only legal bookmakers operate on-course and the course runs its own Tote. All legal off-course betting is done at TAB offices and the hard fact is that, on-course or off it, the Australian punter far prefers betting on a competitive handicap like the Cup than on weight-for-age races for 'better-class' horses.

With admirable realism, the Victorian authorities (each State has a different controlling body) will have no truck with the lily-livered English idea of limiting prize money for handicaps. With Foster's help, they cheerfully raised the Cup prize to $1 million – and who is to say that that money is worse spent than the huge sums we pump into Classic and other Group races, the winning of which already increases the winner's stud value by hundreds of thousands, if not millions.

One massive advantage Australians have over us is the exist- ence of several quite eminent politicians who not only take an active part in racing but actually seem to think it deserves encouragement. Mr Bob Hawke himself was an owner until recently and last year the whole sport was given a priceless boost with the removal of income tax from all racecourse profits. Comparing that with our own government's consist- ently unhelpful attitude over VAT, on-course betting tax and rating, makes you long for a single parliamentarian who does not regard the sport, when indeed he thinks of it at all, as a cheap, if slightly disreputable, method of collecting taxes.

Long before the sweat had dried on At Talaq (which means either 'Swift as a bullet' or 'I wish to divorce you!' – no one seems certain which), the contrasts that are Cup day's outstanding feature were growing wider and wilder. Up in the Committee Box tail coats and elaborate dresses might, as I say, have been at Ascot – except that the lunch was better. But everywhere else (there is only one public enclosure which costs a mere $4 on ordinary days but goes up to $10, still well under £5, for the Cup), joy, drink and dress were unconfined and getting unconfineder every moment.

One observer counted three Popes, seven Father Christmases

and a six-man centipede – and I can add two gorillas, a Mickey Mouse and several Supermen.

The party looked odds-on to outstay the sun when we were carried away and I cannot remember a day's racing when I saw fewer horses or had more fun.

14 November 1986

At Talaq's strapper celebrates the horse's Melbourne Cup win.

SUDDENLY THE SPORT
WE LOVE SEEMS EMPTY
AND UNIMPORTANT

Looking back, this week, down the echoing corridor of Sir Winston Churchill's ninety years, the narrow worlds of horse and hound, of racecourse and of hunting field seem suddenly empty, unimportant, almost childish things. As we contemplate the void left by his death – and attempt to measure what we owe him – the petty preoccupations even of these, the sports we love, pale into insignificance.

And yet, I doubt whether he would have it so. For throughout his long and infinitely varied life, even in those dark days when he carried, almost literally, the cares of the world upon his shoulders, Sir Winston never forgot how to enjoy himself, never allowed the burden of the task to spoil his zest for living.

Blessed with the sort of physical courage that seems to know no fear, he set a high price on daring in any form and, loving the English way of life, recognised the part played in it by the many sports and pastimes which depend, for their existence, on the horse. In many of them – on the polo field, the racecourse and out hunting – he took part himself.

The racing world, in which Sir Winston had, like his father, always taken an interest, remembers with pride his entry into it after the war. And, fittingly, the three best horses who carried his colours, Colonist II, Vienna and High Hat, all had in common with their owner the priceless quality of absolute refusal to admit defeat.

Among the countless Churchill stories being told this week there are two which illustrate, I think, his attitude to racing and the men and animals who are its flesh and blood.

Fred Winter tells, for instance, how, preparing to get up on one of Sir Winston's horses before a hurdle race at Sandown Park, he was discussing tactics with the great man's son-in-law, Mr Christopher Soames, when that deep, unforgettable voice broke in: 'I shouldn't bother to tell Winter what to do,' it said, 'you are talking to a master of his art.'

He who was great in so many fields could recognise greatness in another – and as Fred rode out that day with those words ringing in his ears, I have no doubt he was inspired, as millions before and since have been, by a quality of leadership never excelled in the history of man.

The second story was told to me by a friend of mine who once sat next to Sir Winston in a cinema, watching some epic in which a cavalry charge occurred. Horses were crashing headlong all over the screen and, hearing a mournful rumble from the seat beside him, my friend turned to look at his companion.

'Those poor horses, oh, those poor horses,' Churchill was muttering over and over again – and, as the battle reached its bloody climax, the tears, of which he never was ashamed, coursed freely down the cheeks of the man who charged with Kitchener at Omdurman.

This, then, was the man we mourn today, a man who walked with destiny yet kept the human touch, a man who could admire a jockey, cry for the pain of a wounded horse, win a war – and bear without flinching the rejection of those for whom he won it. A man who, in President Kennedy's memorable phrase, 'mobilised the English language and sent it into battle', a man who never, all his life, allowed considerations of personal gain or loss to deter him from the aims in which he believed.

Such a man was far too generous, far too broad of mind to scorn the amusements of inferior beings. Instead he shared them and as we set out racing or hunting this week he would not, I believe, want his death to cast its shadow on our pleasure.

The shadow will be there, of course – but let it be one of grateful memory, not grief. Let us remember, as we ride or stand and cheer, that, but for him, we might not have the chance to do so.

Our freedom to enjoy ourselves is his memorial.

30 January 1965

SPARE A THOUGHT
FOR THE JOURNALISTS

To every man, woman and child actively concerned in National Hunt racing the period lasting from Christmas to Cheltenham brings, each year, in varying proportions, a mixture of anxiety, boredom and extreme physical discomfort.

Cancelled meetings and missed opportunities double the trainer's normal heavy burden of care; arctic mornings and mad-fresh horses make the lives of his stable lads (and girls) a frozen misery; and as for the jockeys – they must, sometimes for weeks on end, kick their heels, watch their weight and try to keep fit for rides which may never come.

The plight of these unfortunate people has, however, been often and sympathetically described. Less hard – but still quite hard enough – is the lot of the professional journalist who must still cover a given acreage of paper even when there is no current racing on which to lavish his deathless prose.

Thinking along these lines, it occurred to me the other day that the racing press (for fairly obvious reasons!) has less space devoted to it than any of the other cogs in the machinery of English racing.

'A good thing, too,' you will no doubt say – and, as a rule, I would agree. No one wants to read about the exploits, methods, habits and skill – or lack of it – of the men who write about racing for their daily bread, and we, who do the job, are more than content to remain in whatever obscurity our various *noms de plume* can give us.

There is, however, one feature of contemporary racing journalism which seems to me worthy of comment – if not of reform.

For various reasons – some good, some bad – it has now become an all but inviolable rule that the men who ride and train racehorses must *never* be criticised in any but the most lukewarm, qualified fashion.

I should, perhaps, make clear at once (lest you throw down the paper in disgust) that I am not about to say that this tolerant silence is necessarily wrong. My purpose is rather to fill an idle hour with an attempt to show why it exists.

Racing is a sport demanding skills of many different kinds. For the exercise of these skills, and indirectly, because of the entertainment they give the public, men are paid money. And upon these skills large sums of money depend.

To this extent the sport is comparable to all other branches of the entertainment business – to the theatre, the cinema, the television and to all other spectator sports which people pay to watch and enjoy. I am sorry to stress the 'money' aspect, but it is, surely, important. For when an entry fee is charged for a spectacle – or a price paid for a book – those who pay expect value for their money, and if they do not get it they expect to hear the reason why. No one who has attended a professional football match will query the truth of this proposition!

Now all spectator sports and most forms of human entertainment have their commentators in the popular Press. Whether theatre critics or football reporters, their job is to tell the public what has happened and, whether they like it or not, to mould its taste for the future.

It is here that the similarity between racing and its fellows comes to a full stop.

If an actor fumbles for his lines or fails, exactly, to interpret his part, do the critics pull their punches? They do not. Actor, producer and author – all are subjected to a merciless hail of scornful, pitying words, savage enough to make the thickest-skinned man alive sink through the floor with shame, and quickly take up some less exacting profession.

'But that is art,' you say. 'That's different.' Then I refer you to the comments of writers on cricket and football. A Test cricketer on tour in Australia has only to make one poor innings – to bowl a few sub-standard overs – and every detail of his private life is dissected next morning before the eyes of a breakfast-eating world. What time did he go to bed last night? Is his girlfriend taking up too much of his spare time? Has he lost his nerve against fast bowling? Nothing is safe and nothing is unimportant.

If a centre-forward misses an easy goal, you read all about it and the blame for his team's departure from the Cup is placed squarely where the reporter thinks it belongs.

One could go on quoting examples for ever, but nobody who reads even one page of his newspaper will really need to be convinced – and nobody who goes racing will deny the comparative gentleness of those whose business is to report and comment on the day's doings at the track.

There are many ways of losing a race that should be won, and many of these, rightly or wrongly, could be laid at the door of the jockey concerned. Like the actor, the footballer or the cricketer, he *may* have a perfectly good excuse for his apparent lack of judgment, skill or opportunism – an excuse invisible from the stands. But, *unlike* them, he is practically never called to account in print. His mistake – if such it was – is glossed over and the reader who did not see the race is none the wiser.

'So-and-so appeared to lie a little out of his ground'; 'X found himself shut in until too late'; 'Y dropped his hands a stride too soon.' Such are the euphemisms of our trade when what we sometimes mean is that 'So-and-so was half-asleep for three-quarters of the race and woke up when it was over'; 'X went for an opening on the rails which a blind man on a dark night could have seen was hopeless'; and 'Y thought he had won by 10 lengths, tried to be clever, and was caught on the line.'

None of these statements would be libellous and, occasionally, some of them might be perfectly accurate. Whether accurate or not, they would, unfortunately, human nature being what it is, enliven the printed page and attract the notice of sensation-minded readers.

So why is it, then, that racing reporters, almost alone among their kind, muffle criticism in a blanket of understatement, falling over backwards, it sometimes seems, to avoid offence at any cost? Some of our reasons, as I have said, are bad and some good.

First, racing is a close-knit sport in which friends compete against friends and the over-critical reporter would soon find himself in the wilderness. This, it seems to me, is a bad reason – at least in so far as it stifles the honest expression of opinion. For on this hard, practical line of reasoning the temptation is to criticise the small stable – the unknown jockey – and to leave the bigger fish alone.

Another, much less unpleasant, facet of the same reason lies in the generally excellent cooperation which exists between the trainers and jockeys and the press. Without this cooperation – and a certain amount of mutual respect that goes with it – the lists of runners, for instance, could not be compiled and the whole sport would suffer. This situation does not, I believe, exist to the same degree in France, where press criticism is correspondingly more bitter.

To scratch a man's back in the hope that he will one day scratch yours is one thing; to refrain from stabbing the same back because you respect its owner and because you and he work together every day is quite another.

The second reason – a good one this time – is that, whatever you may think, quite a lot of racing correspondents know quite a lot about racing. Even if they have never ridden themselves, they understand the myriad split-second chances which make the difference between victory and defeat, and they realise that to blame a man when these chances run against him is about as fair as beating a tired horse who has done his best and can do no more.

On the great jockey, of course, luck smiles because he makes her smile. He thinks, perhaps, a fraction further ahead than his rivals and is, perhaps, a fraction quicker to seize his opportunity. But even to him, things happen which may seem from the stands to be the result of incompetence. He alone can say whether they are or not – and the man who thinks he knows better is a fool.

Racing correspondents know, too, that a young man trying to get started as a jockey has a hard row to hoe. Owners, unfortunately, often believe every word they see in print, and when someone writes, quite truthfully, that X, claiming 7lb, was hopelessly outridden from the last fence by Fred Winter, X, who was perhaps getting his first chance of a decent ride, may not get a second.

I do not know whether this soft-hearted attitude exists in other sports (it probably does), but I know it exists in racing, and no one, surely, would have it any other way.

The final reason, it seems to me, applies much more to jumping than to the flat. No man can follow and write about – and love – the winter game without witnessing the physical hardships undergone by those who ride for a living. When you see a man take three crashing falls on one cold, muddy afternoon, how can you write next day that, in his fourth ride, he made a mistake which cost his owner the race or showed less than his usual strength at the finish? It may be true, but it just is not worth saying.

Who can blame reporters of N.H. racing if they feel that professional jockeys run quite enough risks already – without the added one of criticism which may or may not be deserved.

These, then, are the reasons for what sometimes appears to be the blindness of the racing Press. They produce a prejudice that is, I think, sometimes unduly exaggerated, and I know from my own experience that it sometimes operates from the wrong motives. But it is, at least, a prejudice on the right side – like the law, it believes that a man should be innocent till he is proved guilty beyond a reasonable doubt.

So when you next see a jockey criticised in this or any other paper, do not fly too hastily to your protesting pen. The criticism *may* be unjust, but it will, at least, be no mere frivolous attempt at sensation.

I apologise for all this long-winded sermonising, but in times like these allowances must be made for the ramblings of the unemployed.

23 January 1960

THE BASIC
UNDERMINING EVIL
OF THE RACING SET-UP

Only one more name now remains to be announced to complete the Board of eight brave men in whose hands, under the chairmanship of Field-Marshal Lord Harding, all the hopes and aspirations of British racing will rest during the next few years. It is, of course, the Betting Levy Board, set up by the Government not only to control the amount of money to be raised from starting-price bookmakers but also, even more important, to dictate the things on which that money shall be spent.

The Board is not yet officially in being and it seems that the first tangible fruits of its labours will not begin to flow until late in 1962. Before that time, millions of well-meant words of advice will be showered upon the Field-Marshal and his colleagues – and doubtless this column will find it hard to resist the temptation sooner or later to add its twopennyworth.

For the moment, however, I want rather to pass on a point of view put calmly and sensibly to me while riding out one recent glorious July morning along a peaceful ridge of the Berkshire Downs.

It was a morning to lift the hearts of man and horses alike and my companion, a stable lad in his early thirties, looked what he is – a man happy in his work, good at his job and content with life in general.

Apprenticed at the age of fourteen, he has been in stables ever since and now, married with two children, is a senior lad in a small mixed yard. He was never light enough – or lucky enough – to ride racing, but is a stronger and better horseman than many so-called jockeys will ever be.

Most mornings this summer this stable lad has, to my knowledge, ridden a mare who not only pulls like a runaway train but who, at least once a day, whips round, dropping her shoulder with a speed, cunning and absence of warning that defies the normal laws of balance and grip.

More than once she has succeeded in her object and put him on the floor – but her coat shines with the results of his long and skilful grooming and although he calls her many unprintable names, any outsider unwise enough to criticise would quickly be told what to do with his opinion!

This, in fact, was a normal stable lad of the highest class – a skilled, experienced tradesman whom any trainer in England would think himself lucky to employ. *His wage, after nearly twenty years in the game, is just over £9 a week.**

Not far from where we rode last week, a dozen of his friends and contemporaries are working shorter, more regular hours in a factory. Unskilled, they can earn, with overtime, almost twice as much as he does. Unlike him, they are protected from sudden dismissal by the full power of a big trade union.

But he speaks of them with pity in his voice. Their faces, he says, are as white as a fish's belly. They long to come back to racing – and would, like a shot, if the money was there. He does not envy them – but might easily have to go the same way if, for instance, his rent went up, another child was born or a couple of rash bets went down.

The life of a stable lad has not – in itself – become any less attractive now than it was twenty years ago. The lures are still there – a healthy life in the open air with horses and the excitement of being connected, however humbly, with the success or failure of a racing stable.

There is no real shortage of boys who want to become

---

* Nearly thirty years later, I quoted these figures in a speech during a House of Lords debate on the plight of racing. Of course, stable lads' pay *has* improved – but not much if you take account of inflation.

The basic wage with agreed weekend overtime is around £130 a week in 1991 – still not nearly enough to support a worthwhile mortgage for an experienced lad who wants to marry and start a family, – which is why so many go out of racing in search of a better paid job.

apprentices, but when, through increasing weight, lack of aptitude or lack of opportunity, an apprentice finally loses hope of becoming a jockey, it is *then* that he weighs the rewards of staying in racing against those of a job in a factory and, in too many cases, chooses the better-paid but less attractive occupation.

The lad to whom I was talking chose the other way. To him, and to many others, love of the life is still stronger than the need for money. And, as he says, this is the only job he knows.

But when trained men leave the game, the gaps have to be filled. And it is this, the growing employment of unskilled lads who have not served their time, of which he spoke most bitterly the other day.

Some of the newcomers, whether boys or girls, are, of course, 'naturals' who learn the job quickly and can soon ride and do their horses as well as any – but some are not and, under the present system, *all* are paid the same basic wage.

It is this, he explained, that is pulling the general standard down. For why should a fully trained, experienced lad give his horses the long, careful treatment he knows they need when, in the next box, some green newcomer is botching the job through idleness or incompetence – and getting the same pay packet at the end of the week?

Trainers, needless to say, have ways to get round this problem. There are many 'perks' that can be put in the way of a first-rate lad, but even so, in too many cases, the grievance remains. With the present basic wage fixed around £9 a week no man trying to make a living out of training fees alone can afford to pay his good lads the wages they deserve.

So here, surely, is the basic undermining evil to the mending of which the betting levy should first be directed. Others will cry out for better stands, bigger bars and cheaper entrance charges.

All are desirable and all should come in time, but surely the first priority ought to be to reward properly the skill and hard work of those for whom racing is a life, not just an entertainment.

There is another, more difficult angle to the same problem. Until at least one 'nobbler' is caught – and his methods discovered – it will be impossible to resist the feeling that the easiest way to 'get at' a favourite horse is by bribing a lad in his stable.

And although it goes without saying that the vast majority of lads would die rather than harm one of their horses, the occasional weak character is made far more vulnerable and approachable because his wage packet is at its present low level.

If, as I hope and expect, the Board decides to try to improve the lot of trainers and stable lads, the question, of course, remains – how best to do it? It has recently been calculated that, with costs as they are, owners and owner-breeders in England and Ireland are subsidising racing to the tune of over £4 million – that being the sum by which the expenses of breeding, rearing and training racehorses exceeds the money to be recovered by way of prizes and sales.

Four million sounds an awful lot, but although many individual owners undoubtedly feel the pinch, there is no evidence at present that the number of people wanting to own horses is on the decrease. From this, I conclude that although it would certainly be wrong to make owners pay more, there is no pressing need to subsidise them directly.

Any measure, therefore, which cuts owners' costs or increases their rewards ought to be passed straight on to the trainers in higher training fees, enabling them first to make a living themselves (without the present almost universal need to bet), and second to pay their lads according to skill and experience so that men 'lost' at present will be attracted back to racing and so that the incentive to do the job as well as it can be done will be restored.

How the Board can best bring about these desirable ends is not the point of this article. Personally I believe that a simple increase in the level of prize money would not only cause considerable discontent in many circles but also have the more serious drawback of affecting only winning owners and not losing ones. Belonging, as I do, to the second group, I feel strongly on the subject!

Probably a better solution would be considerably to increase the allowances already paid towards the cost of travelling horses – or even perhaps to make travelling totally free as it is in France and Ireland.

But whatever the measure, the important thing is to make the racing public realise that it is not designed just to benefit racehorse owners who are, after all, in the business ostensibly for fun.

The owners must pass along whatever windfall may come their way to those who deserve and need it most. And those are not the punters or race-goers so widely championed by the big circulation newspapers – but the trainers and stable lads on whose sweat, worry and skill the whole industry depends. They, I hope, will be the first beneficiaries when, next year, the money begins to flow at long last.

29 July 1961

A TRAGI-COMEDY

On the Wednesday afternoon an extraordinary tragi-comedy was being played out at Worcester, starring a humble selling hurdler called Billy Buck.

Getting rid of his rider at the first, Billy, for reasons best known to himself, plunged headlong into the River Severn – swollen that day to near flood-level by recent downpours.

Horses, it seems, are all good natural swimmers, but although Billy Buck is no exception he was desperately – all but fatally – hampered on this occasion by a 14lb saddle and 14lb of lead.

A boat was hurriedly pressed into service by the course vet, David Denny, but, misunderstanding the aims of his would-be rescuers, Billy Buck swam off – pausing briefly under the rowing club dining-room – and then downstream, out of control, on the flood-tide.

When at length the rescue boat caught up, he was foundering fast and to drag him bodily ashore must have been no mean task. But it was done and, walking calmly back through the Silver Ring, Billy Buck got the shipwrecked survivors' reward of half a bottle of whisky – becoming probably the first horse to be given a stimulant on an English racecourse this season.

His saddle, incidentally, was found to be exactly twice its normal weight when recovered so, having carried three stone for the best part of a mile, he must rate pretty high in the aquatic stakes.

Billy Buck is, of course, by no means the first horse to go for a swim and I know of at least one man who was forced, by the fortunes of racing, to take to the Severn at much the same point.

My grandfather used to recall how, leaving Worcester after the last race one day before the first war, he saw a defaulting bookmaker pursued by a large and extremely angry crowd. Wearing a bottle-green, long-tailed coat and a large white bushy top-hat, the welsher had only a few lengths lead when he came to the bank and, with no time to adjust his dress, took the only alternative to a severe manhandling.

In he went, and away like a frightened otter. The punters, it seems, did not want their winnings that badly – for none of them followed.

And, arriving safe on the far bank, their quarry turned, doffed his white topper (which he had hitherto not troubled to remove) and, with a graceful bow, vanished – doubtless to sup the same restorative that Billy Buck found so effective last week.

Well, that, anyway, was my grandfather's story – and he was a truthful man. A game one, too, if you'll pardon a grandson's pride, for he died at the age of 93, drowned while fishing for salmon in the Wye, after swimming 50 yards with his waders filled. His house was called Abernant – but how the great sprinter came to be given that name is another story . . .

30 November 1963

My uncle, who lived at Abernant, nearly married Miss Buchanan – later Mrs Macdonald-Buchanan. Her husband, Sir Reggie, owned Owen Tudor and, when that horse retired to stud, wrote to my uncle asking for some Welsh placenames.

My uncle replied with a list but Sir Reg wrote back saying, 'I like the name of your house best of all and have therefore called my nicest yearling Abernant.' The great grey sprinter, one of Sir Gordon Richards's all-time favourites, was only ever beaten twice.

IS SUFFICIENT BEING DONE TO COMBAT THE 'ANTIS'?

Although hounds and hunting do not strictly fall within Audax's terms of reference, he might, just once, be forgiven for straying off the beaten track. Kindly, therefore, either turn over quickly – or muster any good will you may have left to bear with the rambling, ill-informed reflections of a non-hunting man on a sport he loves, admires, but hardly understands.

If Whyte Melville were alive today he would, I imagine, find it hard to recognise the English hunting scene. Barbed wire, ploughed fields, spreading towns, motorways and the need to farm each acre to the full – all these would long ago have killed a sport less deeply rooted in the nation's heart – and what follows is not meant as any criticism of the indefatigable men and women who, against tremendous odds, are keeping it alive.

If it ever died, the loss, to all who love horses, the country and the open air, would be irreparable and other equine sports, notably steeplechasing, would suffer too – more deeply, I think, than their supporters understand.

For the moment, at least, the 'antis' are quiescent, but only, I fear, gathering strength for a new assault. When that assault comes, hunting will need all the friends it can get and – here is the point – I do not believe it is doing enough at present to enlist the sympathy of irregulars like myself whose only experience consists of a very occasional day snatched as the opportunity offers.

My own recent attempts in England may, admittedly, not be typical, and the enjoyment of any one day's hunting obviously depends largely on circumstances beyond human control. Even the finest part of Leicestershire, for instance, can be a dullish spot if you fail to find a fox, and no huntsman, however brilliant, can produce scent where none exists.

By far the longest sustained period of hunting I ever enjoyed was as a child with the VWH (Earl Bathurst's), then hunted by Lord Knutsford. He left in my mind an ideal of what the atmosphere should be, never failing to find a kind, encouraging word for us children even when things were going wrong and the cares of a Master must have been pressing hard upon him.

Nowadays, however, the modern facts of hunting life seem all too often to produce a situation in which the stranger is *not welcomed* – and this, to my mind, is suicidal in a world where more than half the populace do not understand the sport.

A leading steeplechase jockey who used to love his hunting told me the other day that he had given up 'because I kept getting sent home'. Well, that, no doubt, was an exaggeration, but he *had* been sent home (twice) for what, in older, bolder days would have been the very pardonable sin of taking his own line.

Understandably, popular packs with a huge list of subscribers must take steps to keep the size of their fields in check – and obviously, since all hunting depends on the good will of farmers, fences cannot be bashed indiscriminately without regard for the cost.

But if, for those who hunt to ride rather than the other way round, hunting is still to be fun, a balance has to be struck between too much control and too little.

No one can help the huge fields and the long frustration of queueing at artificial hunt jumps. What they *can* help is the impression, sometimes given, of a rigidly ordered sequence of events in which age and social precedence count for more than the wish and ability to ride across country fast, to stay near the hounds and the devil take the hindmost.

These reflections, based, as I say, on totally insufficient evidence, may well strike the true hunting man as unforgivable impertinence on my part. But I shall be surprised if there are not some who, in their heart of hearts, find on occasion that the sport is becoming even more artificial than circumstances demand.

This used to be the field in which the ordinary Englishman's love of adventure with a spice of risk found its most natural outlet. Many thousands still get untold pleasure from it, but for some the bonds of control are becoming too tight.

An outsider's view, given with considerable diffidence, is that hunting must at all costs strive to preserve something of its old happy-go-lucky, neck-or-nothing spirit.

Doubtless there are many English packs with which that spirit still flourishes – and many for whom the pressure of 'urbanisation' (what a dreadful word) has made it impossible. There *are* still places in England where men can risk their necks chasing a fox and all I ask is that they should be allowed to do so in as friendly an atmosphere and with as little control as possible.

My own slight discontent is prompted not so much by a few abortive experiences in the modern English hunting field as by four gloriously exciting, infinitely enjoyable days spent recently in the south of Ireland.

It is clearly unfair for a start to compare English with Irish hunting. There are no large towns in Co. Limerick, no motorways, no electric railroads and precious few ploughed fields.

True, they have wire – and plenty of it, often lurking invisible in the top of huge and hairy banks – but no one seems to take much notice. It is just another added hazard to be overcome in what, to startled English eyes, is already a battle quite hazardous enough.

This, indeed, is 'the image of war' and, having never been in a war I cannot vouch for the accuracy of Jorrocks's 'five and twenty per cent' of danger. The percentage, when the Black and Tans are running, might well be higher than this.

Arriving at an Irish meet the first – and lasting – impression is one of gorgeous informality. Clothes, for instance, do not matter much. If you have no boots, jodhpurs will do and gentlemen, arising late after a Hunt ball the night before, have been known, I believe, to set out in dinner jacket trousers!

The hunting-crop – an awkward object I have never really been able to manage – is only carried by those who may need to use it. For the rest, few gates will have to be opened in any case and a stout ash-plant is as good an accelerator as any if your horse may need encouragement.

Probably he won't, for the standard of hunter, even the humble hireling, is incredibly high. In four full days the refusals I saw could be counted on two hands – and most of them were from young horses being taught their business.

The field, by English standards, is tiny – forty would be a big one – but the difference is that here nearly all are 100 per cent active participants. The rule seems to be that if you no longer want to 'go', you stop hunting altogether – and age alone is no barrier.

One gallant lady, well the wrong side of seventy, was pointed out to me. 'After her last fall the doctor said one more would kill her' – but she sailed over bank after bank and was there at the end of the day with the joy of it all in her eyes.

The hunt, when it starts, starts fast – and at once, for a beginner like me, your whole attention is concentrated on getting from A to B in one piece.

Even if you could see the hounds – which in this country of tiny fields and high banks you usually can't – there would be precious little time to speculate on where they were going. They're gone – that's all you know – and, as the leaders disappear from view over the first obstacle, the horse makes up your mind willy-nilly.

Despite your terrified, too-short grip of the reins, he bounds, sure-footed, on to the bank – a sickening pause while you look in horror at the yawning ditch below – and down, leaving you shamefully far behind, to land with his back teeth jarred and you hanging round his neck.

After ten or twenty such experiences you begin to see how it *should* be done – and to realise, too, how men like Pat Taaffe acquire their rock-like seat, unshakable by anything short of an earthquake.

In four days I fell off half-a-dozen times – and learnt more about riding than twenty three-mile 'chases could teach.

Pat Hogan was my host and mentor, an incredible bundle of nerveless energy and drive – and almost certainly the best man to hounds now living in what he would not like to hear called the British Isles.

To watch Pat ride across Co. Limerick is to see an artist at work. Never apparently out of a hack canter, he seems to know what both fox and hounds are doing before they know themselves.

Following Hogan makes even this hazardous form of hunting easy – easy, that is, if you have a horse good enough to do what all his do with such unhurried ease.

At the first check, after ten hectic minutes that seem, looking back, to have lasted a lifetime, another delightful facet of Irish hunting appears. It is the cars – not, as in England, a stream of anxious motorised followers getting in their own and everyone else's way, but a handful, driven by magicians who materialise just when you need them most to produce life-giving food and, more important, drink to bolster your shattered nerves, sustain the tissues and send you on your way a braver, better man.

My day with the Black and Tans is a jumble of memories too many and varied to be described. Bank after bank, a river called the Morning Star – out of which one had to scramble up a perpendicular cliff – falls, loose horses (someone *always* catches them and brings them back), more falls, more banks, and the wild, wonderful hounds themselves, of whom it is said that the six best whips in the world would not hold them back when the scent runs high and the fox is gone.

And then when it is over, the joy of an Irish hunting tea with eggs and bacon that exhausted satisfaction makes taste better than any caviar. This, you feel, is the life; this was hunting as it should be.

Throughout, a stranger, you have been made to feel a friend – made to feel that while it would be nice to catch a fox, your enjoyment is the main object of the excursion.

It is this, I think, that we might learn from Ireland, and if my tangled, grateful recollections can persuade any of you to go and see for yourselves, that, alone, will perhaps excuse the crime of a racing correspondent who, this week, has deserted racing for a subject of which he is even less qualified to write.

29 December 1962

ARE TODAY'S JOCKEYS AS GOOD AS THOSE OF PRE-WAR DAYS?

Almost as long as I can remember it has been the fashion among senior observers of the racing scene to decry the general standard of modern flat-race jockeyship – or at least to compare it pretty unfavourably with that of the period between the wars.

Like most comparisons between one era and another, this may partly have been caused, or anyway influenced, by a common human tendency to praise the past at the expense of the present.

Certainly the onset of middle age is apt to throw a rosy aura of romantic exaggeration around the scenes and heroes of one's youth, and when a fifty-year-old man tells you that they don't make them like Steve Donoghue any more, it quite often turns out, on investigation, that his first and only glimpse of that great man was gained as a boy of twelve at Goodwood on the first day of the summer holidays.

I saw Steve Donoghue, already long retired, riding Brown Jack at Olympia just before the war. I was eighteen or thereabouts, but had already read Bob Lyle's wonderful book three times. It seems to me now that Donoghue – in colours and riding at racing length – put his old friend through an intricate series of graceful manoeuvres, changing leg and gait like a dressage champion. But I was eight, Brown Jack was my hero – and who knows how much time has coloured and enlarged the picture?

Nevertheless, making all due allowance for that brand of distortion, it *is* probably somewhat easier and more meaningful to compare the merits of jockeys in different eras than it is those of the horses they rode.

Although speed is a measurable factor by which, in theory, form over a given course and distance should be comparable, so many other things have changed – going, tactics and starting methods to name only three – that even if we had an accurate time for, say, Bahram's Derby it would be precious little use as evidence to measure him against Nijinsky or Mill Reef.

A film of their three Epsom triumphs would be equally irrelevant – except perhaps as regards the ease with which they won – but film of two different jockeys in different eras should, surely, be far more useful and informative.

Whatever other effects, good or bad, television may have had upon British racing, it has undeniably made possible the study of riding technique in a detail hitherto undreamt of.

Unfortunately we have only just arrived in the age of highly developed slow-motion photography, and what wouldn't I give for just one short clear film clip of finishes involving Fred Archer, Tod Sloan, Danny Maher, Frank Wootton, Steve Donoghue, Harry Wragg and, although his style is unforgettable and unforgotten, Sir Gordon Richards.

But films do exist of that 'golden age' between the wars and it was one I saw recently – allegedly of Brownie Carslake in action – which triggered off these reflections.

I have always been told – and am perfectly ready to believe – that when it came to a finish Carslake could hold his own with anyone then riding – and much more than hold it with most.

He was, I understand, only able to use the whip in one hand, but that mattered far less than usual since he had the good fortune, so far as riding is concerned, to be left-handed.

Well the film I saw was short, jerky and far from clear, but it showed two men riding a finish at (I think) Ascot, and Carslake (if it really was he) got home by half a length, on the horse nearest the camera.

Now it scarcely needs saying that techniques and methods of jockeyship have changed enormously since those days (probably somewhere in the early Thirties) and it is not at all surprising that a jockey riding then should look distinctly odd to our eyes now. But what *is* surprising is that neither of the two jockeys involved in this film looked to me particularly effective.

They rode, of course, several holes longer than any modern

professional – and at least a foot longer than Lester Piggott or Yves Saint-Martin. (But no longer than, for instance, Fred Winter in his heyday over fences and he, if you remember, neither looked, nor was, ineffective.)

It wasn't the length of stirrup, however, which so surprised me – but rather the general lack of style and, more important, rhythm.

Perhaps the film was to blame – and certainly the camera *can* lie – but the fact is that if, say, Joe Mercer or Geoff Lewis could have been superimposed on that finish at Ascot, the other two would have looked, to my eyes at least, like a couple of unpolished amateurs.

It would, of course, be ridiculous in the extreme to draw any general conclusions from one solitary piece of film which may not even have been what it claimed to be.

And before these pages are flooded with infuriated dia-tribes from admirers of Brownie Carslake, let me say I do not suggest for one moment that either he or his many famous contemporaries were either amateurish or ineffective.

But it isn't that film alone which set me wondering whether the standard of flat-race jockeyship really *has* declined as much as some pundits would have you believe.

It is also the result of watching an awful lot of races – some of them more than once and in slow motion – and what that observation suggests to me is that, even if the standard *had* declined since the war, it has now started to improve again and *may even now be as high as it has ever been*.

There are many headings under which a jockey's merit can be measured, but the three I prefer are technique, tactical skill and reliability.

Technique includes all the physical skills ranging from rela-tively simple ones like a balanced seat and the proper use of the whip to such complex, indefinable qualities as 'hands' and the magic knack that makes a horse go kindly for one man when he won't try a yard for another.

Many of these are, of course, invisible and can only be measured by results. But a jockey's general 'style', particularly in a finish, *can* be observed and assessed – and so can his mastery of vital skills like switching the whip from hand to hand.

'Tactical skill' is an equally comprehensive heading, but the most important facet of it is a jockey's ability to adapt himself to the needs of different horses, different races and different circumstances of every kind.

It is all very fine to ride a brilliant waiting race on a doubtful stayer with a turn of speed, but all too easy, having done so once or twice, to get the idea that all horses need the same treatment.

Both the first two headings affect the third because obviously a jockey can only be 'reliable' if he *has* first-rate technique and tactical skill *and* uses them consistently.

The most reliable jockey in this sense is, simply, he who loses the fewest races which he should have won, whether by a tactical error or because his technique is not as complete as that of an opponent.

Granted all this – and it is necessarily oversimplified – how do you then measure the standard of any one generation of jockeys?

Well clearly not by its outstanding figure – or not by him alone. There may conceivably have been jockeys more 'reliable' than Lester Piggott in the sense described above, but although his technique is both personal and inimitable, it is also complete.

I do not think there can ever have been a jockey better able to adapt himself to different tactical problems and certainly there has never been one more in his element on the big occasion.

But while Lester Piggott undoubtedly ranks very high indeed among the greatest jockeys of all time that, in itself, tells us little or nothing about the standard now prevailing.

Piggott's unchallenged supremacy has, in fact, been cited (unfairly in my opinion) as evidence that his contemporaries are mediocre – and certainly there was a time when, in an unwise attempt to copy his uncopiable method, some young riders ruined quite promising careers.

That tendency has now, I believe, been largely halted by the efforts of the comparatively few trainers (Frenchie Nicholson and Ian Balding are two outstanding examples) who have both the knowledge and the wish to teach and produce good apprentices.

And I also believe that there is no longer much, if any, truth in the argument that, as compared with, for instance, Sir Gordon Richards, Lester Piggott has only insignificant opposition to contend with.

Of course Sir Gordon *did* have many famous and formidable contemporaries, but do you suppose that Joe Mercer, Geoff Lewis, Jimmy Lindley and Brian Taylor are *all that much* easier to beat than Steve Donoghue, Charlie Elliott, Harry Wragg and Tommy Weston?

The four I have named above are chosen solely as good examples of traditional English jockeyship as it has now been developed and altered to fit the needs of the 1970s.

Unlike Lester Piggott's, there is nothing exaggerated or unnatural about their style – based as it is on a firm, balanced seat and, in the finish, on a rhymthmic drive, powerful but without violent or unnecessary movement of any kind.

If you want to see what I mean, just watch carefully the next time Joe Mercer gets involved in a finish on TV. In my carefully considered opinion it is very hard indeed to believe that a more effective, more stylish or more aesthetically satisfying method exists of persuading a Thoroughbred horse to go faster.

But four – or five – jockeys, however excellent, still don't prove my thesis, especially since they are all comparatively senior. A healthy tree must have roots and buds – and it is here, I believe, that the past two seasons have been such a dramatic improvement, because they have seen the emergence of two young men, Tony Murray and Willie Carson, quite capable of standing comparison with their counterparts in any previous era. And, hard on their heels, Philip Waldron and Patrick Eddery are steadily developing the same soundly based, highly effective method.

In any article such as this it is both dangerous and invidious to name names, because by doing so you have to leave out so many others. But since the suggestion being put forward here is that the current crop of flat-race jockeys is, as a whole, worthy of this country's long tradition, I can only hope that those I have not mentioned won't consider it an insult.

24 September 1971

FROM DREAM TO REALITY

The first point-to-point is only six short weeks ahead and, between now and February, how many nights, I wonder, will be spent all over Britain dreaming of triumphs to come on some muddy or sun-baked stage?

Plenty, I hope, for, with me at least, anticipation has, from the earliest days, been a major part of all the untold pleasure I've got from various sorts of riding.

Can't you, for instance, remember those anxious bedtimes long ago when a pile of hunting clothes laid ready across a chair spoke of the thrills to come next day – when, in your dreams, your pony jumped a five-barred gate as big as himself in front of all the field, when they killed in the open and you the only one with hounds?

Reality, of course, is seldom quite the dream, whether hunting, racing or in any other field of human endeavour. But that doesn't stop you dreaming – or, when it *does*, it's probably time to hang up your boots and dream instead about the past.

So sleep sound, you would-be jockeys, and dream not of falls and failure but of victory. In the cold light of day you'll doubtless get plenty of the former, but the latter's hard to come by and to win in the imagination is far better than not to win at all.

Between the dream and its achievement there is, unfortunately, a great deal of hard work and, almost certainly, bitter disappointment. Yet the memory of them will be swept away when, one day, you come to the last fence in front.

At that moment all the hardships and disasters of the past will seem worthwhile – and so they were – but perhaps, just possibly, some of them could have been avoided.

Having once decided that you want to ride in point-to-points, the first step is to find at least one suitable conveyance and, unless you are lucky enough to have some extremely indulgent friends or relations, that probably means the purchase of a horse.

Almost certainly, so far as this season is concerned, you've got him already, in which case don't let anything I say discourage you – but, nevertheless, in choosing a horse 'to learn on' there are a few principles worth bearing in mind.

The first is that, other things being equal, a good horse costs no more to keep than a bad one – considerably less, in fact, if he happens to win a prize or two. And, even more important for the beginner, a *bad* horse, however safe, will teach you precious little – for the simple reason that he is probably too slow to let you take part in the business end of a race.

It is over the *last* six fences – not the first – that you really start to learn and if, by that time, the others are specks on the horizon, you might just as well have stayed at home.

I speak from experience here, for my first rides were on a twenty-year-old heavyweight hunter and a mare who cost £40 and wasn't really worth it. I loved them both dearly but they didn't, to be honest, get me much nearer the fulfilment of my dream!

Perhaps, on reflection, one or two such rides are no bad thing – certainly better than nothing and even more certainly better than a tearaway five-year-old you can't control. At least they probably get you round intact and, however far behind you finish, you have learnt the unfamiliar routine of changing, weighing out, getting to the start – and leaving it.

But the principle remains. Nine point-to-points out of ten nowadays are run at or very near steeplechasing pace. They are *races*, and to take a serious part in them you need a racehorse.

By all means run your faithful hunter in the members' race,

but, unless he's more than just a faithful hunter, don't expect him to do something for which he was never designed.

The second principle is that two novices together make a highly undesirable mixture, dangerous both to themselves and to their rivals.

Of course there are young horses who, from the first, make perfectly safe, easily controllable rides, but they are the exception rather than the rule and, to begin with, a bit of real experience *under* the saddle is highly advisable to make up for the lack of it on top.

But that's all very well to say – not half so easy to secure. The tremendous, ever-growing demand for young potential 'chasers has in the past few years wrought a big and not altogether healthy change in British point-to-points. More and more, in Ireland and England, the suitable animals are being snapped up as three- or four-year-olds by professional trainers with four-figure sums at their command.

If you look at one of the huge, over-crowded fields for a novice hurdle race nowadays, you will see dozens of big, backward youngsters who, ten years ago, would probably have been out hunting, learning their trade in a few point-to-points and only *then*, if they showed sufficient promise, graduating to the world of National Hunt.

Some, of course, still follow that sensible, well-trodden path, but all too often the modern would-be owner is not prepared to wait.

One result of this, I believe, is that the overall stand- ard of point-to-points has probably fallen – and another that more and more old retired 'chasers are being quali- fied when no longer good enough to earn their keep under Rules.

Personally, I have slightly mixed feelings about this practice. It all depends, of course, on the horse himself. Some racehorses are unhappy in idle retirement, enjoy hunting and probably have no objection to going round in a few point-to-points. There can, however, be something both sad and undignified about the sight of a once formidable 'chaser fallen, so to speak, on evil days.

In any particular case the only person able to judge one way or another is the man who knows the horse. I would, for instance, no more think of running Taxidermist (who seems to love his hunting) in a point-to-point than I would of asking him to pull a plough.*

On the other hand, I have no such scruples about a moderate animal called Southern Fort, for whom point-to-pointing will be no more of a disgrace than some of his recent efforts under Rules.

To the former I owe an unpayable debt – with the latter, if anything, it is the other way round.

But all that is a digression. To return to your choice of a horse, an old 'chaser may well be as good an answer as any, provided you can control him and provided (which is not always the case) that he regards point-to-point fences with sufficient respect to be a reasonably safe conveyance.

You have got to have falls some time, but later is better than sooner and to start on anything but a good jumper is asking for unnecessary trouble.

Once found, bought and qualified, the horse has to be trained – and this is far too wide a subject to be treated here even if I knew what advice to give.

All I *do* know is that while long, slow work never yet lost a race, galloping loses thousands.

At all costs resist the temptation to 'see what he can do' at home. A horse that has been reasonably fairly hunted ought to be pretty hard by Christmas and the only 'fast' work he will then need is two or three spins to clear his wind. And even then, unless incurably lazy, he should never come off the bit.

No rules can be laid down, but by and large one gallop too few is better than one too many. If your horse gets tired first time out, *pull him up*. There will always be another day. But there won't be *any* day if he arrives at the races in February already stale, tired and sick to death of galloping.

Too much work may spoil *him* but it certainly won't spoil *you*. The only known way to get *thoroughly* fit for race-riding is – race-riding. But, since this, in the first instance, is impossible,

---

* On the other hand, Sir John Thomson gave me and my daughter Sara both Tuscan Prince and Lean Forward when they retired from racing. Tuscy – still alive, touch wood, aged twenty-seven – was a marvellous schoolmaster in Sara's first point-to-points and Lean Forward won several times later on.

you must resort to substitutes – and hunting, hacking and riding work are simply not enough.

The muscles that matter are those of your thighs, back and arms and by far the best exercise I know is bicycling, preferably uphill, with your seat off the saddle. Three miles over fences is a long, long way, so work till it hurts and go on working after that. Then at least you will know you've done your best and if you set out *believing* you are fit the battle is half won.

So there you are, one reasonably fit horse and one reasonably fit man. The great day approaches – but there is a great deal more to be done.

First, equipment. This is vital and, alas, expensive, but money was never better spent. Sound, rubber-covered reins are the most important feature of your bridle. There are various drop nosebands which help to hold a puller, but keep the ironmongery to a minimum. If you can't control him in a snaffle, you've probably got the wrong horse.

Good, comfortable racing saddles are surprisingly rare but worth their weight in gold. *Comfort* is the aim – for the horse as well as yourself.

A breastplate (not too tight) is almost always a worthwhile safeguard and if you have to carry lead put it well forward, in front of your knees if possible, not under them.

For your own turn-out comfort again is all that really matters but, if you can afford it, at least set out *looking* like a jockey. It will help both your own morale and that of your backers – if any.

Racing boots and breeches may not be absolutely essential, but light kit, even if your weight's no problem, gives the necessary freedom of movement and heavy hunting boots are a very definite drawback.

Whatever you wear on your feet, for goodness sake see that the stirrups are big enough – but not too big.

Either inside or outside your breeches wear a pair of elastic leggings – the sort they sell for varicose veins – and, if your breeches have buttons, make sure these are not between the shin-bone and the saddle. That way torture lies!

The coloured jersey should be tucked *inside* your breeches and the scarf around your neck is *not* just a useless adornment. It has saved men's lives before now and will again.

Crash helmets are, thank heaven, nowadays of uniform design, but they still need to *fit* and see that the chin-strap buckle is secure.

Your whip should be plain with an elastic band at the point of balance to stop it slipping through your fingers. Two more elastic bands around your wrists – and there you are, ready for anything.

So now it's the morning of the race. Feeling, probably, rather like a condemned man, you can, if possible, eat a hearty breakfast, but lunch merely clogs the works and a fairly empty stomach (nature and nerves will see to that) helps the wind and clears the brain.

Get there early – agonised minutes in a traffic jam are a quite unnecessary nervous strain – and when you get there walk the course.

I'd got this far before the recent Cheltenham meeting and, remembering what happened there, you may consider any further advice an unforgivable impertinence! [*See page 336.*]

For walk round was precisely what I hadn't done before the Whaddon Amateurs' 'Chase – and the nightmare outcome of that omission is all too common knowledge.

I would have sworn that I knew my way round Cheltenham blindfold, but things happen fast at 30 m.p.h., there is precious little time to think and, unless you really *know*, the result, though most unlikely to be quite as disastrous as my idiotic behaviour, is apt to be delay or loss of ground you can ill afford.

Don't bother too much about the fences themselves. It's the line you take to them that matters – and the straightest line is usually best.

Every course has its own problems and, on nine point-to-point courses out of ten, priceless lengths can be saved by going the shortest way. This is usually, but not quite always, the inside. It is no good galloping flat out into a sharp bend on the inside and then skidding wide like a badly driven motor car.

Besides walking round, much can be learnt by watching races run before your own. Look for the mistakes of others and avoid them and if some acknowledged expert like Guy Cunard is riding take note of the path he chooses.

When you arrive at the start try your girths and, if necessary, ask the starter to pull them up a hole. The length you ride is up to you, but here again comfort is the most important thing.

The shorter you ride, the greater the strain on your thigh muscles and, probably, the less secure your seat. Too long, on the other hand, and you may literally deserve to be called a 'bumper'. The golden mean that suits you best can only be found by trial and error but, basically, better a hole too long than a hole too short.

Tactics depend so much on individual horses that nothing I could say in the short space left would be much help. But if someone in authority gives you sensible orders, *obey them* come what may. That way, win or lose, you are more likely to be asked again.

The most important single thing throughout the race itself is to *sit still*. The slightest unnecessary movement has to be countered by your horse and he has quite enough to do without being worried by a shifting burden on his back.

Don't, to begin with, be in a hurry. For more races are lost by coming too soon than too late and, without dropping right out, almost all horses jump better if they have a lead. But they also need to *see* the fences and to get a bit of daylight it's well worth going a yard or two farther round.

Four or five strides off each fence your way should be clear and you should, in theory, know where you want to take off. This, unfortunately, can only come with practice. If you feel you are meeting it right push on – but not too hard. If not, sit still and, whatever happens, be ready to slip your reins if you are left behind. Too tight or too short a hold may, if the horse pecks, catapult you between his ears. Worse still, even if you stay on it will mean, for him, an agonising jab in the mouth – and this is the one really unforgivable sin.

The perfect, all-purpose seat for crossing a steeplechase fence at speed can best be learnt not from textbooks or theory but by watching the men who do it a thousand times a year to earn their daily bread.

Watch them and you will see that, except when disaster threatens, nothing they do is exaggerated. The only necessary movement is a slight forward thrust against the stirrup as the horse takes off. Apart from that, once again *sit still* – and let him do the work.

Sooner or later, if you persevere, the long-awaited day will come when you arrive at the last few fences with a chance. Perhaps you are in front, perhaps there are a few lengths to make up. Either way this, for any amateur, is by far the easiest time to make a fool of yourself and your horse. He, almost certainly, is tired or getting tired and so, more than likely, are you.

Now more than ever unnecessary movement on his back will unbalance and exhaust him. So shorten your reins to 'pick him up', squeeze with your legs and *gently* begin, with your hands, to follow the rhythmic rise and fall of his neck.

Forget about the whip, except perhaps to slap him down the shoulder without moving your hand from the reins.

At all costs *keep in time*, don't go faster than he can and then at least you won't be hampering his efforts.

The average ignorant punter almost always confuses movement with effectiveness and the highest compliment a beginner can be paid is to be sworn at for 'not trying'.

The man who gets beaten half a length sitting still, going with his horse, has something to be proud of. The one who gives a bad imitation of Sir Gordon Richards – brandishing the whip and flopping about like a fish out of water – *may* win, but only because his unfortunate horse had about two stone in hand.

These have been the random reflections of someone whose only right to speak lies in the number of mistakes he has made himself. If they help bring one single dream a fraction closer to fulfilment then they won't be wasted.

The writer is still dreaming – and still making most of the mistakes against which he so glibly warns.

There is no short or easy road to victory but, to all who set out, I wish the very best of luck.

2 January 1965

FILM STAR JOE
WOULD HAVE
THE WHIP HAND

When the Jockey Club issued its exhortations to local stewards on the subject of the whip last week, there were quite a few jockeys, I've no doubt, who thought it, at best, a fuss about nothing and, at worst, an unjustified slur on the profession in general and themselves in particular.

In some cases that feeling is perfectly understandable because most of the best jockeys – those who have worked hard and long to learn their trade – do not, as a rule, abuse the horses on whose cooperation they depend.

But, even among that elite, opinions about the whip and its efficacy vary widely and what, to one, might seem a useful and essential minimum, might to another – or to a watcher in the stands – look excessive if not downright cruel.

But anyway, even if some jockeys did feel themselves unjustly 'accused' (at least by implication), that does not alter the fact that the stewards of the Jockey Club were absolutely right.

Even if, as may well happen, some overzealous local stewards caution jockeys undeservedly for 'excessive use', their hurt feelings and injured pride will be far less important than the multiple disgust which can be caused by one genuine case – particularly one which happens to be shown on television. Because what all of us involved in racing need constantly to be reminded is that we are in the entertainment business. If the audience is not entertained, the show, at least as we know it now, would not go on.

No doubt you could stage some kind of gambling game dependent on horses to keep the betting shop in business –

on, for instance, an 'all-weather' course designed for endless mediocre hurdle races and freezing winter afternoons! But, in so far as it is still trying to provide a spectator sport as well as a gambling medium, racing simply cannot afford anything (avoidable) which spectators or potential spectators are likely to find repulsive. And excessive – or what looks like excessive – use of the whip is undeniably both avoidable and likely to repel.

Well, if you want to avoid it, why have whips at all? It is a perfectly good question and not, in my opinion, really as easy to answer as you might at first sight suppose.

No one denies, of course, that the whip, properly used, is a useful and effective aid. It can send many different signals to the horse – wake up, concentrate, go faster, take off, go left, go right, stop going left or right or stop pretending that log by the side of the road is a crocodile about to bite you.

No doubt in dressage and in *haute école* there are thousands more and anyone who sets out to educate a young horse without a whip or stick would be giving himself a pointless handicap.

The whip, let's face it, may also be needed for punishment – although that use is nothing like as easy as it sounds and, if attempted inexpertly on a determined horse, usually ends in undignified disaster!

But the question has still not been answered. All I have said applies to schooling young horses and most of it to other forms of equitation. But why necessarily to racing? If all you are trying to find out is which of several man–horse combinations can travel fastest from A to B, then surely all you need to ensure is that they start and finish at the same places, follow the same course, carry (not counting handicaps) the same weights and that *the riders are allowed to use roughly the same equipment and aids to propulsion.*

So if one of those aids is doing more harm than good to racing, why not simply forbid its use? It would, after all, be the same for everyone and if the change led to happier horses and more contented spectators, what harm would be done?

You might well need a slightly different sort of horse, differently – and almost certainly better – trained and educated. Different jockeys might come to the top and those who did would almost certainly ride a few holes longer. To begin with, admittedly, jockeys under both codes might find it harder to keep horses straight and jumping jockeys would undoubtedly miss the 'slap down the neck' which many of them use – and many horses expect – as a final command to pick up.

But I honestly cannot find any unanswerable reason there for regarding the abolition of whips on the racecourse as an unthinkable, impossible, end-of-the-world-as-we-know-it revolution.

In Scandinavia the length of whips is already limited and in Norway the jockey is only allowed to pick up and wave his whip in order to correct an obvious tendency to hang.

In a perfect world, of course, none of these rules would be needed and there would be no point in even discussing prohibition.

But the racing world is not perfect; not all jockeys are either very experienced, very skilful or very scrupulous. Some of them, even the good ones, occasionally lose their heads and some feel compelled, in defeat, to 'prove' how hard they are trying for the benefit of owners and/or trainers in the stand. All too often the 'proof' they choose is repeated and ill-directed use of the whip.

So that is why I welcome the stewards' pronouncement – and believe that they should at least hold in reserve, as an ultimate deterrent, the outright prohibition of the whip or at least of its use in any but the 'carrying' position.

In fact I would like to see that last rule introduced now in apprentice and opportunity races or at least those confined to jockeys claiming the full allowance.

Riders in these should by all means, as things are now, be allowed to *carry* whips but not to use them, except while still holding the rein, on the horse's neck.

As things are, the use of the whip is undoubtedly an art and, wielded sparingly, ambidextrously and rhythmically, it is a vital and powerful weapon in the armoury of a top-class rider, but most if not all of them would, I believe, agree that, except on an exceptionally lazy horse, it is only worth using – applying, that is, as opposed to waving – a certain number of times.

On the flat that number depends, of course, in how far from home a jockey has to start riding a finish – but 'excessive use' is not really so much a matter of frequency as of the force employed.

After all, horses in a flat-race finish are very seldom tired in the sense that a three-mile 'chaser may be, slogging up the hill at Cheltenham or Sandown.

Joe Mercer and John Oaksey at Doncaster.

For a three-year-old colt with his blood up, a few flicks on the not very sensitive skin of his quarters hardly amount to cruelty.

In this as in so many other questions of style and method, Joe Mercer is my ideal and it is entirely appropriate that Peter O'Sullevan (no mean stylist himself) should choose the end of Joe's first championship season to launch his campaign against excessive or unnecessary use of the whip.

Peter's wise words were fully supported by the new champion himself, but Joe does not really need to talk about it. You only have to watch him ride and once he has settled into the classical rhythm of his finishing drive the whip (if he picks it up at all) keeps such perfect time with the horse's stride that you cannot be sure whether it is actually making contact or merely being swung.

In fact, as his long-time employer Dick Hern confirms, Joe's method has always consisted of a few slaps interspersed with a lot of rhythmic swinging.

According to Dick, the horses he rides practically never come back with a mark on them – and even if they did it would always be gone (and forgotten) next day. 'It doesn't matter how important the race or how close the finish,' Dick says. 'He rode Bustino against Grundy in the "King George" just the same way.'

No one who watched that race can suppose for a moment that any other jockey could have got an ounce more from Bustino – and no one in his senses could claim that Joe Mercer lacks strength in a tight finish.

So if the stewards are worried – as they clearly and rightly are – about the whip and its use, I suggest that they should make and circulate as widely as possible an instructional film on the subject.

First it would show some X-certificate action-replays in which misguided jockeys (who will not necessarily be either obscure or unsuccessful) repeatedly suspend the whole operation of riding a conventional finish while they hit, unbalance and generally abuse their unfortunate steeds.

Sometimes they win, sometimes they lose, but *always* they are a deeply ungraceful, unattractive sight.

Then the film will cut to Joe Mercer and (if I was directing it) Fred Winter in action. It will show how every ounce of strength and speed can be extracted from a flat-race horse by rhythm, balance and timing in place of violence – and how an exhausted jumper can be held together, lifted and actually *helped* by the strength of a man's legs, back and arms.

The film should be shown, together, if possible, with one of himself, to any jockey whom the stewards or their secretaries consider to have misused the whip. Not all that many, alas, will have the strength, balance and coordination to copy Joe or Fred precisely, but at least they will see how far short their own efforts fall of the ideal.

For boys still learning their trade, such a film would be even more valuable. Racing simply cannot afford to let slip the priceless opportunity of having as champion jockey a man capable of setting such a superb example. Joe Mercer has already done racing great service, but with any luck, if proper use is made of him, his reign as champion could usher in a golden age of stylish, effective jockeyship which, even at its strongest, is still a pleasure to watch.

25 January 1980

JOCKEYS SHOULD BE INNOCENT UNTIL PROVEN GUILTY

The whole vital question of local stewarding will be in the spotlight next week when General Blacker and his committee produce their report. Since the General is a wise and hugely experienced man who has heard evidence from a wide range of interested parties, his recommendations will, without much doubt, greatly improve the selection, training and treatment of the amateur volunteers on whom British racing discipline chiefly depends.

They will also, I hope and expect, underline the importance of having stewards' secretaries – and as many actual stewards as possible – who have personal experience of the methods, techniques, problems and split-second tactical decisions which are involved in race-riding.

There may not be all that many retired jockeys who would either be prepared or suitable to do the job but there *are* some – the brand of retarded blimpery that refused Fred Winter's application to be a starter on the grounds that he 'might not have sufficient control over the jockeys' must never be allowed to 'lose' good men again – and to ensure that, there will, no doubt, have to be a considerable improvement in the salaries paid to stewards' secretaries.

I shall also be surprised if amateur stewards themselves are not paid travelling expenses and, quite possibly, a loss-of-earnings allowance like those now given to local magistrates.

But even with all these and other improvements, the lot of the local steward will still, in my opinion, be an unhappy and often impossibly difficult one while the Rules in general – and

Rule 153 in particular – remain in their present form. Journalists are often, and rightly, criticised for mere destructive criticism and no one who goes racing regularly can be surprised when different groups of stewards with widely varying experience reach different decisions and impose what seem inconsistent penalties.

The same thing happens daily in courts of all kinds and is even less surprising when the chief evidence is something as difficult to interpret as a race patrol film.

But more often than not, I believe, confusion and inconsistency arises from the Rules themselves – and from the current Jockey Club instructions on how they should be enforced.

Take the following imaginary incident. Horse A interferes, slightly and 'accidentally' (i.e. the jockey could not have avoided it) with horse B. That interference costs B, at most, one length and A goes on to win decisively by six lengths. In the meanwhile, however, horse C, who has not been involved in the incident at all, gets up to beat B a short-head for second place.

Now at present Rule 153 reads as follows: 'When a horse or his rider has caused interference by accident . . . the horse shall . . . be disqualified or placed behind the horse with which it has interfered unless the stewards are satisfied that the interference had no effect on the result of the race . . . when they may . . . order that the placings remain unchanged.'

The present practice is that, in this context, 'the result of the race' means the placings of the first four horses. So, getting back to our example, what happens when the stewards decide that the interference was accidental or unavoidable?

The next question is: 'Did it affect the result?' And, since, because of the interference, B has lost second place to C, the answer has to be, 'Yes'. So A, the decisive winner on merit, is placed 'behind the horse it interfered with' – in third place, with C becoming an utterly undeserving winner.

Well, that scenario has not yet happened in a Derby but, as the Rules stand, it easily could – and even if an angry crowd of aggrieved punters did not burn down the Epsom stands, the stewards, the Rules and racing itself would all be made to look immortal asses.

But here, with respect, is a rewording of the Rule which seems to me at least a partial solution.

In place of the present double negative – 'unless the stewards are satisfied that the interference had *no* effect on the result', I suggest the Rule should read, 'The horse shall not be disqualified IF the stewards are satisfied that the interference HAD NO EFFECT ON THE RELATIVE PLACINGS OF THE HORSES INVOLVED.'

The first purpose of this alteration is to shift the burden of proof. Substitution of a positive 'if' for the complex double negative of 'unless' and 'not' means that a jockey alleging interference would have to satisfy the stewards: (a) that it happened and (b) that his horse's prospects were affected.

At present, by contrast, the jockey whose horse is 'accused' has to prove not only that the interference was unavoidable and accidental, but also that it did *not* affect the other horse.

In this, and in other instances, in fact, local stewards are being told to ignore the age-old principle of natural justice – that any man (or horse) is innocent until proven guilty beyond reasonable doubt.

The second change to Rule 153 is designed to avoid as far as possible the ridiculous and deeply unpopular situation in which a deserving and decisive winner can be disqualified for some minor peccadillo which had nothing to do with his victory.

Instead of 'had no effect on the result', my suggested wording is: 'affected the relative placings of the horses involved'. In our example above, A's interference with B could not possibly have prevented B from finishing in front of A – so *their* 'relative placings' were clearly not affected. Horse C, on the other hand, was not involved in the interference. Admittedly, he profited by it (finishing second instead of third), but that is a far lesser evil than giving him a race to which, on merit, he had no right whatever.

To some extent, of course, this runs parallel with Phil Bull's long-held conviction that interference, even the non-accidental sort caused by careless or reckless riding, should *never* get a horse disqualified. In Mr Bull's view only the jockey should be blamed and punished.

I still disagree with this extension of the theory because the

Jockey Club Rules run across the board and in small races involving unfashionable jockeys who get few rides there is no punishment stewards could impose which would be an effective deterrent to 'no holds barred', 'stop at nothing' tactics.

If an unscrupulous gambler bets enough on a humble selling hurdle, he may offer Joe Bloggs, who has about five rides a year, an inducement more than sufficient to repay him for a long or even permanent suspension. The only sure-fire deterrent to such foul play is to disqualify the horse and make sure the crooked gambler does not collect.

But that still does not justify the present atmosphere in which, in supposedly the interests of 'safety', the slightest interference or contact between two competitors is apt to earn a jockey an expensive suspension.

For one thing, when did you last hear of a jockey getting hurt in the sort of 'last two furlongs' incident governed by Rule 153? Not for a very long time is the answer, and although, of course, the stewards can say that their Rules are responsible for this admirable record, it goes back long before the patrol camera and the modern atmosphere of which I complain.

My chief complaint on the jockeys' behalf again concerns the burden of proof and benefit of doubt in 'interference' cases. Among the questions local stewards have to answer about any suspected interference are:

(1) Did it occur?
(2) Was it accidental?
(3) If so, did it affect the result (or in my version 'relative placings')?
(4) If not, was it caused by careless riding? and
(5) Was the riding reckless – i.e., did it involve an element of intent or risk to others?

In all these questions it seems to me the stewards should constantly remember the countless chances and uncontrollable factors involved in riding a finish. Far too often, instead of giving jockey or horse the benefit of the doubt, which so frequently, in the nature of races, must exist, they seem to consider them 'guilty unless proved innocent'.

The result, anathema to the racing public, is that jockeys who try a fraction too hard and get unlucky are constantly punished far more severely than those who for whatever reason do not try hard enough.

27 September 1985

One of the most controversial instances of Rule 153 in action was the 1988 Ascot Gold Cup . . .

JUST *WHO* WAS CARELESS?

Maybe they will put up a statue to Royal Gait in Madrid and call him 'The avenger of the Armada'.

His superiority over the English was certainly just as total last week as Gladiateur's in 1865 and even if, for some reason, you agree with the Ascot stewards that Cash Asmussen rode him 'carelessly', there is not the shadow of a doubt that Royal Gait won the Gold Cup strictly on merit.

He won it in record time, what's more, thanks largely to the suicidal early gallop set by Tony Clark on Sadeem's pacemaker El Conquistador. It was, of course, the latter, rolling about like a drunkard in the straight, with whom Royal Gait was held to have interfered.

If Clark had stayed aboard El Conquistador, I rather doubt if the Ascot stewards would have felt the need to disqualify, but the jockey, shaken but unhurt, said afterwards that he 'would have been very disappointed if Sadeem had not got the race'. His evidence in the stewards' room seems unlikely to have helped Asmussen!

The whole question of pacemakers seems to me to put local stewards in a difficult position. Clearly pacemaking is 'allowed' but no one with eyes could possibly say that Tony Clark 'took all reasonable and permissible measures . . . to ensure that El Conquistador was given a full opportunity to win or of obtaining the best possible placing'!

That is what Rule 151 (ii) requires and, by riding El Conquistador (who was tipped to win on the front page of the *Sporting Life* and not by any means the worst horse in the race) with such excessive zeal that he was beaten fully a mile from home, Clark broke it in half-a-dozen ways. Without misusing the language, in fact, you could almost call his riding 'careless'.

The whole regrettable incident strongly reinforces Phil Bull's oft-stated conviction that, when interference is caused in a race by careless riding, it is the jockey responsible who should be penalised – and no one else.

Royal Gait and Cash Asmussen being led in after the 1988 Ascot Gold Cup.

Why on earth, Mr Bull has always asked, should the owner, trainer and backers of the best horse in a race be punished (by his disqualification) because his jockey has broken the rules?

It seemed a pretty good question at Ascot last week – and, without going into all the old arguments for and against, I still think that, as long as Rule 153 is enforced in its present form, it is only a matter of time before British racing makes an even bigger fool of itself than it did on this occasion.

23 June 1988

When the Disciplinary Committee rejected appeals made on behalf of Royal Gait and Cash Asmussen last week it was, you might think, the last chapter in the sad story of the 1988 Gold Cup. But no. For the first time in a controversy of this kind, the Jockey Club decided to put their cards publicly on the table, asking the senior Stewards' Secretary, Peter Steveney, to examine the race again on BBC TV with Julian Wilson.

It was, at first sight, a bold and admirable move. As Julian said, the racing public, or a large part of it, has been wondering how on earth the stewards (two separate lots of them) arrived at their decision. It was obviously desirable that someone should be given the chance to explain their reasoning in detail.

I wish I could say that it worked – that a satisfactory explanation was forthcoming – but, alas, the exact reverse occurred. During the Wilson–Steveney exchange, we saw no fewer than six versions of the Gold Cup incident – filmed from all the different angles which the stewards had at their disposal.

And the sad truth is that, during nearly eight minutes of film and discussion, nothing, repeat nothing, was either seen or heard to weaken my original conviction that the stewards were wrong.

At least Major Steveney made clear the grounds on which Asmussen was convicted of careless riding. 'There was only a minimal gap and he [Cash] should not have gone for it. When he did, he bumped first Sadeem and then El Conquistador. The bump caused the horse to unship his jockey – and that's careless.'

Fair enough, but a moment later, watching a film just before the fatal contact with El Conquistador's quarters, the Major says: 'There, you can see him KICK ON INTO THE GAP.'

What we actually saw was Asmussen sitting as still as a statue on Royal Gait, with Greville Starkey tight outside him on Sadeem and El Conquistador falling back exhausted in his path. There was not, with respect to Peter Steveney's experienced eyesight, the tiniest sign of a 'kick' or any other form of encouragement.

It seems to me that the following relevant points appear from Sunday's interview and the films which it included.

- From well before the turn, Cash Asmussen, on the rail with first Chauve Souris and then Sadeem outside him, never had a chance to pull Royal Gait out.
- Greville Starkey turned for home on Sadeem at least three horses wide – on course to go outside Sergeyevich. Had he done so, Royal Gait would have had plenty of room and the incident would never have happened.
- Starkey was fully entitled to steer in behind Sergeyevich, closing the gap through which Royal Gait was pulling his way so strongly. But it was his decision to close the gap – and the relentless vigour with which he did it – which caused not only the alleged contact (never visible on Sunday's films) between Sadeem and Royal Gait but also, far more important, the contact between Royal Gait and El Conquistador's quarters.
- When that occurred, El Conquistador, who had been hard ridden for at least two furlongs after setting a harebrained pace, had come a full horse's width off the rails. If he had stayed tight on the inner there would have been an even wider gap – except, of course, that Sadeem would presumably just have come further across to close it.

So there it is. Nothing we saw or heard on Sunday explained the Ascot stewards' decision to disqualify a thoroughly deserving winner and, frankly, the BBC interview made it even harder to see how the Disciplinary Committee felt able to confirm that disqualification.

Its three members, the Ascot stewards and Major Steveney, are all experienced men with the good of racing thoroughly at heart.

I believe that their own strict interpretation of Rule 153 led them into an untenable position and I am more than ever convinced that the Rule, in its present form, must go.

Racing is supposed to be the fairest possible way of finding out which horse runs fastest. The disqualification of Royal Gait struck a damaging blow at that reputation for fairness and if Rule 153 is left unchanged it will not be the last such blow we suffer.

30 June 1988

WHY NOT LET THOSE LEATHERS DOWN A HOLE OR TWO?

One of the great unsolved mysteries of modern racing is why, almost throughout the twentieth century, jockeys all over the world have tended to ride with shorter and shorter stirrup-leathers.

At least I have never heard a convincing explanation and, to tell the truth, if a fairy godmother offered me some racing wishes, one would certainly be that the tendency should stop. In quite a few cases, in fact, I would ask her to reverse it.

When it all started, the change was easy enough to understand. Tod Sloan may have been jeered at as 'a monkey on a stick', but he very soon demonstrated that monkeys are easier to carry than mounted policemen. What he brought from America was a method which shifted the jockey's weight forward towards the horse's centre of gravity.

He and his imitators did not, of course, ride in anything like the modern style, but from the horse's point of view there was almost certainly at least as much difference between Fred Archer and Tod Sloan as, for instance, between Tod Sloan and Joe Mercer.

Without extensive experiments in a wind tunnel – which have, so far as I know, never been carried out – it is hard to measure the value of streamlining. No doubt it played a part in the phenomenal success which Tod Sloan enjoyed against rivals who, in those days, sat almost bolt upright.

But Lester Piggott's career does not seem to have been very gravely handicapped by the fact that, compared with, say, Steve Cauthen, his long angular body sticks out from an average field like the Eiffel Tower in a village of bungalows.

Lester Piggott winning the 1954 Derby on Never Say Die.

Lester Piggott winning the 1983 Derby on Teenoso.

Anyway, no one any longer questions the fact that a race-horse finds weight of any kind easiest to carry if it is poised as firmly as possible above or just behind his withers. His progress is definitely impeded if the burden is further back and the last thing he wants at any stage of any race is to have it bumping about on his loins.

Obviously when that truth was first recognized, jockeys had to adapt their methods to the new position and, not surprisingly, jumping jockeys were much slower and more reluctant to do so than their colleagues on the flat.

But under both codes, until well after the last war, no one rode with his knees above the horse's withers. Whether you used them to grip or steer or make the horse go faster, the lower half of both your legs was in more or less constant contact with his sides.

It is here that the greatest and, in my opinion, least explicable change has come, for the average top-class flat-race jockey now rides with his knees well above the withers, and although Andy Turnell is still an exception rather than a rule in the jumping world there are several others at or near the top – Tommy Carmody, for instance, and to a lesser extent Jonjo O'Neill – who seem to ride only a few holes longer than he does.

With only minimal and extremely amateurish experience on the flat, I am not remotely qualified to comment on the judgment regarding style of experts like Lester Piggott or Yves Saint-Martin. They have both decided to use the 'ultra short' method and their success speaks for itself.

So, I suppose, does the fact that Lester seems to have ridden shorter and shorter almost throughout his long career. Certainly the seat he employed on Never Say Die was a positive model of convention compared with the precarious-looking perch he has now developed!

The trouble is, of course, that such champions are inevitably copied – and the extraordinary methods of a genius can be disastrous when attempted by lesser men. You only have to inspect a big flat string being exercised at Newmarket or Lambourn to see the widespread and, in my opinion, catastrophic effect which the fashion for short stirrup-leathers has had on the standard among British stable lads.

There are, of course, many glowing exceptions but, quite apart from being extremely insecure, the only meaningful contact which some lads have with their unfortunate horse is apt to be through its mouth. When something goes even slightly wrong, that 'contact' is all too often a violent jerk as the lad hauls himself back into the plate.

The effect on a young, impressionable Thoroughbred can all too easily be imagined and I know more than one trainer who reckons that by far his biggest problem is to get his horses even halfway decently ridden at exercise.

Similar horrors arise, of course, when inexperienced or lesser jockeys attempt to imitate Lester Piggott in a race.

One of the many reasons for welcoming Joe Mercer's emergence as champion jockey last season is, in fact, the hope that he will be used as an example.

Joe, needless to say, is no 'mounted policeman' but nothing about his style is exaggerated and if the next few generations of apprentices would only copy him in every detail his first championship might be the foundation stone of a golden age.

Anyway, although no one seems to be able to explain their reasoning, flat-race jockeys have evidently come to a collective conclusion that the ultra-short style is the most effective way of getting a horse from A to B. And, as I've said, very few people are qualified to disagree – at least with those whose success proves their point.

But to apply the same conclusion to jumping seems to me an entirely different kettle of fish. Nothing said here is meant to suggest that the method I used to employ (once described by Fulke Walwyn as a 'fine example of Old English Lavatory seat') had anything much to recommend it. But twenty years did teach me that riding over fences involves many problems quite different from those you encounter on the flat – and those problems are no more easily or effectively solved with your knees pulled up to your chin.

Presuming that a jumping jockey's weight is so positioned that it does not upset the horse's balance or waste his energy while galloping (there is no great difference here from the flat), the length of his stirrup-leathers may affect his own effectiveness (and his horse's chance) in the following ways.

Security. You cannot win if you don't get round and a jockey's first duty is therefore not to fall off. The conventional, 'accepted' wisdom is that the shorter you ride, the easier you are to dislodge, and this seems to be borne out by the fact that many jockeys, even nowadays, let their leathers down a hole or two at Aintree.

On the other hand there are limits and some experienced jockeys who have given the matter serious thought – Stan Mellor and Bob Davies, for instance – put the point to me that riding reasonably short may actually help you survive a blunder.

What often ejects you when a horse hits a fence and lands too steep is, after all, the impact of his hindquarters on yours. So, their argument goes, since short stirrup-leathers tend to raise your bottom, they may therefore lessen the impact.

Well, having never tried it, I can't tell – but I can certainly testify to the explosive effect of even a minor mistake on the middle-aged bottom of someone riding comparatively long! So maybe Stan and Bob do have a point.

But their argument does not alter the fact that a jockey riding like Andy Turnell needs Andy's incredible balance and speed of reaction to survive.

Andy Turnell and Bird's Nest.

So, with these slight qualifications, the 'accepted' wisdom is probably more or less right. Surviving mistakes depends on luck, quick reactions, grip (or strength) and then more luck. But a jockey riding very short almost certainly needs even more of those priceless commodities than his less 'fashionable' colleagues. He will also get more grandstand criticism when he does fall off – but that is by the way.

The next, not unconnected, category, is the jockey's ability to present a horse at a fence, his position during the leap and the speed with which he gets away. I am speaking mainly of steeplechasing, but this applies to hurdling too.

The art of 'seeing a stride' and choosing where to take off has nothing to do with the length you ride. These are knacks, inborn or acquired, and you either have them or you don't. Or, more exactly, sometimes you have them and sometimes you don't!

When it comes to putting these knacks into practice – asking the horse to take off – a man with his ankles on the saddle must necessarily, be at some disadvantage. I would not personally put it all that high, but you need legs and heels to kick with and some horses do need a very definite kick.

When things go according to plan a jockey riding short can look – and be – perfectly placed in mid-air. And, on landing, he will probably regain the racing position more quickly than someone sitting even a little further back.

But when things do *not* go exactly right – when the horse screws or makes even a slight mistake – the opposite is apt to happen. The conventional safeguard against hitting a fence is to slip your reins and thrust your legs forward against the stirrups. 'Get them up on the mantelpiece,' Dave Dick used to say – but if you attempt that well-tried shock-absorbing method with short leathers, your bottom is apt to end up landing far back (with a thump) on the horse's loins and that, as we've seen, is no help to him whatever.

So over the fence, to my mind, the balance of 'advantage' is firmly on the side of riding a conventional length. Provided of course, that 'conventional' does not mean ultra-short!

If asked to define it at present I would point to John Francome and Jeff King as the best contemporary examples of the conventional English method. And that is the first time I ever called Jeff 'conventional'!

In the third and final category, however, he is, in my opinion, supreme – the nearest thing, at his best, to Fred Winter, who was, and still is, my ideal of a jumping jockey.

Because that category is the finish and it is here, in jumping, that the ultra-short method seems to me to suffer its worst defeat.

I am not speaking of finishes in which the winner is still full of running or producing, in a well-timed burst, a superior turn of speed. I mean the slogging, exhausting drive from the second last when a tired horse needs to be lifted and held together.

In the first sort, Andy Turnell and Tommy Carmody look superb – motionless, posed and, if Jeff King or Ron Barry happen to be struggling close behind, even they look almost uncouth.

But in the second, more common, sort of finish, the man riding short is physically unable even to attempt the method which made Fred Winter supreme.

His legs grinding inwards, almost motionless, used to provide a fulcrum from which his arms and shoulders and back could work and thrust and drive in time with the horse's stride.

Jeff King can do something very like it still – and one or two others are trying. But the ultra-short brigade will never get within a mile of it. In heavy ground on a tired horse you can forget them – unless the horse has 7lb or 20 yards to spare. That is why I would implore my fairy godmother – at least as far as jumping is concerned – to put the clock back again and get the stirrup-leathers down again.

There is one other reason which applies equally to flat racing and jumping. It is the whip, and I believe wholeheartedly that the fashion for riding ultra-short has made jockeys of every sort and class rely on it more than ever before.

The explanation is not hard to find. If you cannot encourage a horse with your legs, the obvious alternative is the whip – and unfortunately, all too many jockeys nowadays seem to think that waving it in time with a horse's stride is not enough.

Worse still, instead of a rhythmic swing (as practised by Joe Mercer or Fred Winter), they tend to suspend all other operations while they turn in the saddle to apply it.

Lester Piggott (who typically makes his whip work miracles, and according to the trainers he rides for, seldom hurts a horse nowadays) is again 'to blame' for his 'example' here.

Trying to copy him, rather than, for instance, Joe Mercer, has produced some deeply unattractive spectacles and, for even less skilful and experienced jockeys at small jumping meetings, the temptation is to show everyone how hard you are trying by 'doing a Lester Piggott' seven or eight times between the last obstacle and the line.

To 'do a Fred Winter' – or even attempt it – would need a degree of strength, fitness and coordination which they may well not possess. And even if you had all those qualities they would still do you no good with your ankles on the saddle flaps.

I have a good deal more to say, one day, about the whip and how its use should be controlled but, for the moment, a happy New Year and let's hope, at the very least, that 1980 sees the stirrups go no higher.

28 December 1979

THE CHRISTMAS PRESENT

So far as I know, this story never happened and the man I've called Joe Bell does not exist. But I've known men very like him and to all of them, with heartfelt admiration for their cheerful courage, what follows is respectively dedicated.

It was in the Turkish baths I saw him first. The morning of Christmas Eve, he was sitting on a marble slab between two fat businessmen and he looked like one of those Oxfam pictures that make you ashamed of eating three square meals a day.

When you see a thin man in the baths it's never long odds against his being a jockey and you didn't need Sherlock Holmes to tell you this one hadn't come in just to sweat out last night's hangover.

You can't see much through the choking fog of the steam room, but a little later in one of those outsize ovens with long Latin names, when you need wooden sandals to keep your feet from burning, I got a better look.

The sweat running down his chest made the ribs stand out like timbers on a shipwreck and his body was very white, except for a big blue scar across one collar-bone.

The reddish brown of his face stopped short halfway up the forehead where a cap had shielded his skin from the wind and rain of a thousand early mornings and there wasn't a pinch of flesh on him anywhere – just muscle, bunched hard behind his shoulders and running along the tops of his thighs.

He had grey hair, cut very short, blue eyes and a nose that had changed for the worse since his first birthday.

He might have been anywhere from 35 to 60, but that morning, sweating hard and hating it, he looked an old, tired man.

The soggy *Sporting Life* he was reading settled my last doubts about his reason for being in the baths and, glad to find a fellow sufferer, I asked him how much he had to get off.

'Four more pounds if I'm lucky,' he said and then, looking hard at the *Chaseform* on the bench beside me, 'I've got ten to four in the seller at Wincanton.'

Well it just so happened that I had my own rather moderate 'chaser in that race – and thought he could just about win it if the dice rolled right. So I looked down the probables and the only jockey booked to ride I didn't know was J. Bell on Piper's Hat.

The horse was thirteen years old and I'd never heard of him either, but it was going to be a long morning so just to keep the conversation up I asked him what he rode.

'An old yoke of my wife's called Piper's Hat,' he said, then quietly, not boasting, just stating a simple fact, 'And he'll win too if his legs hold up.'

Well, it always pays to know your dangers, so I asked about the horse and this was the story Joe Bell told me, sitting in a fug of sweat and Jeyes fluid two furlongs from Piccadilly Circus talking in a slow, soft brogue with Limerick or maybe Co. Cork jumping out of every word.

'I know you,' he began, 'you write for the papers – but don't write this – not till after he's won anyway.'

His wife had bred Piper's Hat, it seems, and eight years ago, just before she married Joe, won four point-to-points on him in the south of Ireland. Joe was a schooling jockey for one of the big stables then. He'd ridden thirty winners as an apprentice on the flat, but got too heavy and never really made it over fences.

'So I went hunting when we got married,' he said. 'We had a little farm near Hospital, kept a few hirelings, broke young horses – you know the sort of thing.'

The blue eyes smiled and under them I noticed for the first time those little criss-cross white lines that the blackthorns leave on the faces of all who ride much across that fearsome country. 'They were happy times,' Joe said. 'Mary had two boys and the money was short, but they were happy times.'

He wiped the sweat out of his eyes and looked down the empty baths remembering very different memories. 'She never weighed more than seven stone soaking wet, but there wasn't a girl in all Ireland went better across the banks. But then' – his face creased up, and he took a long drag from his cigarette – 'then this day with the Tans from Elton, Piper gets caught up in wire on top of a double.

'It wasn't his fault at all, but he turns clean over in the dyke with Mary under him, and when we drag him off her back is broken.

'She was a year in bed, but the use of her legs never did come back, and they told us she wouldn't walk again.

'Then I hear of this fella in England they say does miracles, so we sell the farm and all the horses and come over here to find him. Only Mary wouldn't sell Piper, so he comes too – and breaks down bad winning a novice 'chase on the hard at Market Rasen.

'Well, we hadn't much cash, but I've been doing my two with Mr X [he named a kind-hearted trainer] and at first this doctor fella thinks he can get Mary mended.

'It took him more than a year to find out he was wrong, and two months ago she comes home, wasted like a sparrow, poor darlin', stuck in this big wheelchair they gave her, but still smilin' fit to bust your heart.'

His voice had gone very quiet now and he moved up politely as a big man, still half-drunk and covered with black curly hair, slumped down on the slab beside him. We moved into a cooler room and after a bit he went on.

'When I went to Mr X I'd asked him to take Piper as a hack and the first thing Mary did when she came home was wheel herself up the yard to see him. She just sat there feedin' him carrots and the old divil knew her plain as day.

'The guv'nor was off at the races next morning so I rode Piper at work. We were meant to lead Red Splash – you know, the yoke that won at Sandown – but when he comes up to me after a mile I'm sitting there with a double handful. We finished together like that – me giving him half a stone too – and as we walked back I suddenly thought, "Joe, me boy, there might be a race in this old divil yet!"

'Well, I ask the guv'nor and he says, "Why not?" So we enter him up in Mary's name and I get a licence out. They didn't much want to give it me at first, but the guv'nor promised me a few spare rides and one of his owners is a Steward.

'So Boxing Day's the day, but we haven't told Mary yet. It's sort of a Christmas present, you see.'

He was almost talking to himself by now and when I mumbled something meaningless about good luck he hardly seemed to hear. So, 'See you at the track,' I said, and walked away with my own little swamp of self-pity – unpaid bills, unwritten articles and an empty stomach – suddenly cut down to size.

I lay for a while being pummelled by a talkative masseur with a Manchester United fixation and when I got up to go, Joe Bell was still sitting in the second hottest room staring at the white-tiled wall and looking older and lonelier than ever.

It froze pretty hard next day and all over England anxious men were leaving Christmas parties to prod the ground and curse the weather. Picking moodily at a sliver of dried-up turkey, I thought about Joe Bell, wondering if he'd told Mary yet and whether they'd race at Wincanton.

Well, they did. It was touch and go, but the frost hadn't really got into the ground and on Boxing Day the sun came out in time to thaw all but a few dodgy yards close in under some of the fences.

The selling 'chase was first on the card and when I got to the weighing room with an hour still to go Joe Bell was there already, putting on a pair of borrowed boots in a corner by the tea-bar. The flood of cheerful back-chat flowed around him and I thought, not for the first time, how a N.H. weighing room, which is the friendliest place in the world, can also be the loneliest.

No one there but me had even set eyes on Joe, no one asked *him* what sort of Christmas he'd had or whether he fancied his chances. He just sat there quietly going through the old routine – stockings, breeches, boots, no sweater under his colours because of the weight, elastic bands around his wrists and a scarf knotted round his neck by a valet far too overworked for conversation.

As he stood on the trial scales with a postage stamp 3lb saddle over his arm, I said hello and he answered in the croaking voice of a man whose dehydrated mouth tastes like the bottom of a parrot's cage.

I knew the taste and I knew how he was feeling – as old as the hills, weak as a half-drowned cat and wondering why the hell he wasn't at home in front of a nice warm fire.

But I had worries of my own – 2lb overweight and a justifiably critical trainer to satisfy – so I didn't see Joe again until they called us out and we walked reluctantly, shoulders hunched against the cold, into the crowd-ringed paddock.

There were only eight runners, mine was favourite and the only danger, on form, was a very ordinary plodder. So, wanting him back if he won, I'd had a few quid on and was thinking about how to ride the race when Joe walked past in a thin old coat that had seen a lot of better days.

I wished him good luck again, but he didn't seem to hear. He was staring across the parade ring with the same smile I'd seen in the Turkish baths and as X pushed the wheelchair down to meet him he looked a happy man for the first time that day.

All you could see of Mary Bell was a small face peering out from a huddle of rugs, but it was a sweetly pretty face and the eyes were as bright and blue as Joe's.

I hadn't told anyone about Piper's Hat, but now, watching him walk round, I remembered those quiet words – 'He'll win, too, if his legs hold up' – and understood them better.

Of course I knew that if he could really give Red Splash weight and stay with him, the race was as good as over – but a broken-down thirteen-year-old who's been off the track for three seasons doesn't *sound* very formidable opposition and I'd reckoned that Joe Bell's confidence was probably based more on hope and sentiment than fact.

But now I saw what he meant. Piper's Hat was a bright little bay with a lovely, bold, sensible head and no one that day would have guessed his age. The bandages on his forelegs were the only sign of the past and, dancing along on his toes, he made my poor old plug and the other six look precisely what they were – a bunch of humble platers.

Then it was 'jockeys up' and, swinging down to the start with the cold air biting your face, you soon forget the dangers. On a one-paced horse, whose only weapon was fast, clean jumping,

I had decided if possible to make it all – and set off in front without a care in the world.

Fence after fence flashed smoothly by and until we started down the back side second time round I neither heard nor saw the others. But then with a crash and a grunt they were there beside us – a rank outsider already well off the bit and Piper's Hat, cruising smooth as silk, with Joe's hands steady on his neck.

The jockey on the outsider was a friend of mine and, as Piper's Hat went half a length ahead of us, he said, 'Jesus, John, what's that? We've got *no* chance.'

That was how it looked to me and, niggling to keep a place, I thought briefly of Mary in the stands – and said goodbye to my money without regret.

Then, at the open ditch – maybe there was a patch of frosty ground or maybe being in front took the old horse's mind off his job. Anyway he didn't lift a leg – just barely cleared the ground-rail and floundered headlong on his nose, tail flying high.

For nine 'chases out of ten it would have been the end, but they learn the hard way in Co. Limerick and somehow, from somewhere, Piper's Hat got a foot out in the nick of time.

And Joe – well, he called himself a flat-race jockey and a failure over fences, but you never saw a man sit tighter. Feet thrust far out to take the shock, back straight, reins slipping to the buckle, he made a horseman's nightmare look like child's play, and as we swept by, my friend – whose vocabulary is a trifle repetitive – said, 'Jesus, John, did you see that?'

But *he* fell at the next and down the hill alone in front once more I slapped my fellow along the neck and set all sail for home.

There were only two to jump, the way seemed clear and I was counting chickens cheerfully when, going to the second last, unbelievably, Piper's Hat came past us as if we were stuck in glue.

You could hear the crowd now. Joe hadn't moved – the race was over bar a fall – and then it happened. One moment we were chasing a smooth, well-oiled machine, the next a struggling, beaten cripple.

That dreadful blunder and the effort of recovery had been too much for the old fired tendons of Piper's Hat's off-fore.

As he faltered, Joe picked up the whip – and put it down unused. Twice in my life, both times on horses I dearly loved, I've known what he was feeling – the awful punctured-tyre sensation of a total breakdown. To win, for Joe, with Mary in the stands, meant all the world, but the pain of their old horse meant even more. So he sat and suffered, motionless, and I caught him on the flat.

An hour later, changed, with a stomach full of tea and buns, I stood outside the weighing room and a red-faced, loud-voiced punter clapped me on the back. 'Well done,' he said, 'but you were lucky, you know. If that fellow could ride worth tuppence you'd have got beat for sure.'

A very rude word rushed into my head, but then, over his shoulder, I saw a man in a thin old coat pushing a wheelchair towards the car-park. So I held my tongue and walked away. What was there left worth saying?

29 December 1967

INDEX

Page numbers in italics refer to illustrations